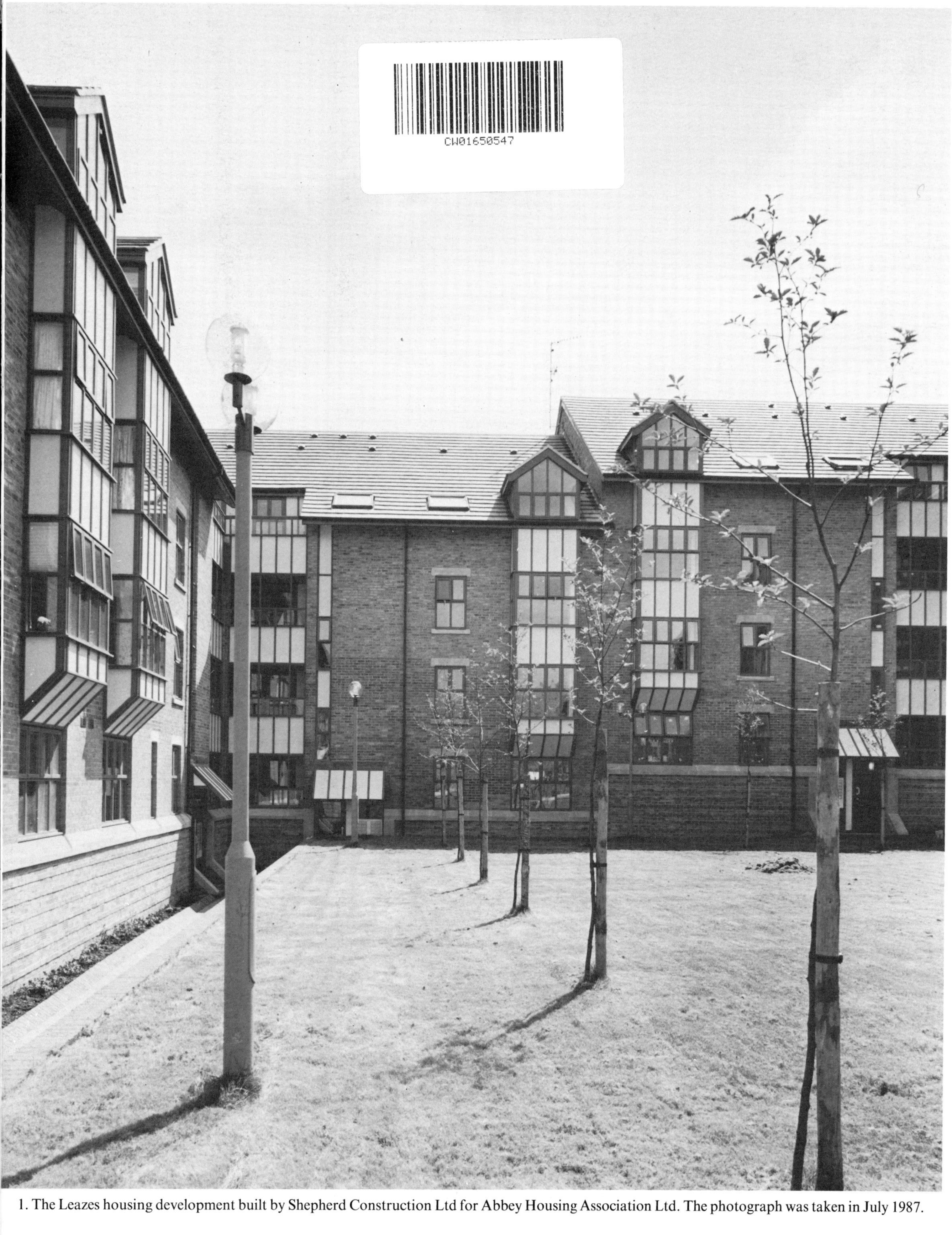

1. The Leazes housing development built by Shepherd Construction Ltd for Abbey Housing Association Ltd. The photograph was taken in July 1987.

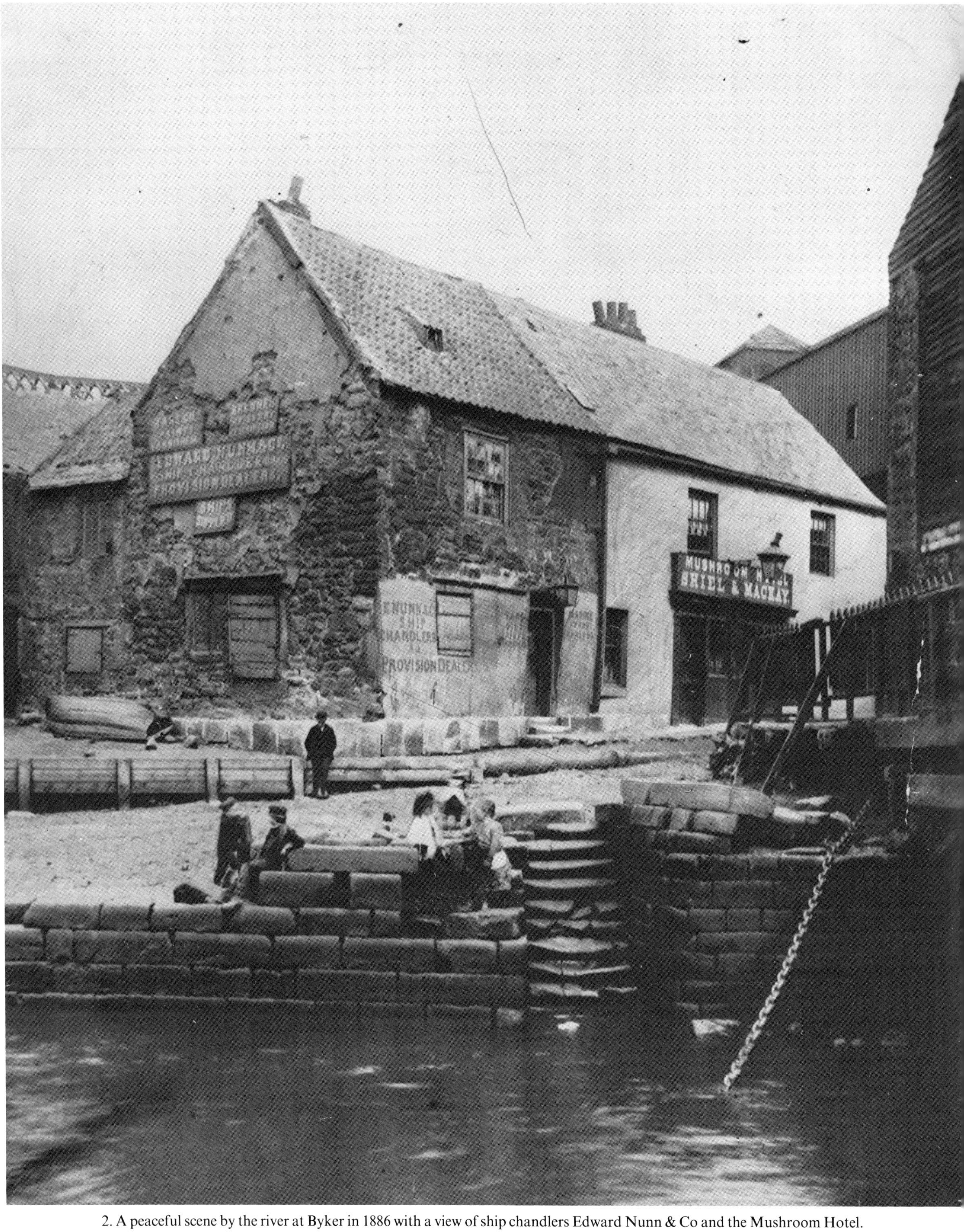

2. A peaceful scene by the river at Byker in 1886 with a view of ship chandlers Edward Nunn & Co and the Mushroom Hotel.

Newcastle in Focus

including

Byker, Walker, Jesmond, Gosforth, Fawdon,

Denton, Walbottle, Newburn, Scotswood, Elswick

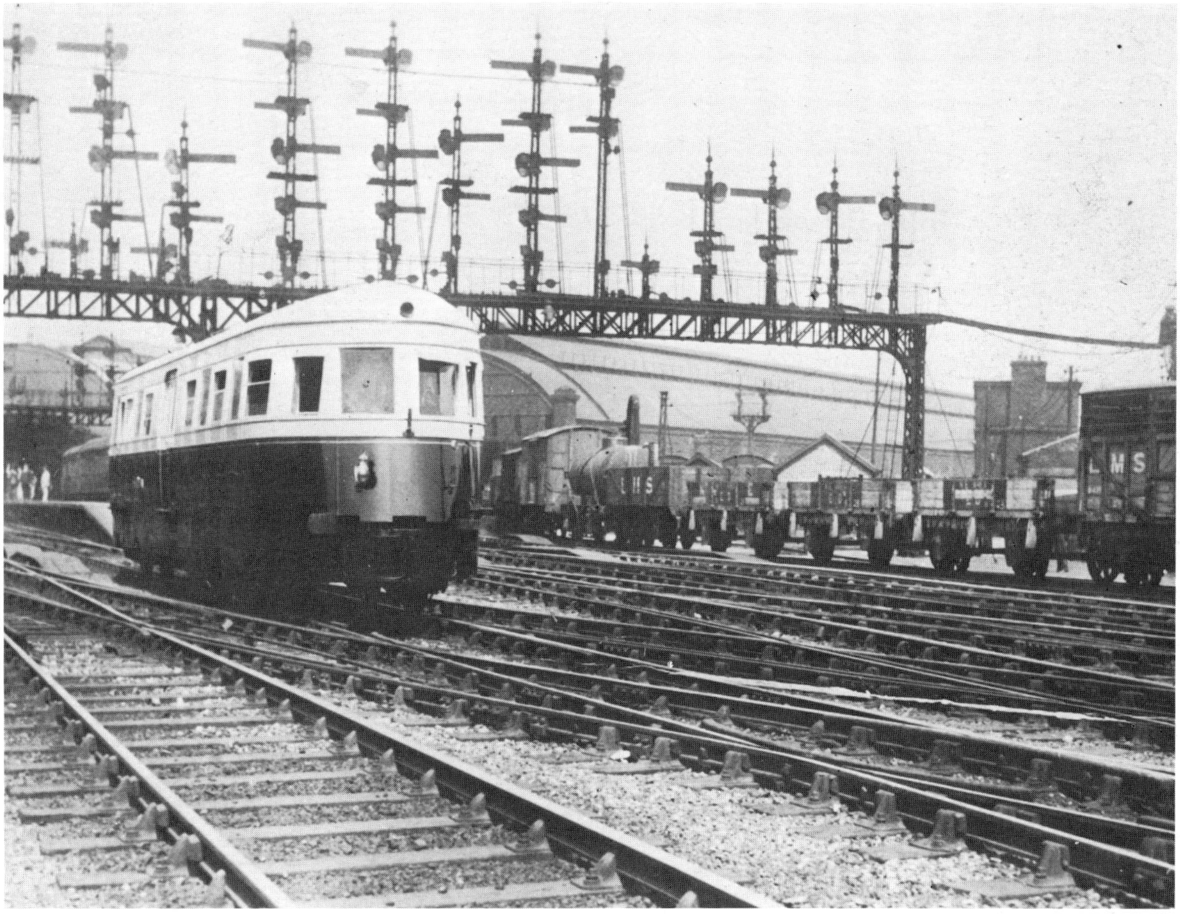

3. An Armstrong Whitworth railbus approaches the Central Station some time in the 1930s. The LNER had bought its first Armstrong railcar in 1932 followed by two more in April 1934. These three railcars were named *Tyneside Venturer, Lady Hamilton* and *Northumbrian*. In June 1934, Armstrongs were paid £2,500 for the sixty-seater diesel-electric railbus pictured above. No others were built because the war prevented further development.

Clive Hardy

First published in 1990 by
Richard Netherwood Limited
Fulstone Barn
New Mill
Huddersfield
West Yorkshire HD7 7DL

in association with

The Newcastle Chronicle & Journal
Thomson House
Groat Market
Newcastle-Upon-Tyne

Printed in the UK by
B.L. & U. Printing Limited
Wellingborough, Northants

© 1990 Text: Clive Hardy and Newcastle Chronicle and Journal
© 1990 Photographs: Newcastle Chronicle & Journal

Designed by Clive Hardy

ISBN: 1-872955-05-3

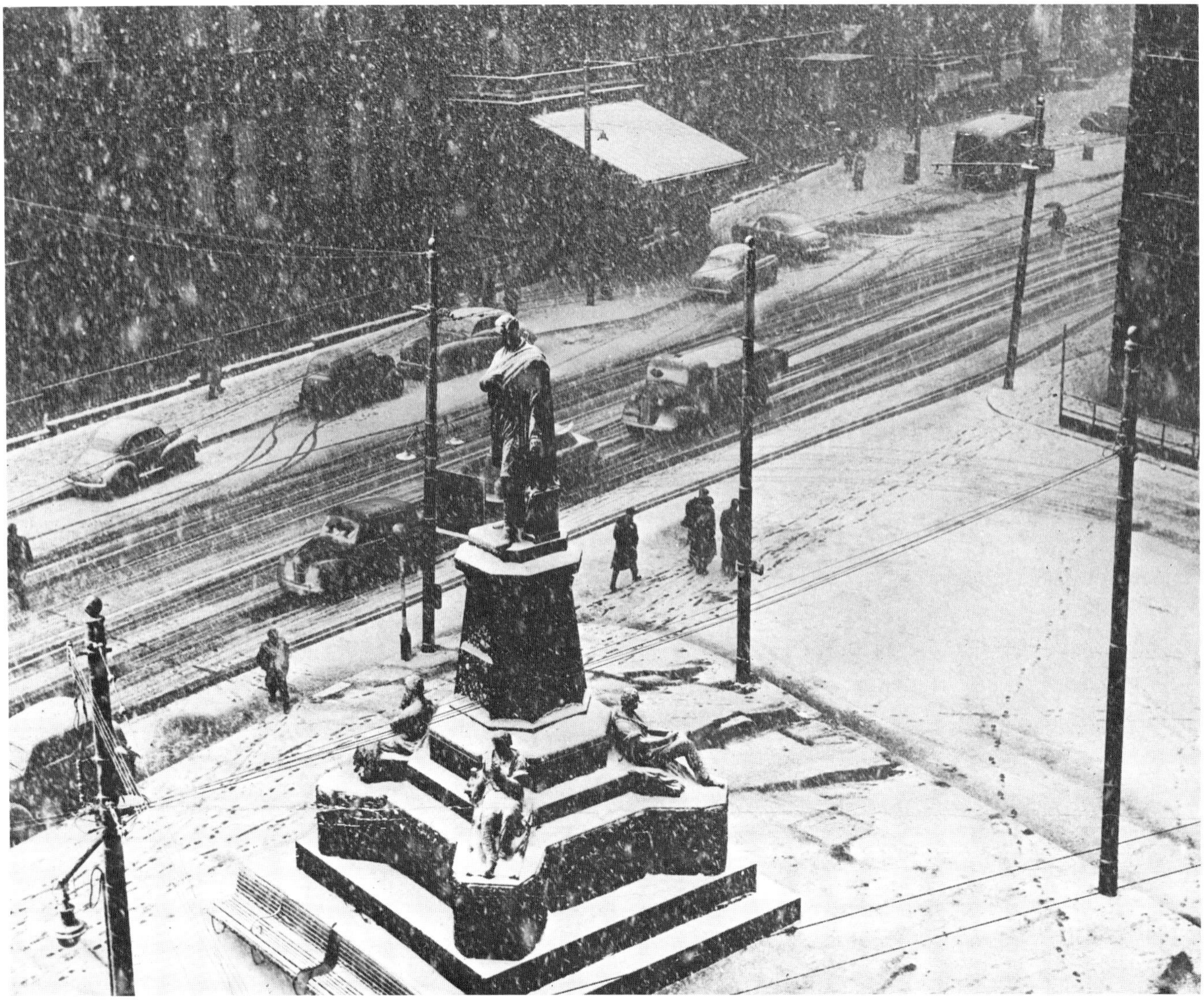

4. 18 February 1955 and the snow is falling heavily on the city. This was the scene around the Stephenson memorial, the photograph being snapped from an upstairs window in *Kemsley House*.

Introduction

Newcastle in Focus is the fourth title in the *Evening Chronicle* and *Richard Netherwood* series on Tyneside, Wearside and Durham City, covering people, places and events over the last hundred years. The earliest photographs in this book date from the 1880s, the latest from 7 March 1990.

We begin our journey on the Quayside in the 1890s, pausing for a drink at the Three Indian Kings and a bargain at the Sunday market before heading off in the direction of Byker, Walker, Jesmond and Gosforth where we are a little too late for placing a bet on the 1950 Northumberland Plate or the 1986 BBC Radio Newcastle Handicap Stakes.

Then it's off to Fawdon, Kenton, Denton and Newburn where Tommy Ward is busy dismantling the defunct steelworks. From Newburn our journey continues via Lemington, Scotswood, Elswick and Benwell to Newcastle General Hospital's high dependency unit and the Royal Victoria Infirmary's cancer research centre as it looked in 1937.

On Town Moor we have photographs dating from Barnum & Bailey's circus of 1898 to the Tyneside Summer Exhibition of 1987. Then we set off in the general direction of Jesmond, Shieldfield and Manors where we turn and head towards the city centre.

These books are not the work of one person; they also represent the combined efforts of *Newcastle Chronicle and Journal* photographers and journalists both past and present including Tommy Mackin, Malcolm Hepple, Paul Dodds, Geoff Hewitt, Paul Norris, Eric Burns, Stuart Outterside, Lawrie Wilson, P Schaill, George Swift, D McStea, F Hulme, J Napier, Dick Jones, W R Gray, Ian Robson, Ian Woodhouse, John Tunney, David Whestone, Arthur Steel, D Webb, Mike Blenkinsop, D Denholm, Alan Haydock, Walter Rich, Denzil McNeelance, Eddie Brown, Maureen Cozens, Fiona MacBeth, Oswald Peterson, Alan Southwell, Ian Winter, Fraser Davie and Suzanne Heron. Also, special thanks are due to Sandra Ramsdale and to Dennis Forman, Chief Librarian, and his magnificent staff for their help.

Clive Hardy
March 1990

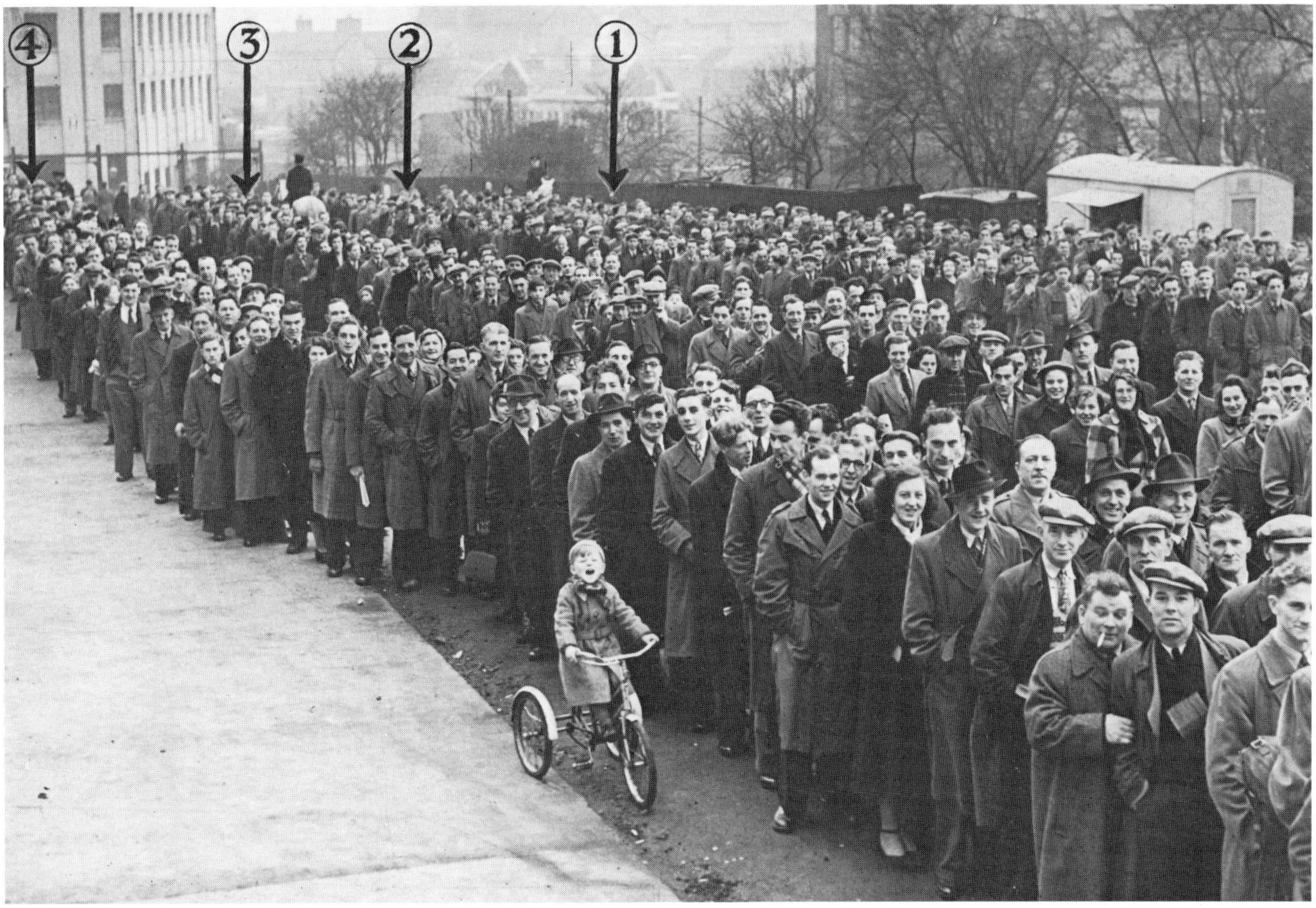

5. The queues (four of them) were long and time seemed to go so slowly at St James's Park in March 1952 but there were still smiles in anticipation of obtaining a ticket for the FA Cup sixth-round clash against Portsmouth. The game, played at Portsmouth on 8 March, was destined to become a classic. United were the Cup-holders and both sides were on form and in the top five of the First Division. After only three minutes Pompey went ahead, but by half-time the score was level at 1-1 thanks to Jackie Milburn. In the sixtieth minute George Robledo put United ahead but he then had to suffer the disappointment of his effort being adjudged offside. However, almost immediately Jackie Milburn made it 2-1. Pompey were soon back in the hunt having an appeal for a penalty turned down but then getting the equaliser when Ronnie Simpson dropped the ball at the feet of Duggie Reid. Pompey continued to pile on the pressure and defender Bobby Cowell saved United from going behind with a superb off-the-line clearance of an almost certain goal. United fought back and in the last fifteen to twenty minutes gradually took control, and with ten minutes to go Milburn scored his hat trick with a blistering 30-yarder which flew past the Pompey goalkeeper. With two minutes to go George Robledo scored United's fourth and the Magpies were once again on the Wembley trail. In the semi-final the Magpies met Blackburn Rovers, winning the replay at Elland Road thanks to goals by Mitchell and Robledo and it was George Robledo who scored the only goal in the final against Arsenal.

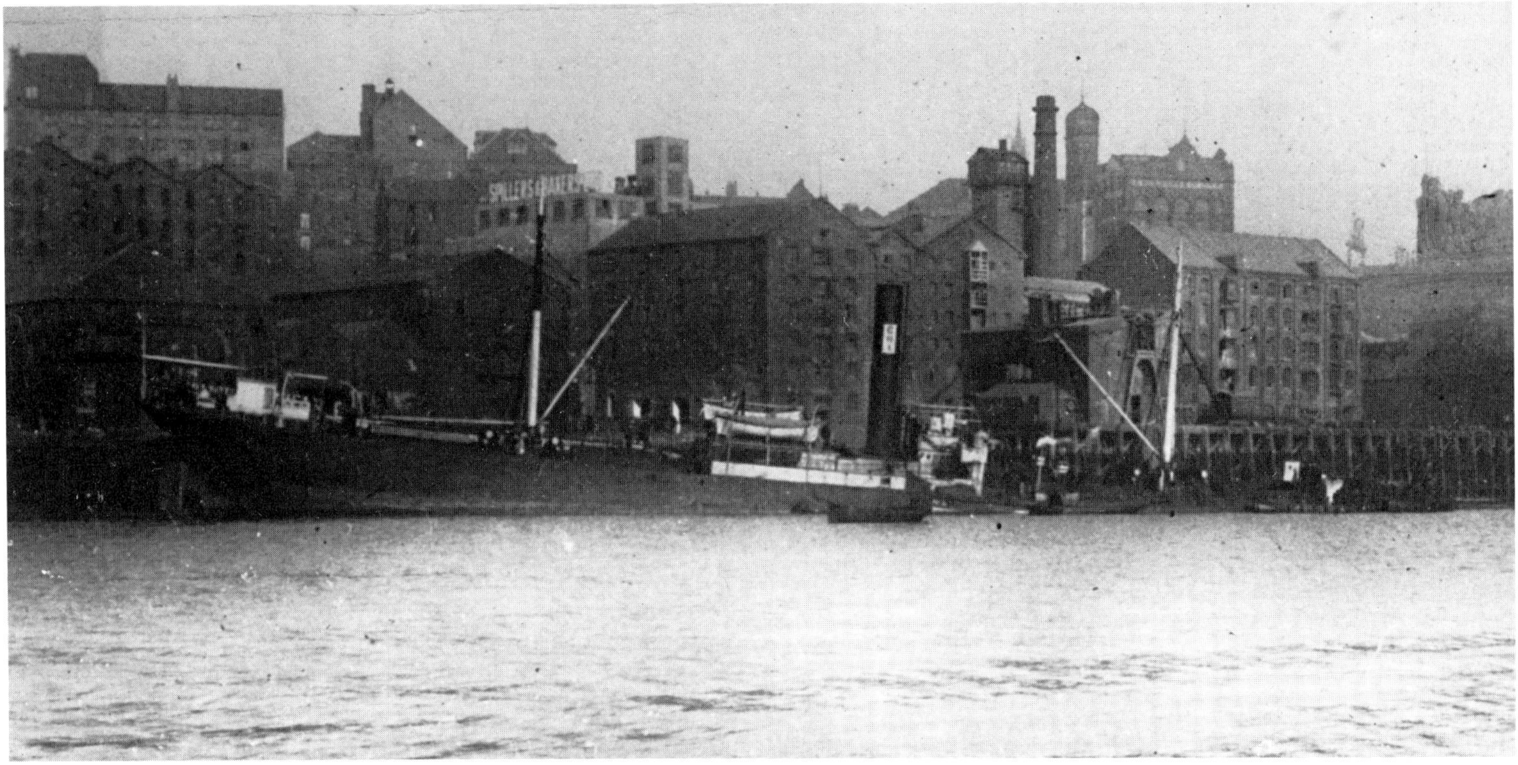

6. What a draw for sightseers around the turn of the century this half-submerged cargo ship must have been. The vessel is pictured alongside the old Spiller's Quay to the west of the High Level Bridge. The photograph was published in the *Evening Chronicle* in June 1957.

7. *Right:* The Three Indian Kings Hotel was an old inn just off the Quayside. The photograph is thought to have been taken in January 1932 when the inn had already been closed for a number of years.

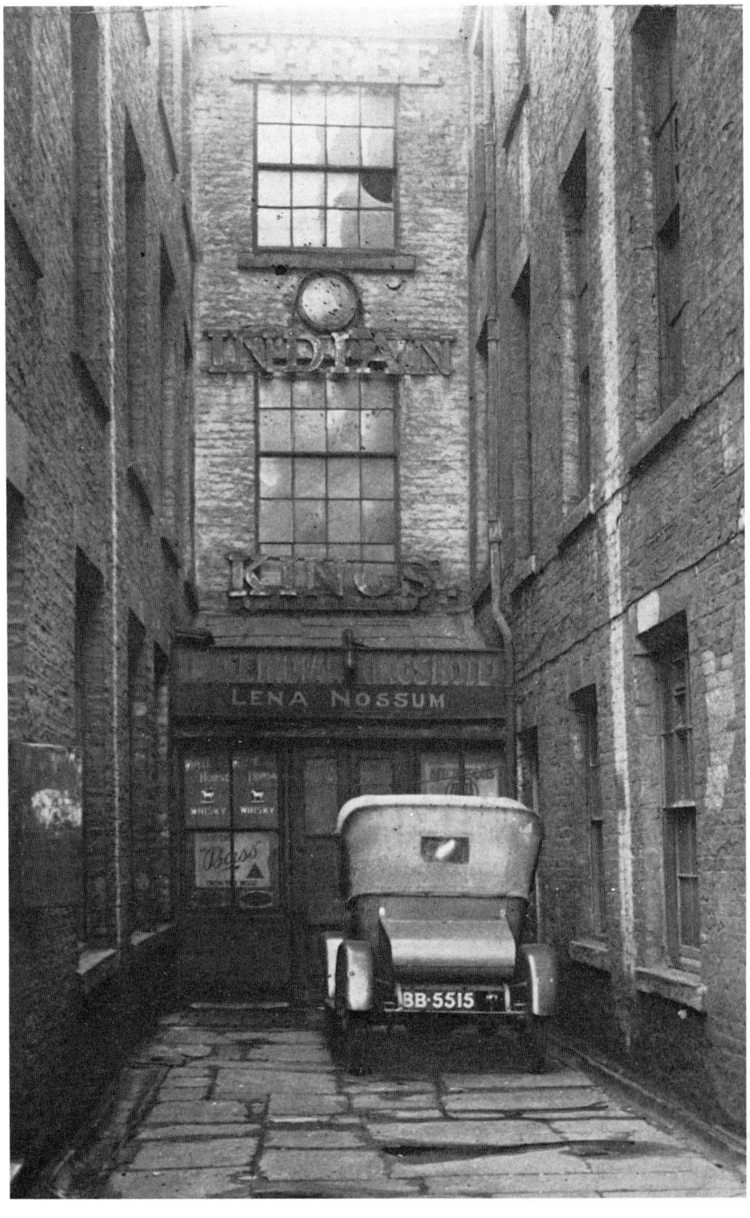

8. *Below:* Newcastle Quayside in 1896 from the site of the Tyne Bridge. The Corn Exchange is to the right of the iron-hulled cargo steamer and have you noticed the steam locomotives standing on the High Level Bridge awaiting their call to duty? *Courtesy:* The collection of M Higgins.

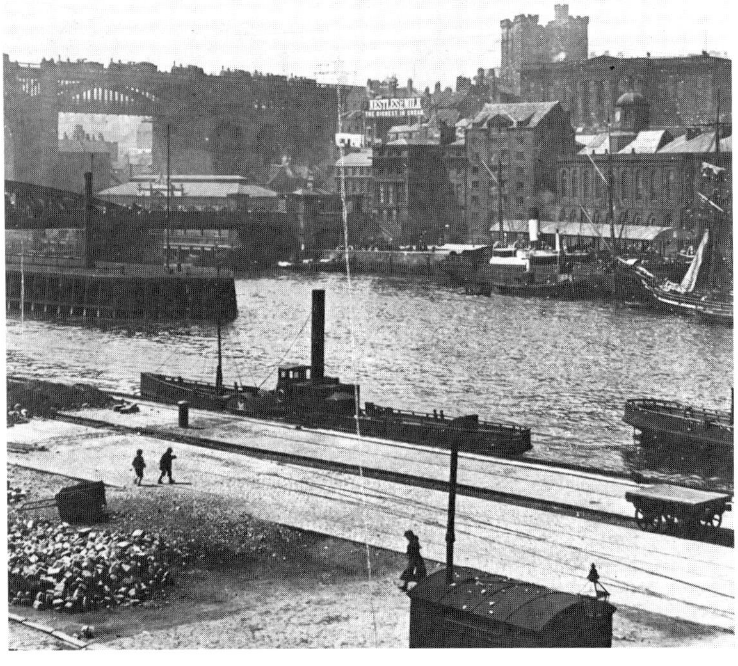

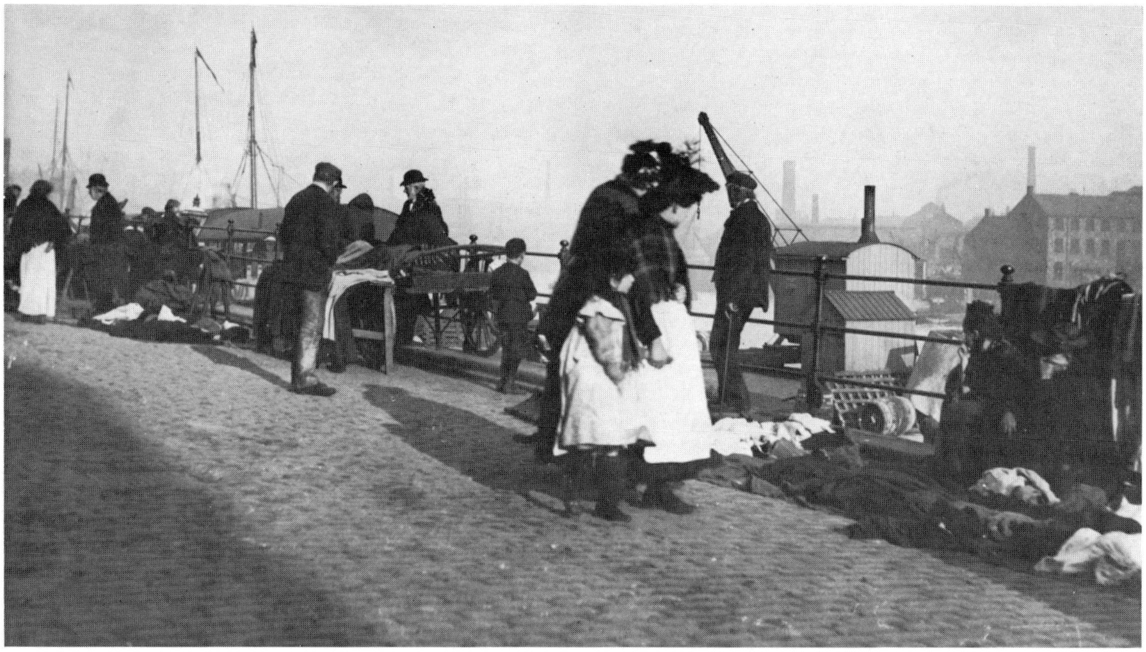

9. Clothes being sold from hand-carts at the Quayside. Was this a scene from *Paddy's Market*?

10. *Centre left:* Sunday morning market. The best of the Quayside traders, silver-tongued mesmerists all, could part the wary from their money within a twinkling of their acquisitive eye, and at the turn of the century there were plenty of them around.

11. *Centre right:* Book buyers browse in June 1936.

12. *Bottom left:* A bargain in handbags in December 1949.

13. *Bottom right:* "A typical grey January Sunday morning . . ." ran the original *Evening Chronicle* caption in January 1973. However, the photograph had in fact been taken in November 1972.

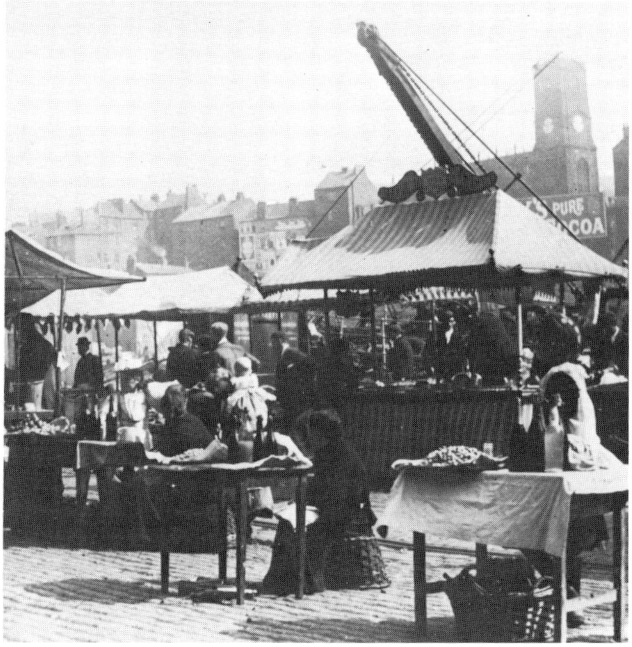

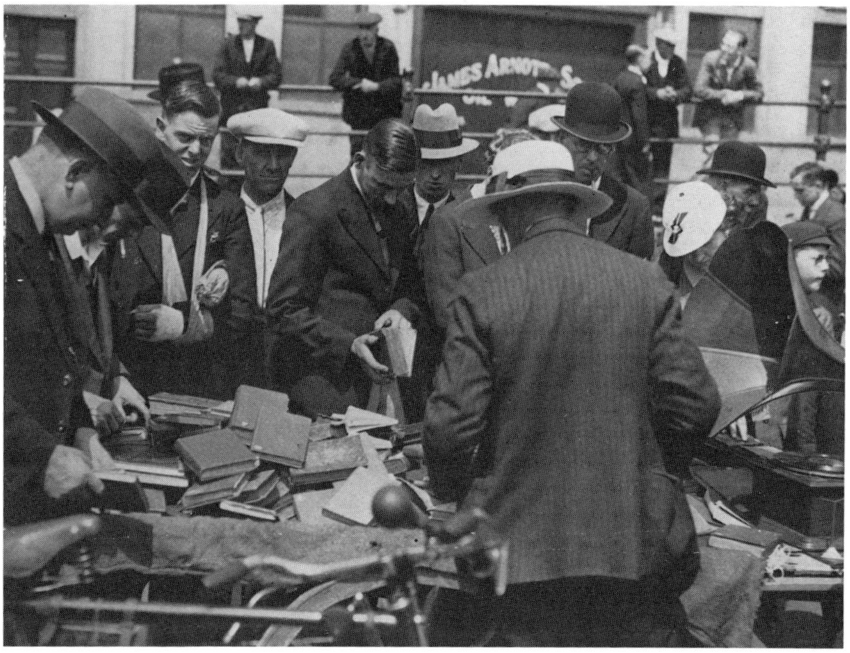

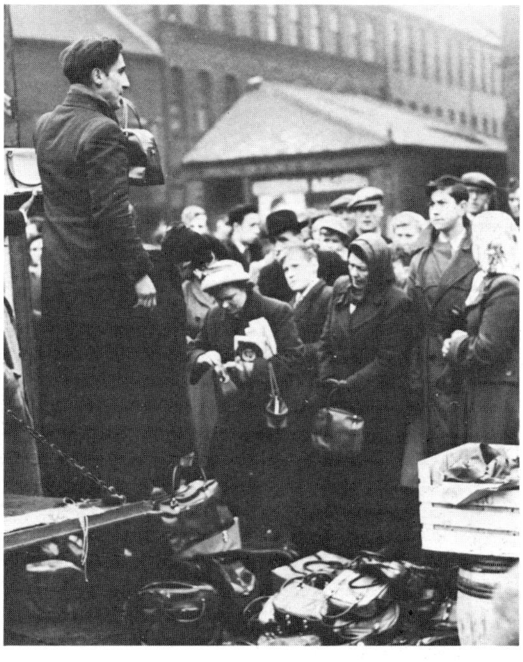

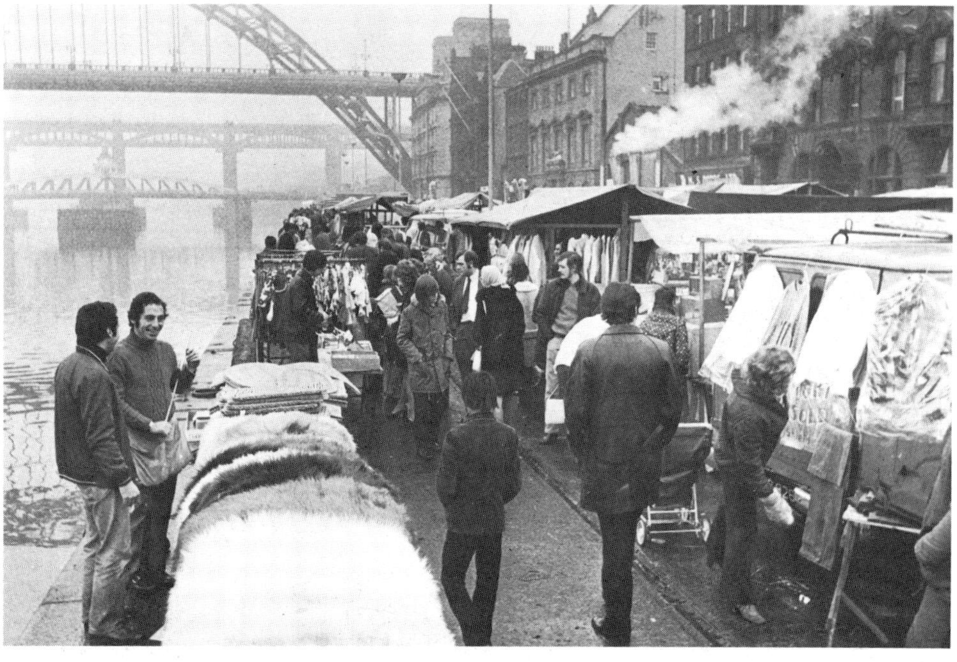

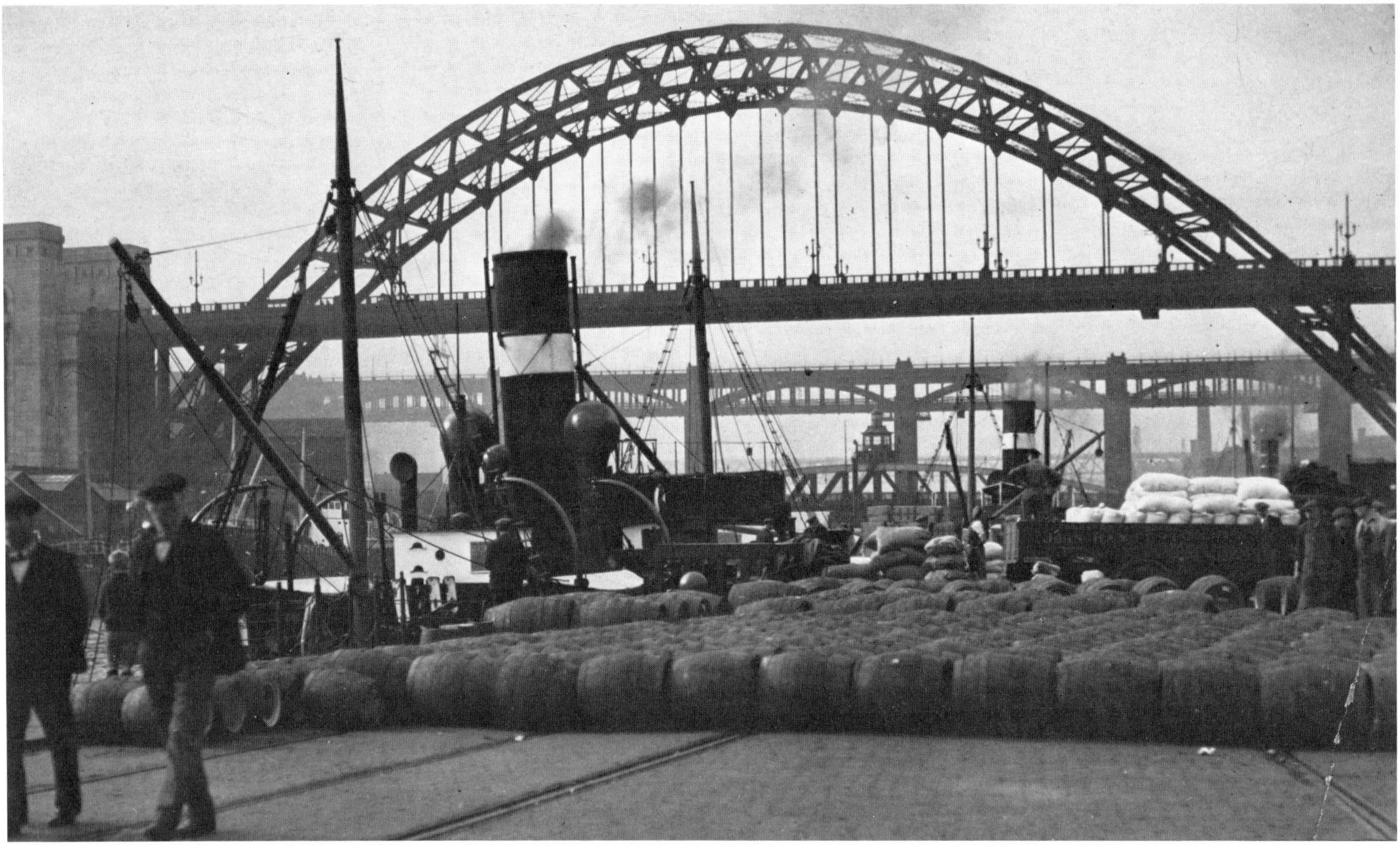

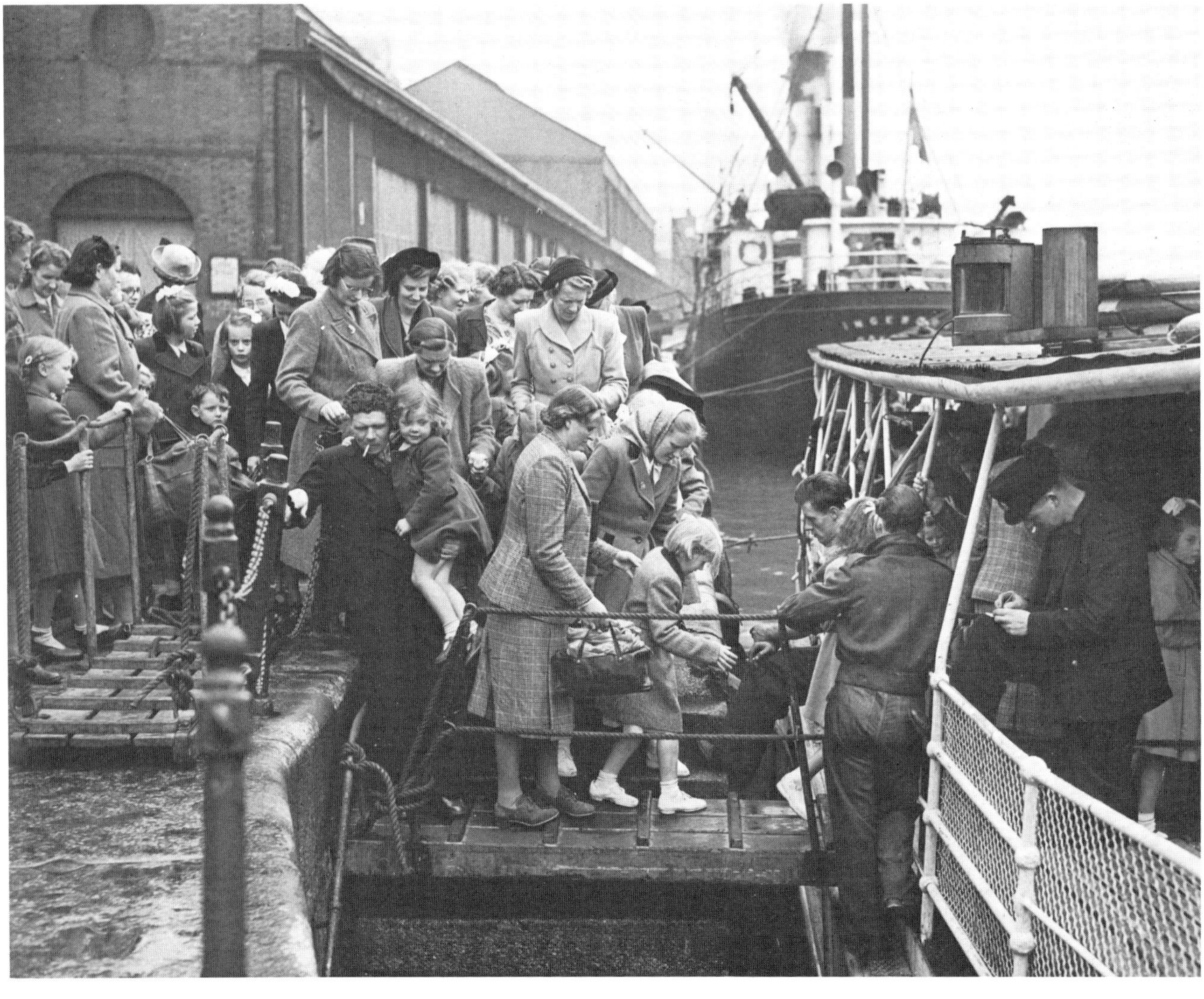

14. The Quayside in February 1939.

16. *Opposite page:* A dramatic view down the Tyne snapped by Malcolm Hepple in February 1978. The new Metro bridge can be seen inching its way across the river.

15. Schoolchildren embark with their parents for a trip down the Tyne to South Shields in July 1950.

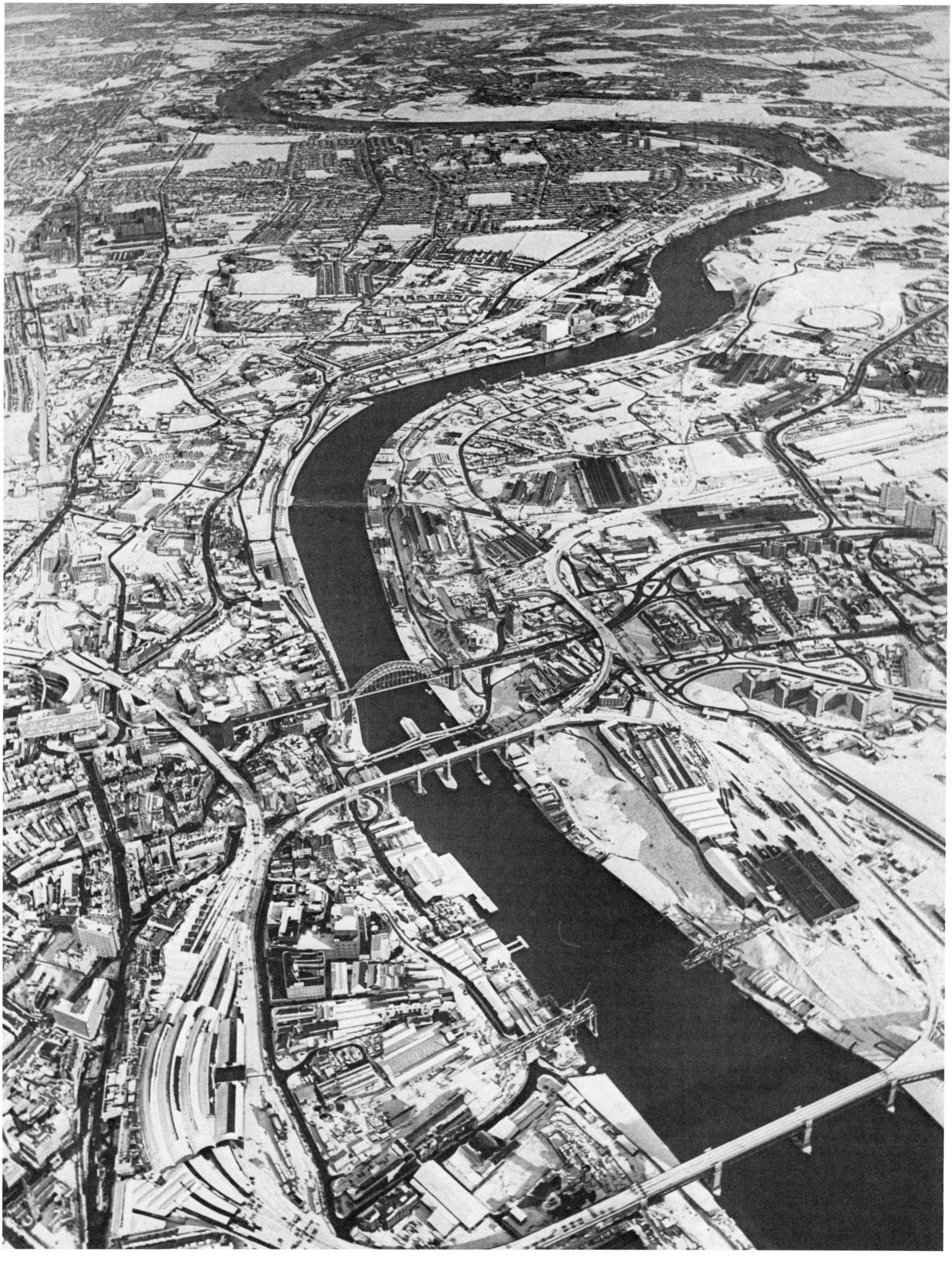

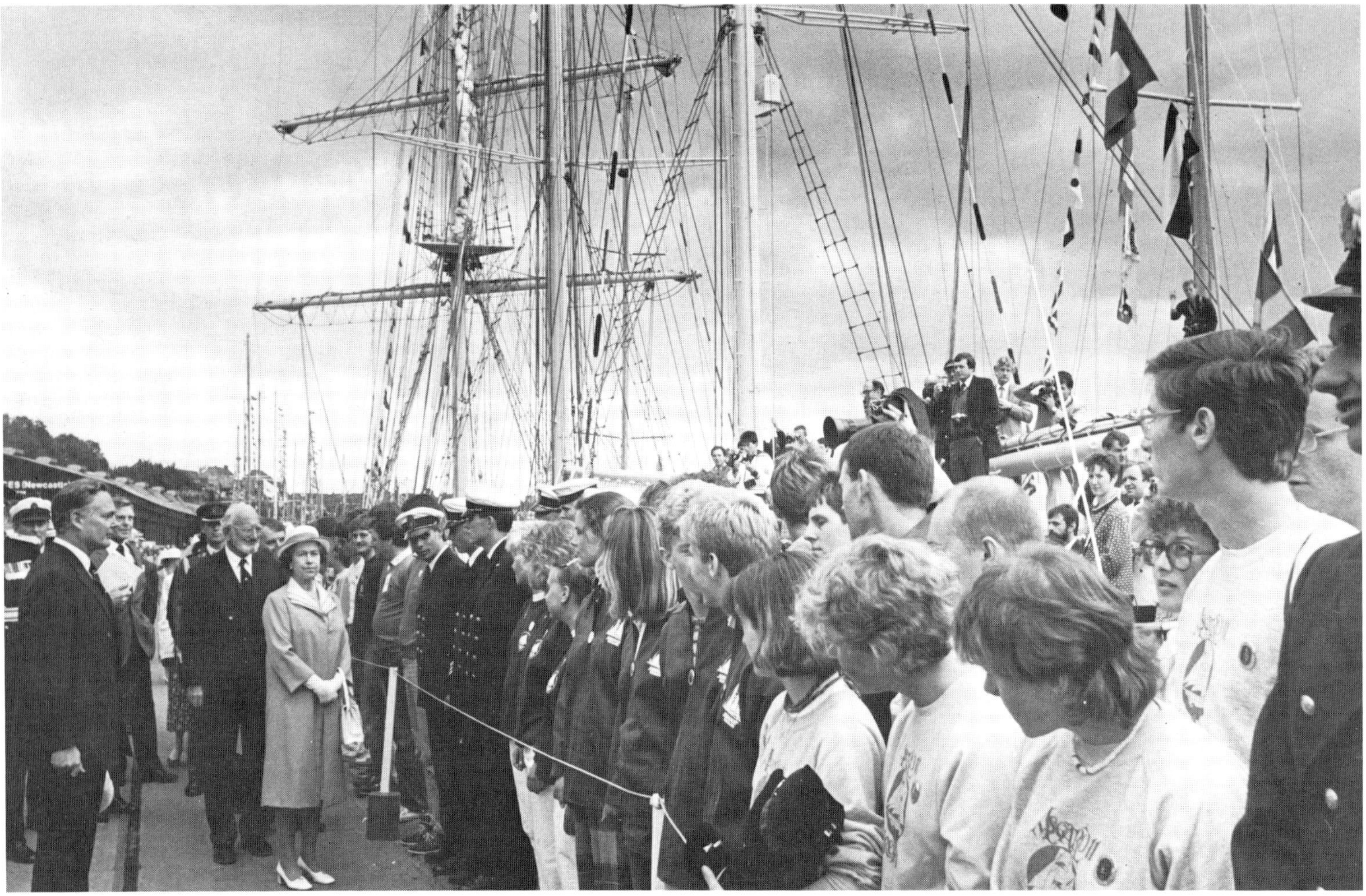

17. Her Majesty Queen Elizabeth II pays a visit to the Sail Training Association vessel *Sir Winston Churchill* at the Quayside in July 1986.

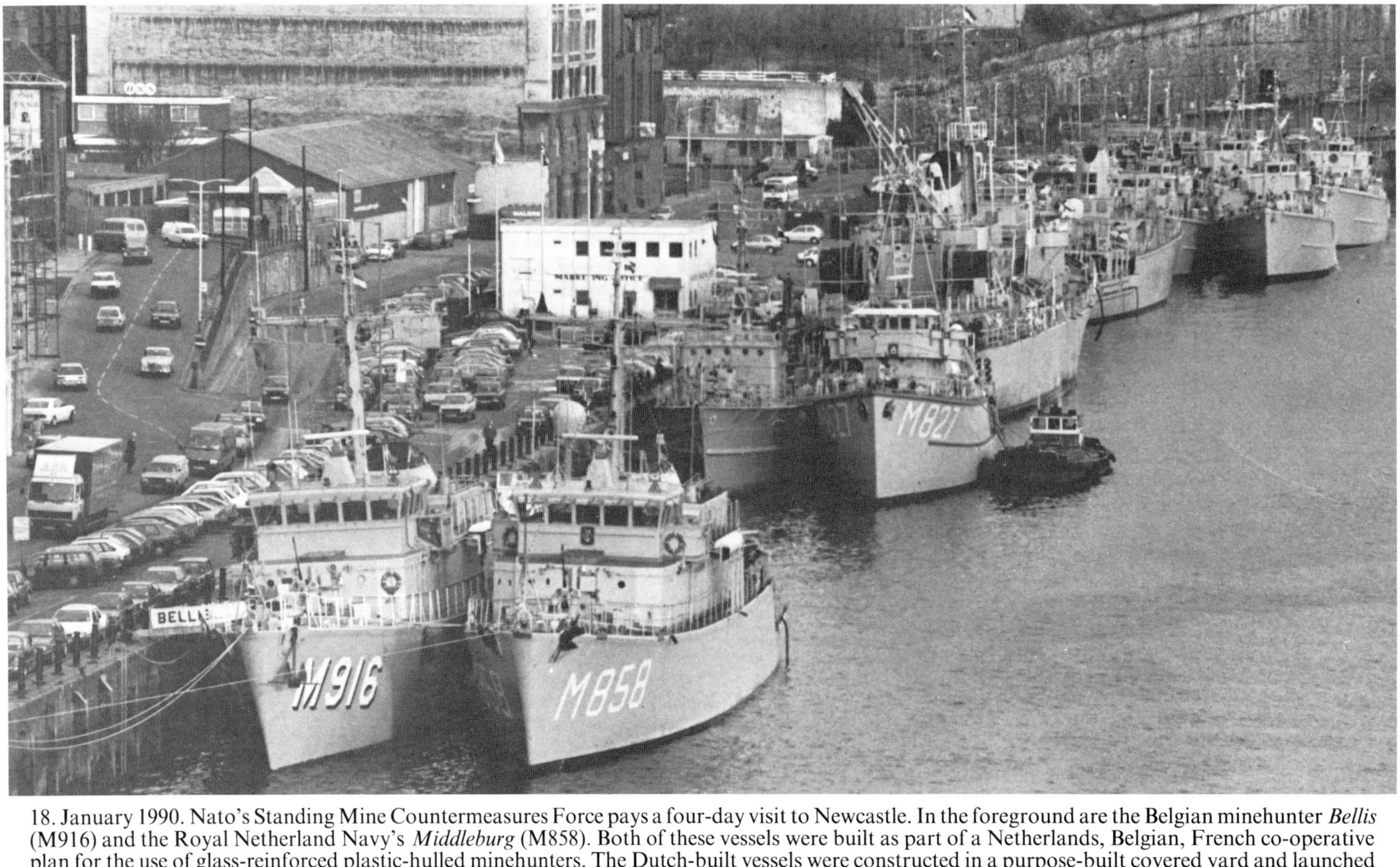

18. January 1990. Nato's Standing Mine Countermeasures Force pays a four-day visit to Newcastle. In the foreground are the Belgian minehunter *Bellis* (M916) and the Royal Netherland Navy's *Middleburg* (M858). Both of these vessels were built as part of a Netherlands, Belgian, French co-operative plan for the use of glass-reinforced plastic-hulled minehunters. The Dutch-built vessels were constructed in a purpose-built covered yard and launched virtually ready for sea trials.

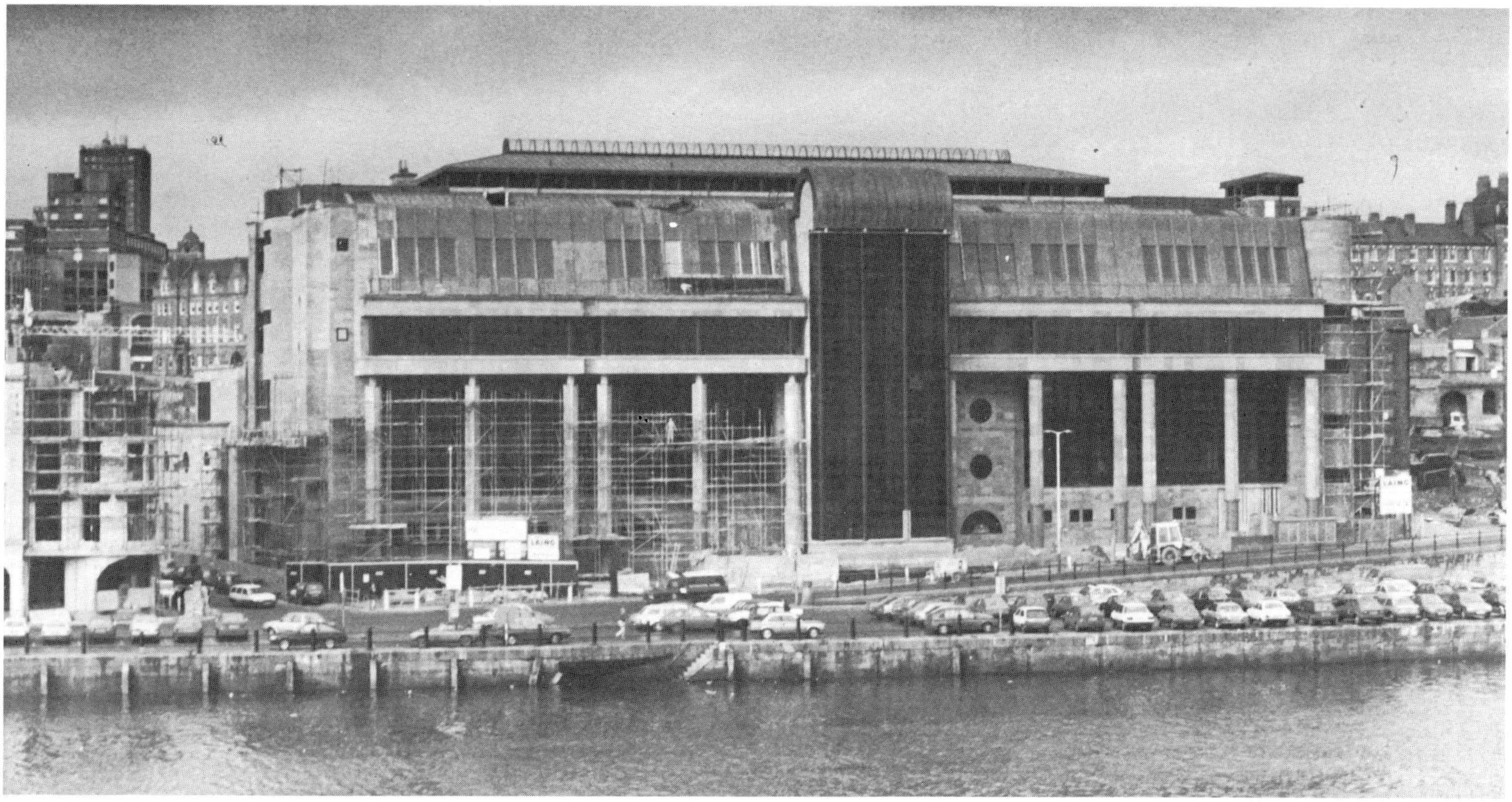

19. A central feature of the Quayside redevelopment is the new law courts building seen here in an advanced state of construction in January 1990.

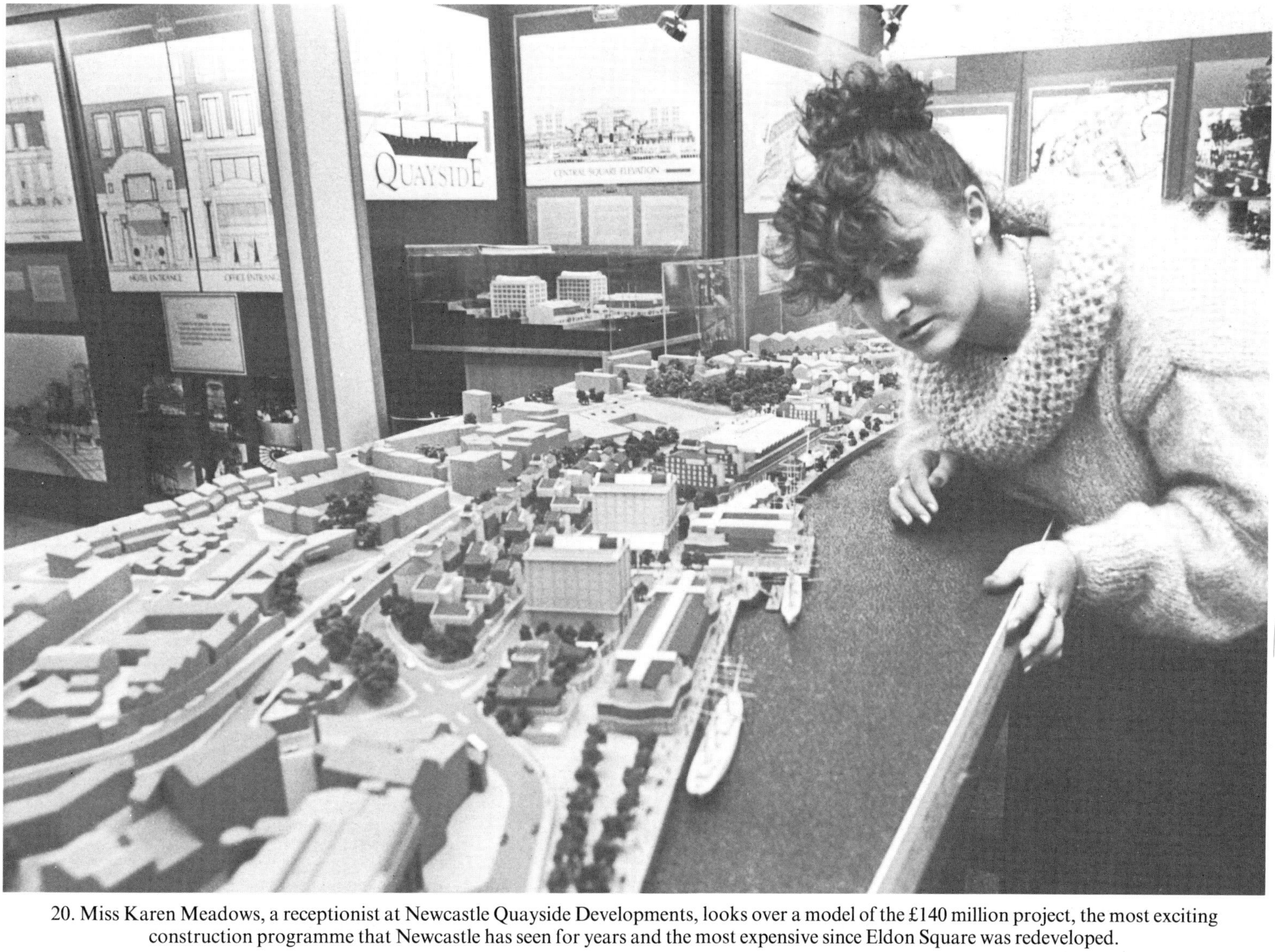

20. Miss Karen Meadows, a receptionist at Newcastle Quayside Developments, looks over a model of the £140 million project, the most exciting construction programme that Newcastle has seen for years and the most expensive since Eldon Square was redeveloped.

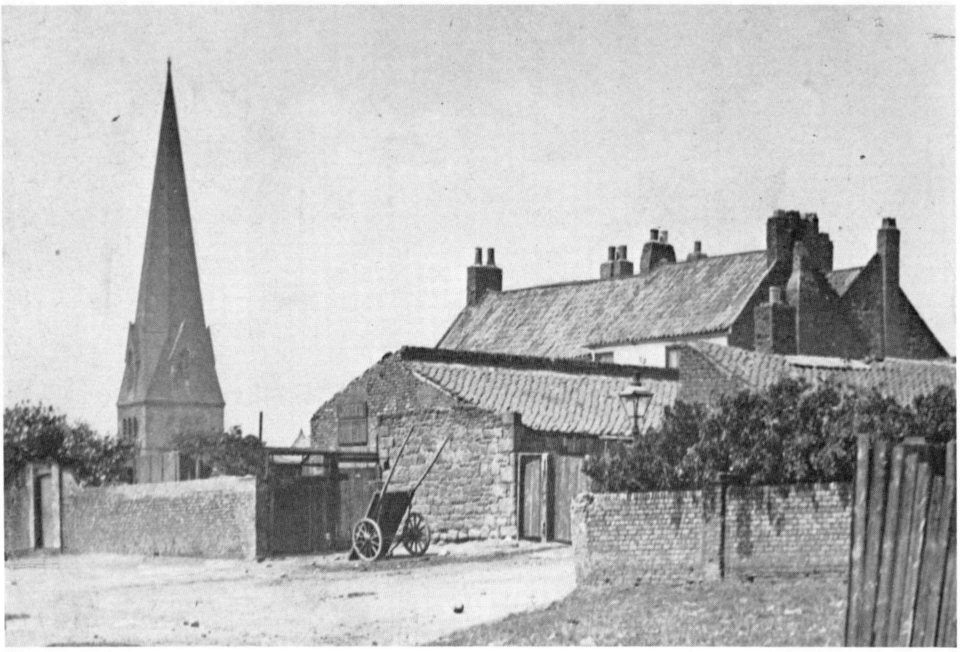

21. Believe it or not this is Byker, before the church and the village houses were demolished to make way for a children's playground. The date of the photograph is unknown though a zinc block was made in November 1930 so that it could be reproduced in the *Weekly Chronicle*. The picture also appeared in the *Sunday Sun* in July 1971.

22. Quality Row, Byker, in September 1930 was one of the streets scheduled for demolition under Newcastle Housing Committee's five-year redevelopment programme. This picture has appeared in the *Sunday Sun* (1972) and the *Evening Chronicle* (1978).

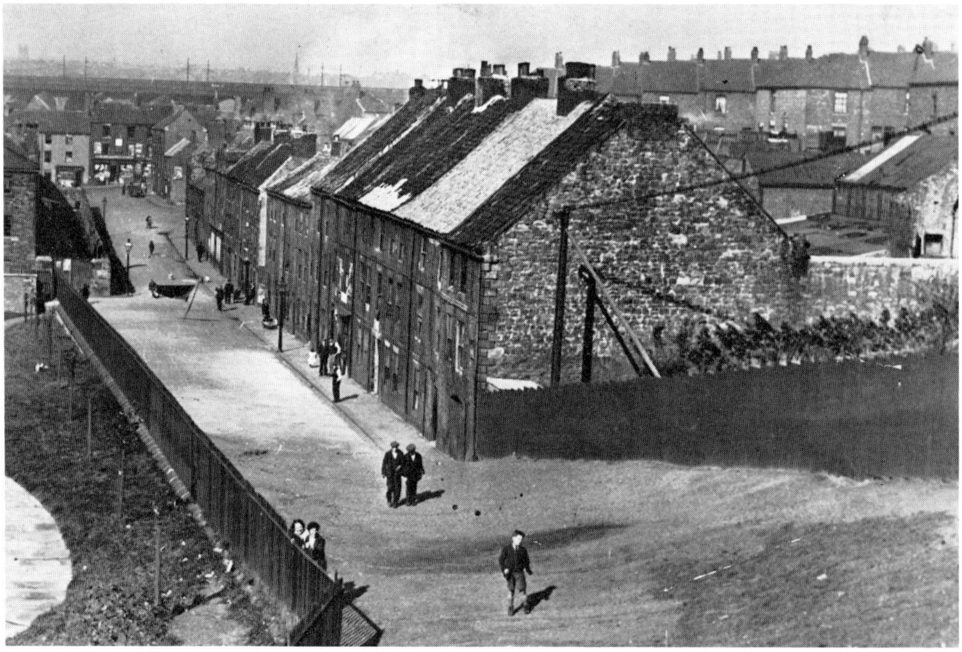

23. The rooftops of Byker looking towards the city centre. The photograph dates from the 1950s and appeared in the *Evening Chronicle* in November 1984.

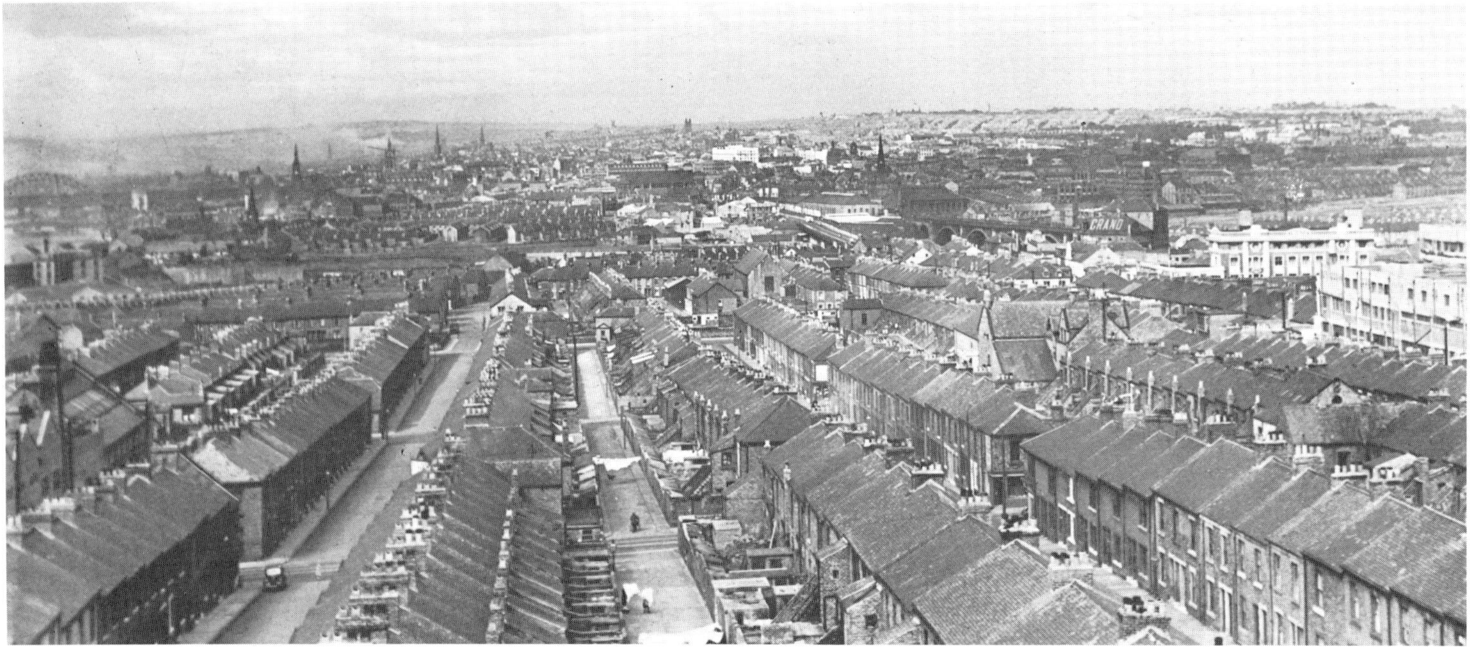

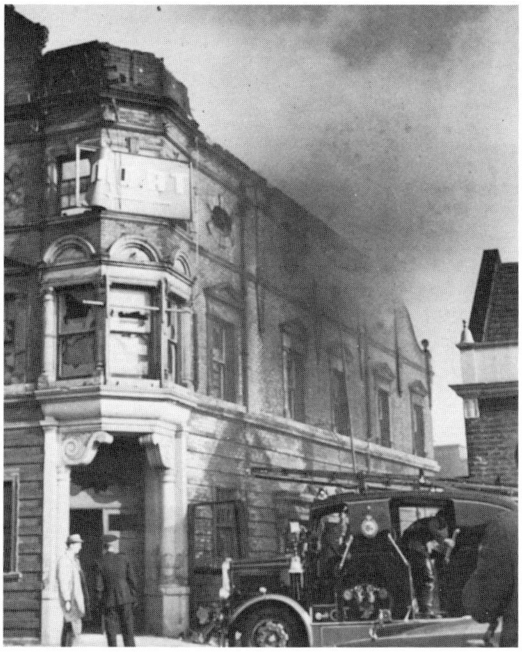

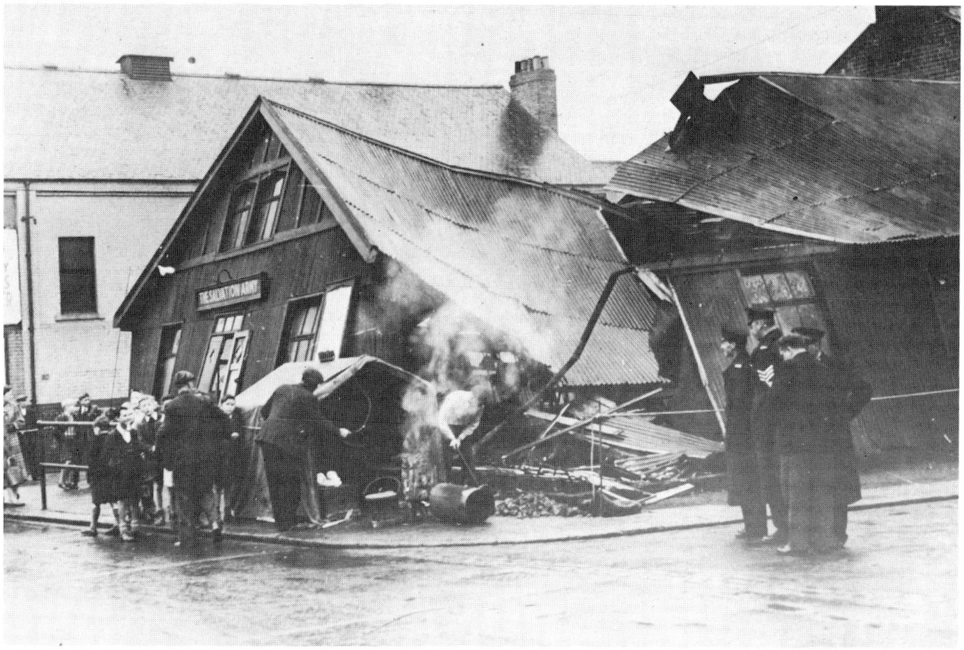

24. *Above:* Smoke belches from the roof at the Grand Theatre, Byker, in April 1964.

25. *Above right:* Tragedy came to the Byker Corps of The Salvation Army the day a double-decker bus skidded and demolished the Citadel in Shields Road.

26. *Right:* Byker Bus Depot in September 1948. The photograph was taken for publication in the *Weekly Chronicle*.

27. *Bottom right:* A scene at the Byker Depot from a more elegant age of travel. Byker was the largest depot on the tramway network.

28. *Below:* Not all tramcars carried passengers; this is one of the service vehicles.

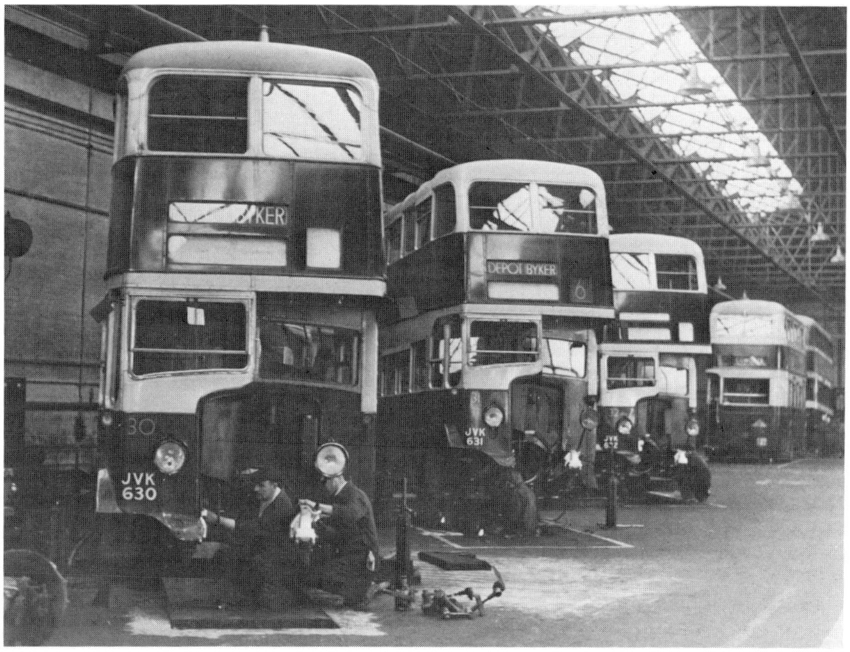

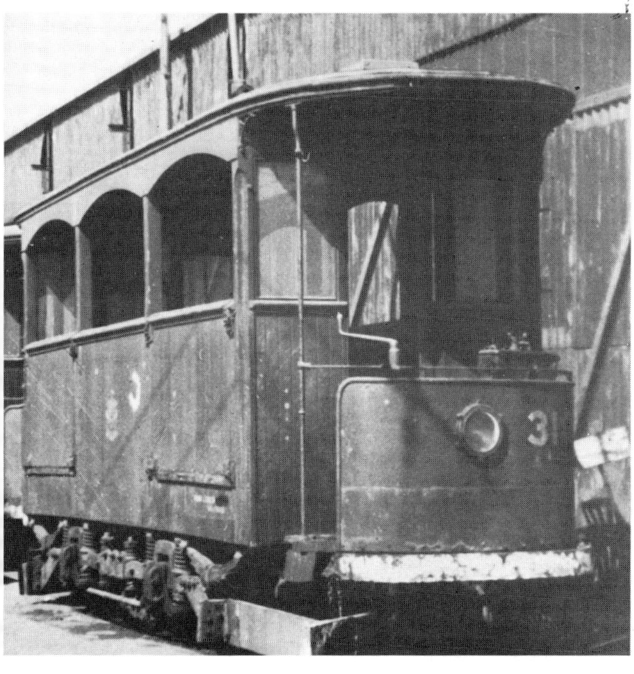

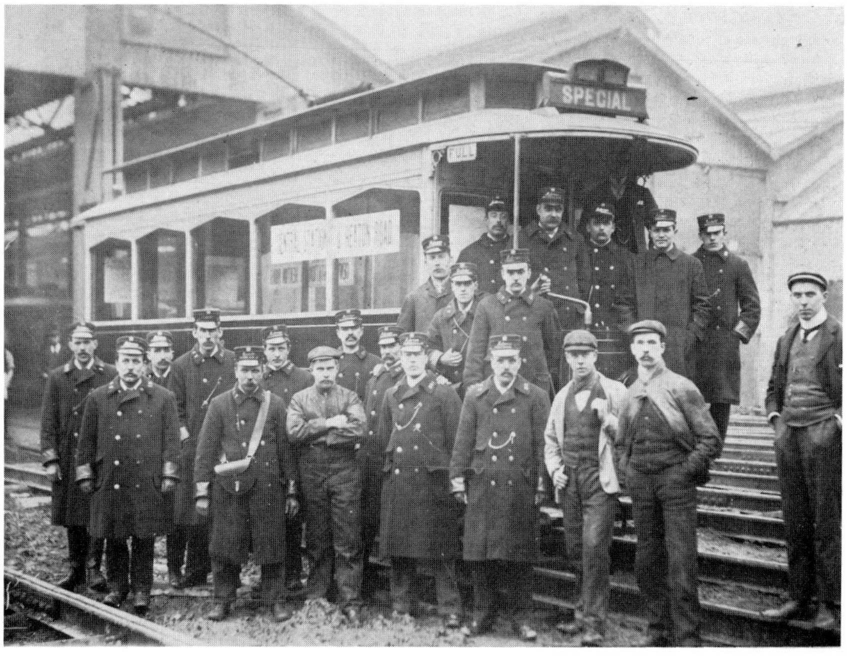

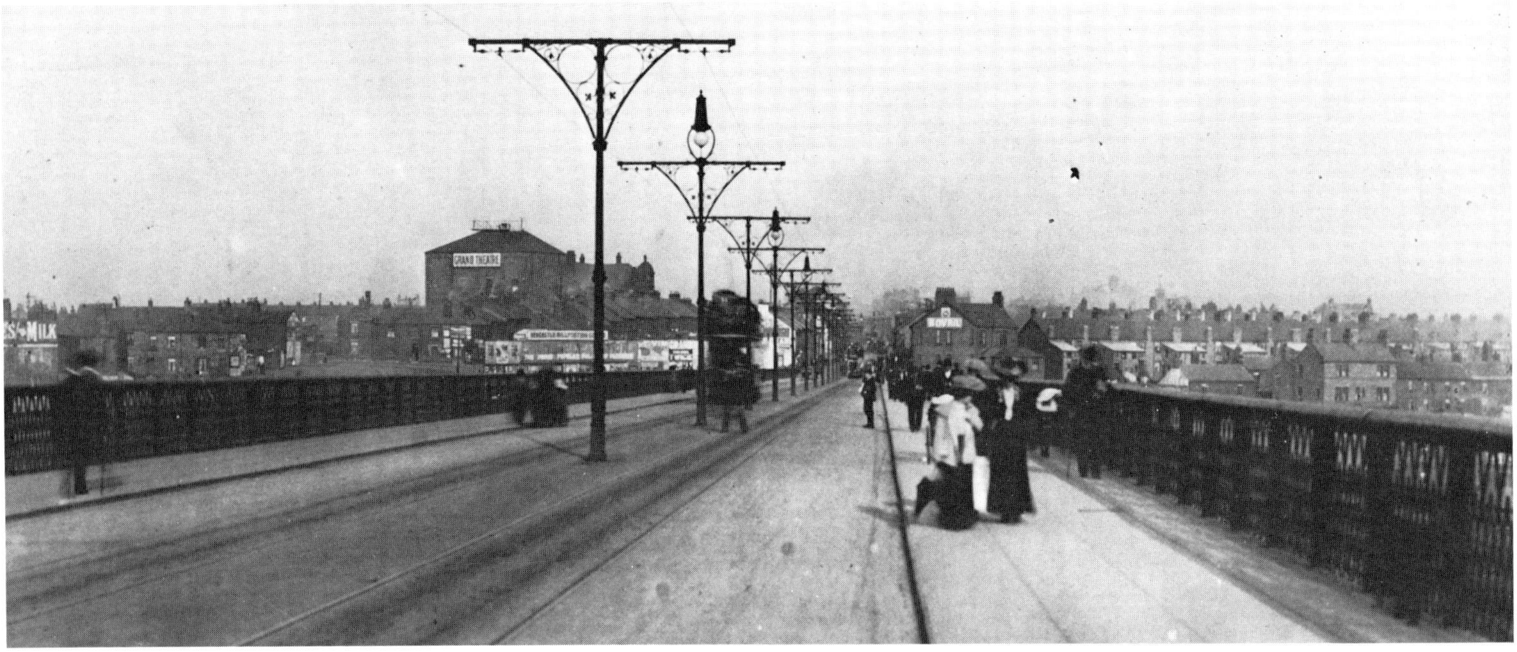

29. Byker Bridge in about 1910.

31. *Right:* The old meets the new in Byker in August 1989. To the right lies the Byker Wall – a housing development which became one of the most talked-about in the country when it was built. The Wall snakes down the picture like some sort of medieval fortification – only the moat is missing. To the left Shields Road runs straight as an arrow, wobbles slightly, then continues as Fossway. Also sneaking into the picture are NEI Parsons and Brough Park Greyhound Racing Stadium.

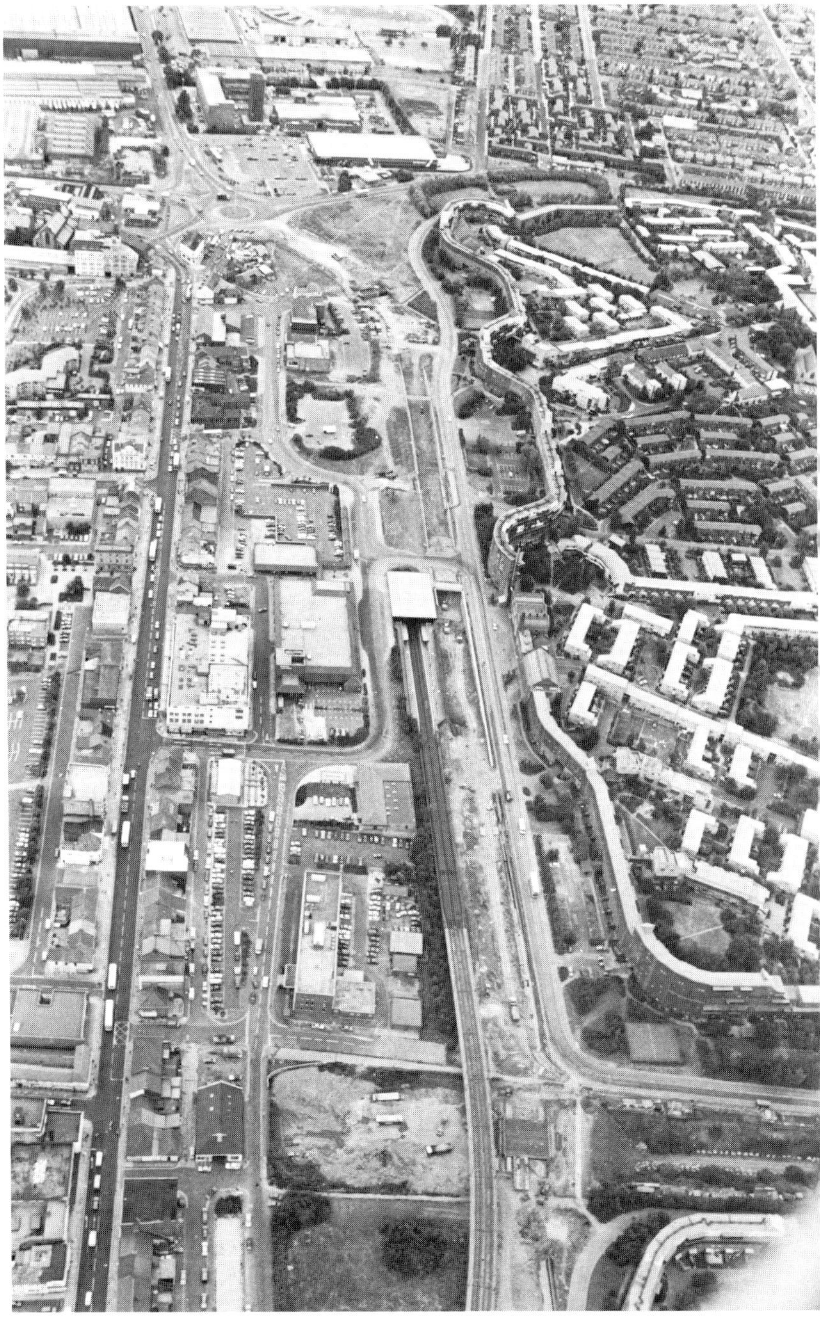

30. A Metro train climbs across the Byker viaduct on a test run in November 1982.

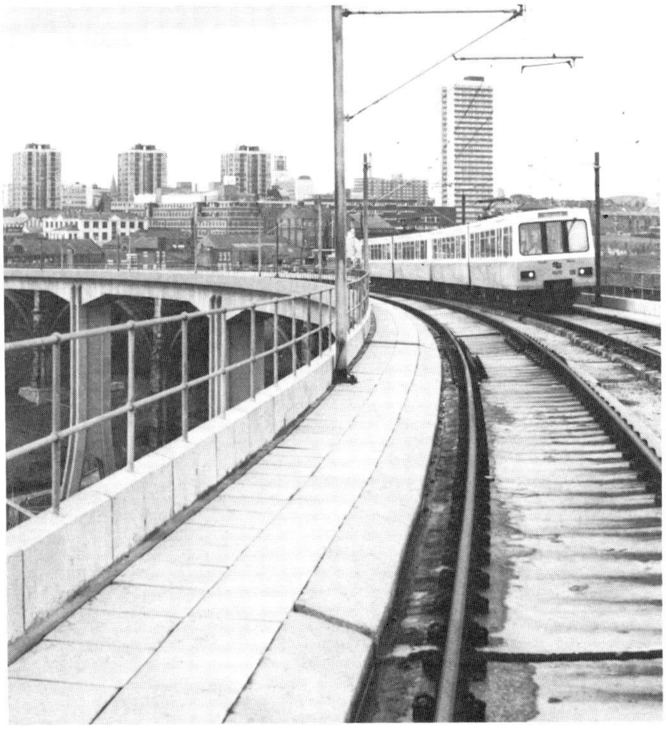

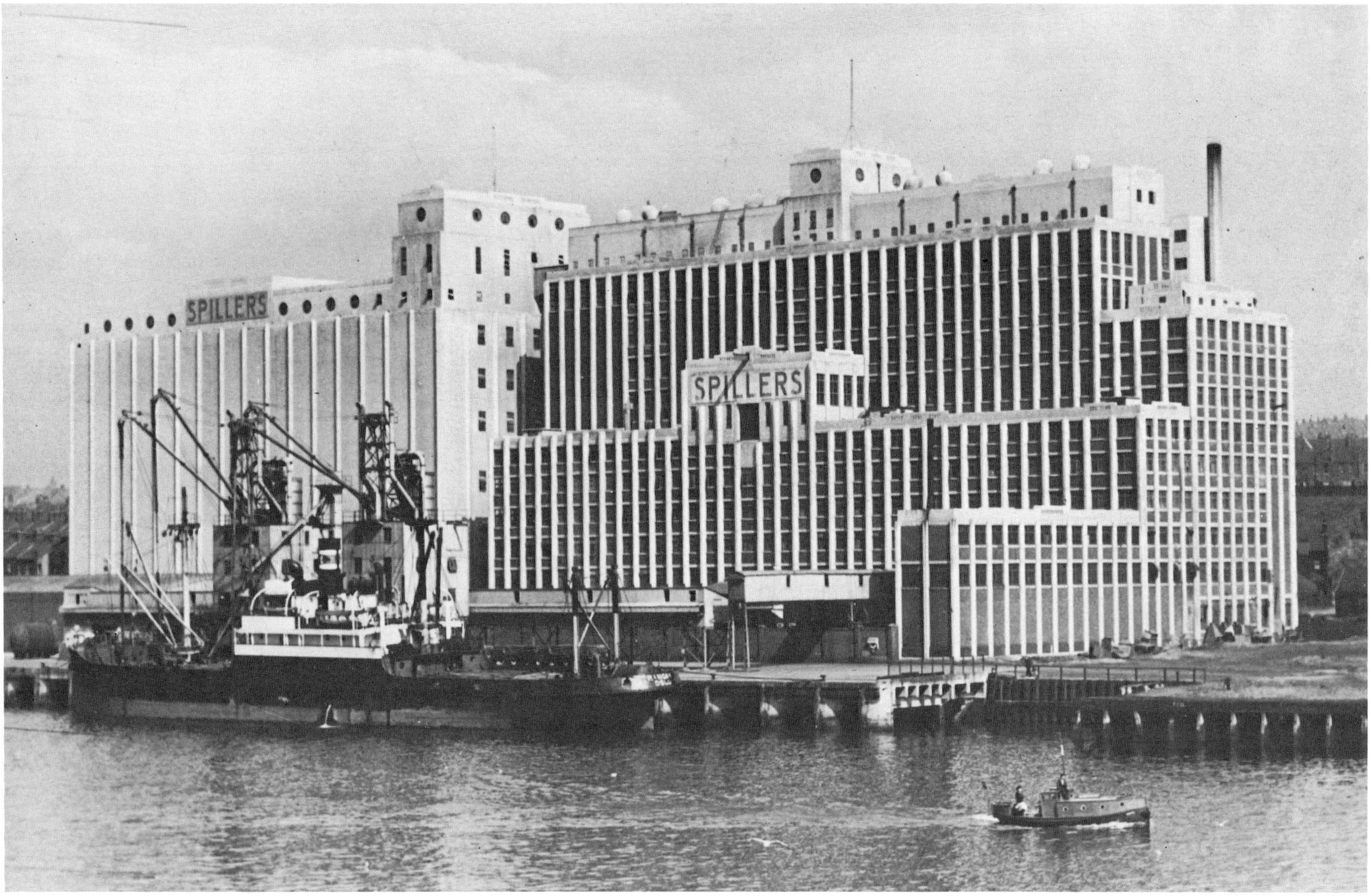

32. Back to the Quayside for a view of Spillers Mill as seen from the Gateshead side of the river in September 1951.

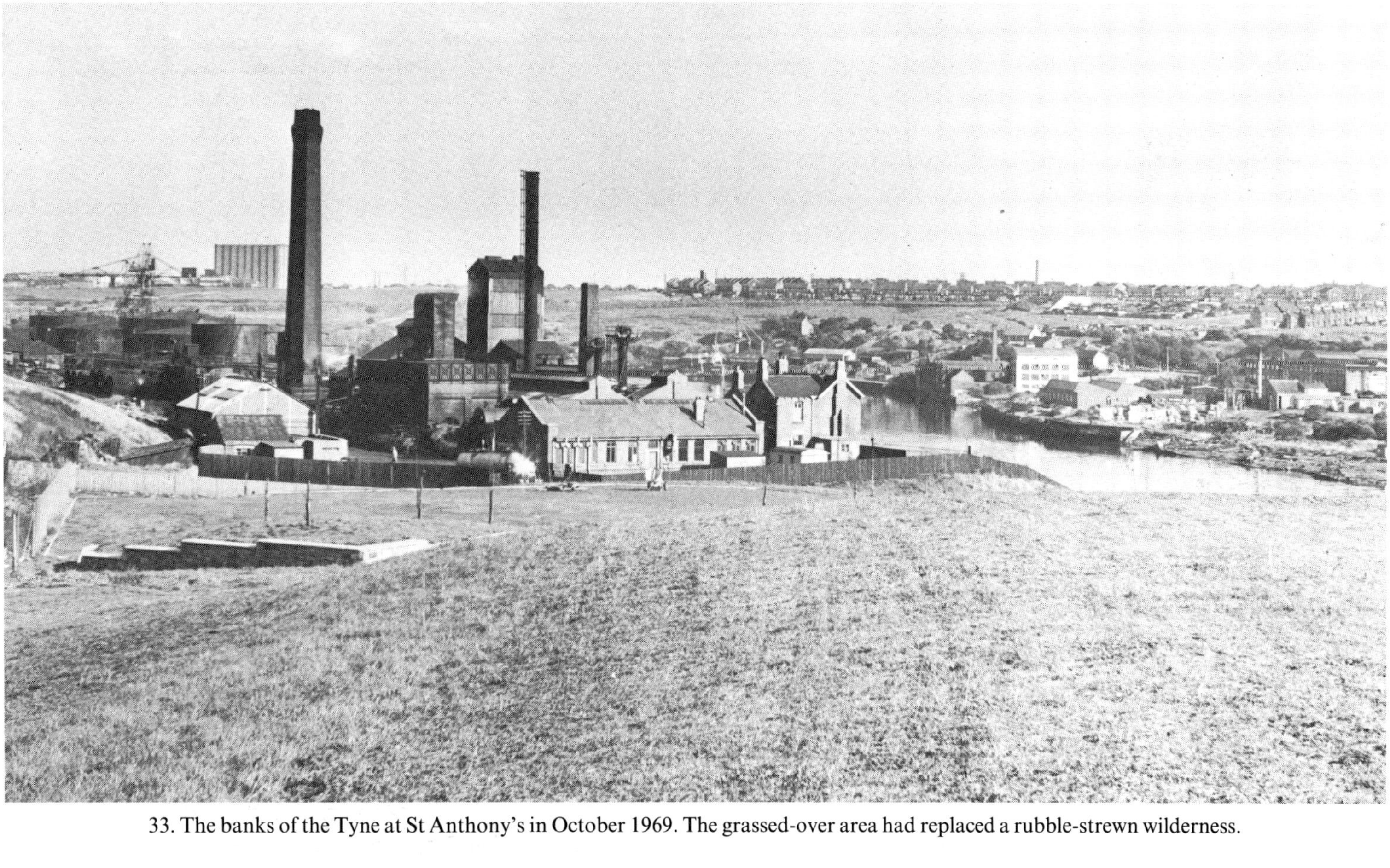
33. The banks of the Tyne at St Anthony's in October 1969. The grassed-over area had replaced a rubble-strewn wilderness.

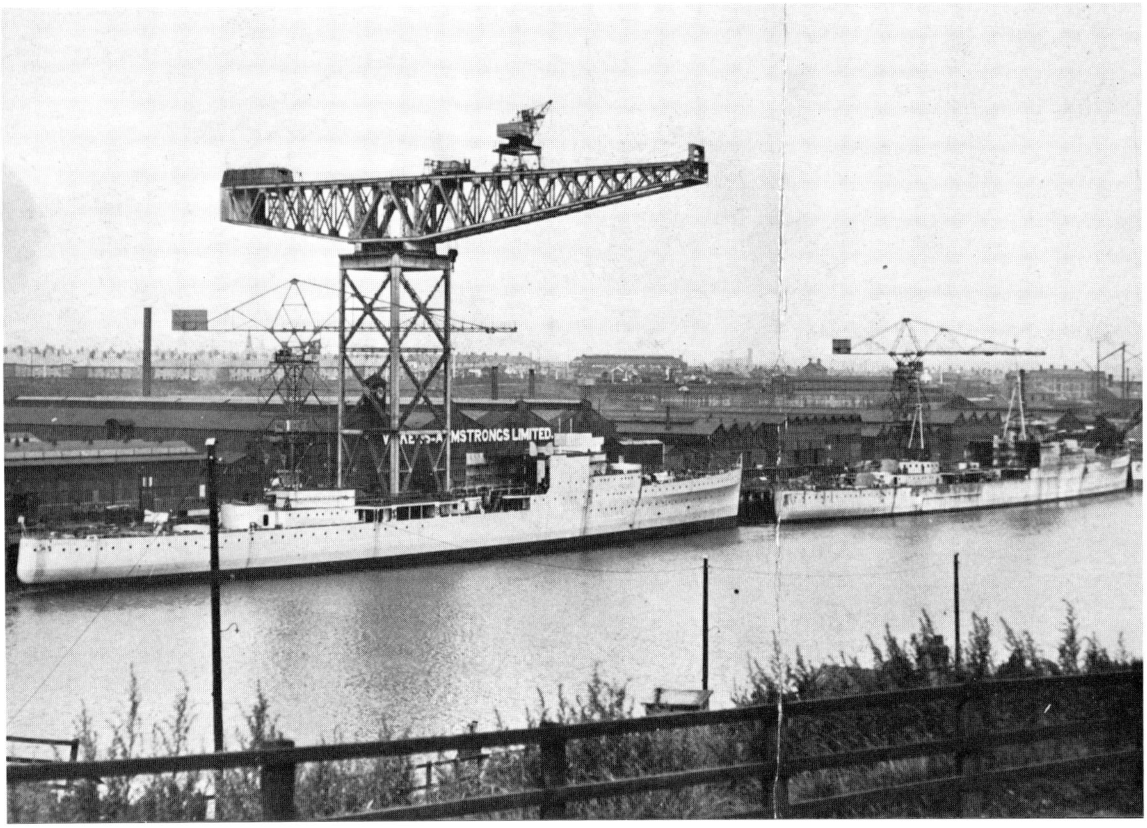

34. A view of the Walker Naval Yard in 1936 with the cruisers *Newcastle* and *Sheffield* (nearest camera) alongside for fitting out. Both vessels belonged to the *Southampton* class, displaced 9,100 tons and were armed with 12-6in guns mounted in triple turrets. During the war *Newcastle* served with the Home Fleet until 1941 and then in the South Atlantic prior to going east of Suez where she became flagship of the 5th Cruiser Squadron. *Newcastle* was scrapped at Faslane in 1959. *Sheffield* served with the Home Fleet and then Force 'H', taking part in the hunting down of the German battleship *Bismarck*. On 26 December 1943, whilst on convoy escort duty, *Sheffield* came into contact with the German battlecruiser *Scharnhorst* but with the help of the cruisers *Belfast* and *Norfolk* succeeded in driving the enemy off. In June 1944 she went to the USA for a much-needed refit returning home in June 1945. She was broken up in 1967.

35. March 1957. Shipyard workers stand around the Stack Hotel, Church Street, Walker, waiting to sign on for union benefit.

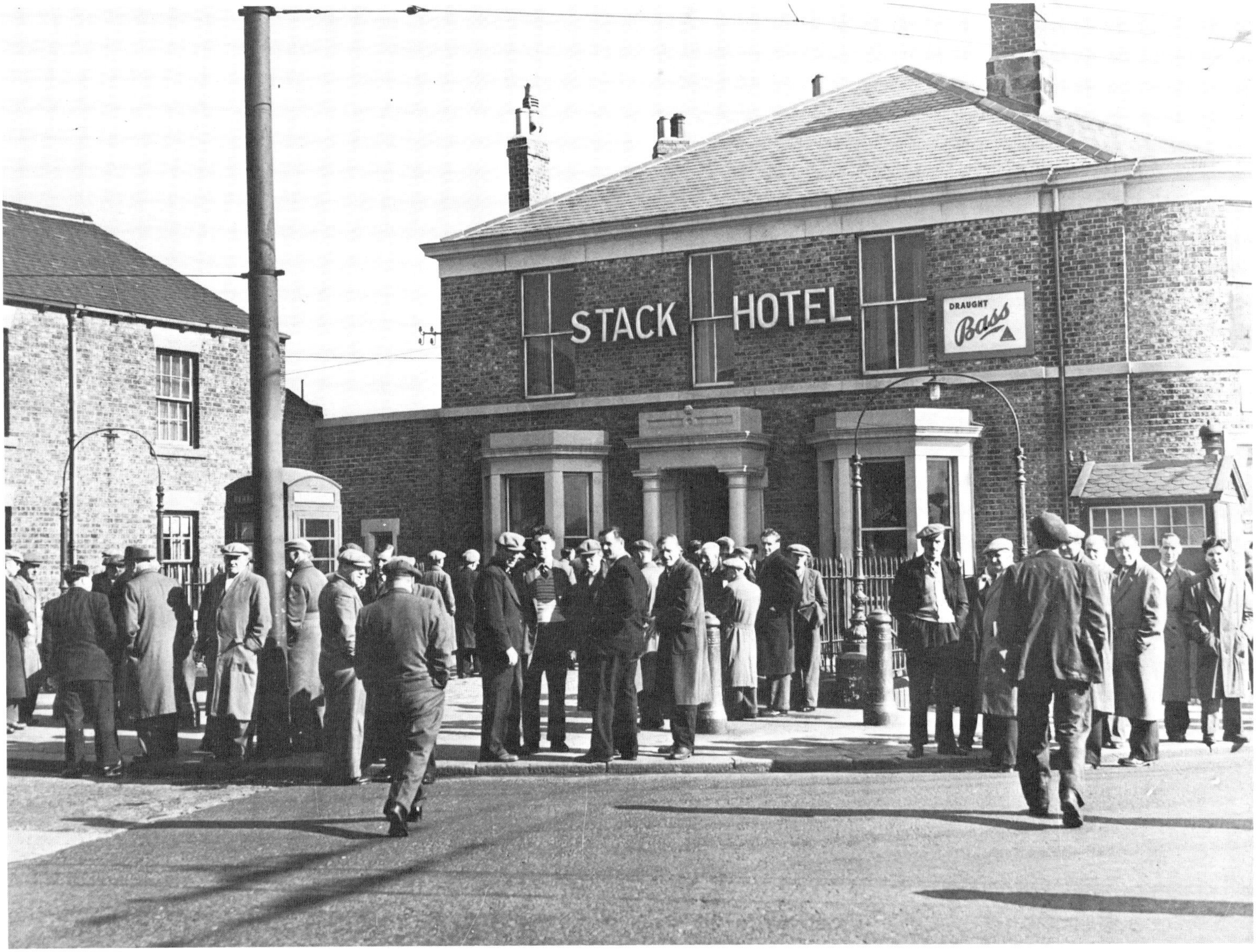

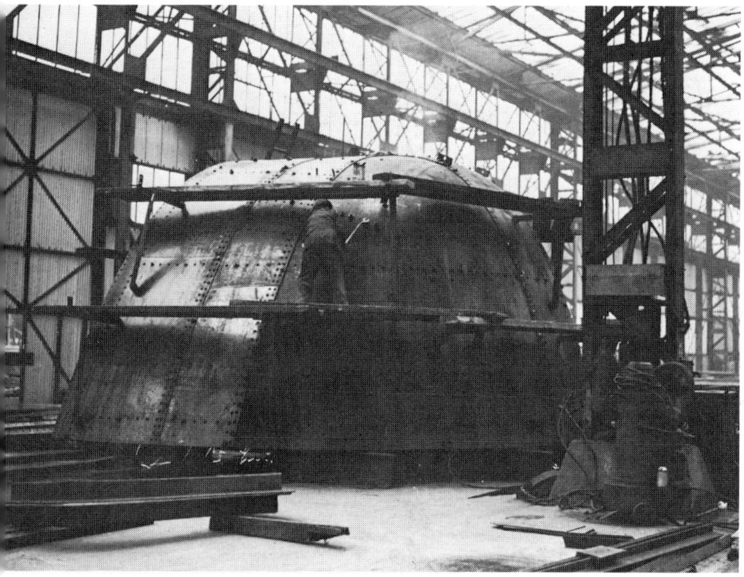

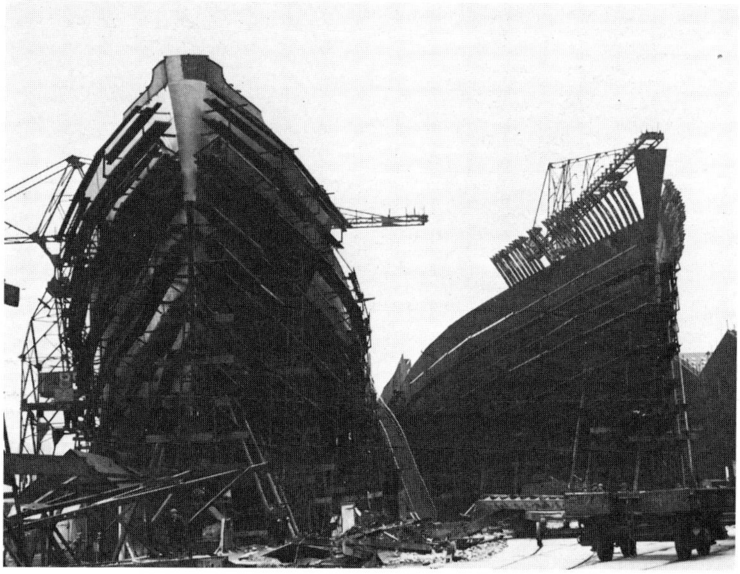

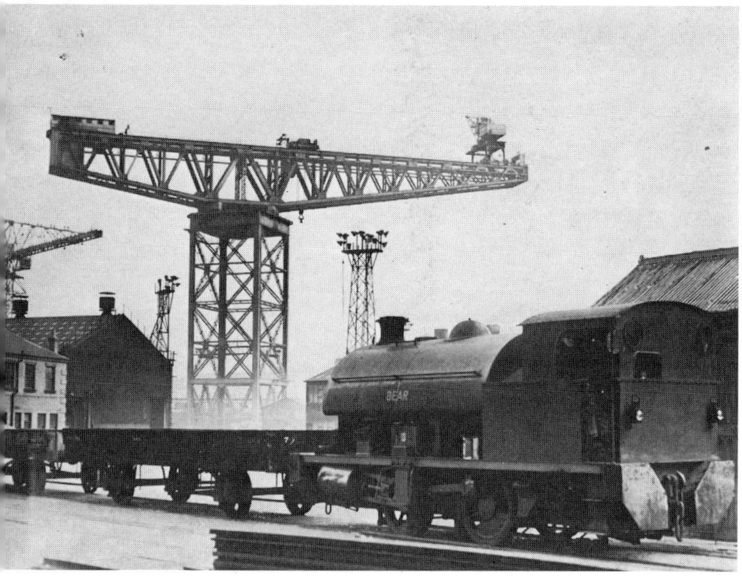

36. *Top left:* The stern section of a merchantship takes shape at the Walker Naval Yard c1946. *Courtesy* Vickers.

37. *Top right:* A busy scene at the Walker Naval Yard in 1946. The vessel on the left is thought to be the *Nova Scotia*, one of a pair of sisterships built for Furness Warren's Canadian service operating out of Liverpool.

38. *Left:* The big crane and the *Bear* in January 1958.

39. *Below:* Waverdale Avenue Camp as it appeared in July 1954 when the *Journal* carried the story that the former army base might soon be closed and the families there rehoused.

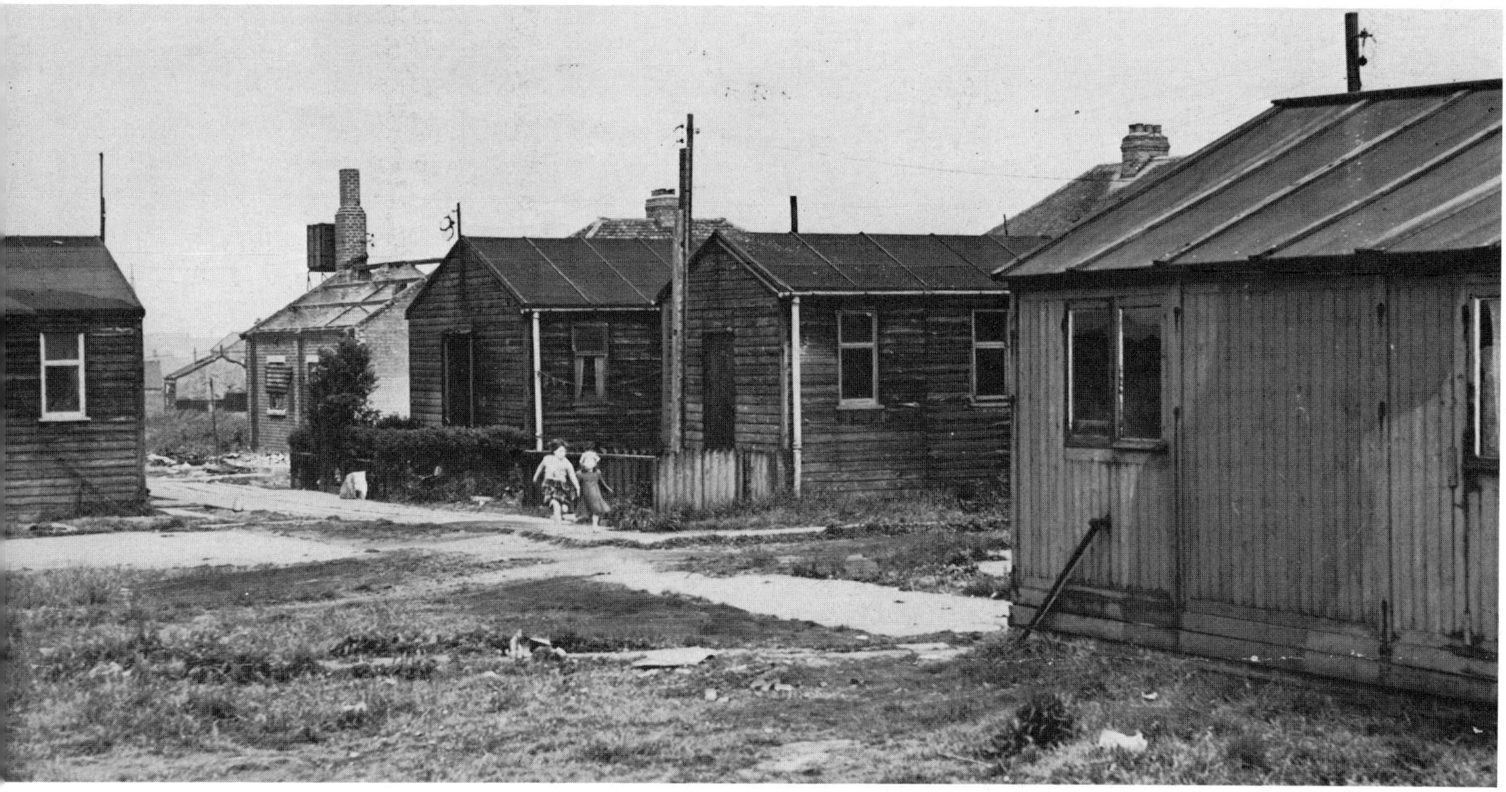

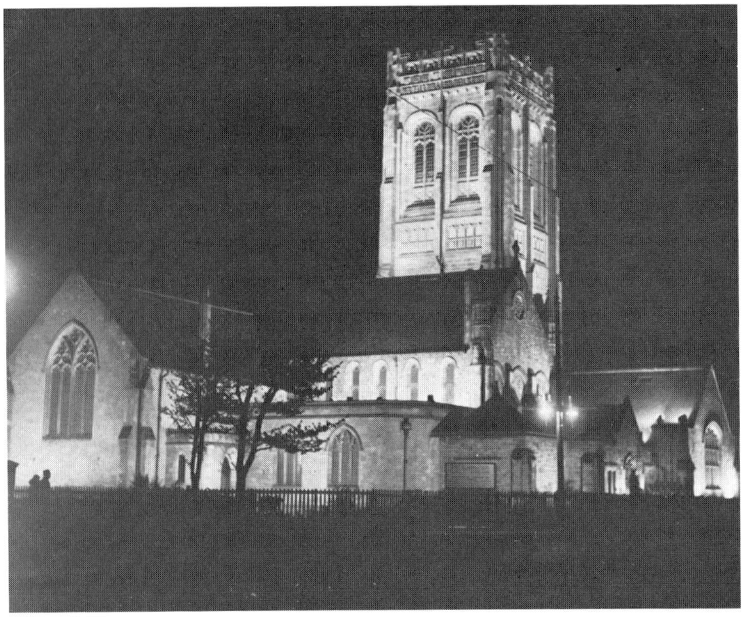

40. St Gabriel's Church, Heaton Road, floodlit for the Coronation of King George VI.

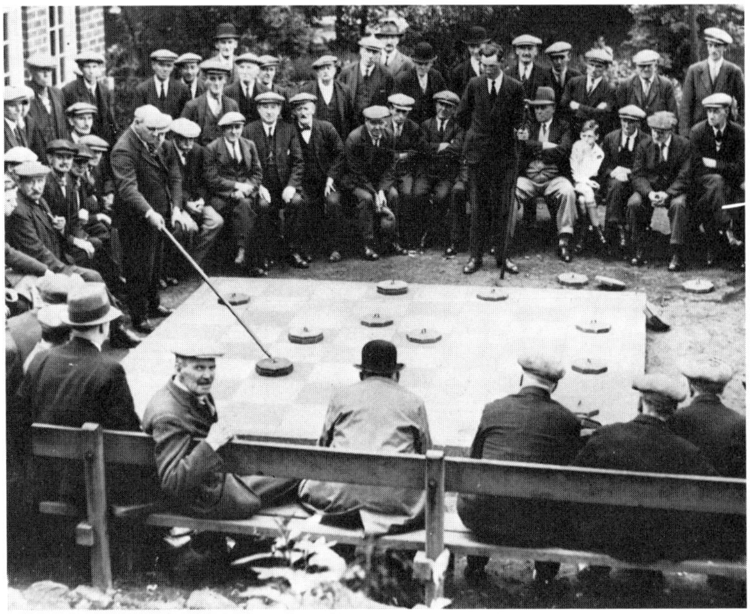

41. The giant draughts board in Heaton Park, August 1932.

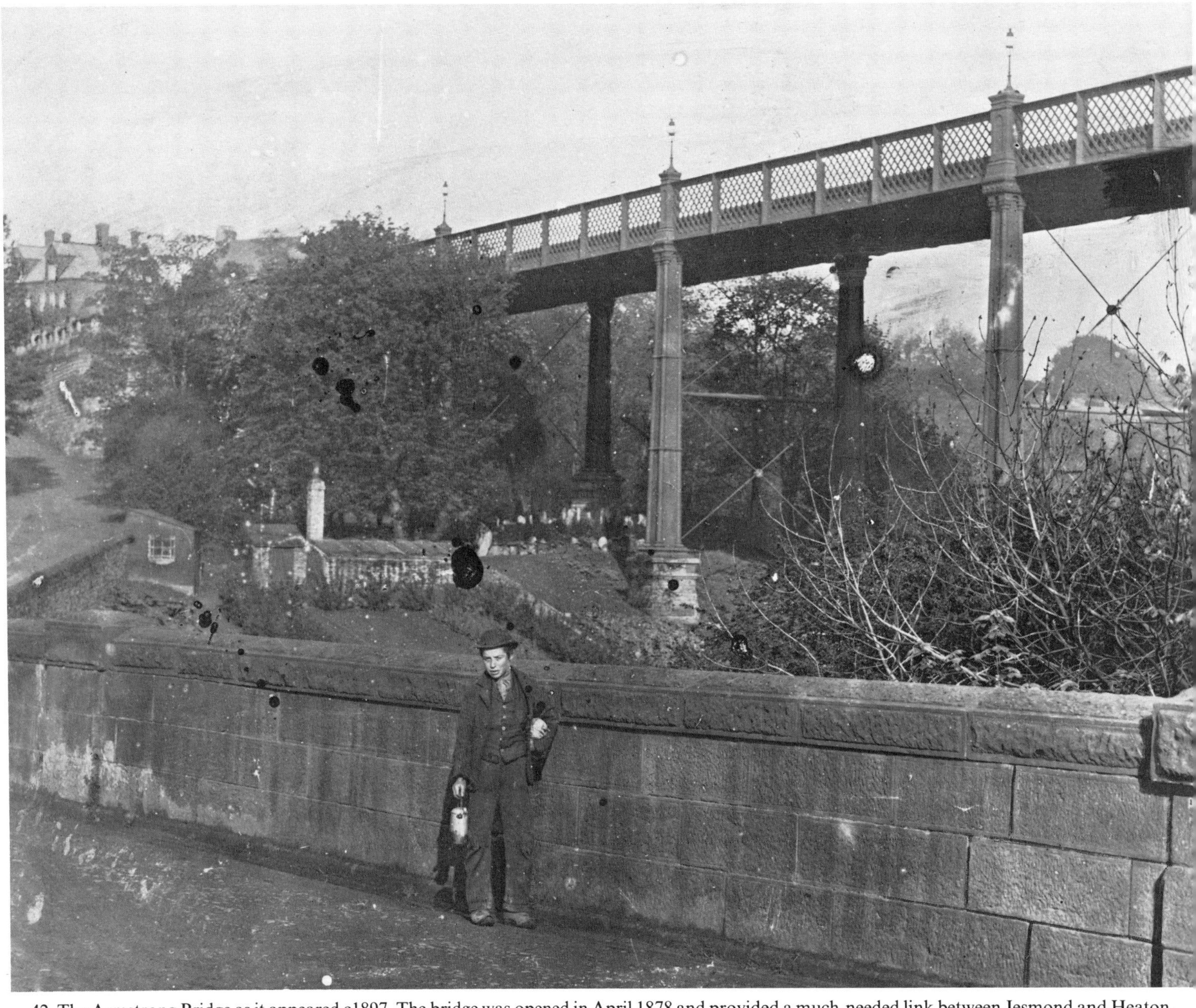

42. The Armstrong Bridge as it appeared c1897. The bridge was opened in April 1878 and provided a much-needed link between Jesmond and Heaton. On the left of the picture is what used to be known locally as *Tippy-toe Bank*. *Courtesy:* The collection of M Higgins.

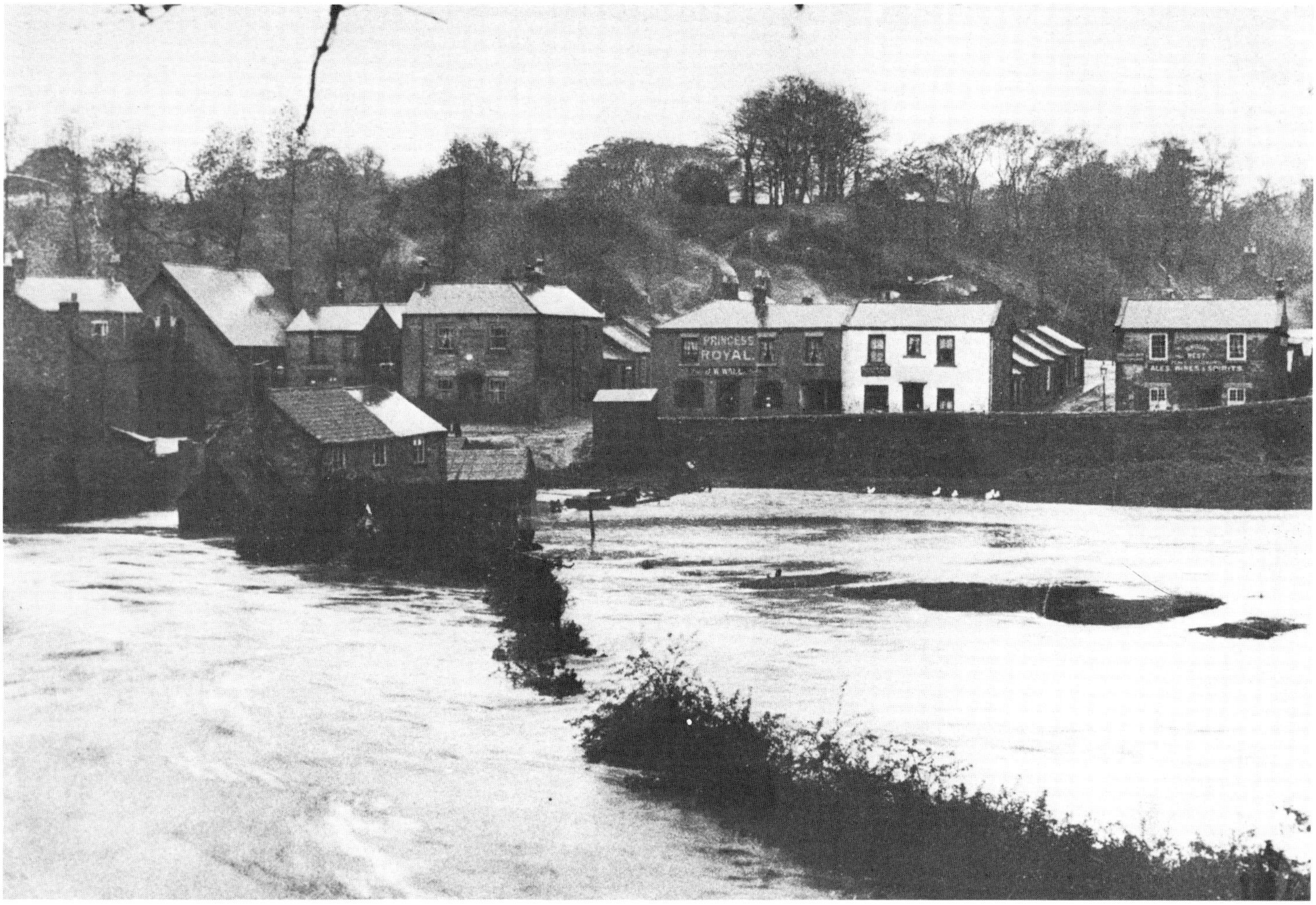

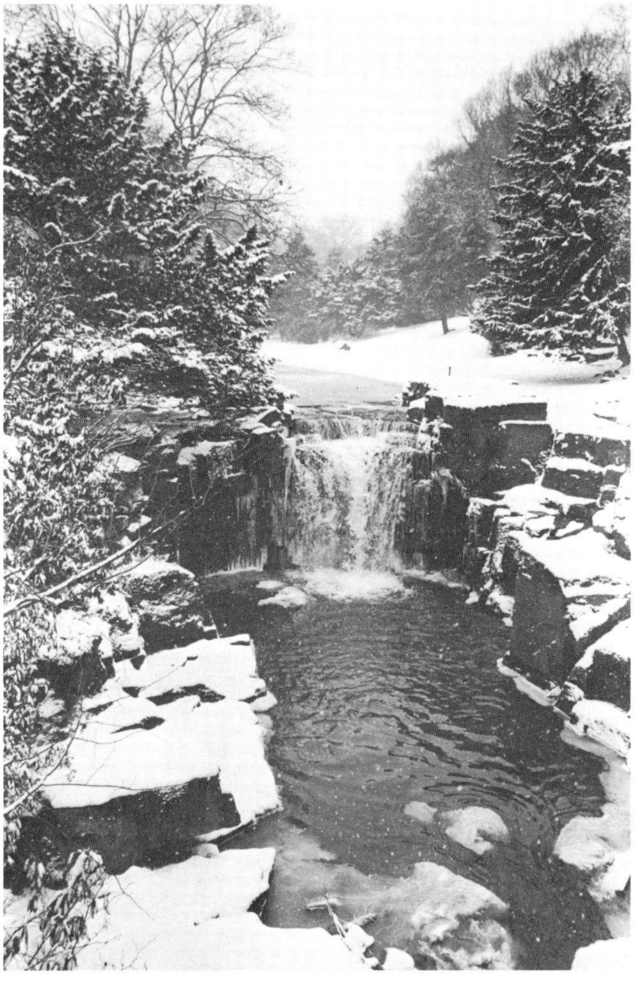

43. Recognise the view? This is Jesmond Vale and the stream is the Ouseburn in flood c1903. The photograph was taken by Mr J Blacklock, an official photographer during the Boer War who came to live in the Vale. Apparently the Ouseburn rose even higher and people in the cottage in the foreground were marooned. They were rescued by a horse and cart – the poor horse swimming all the way.

44. January 1987. Photographer P Schaill might well have been walking in a winter wonderland when he snapped this picture in Jesmond Dene.

45. *Below:* Jesmond Dene in March 1936.

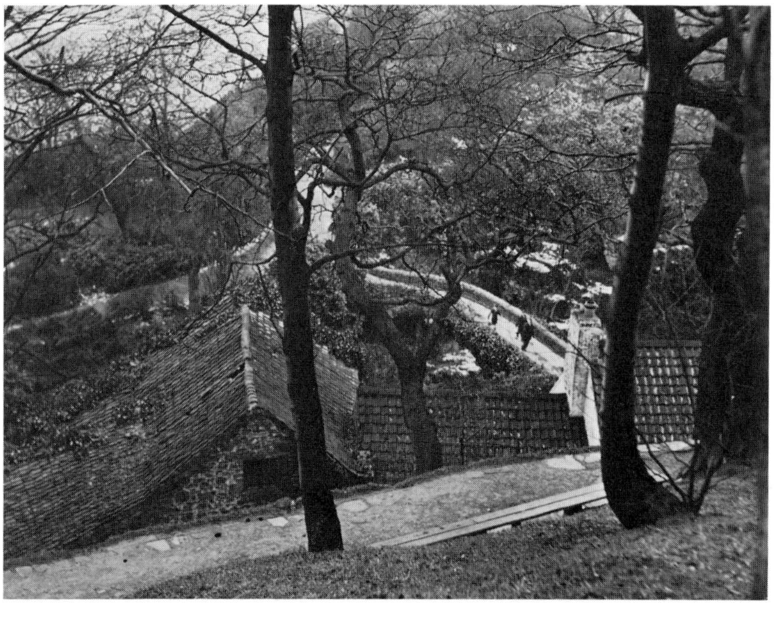

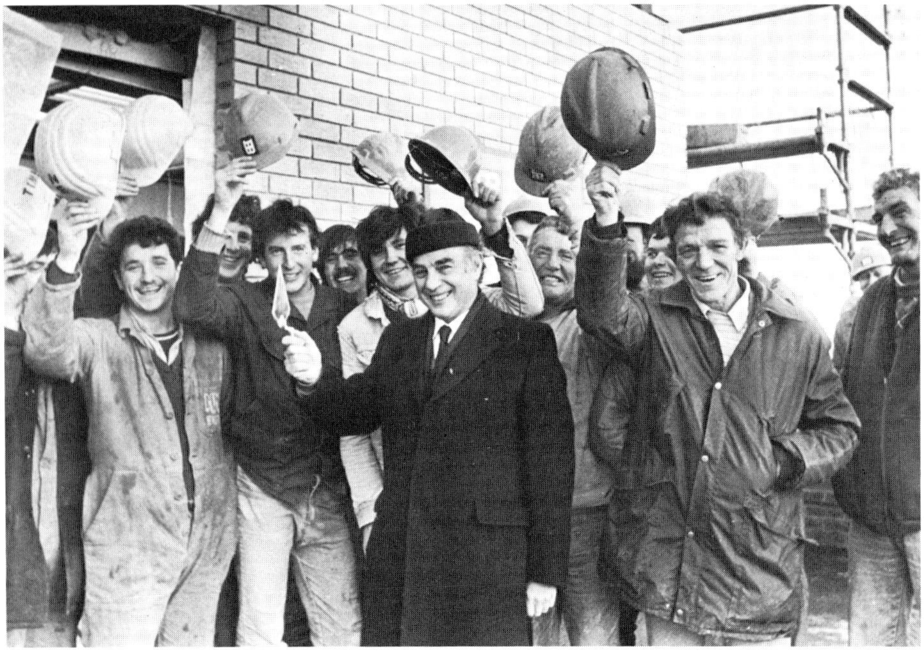

46. Mr Arthur Taylor, chairman of Newcastle Health Authority, tried his bricklaying skills at the topping out ceremony at the Freeman Hospital in November 1985. The new £3.7 million facilities house the ear, nose and throat department, regional medical physics and a new theatre sterile supplies unit.

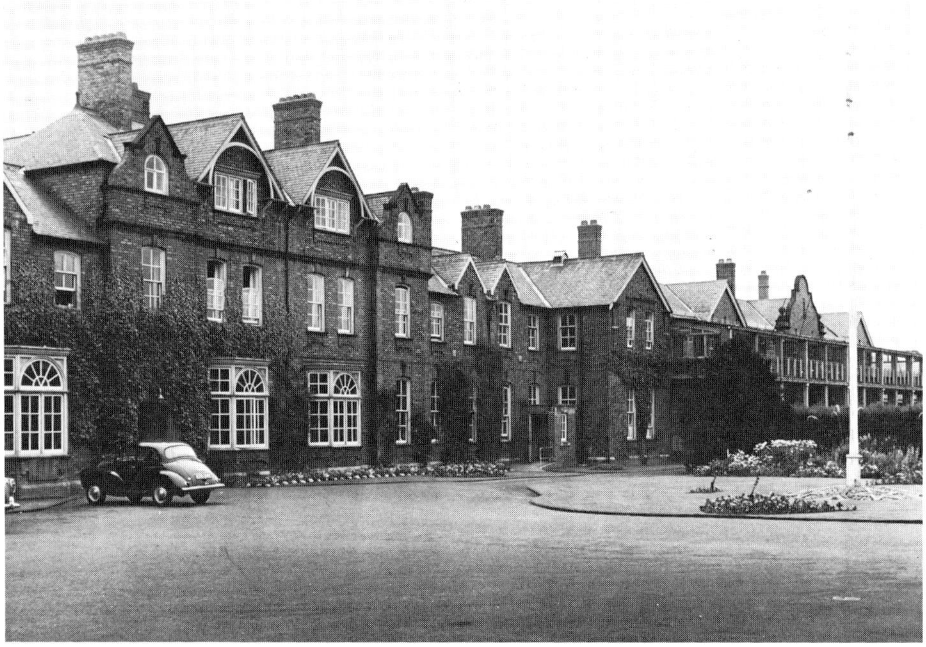

47. Sanderson Orthopaedic Hospital, Gosforth, July 1961.

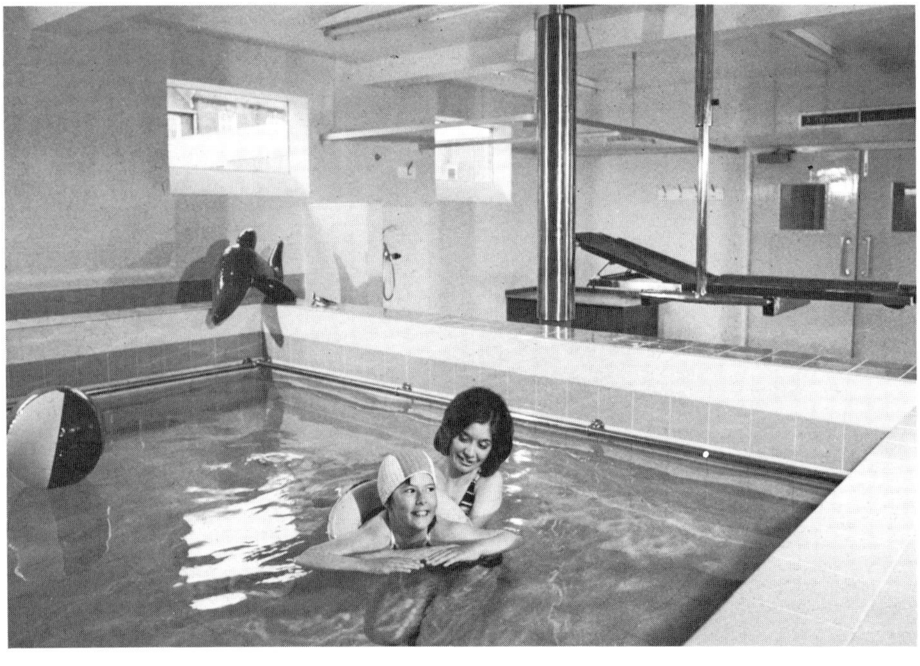

48. In July 1975 a new hydrotherapy pool was opened at the Sanderson orthopaedic Hospital and School for Children. In the photograph, physiotherapist Diane Coggins helps give treatment to nine-year-old Sharon Laskey. *Courtesy:* Turners (Photography) Ltd.

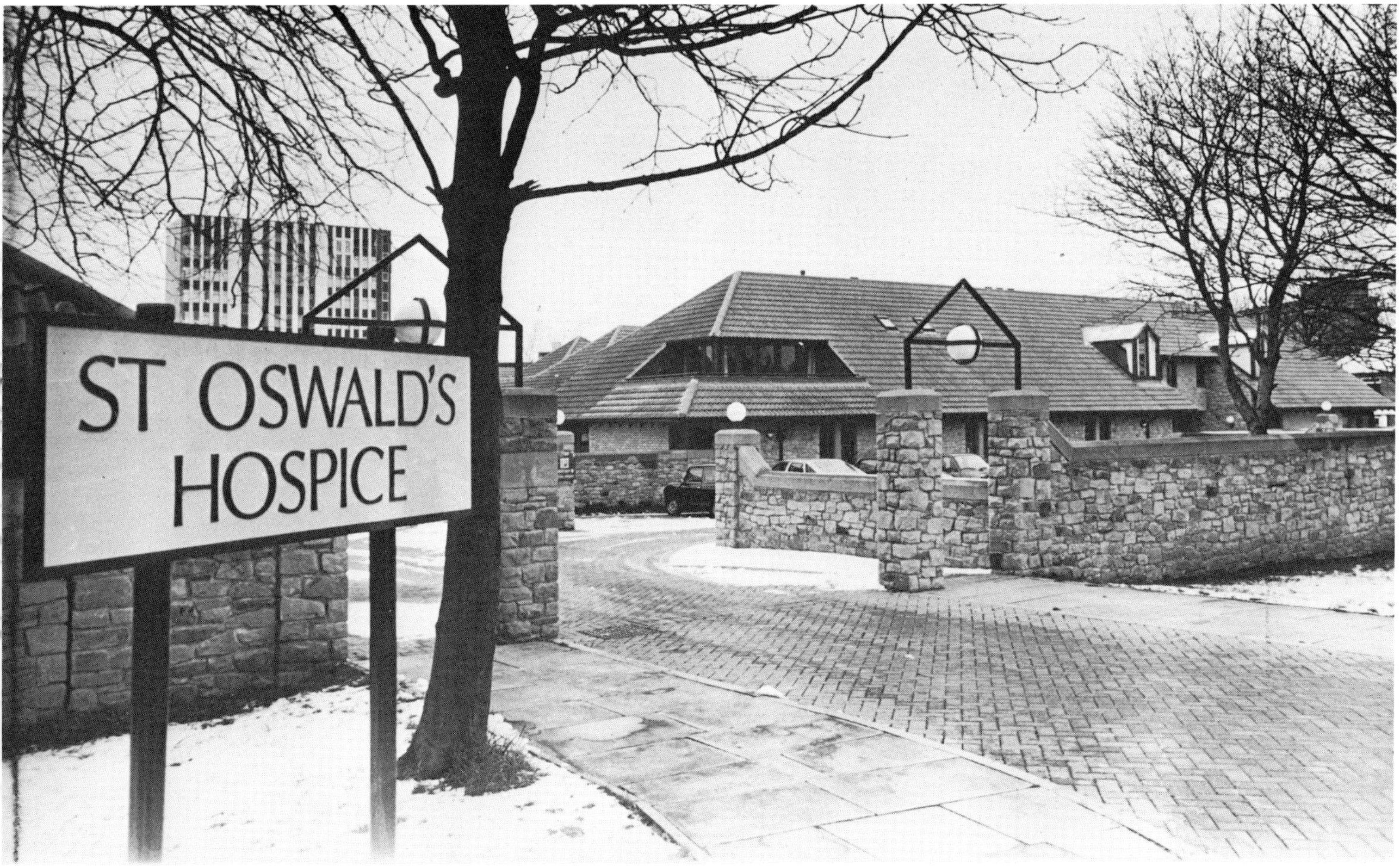

49-50. St Oswald's Hospice opened its doors in July 1986 thanks to a £1.8 million fund-raising campaign. St Oswald's nailed the misconception that hospices are by nature dark and dreary places where the old go to die in loneliness and despair. As medical director Dr Claud Regnard said "A good hospice is a place which is alive . . . We want to try to help people live with their cancer. That might be for weeks and months, sometimes even years, before they die. *Below:* Dr Claud Regnard and his staff photographed by Tom Mackin.

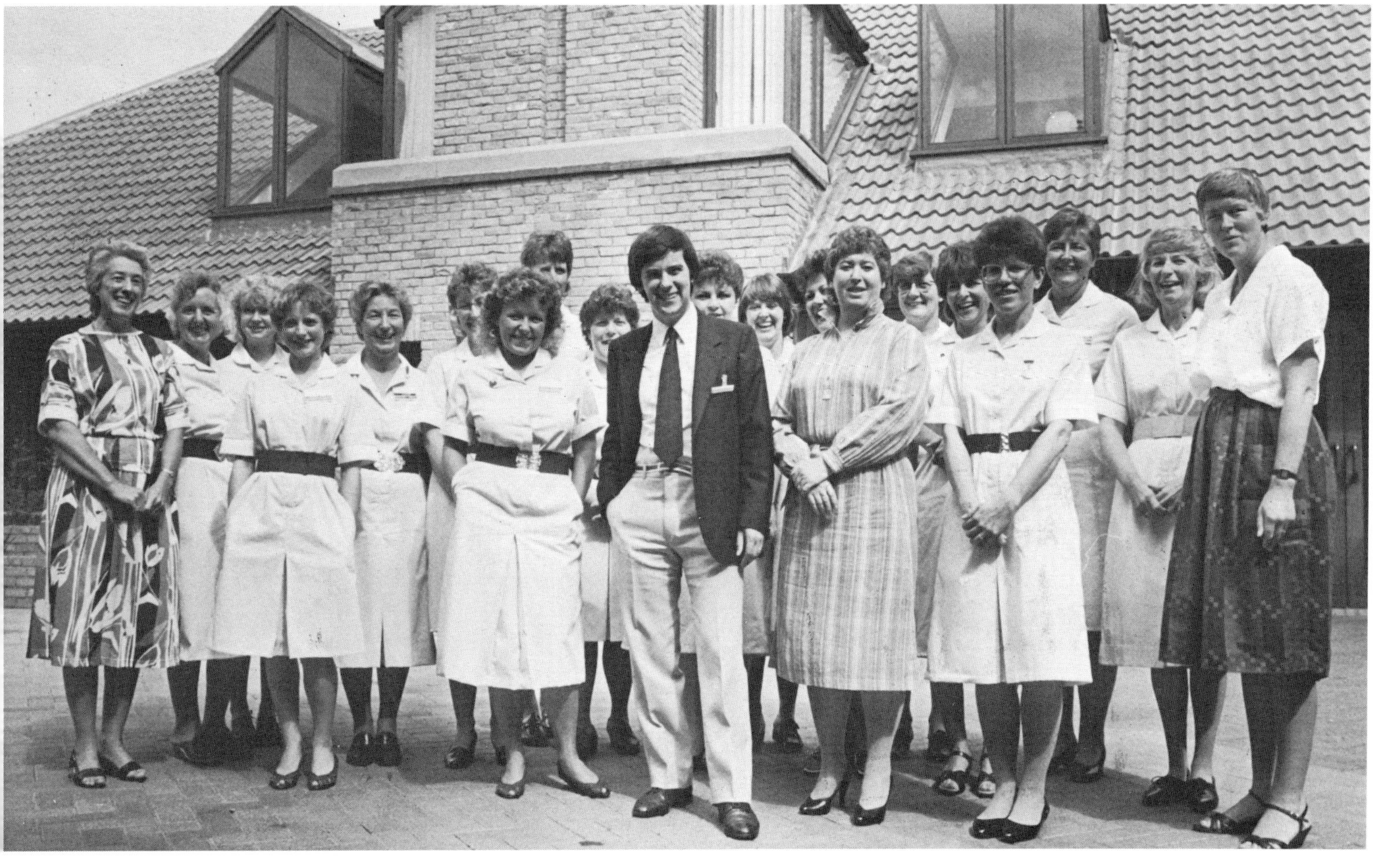

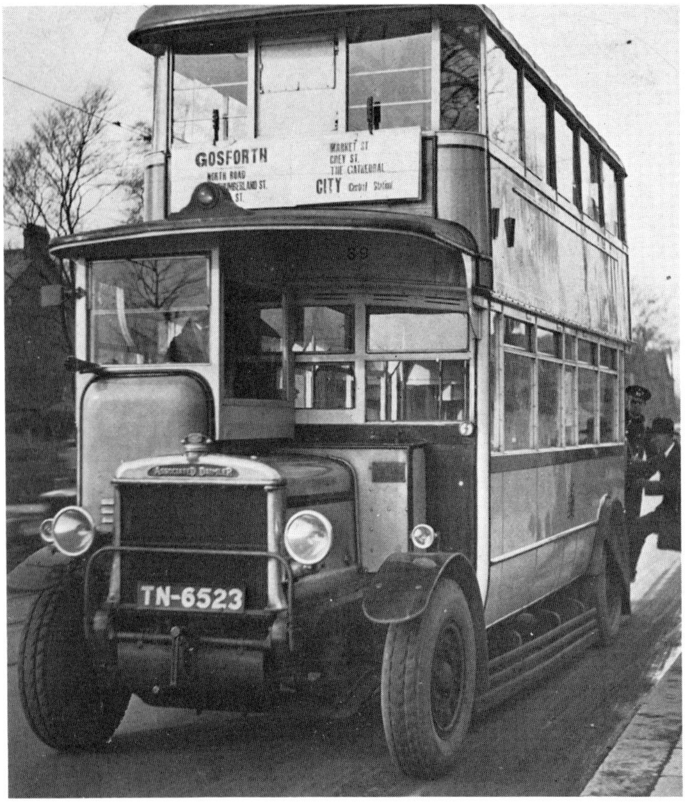

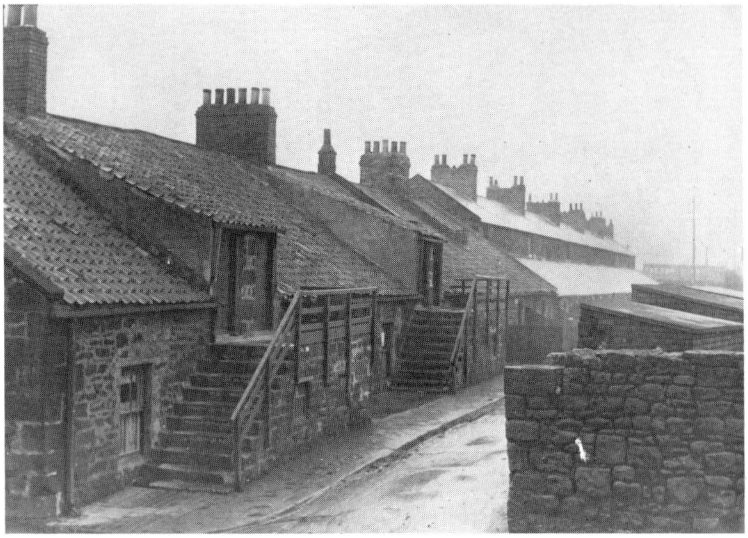

52. If you wanted to buy a village in February 1933, then a call to the Seaton Burn Coal Co would have been in order. Up for sale were fifty stone-built cottages built at the site of Brandling's Gosforth Colliery.

51. *Left:* The blue bus express service linking Gosforth with the city centre offered an alternative to rail transport for business people and office workers.

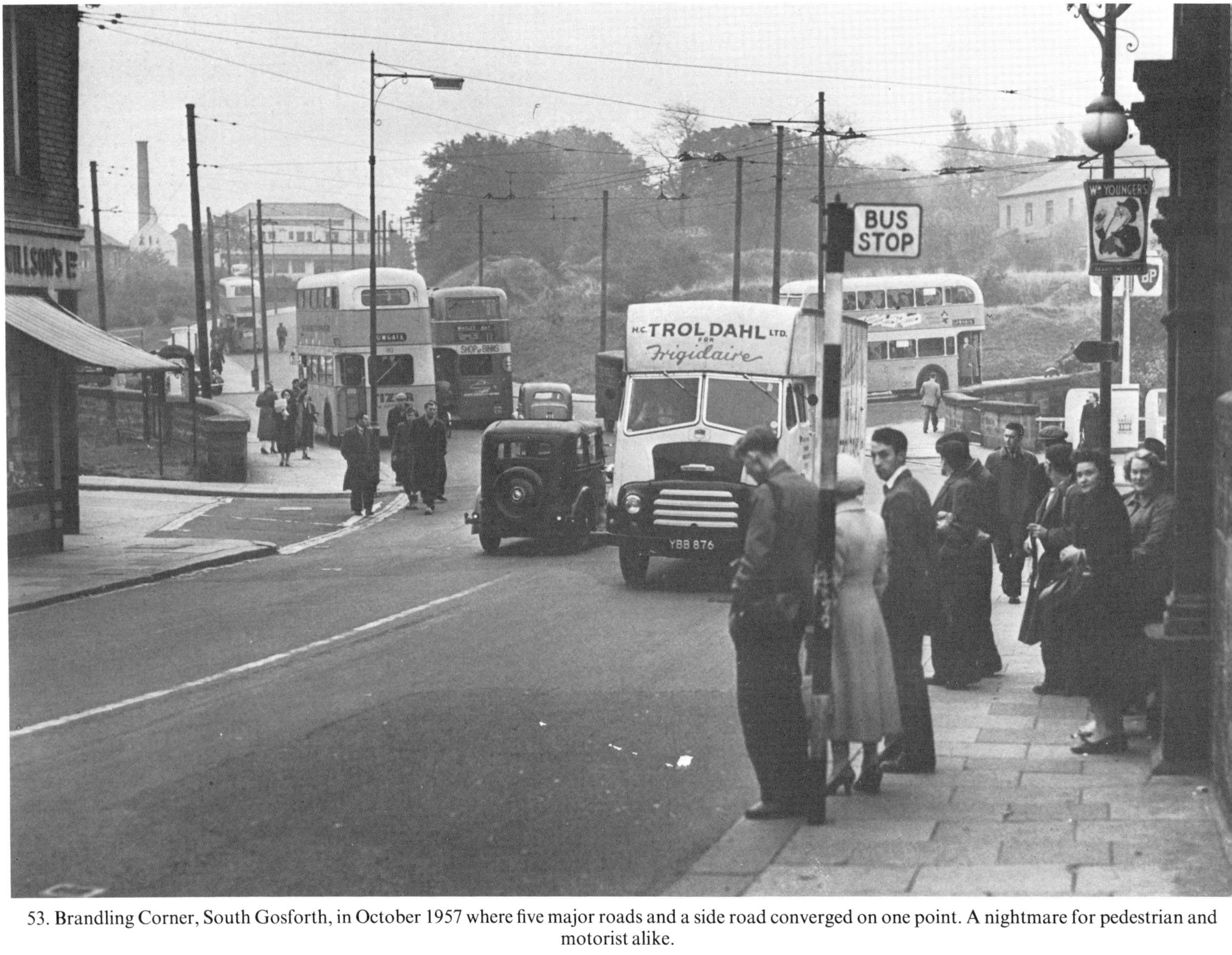

53. Brandling Corner, South Gosforth, in October 1957 where five major roads and a side road converged on one point. A nightmare for pedestrian and motorist alike.

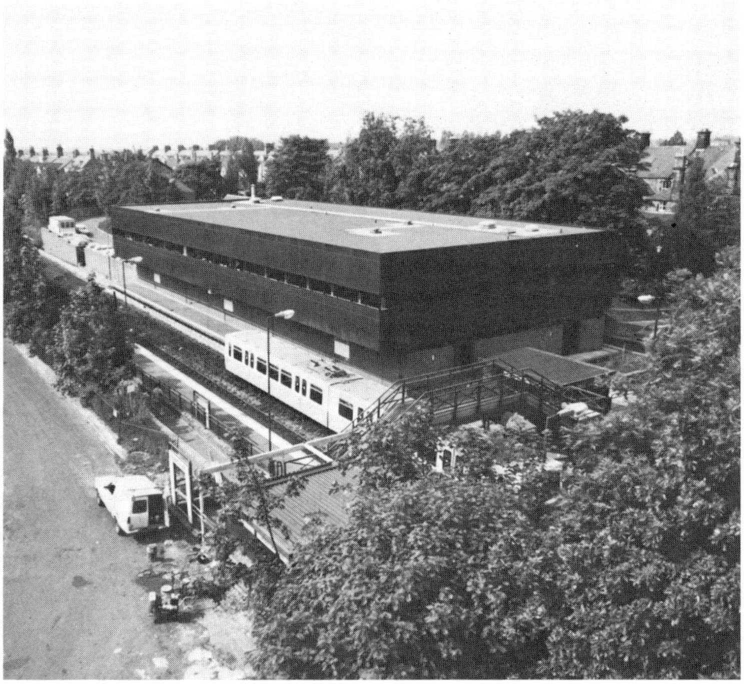

54. September 1980. South Gosforth Station had had a facelift as part of the transformation of the old Coast Line. It was now the nerve centre from which Metro operations were controlled.

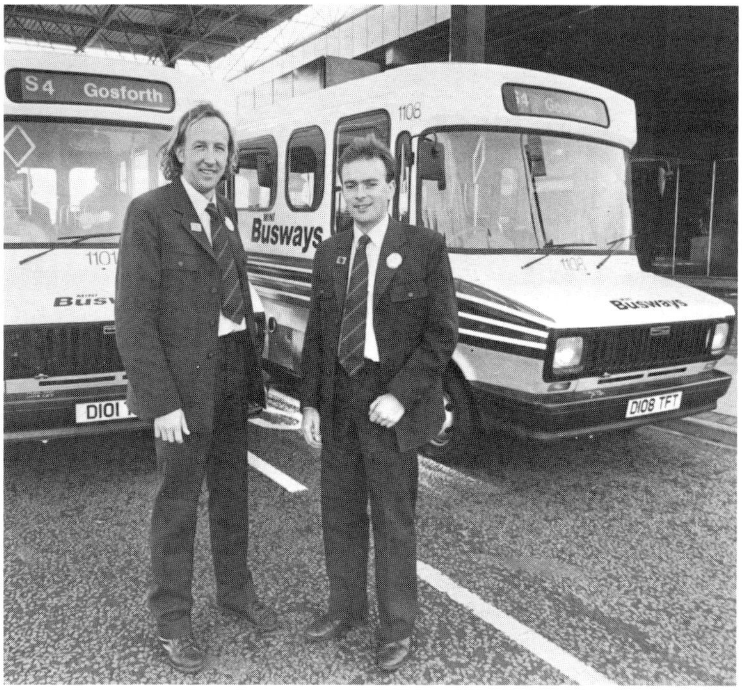

55. Minibuses come to Gosforth in October 1986. Drivers Paul Dyson (*right*) and Alex Gibson prepare to head 'em up and move 'em out.

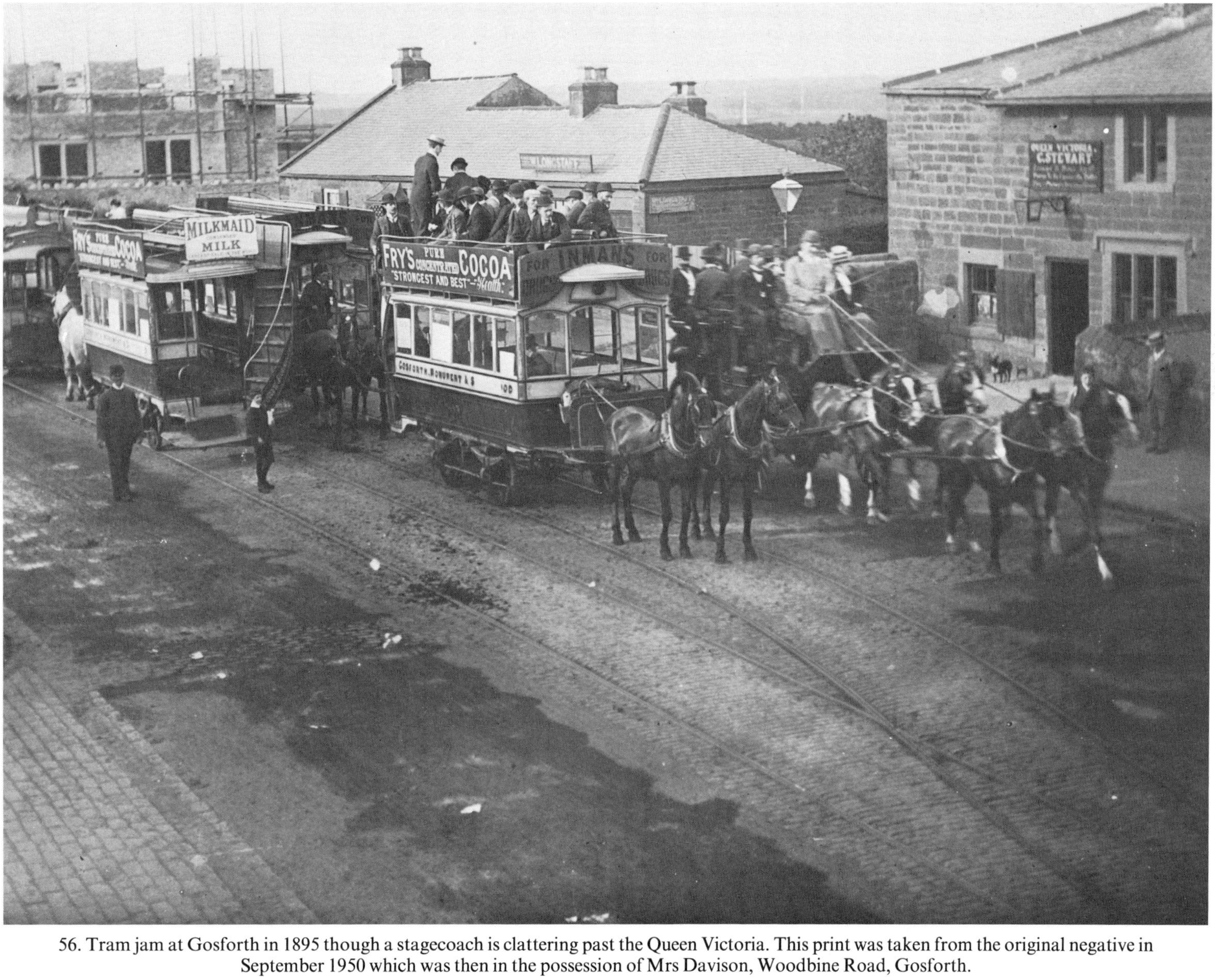

56. Tram jam at Gosforth in 1895 though a stagecoach is clattering past the Queen Victoria. This print was taken from the original negative in September 1950 which was then in the possession of Mrs Davison, Woodbine Road, Gosforth.

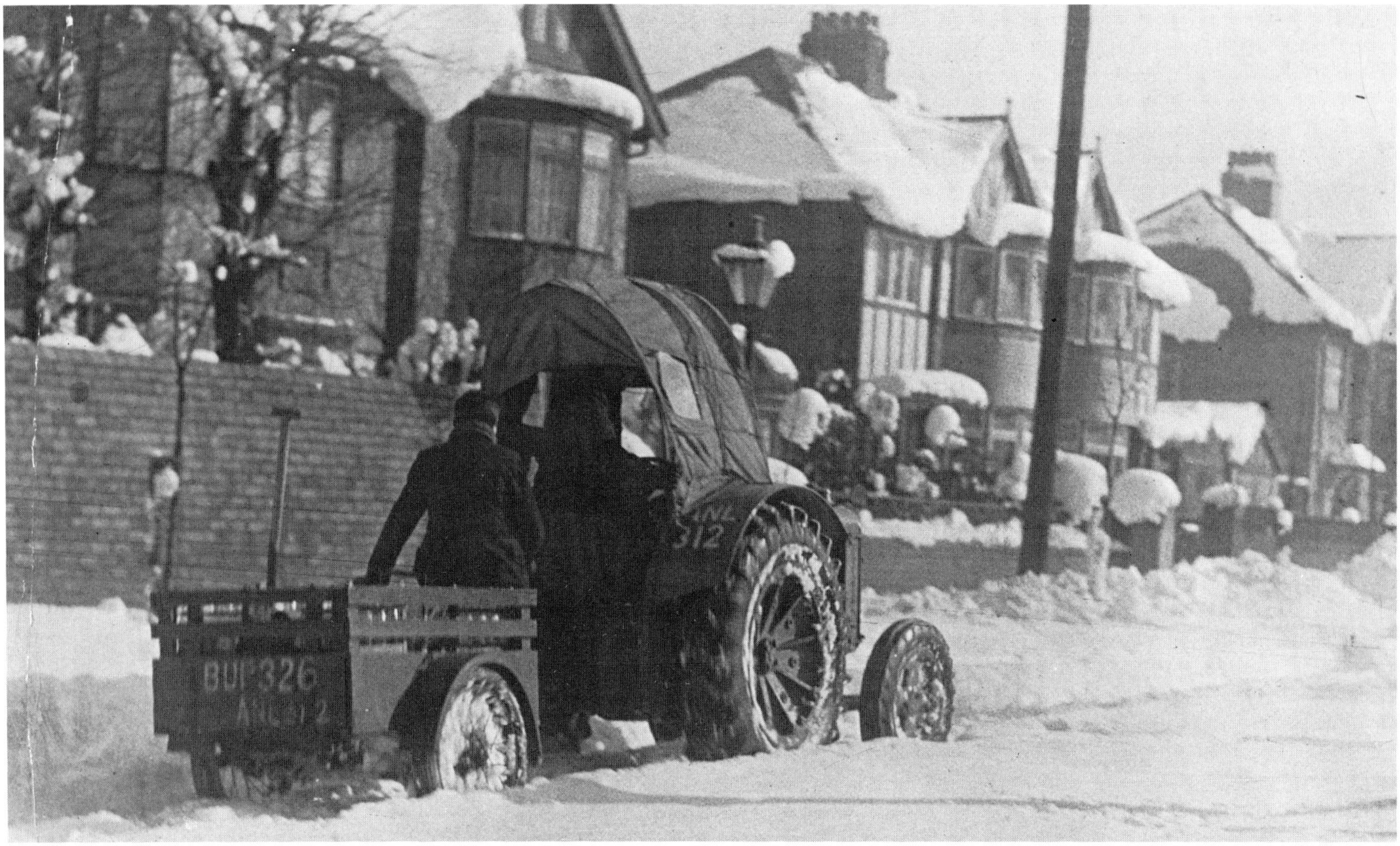

57. Delivering the milk in February 1941. Here's how one enterprising dairy farmer reached his Gosforth customers.

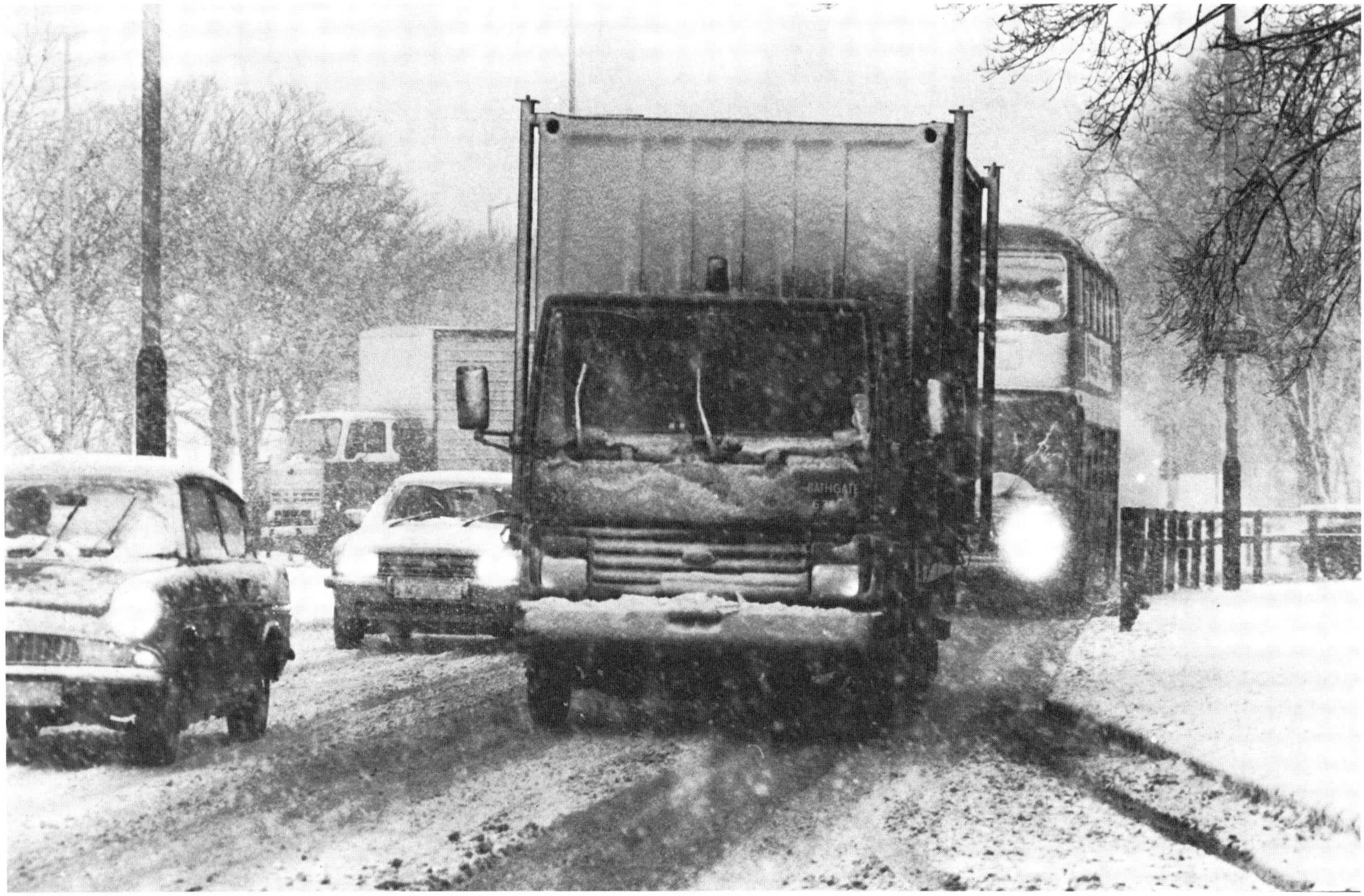

58. Forty-three years on. The snow is snowing, the wind is blowing, the traffic is flowing – well sort of – into Gosforth on the Great North Road.

59. November 1988. Gosforth said a spectacular farewell to the roadworks that had plagued the High Street for three months. Lord Mayor Derek Webster cut the ribbons along the road to officially open the newly-repaired highway. Cheering crowds lined the street as a procession of decorated diggers and construction vehicles left to the accompaniment of jazz bands. What a marvellous day!

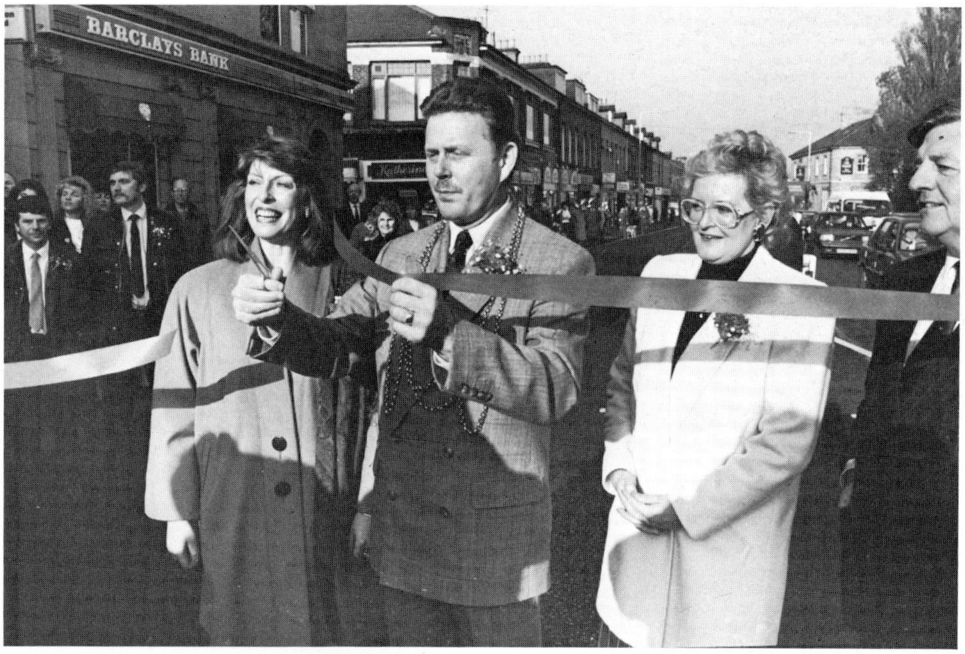

60. OK, who said lightning never strikes twice? Just when people thought it was safe to go out again, the curse of the cones struck in Gosforth High Street. Within a matter of days of pic 59 being taken, British Gas were digging things up some two hundred yards north of the rebuilt section.

61. Gosforth's fire brigade in pre-traffic cone days, showing Superintendent Jack Hann (*front row, far right*) and his gallant band.

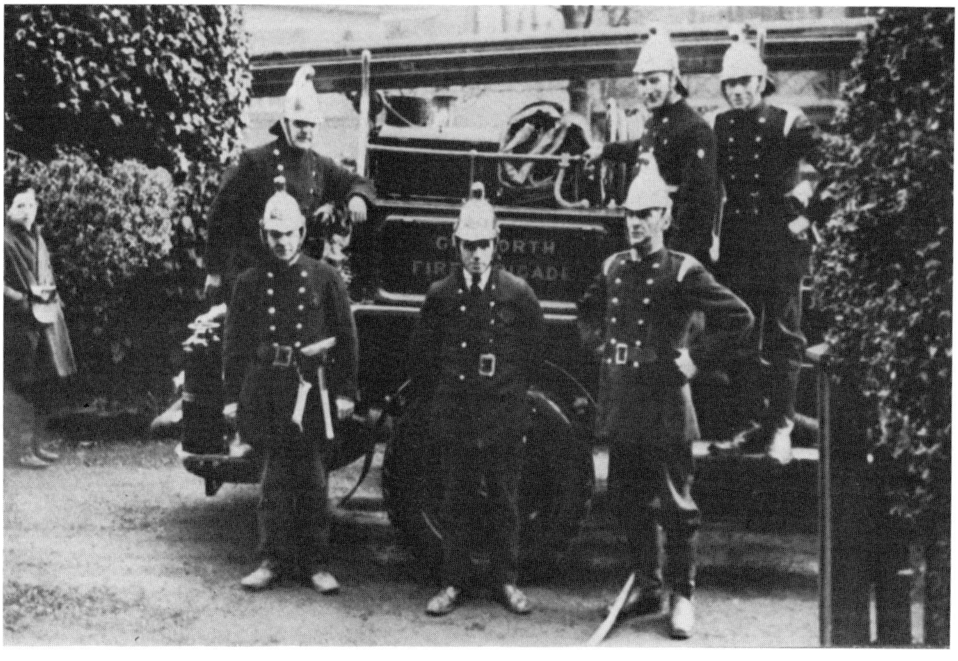

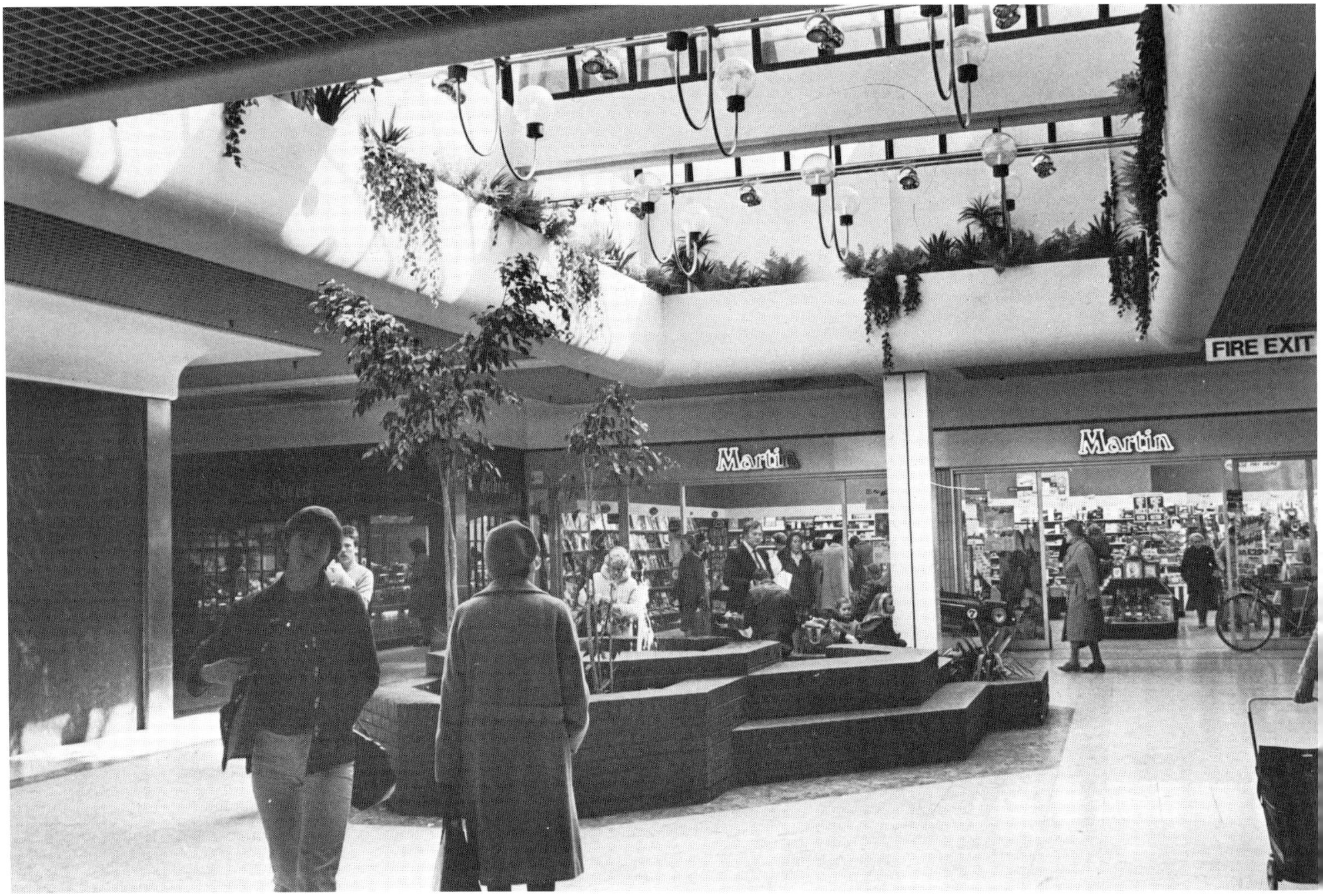
FIRE EXIT
Martin
Martin

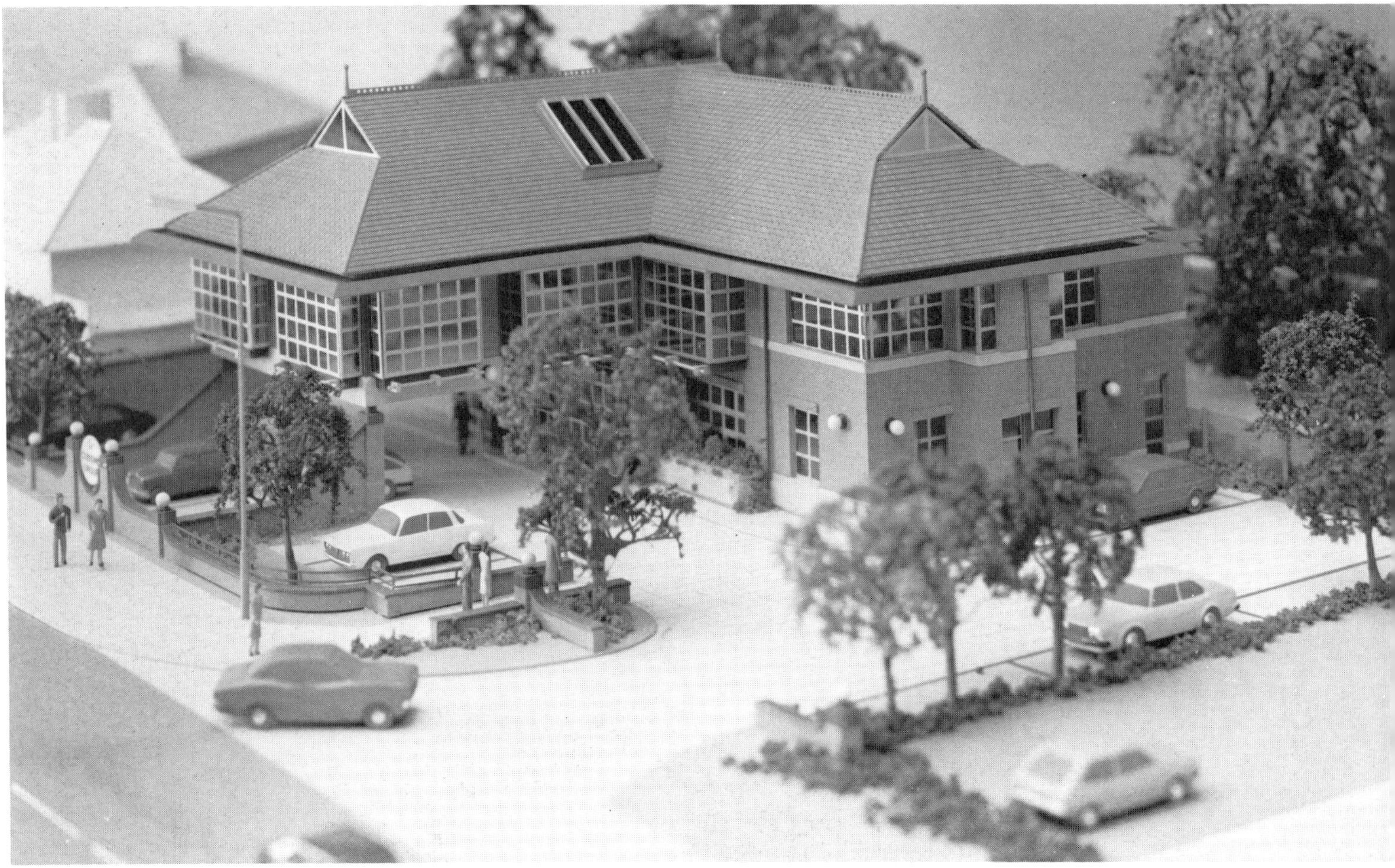

64. *Right:* This photograph appeared in the *Weekly Chronicle* in September 1950 and shows some of the fifty two-storey prefabs built in Glanton Wynd.

62. *Opposite page, top:* Gosforth shopping precinct, May 1983.

63. *Opposite page, bottom:* Proposed new headquarters building for developers Cussins Property Group plc designed by Jim Livingston and to be built at 157 Great North Road. January 1990.

65. *Below:* July 1988 and Gosforth Central Middle School makes the news having scooped first prize in a World Wildlife Fund/Citizen Printers competition called Pictures from Numbers. Competing in the secondary section against 1,200 other schools the youngsters won with their 62-page report Underfoot-Grass, a project to investigate the trampling of same in school grounds. And the winners are *back row:* Kit Young, Andrew Whitelaw, Richard Smith, Edward Powell, Jamie Portsmouth. *Middle:* Joanna Storey, David Brooks. *Front:* Jane Cassie, Mary Hopkins, Louise Heppell, Christopher Martin, Andrew Bogan, Paul Fahy, Mark Thompson, Rhonda Gregson, Gordon Lowery and Nigel Brown.

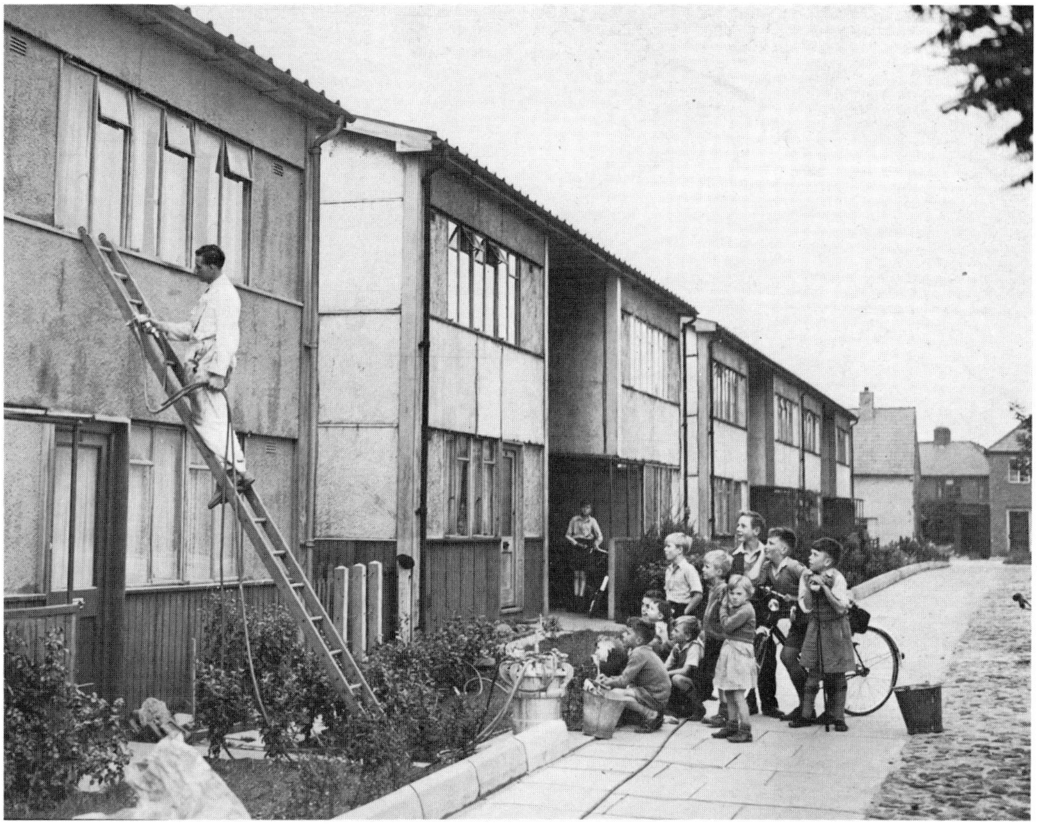

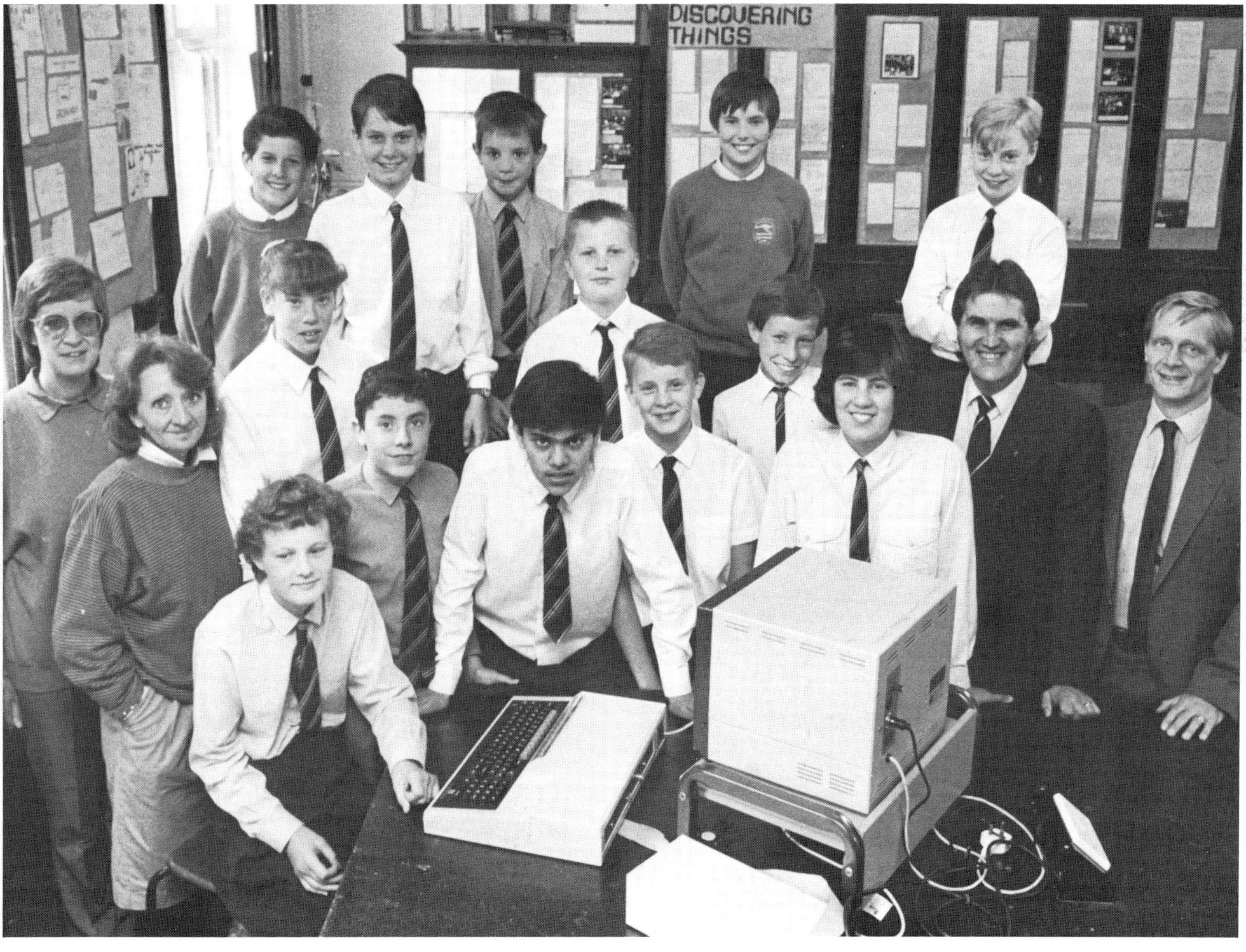

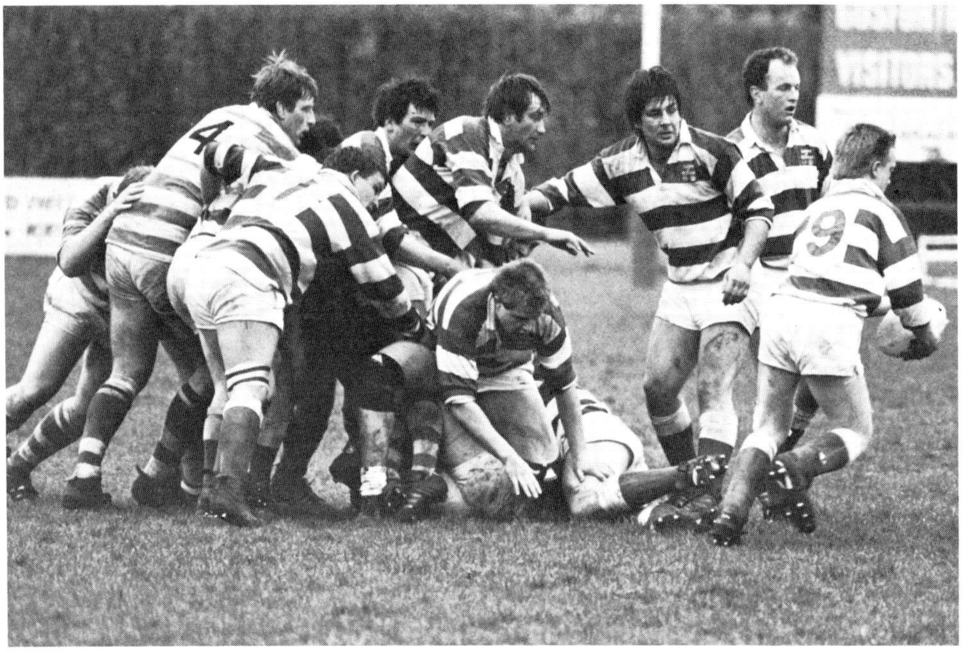

66. This sporting life. Tynedale scrum-half Simon Clayton-Hibbott breaks from a maul in Cup semi-final against Gosforth. April 1989.

67. *Right:* This photograph appeared in the *Sunday Sun* in July 1938. Scouts from far and wide gathered at the Gosforth Park camp site. Their singsong was broadcast by the BBC.

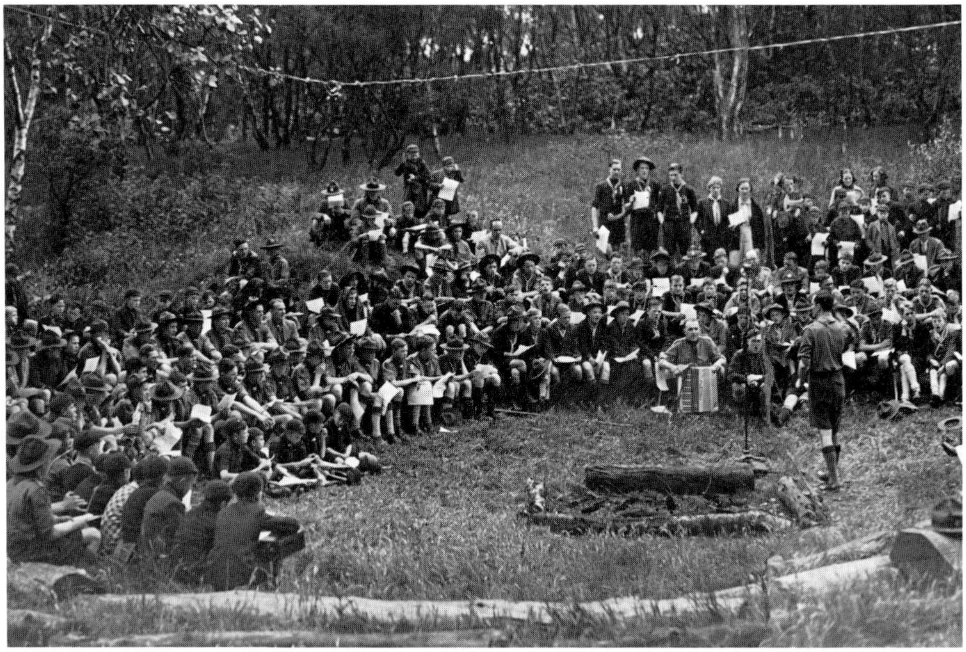

68. *Below:* Racegoers queue for trollybuses, June 1948.

69. *Below right:* Race Sunday at Gosforth Park. It is thought that this photograph might well have been taken at the very first meeting held at Gosforth following their transfer from Town Moor.

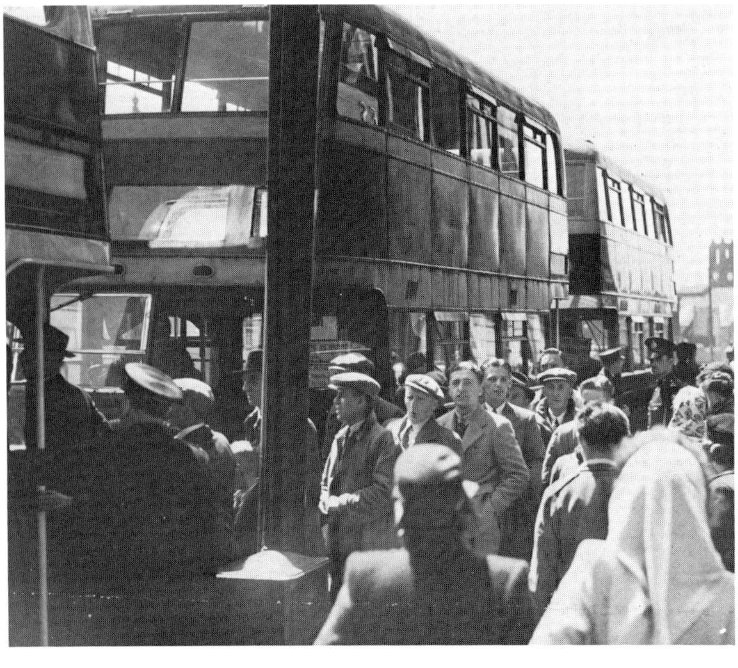

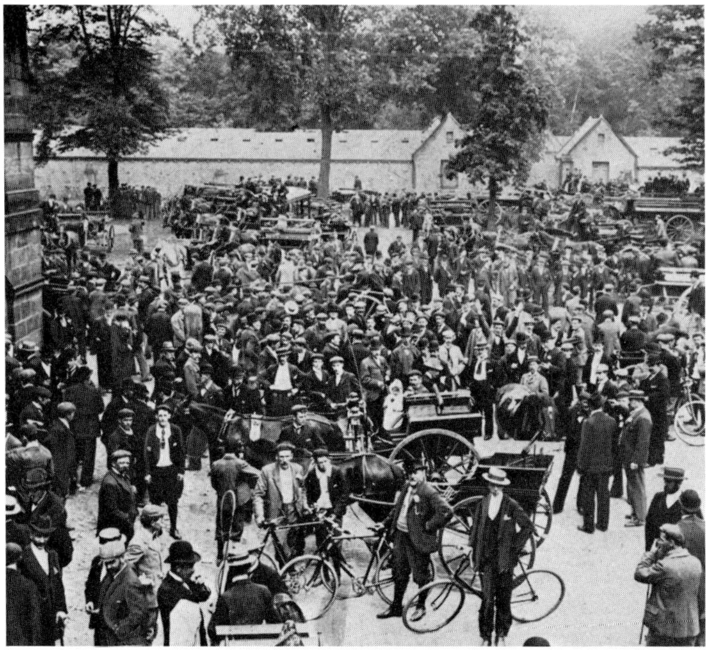

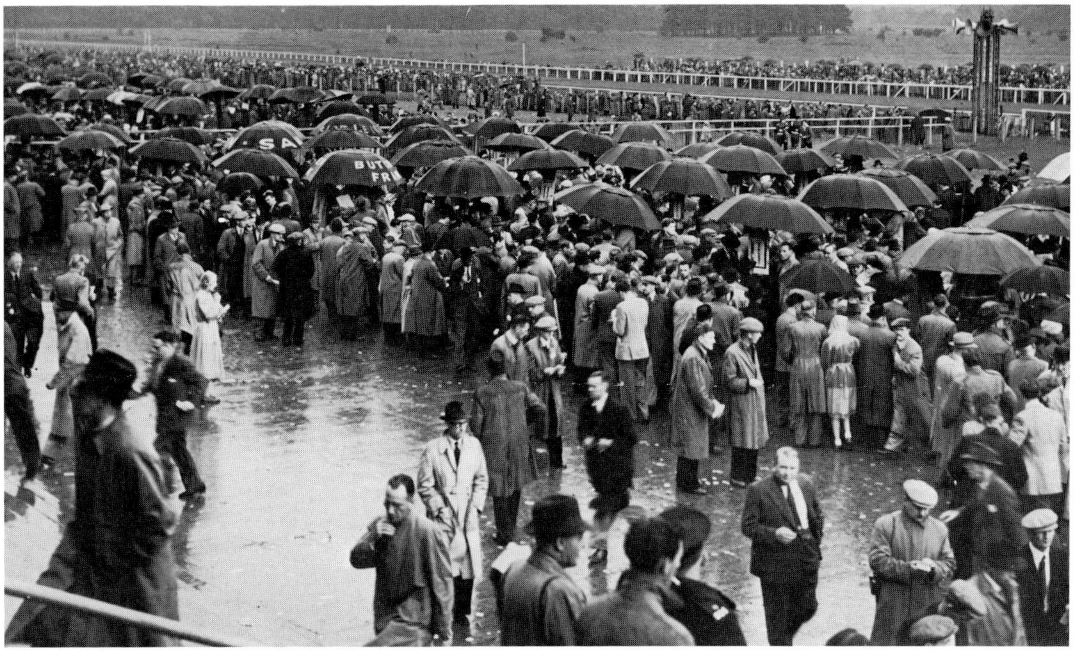

70. Plate Day, June 1950. There was a little sunshine and a lot of rain.

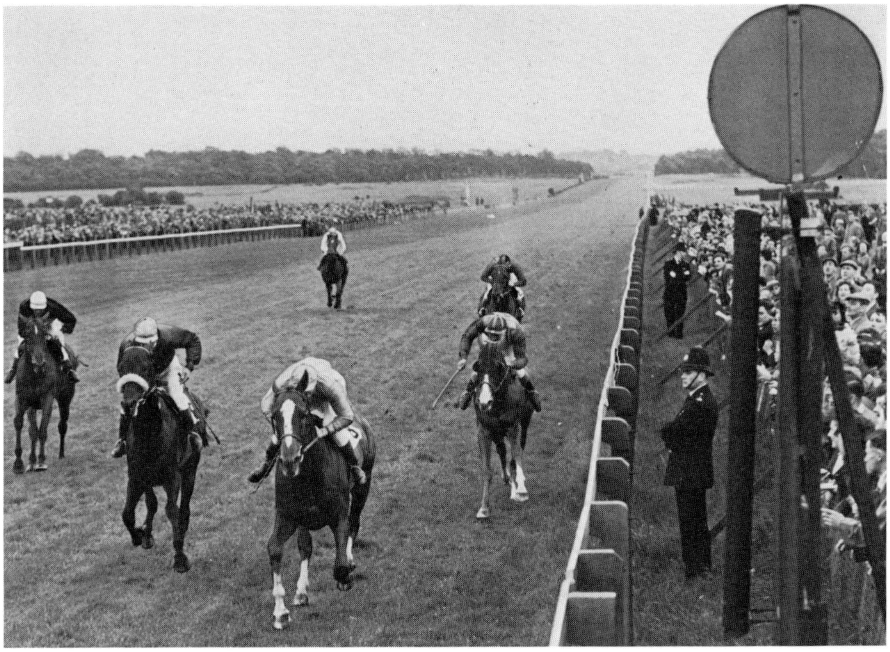

71. There was consternation amid the racing fraternity at Gosforth Park during the running of the 1954 Dobson Peacock Handicap when the runners disappeared behind the trees and didn't reappear. It was later learned that the field had returned to the starting gate – much to the surprise of the starter – who told the jockeys that all had been in order. Apparently, the chap with the red flag who re-calls the field in the event of a false start, had inadvertantly shown his flag and the jockeys had pulled up their horses. Of course, it goes without saying that the result differed. *Criticism*, last to leave the gate the first time, jumped off in front at the second attempt and stayed there throughout the race to win by one-and-a-half lengths from the favourite *Prince Yaky*.

72. *Below:* Photographer Paul Dodds faced a cavalry charge when he took this picture of the 1986 BBC Radio Newcastle Handicap Stakes. At far right Dennis McKeown and *Sharon's Royale* strike the front from the big field. Third from the right, Willie Carson and *Sharp Shot*, stay the course to finish second.

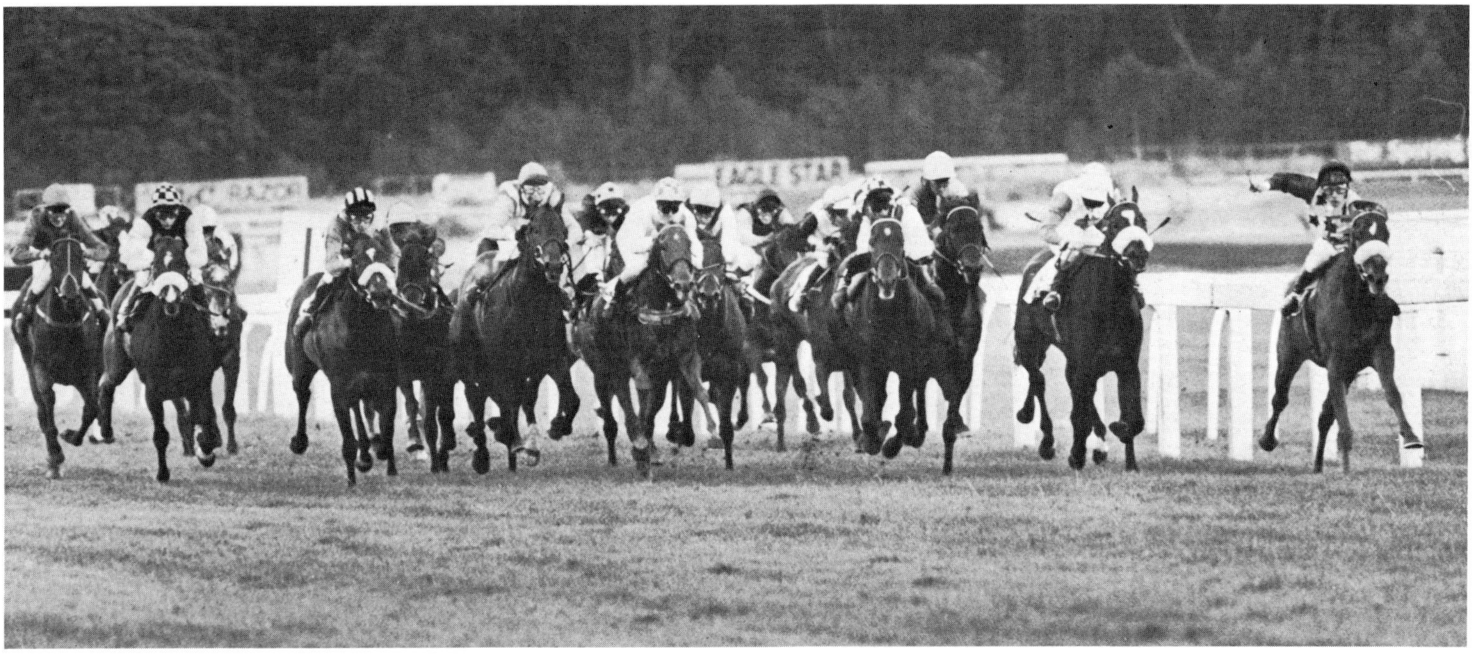

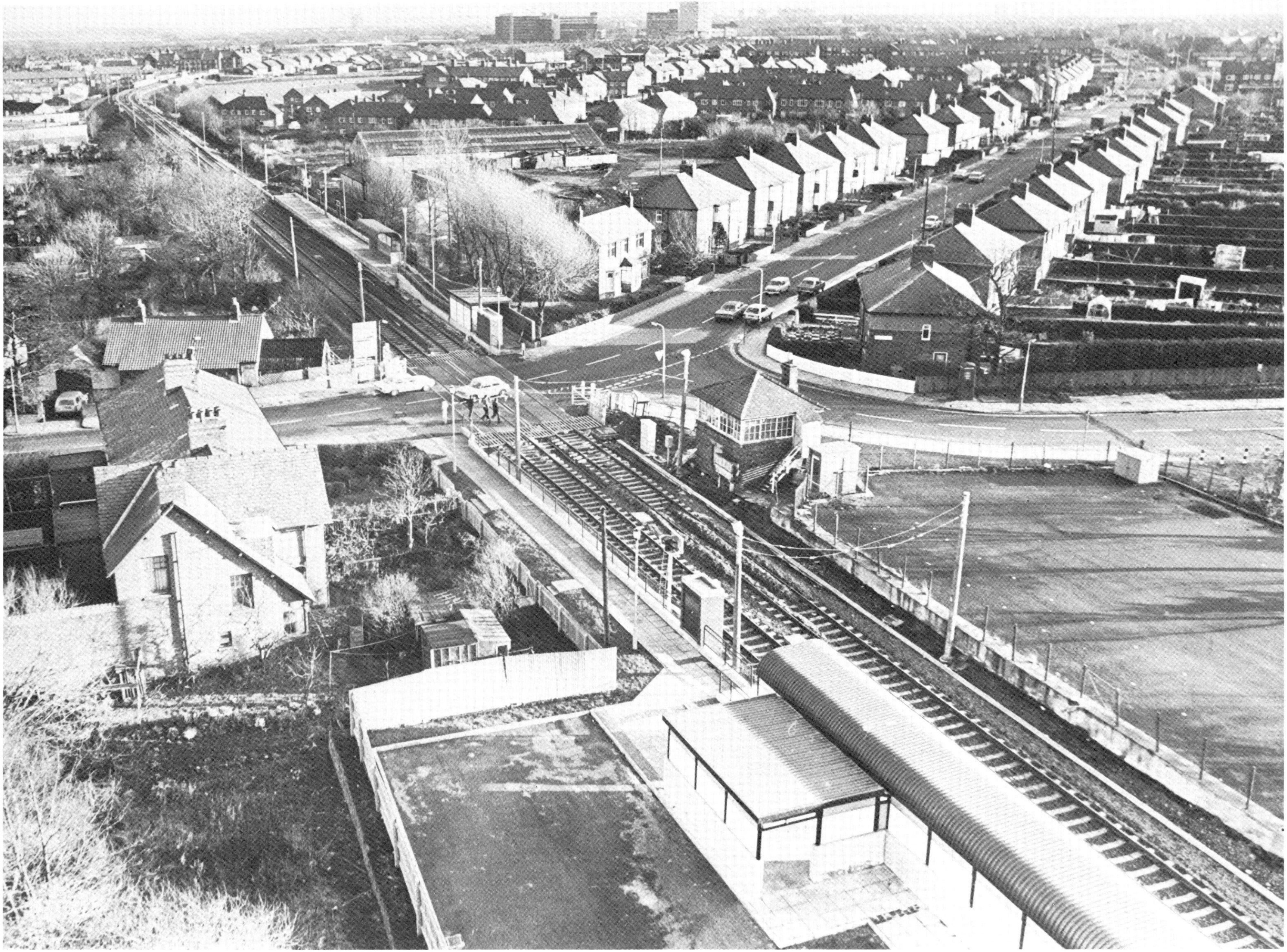

73. Fawdon level crossing on the Metro system.

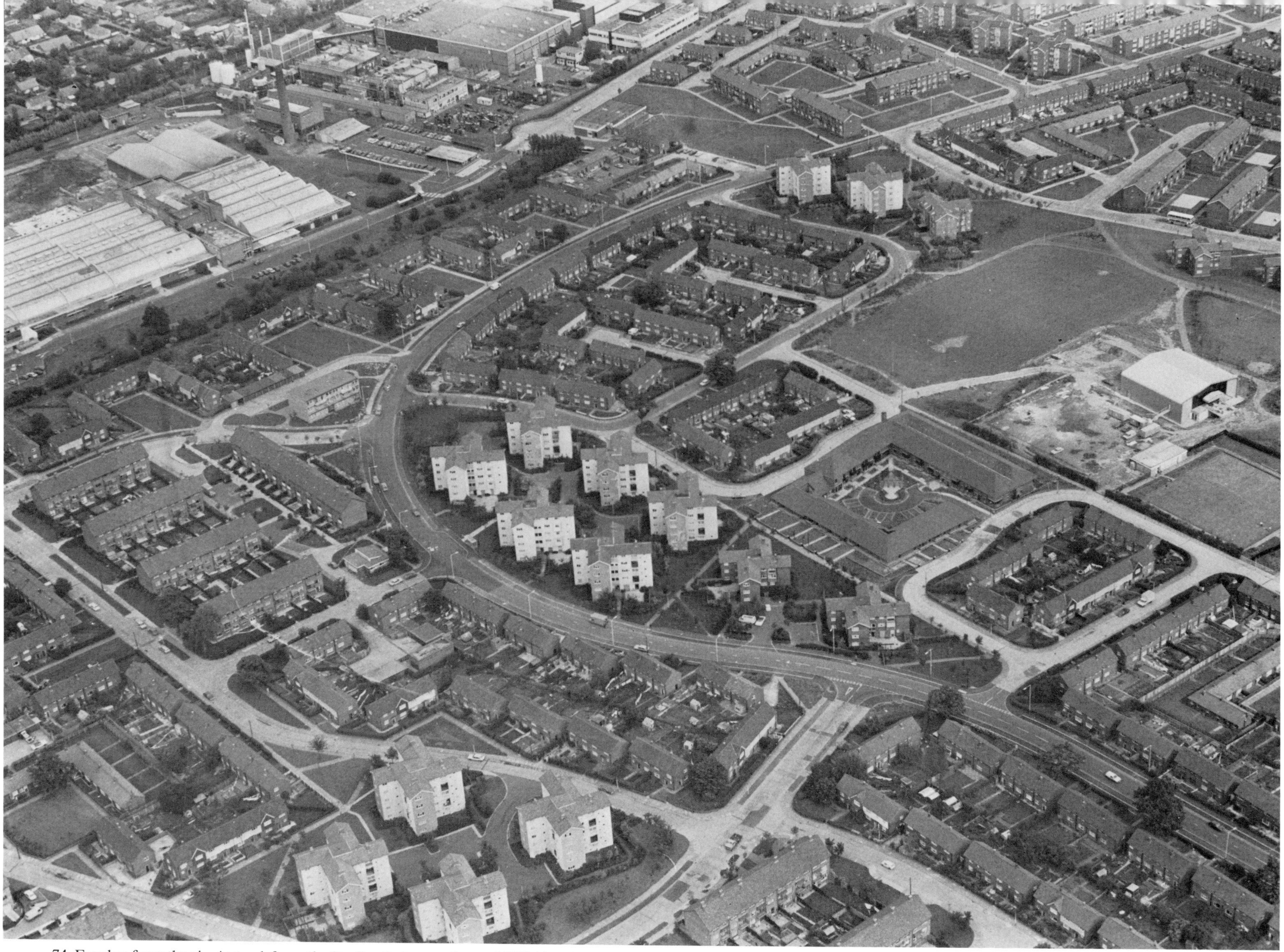

74. Fawdon from the air. At top left are the Sterling Laboratories, and Hillsview Avenue winds its way from bottom right to top right. St Oswald's Hospice is in the centre of the picture.

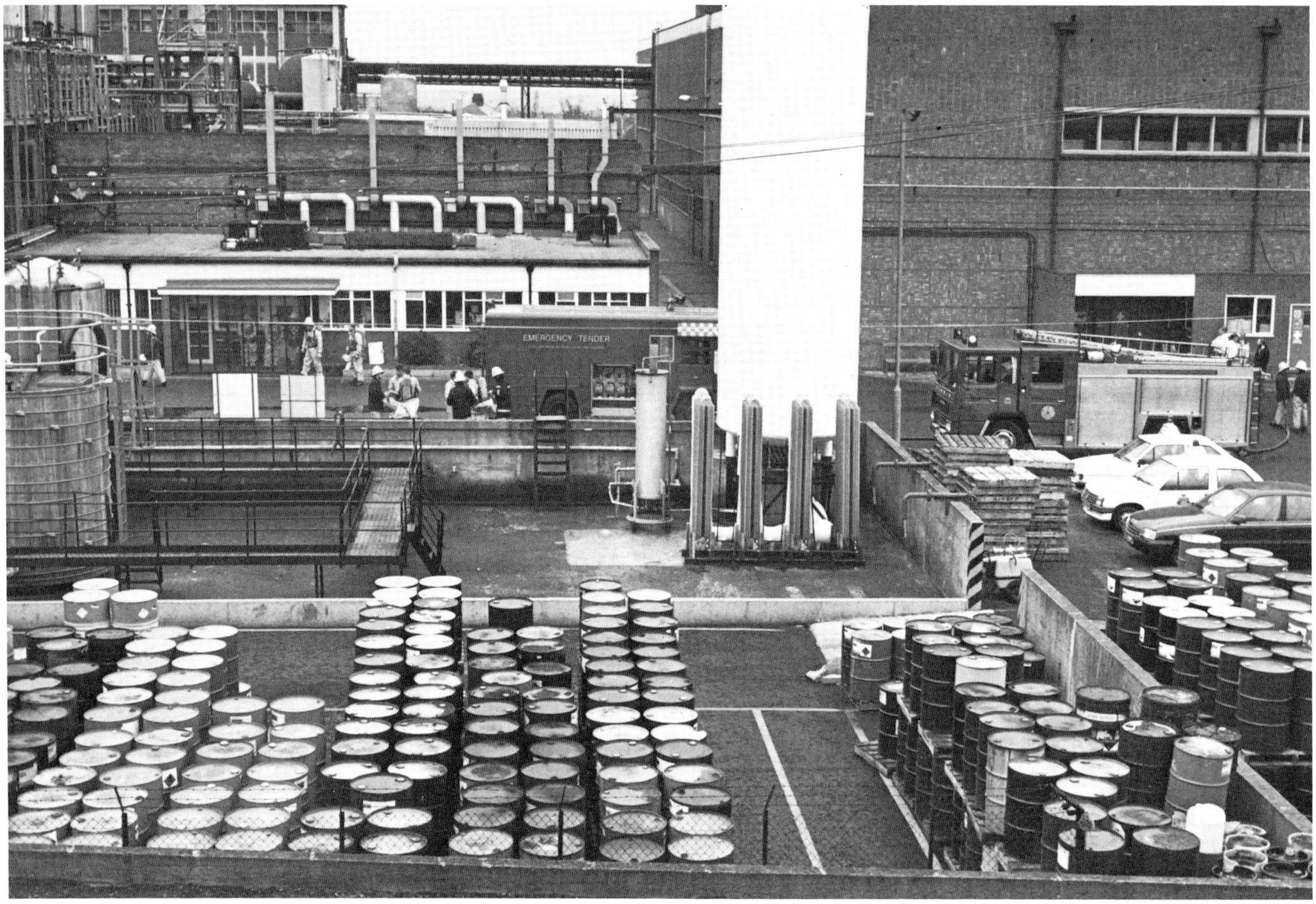

75. Firemen were called to the Sterling Winthrop Laboratories in March 1989 to deal with a gas leak.

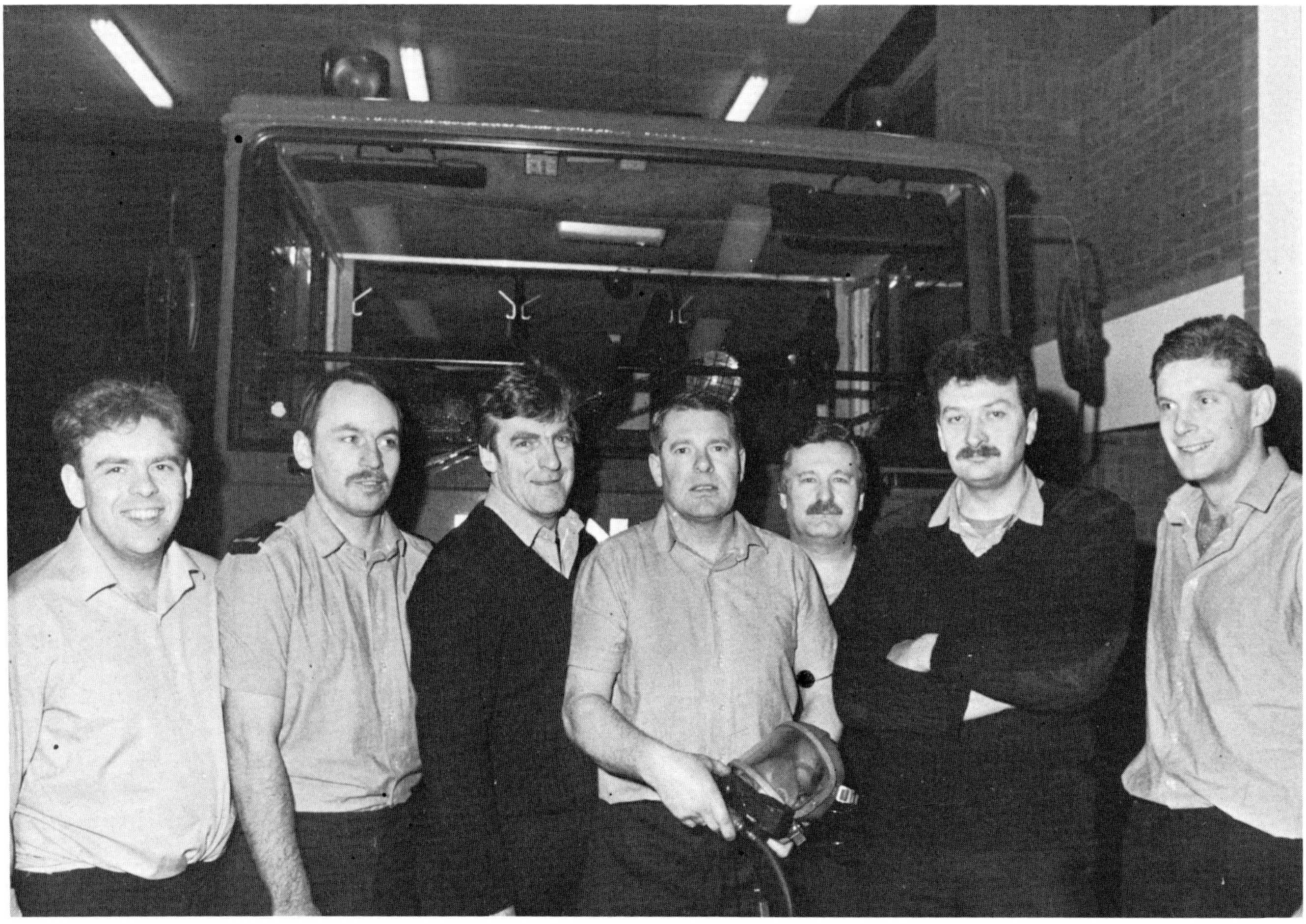

76. Firefighters Michael Ritson, Dennis Kiernan, Jackie Johnson, Charlie Neasham, Peter Gransbury, Paul Murley and David Newman escaped death by seconds when attending a fire at Kielder House in Dorrington Road, Fawdon, in January 1990. The incident happened as firemen reached a wooden internal stairway leading to the roof of the five-storey building. Suddenly there was a flash-over and the roof collapsed, sending large ceramic tiles and heavy wooden joists crashing down around them. Two firemen were injured and taken to hospital.

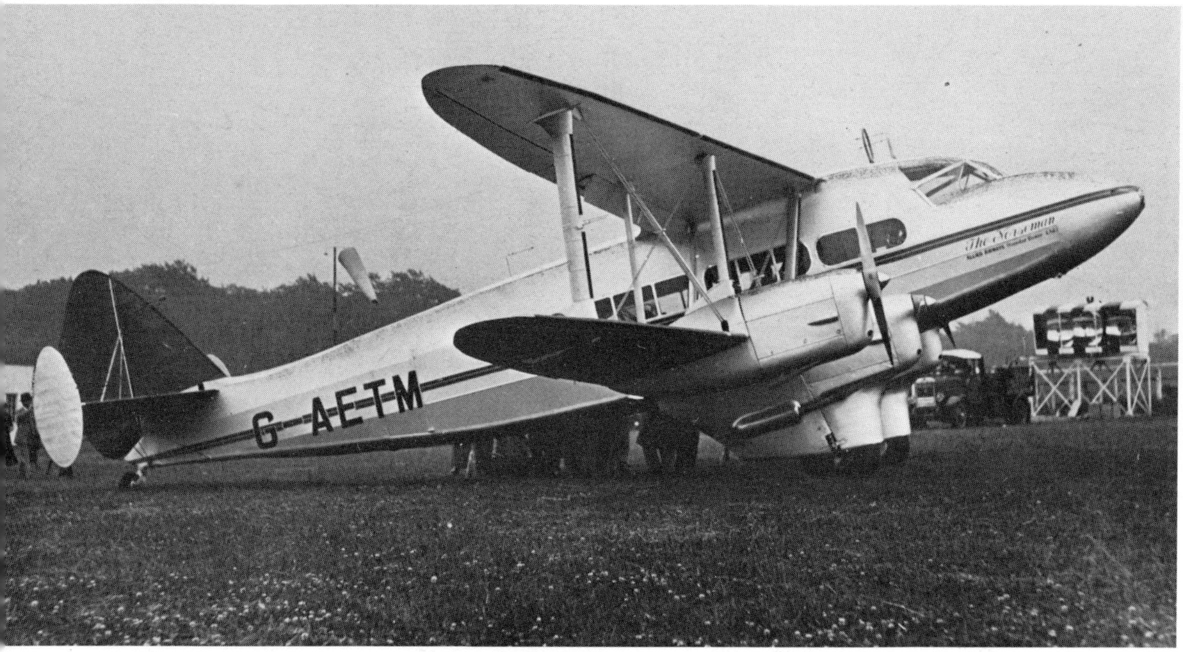

77. Newcastle Airport July 1937. The original caption reads 'The giant plane *Norseman*, which left Newcastle Airport for Stavanger today, on a trial flight in connection with the service which starts next Monday.'

78. *Below:* Did the plane take the strain? This Elizabethan airliner pancaked at Newcastle Airport in March 1960. The picture was published in both the *Evening Chronicle* and *The Journal*.

79. *Bottom:* Snowscape at Newcastle Airport in 1985.

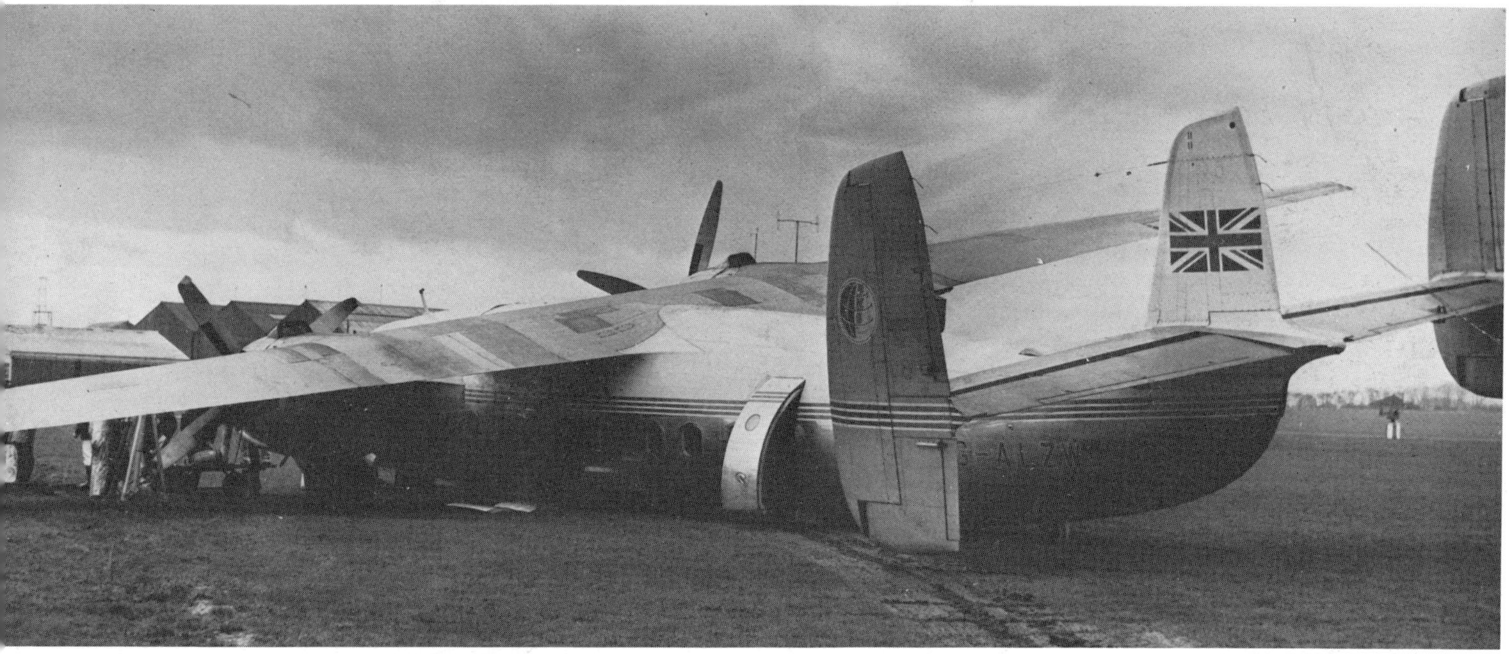

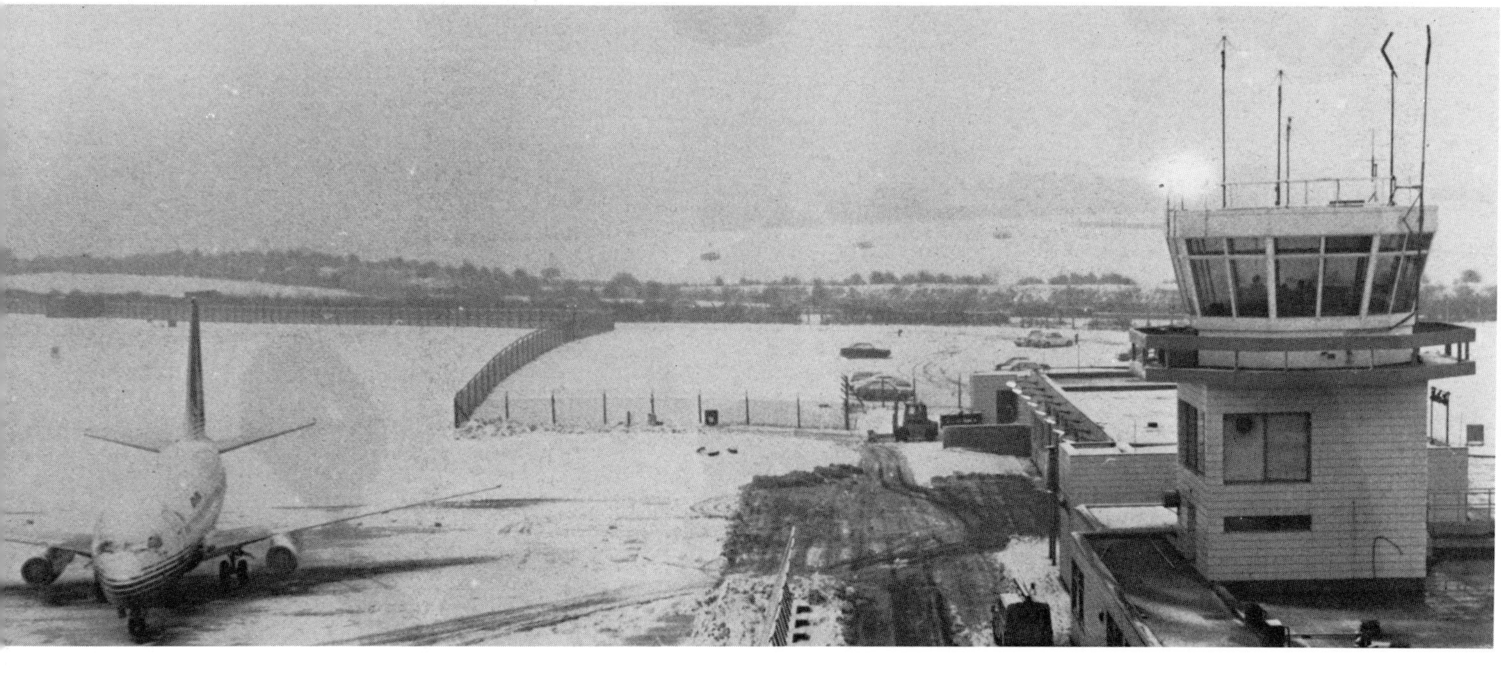

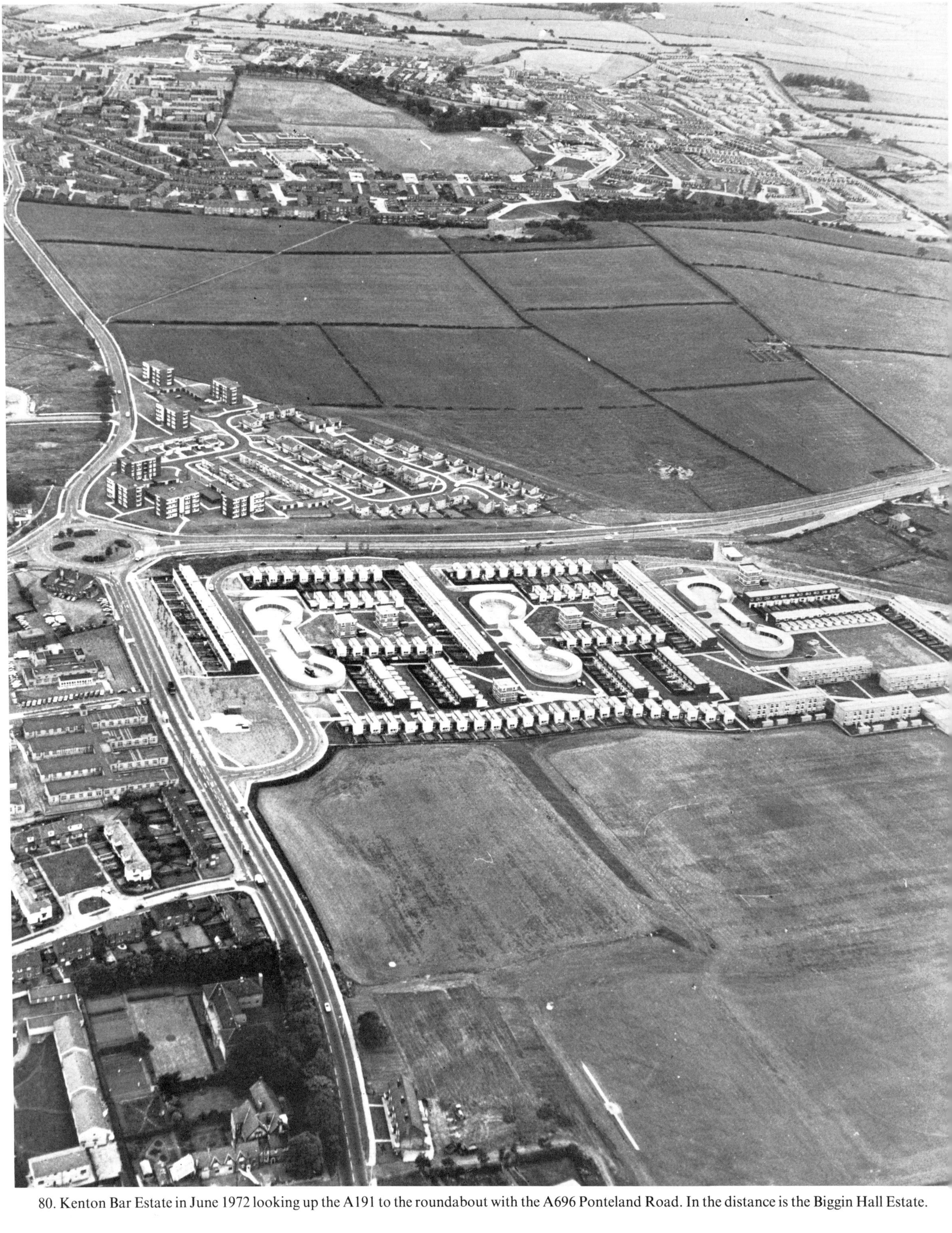

80. Kenton Bar Estate in June 1972 looking up the A191 to the roundabout with the A696 Ponteland Road. In the distance is the Biggin Hall Estate.

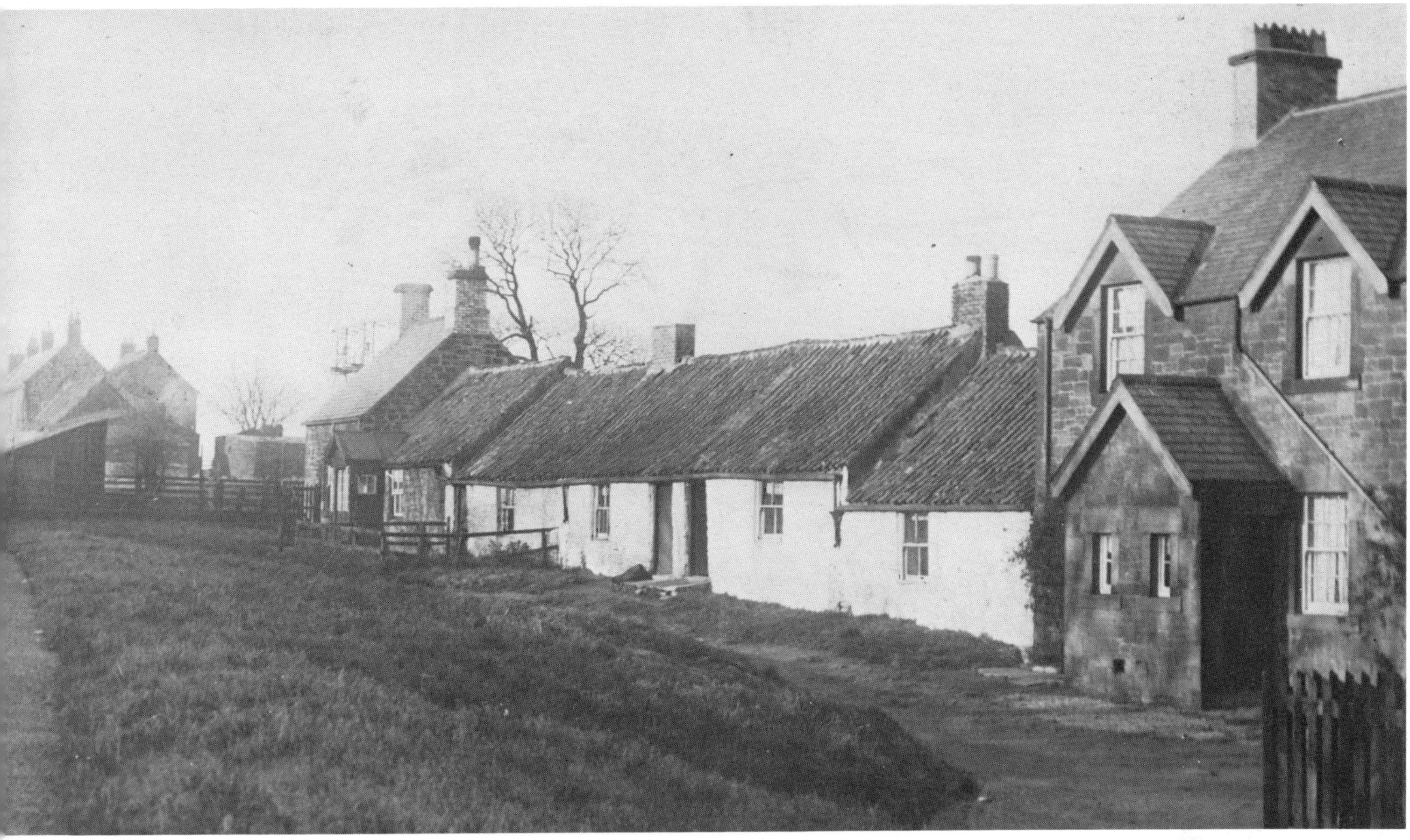

81. This picture appeared in the *Weekly Chronicle* in November 1931 and the *Sunday Sun* in August 1971. These old white cottages stood in Kenton Village – not far from the Thirties-built council houses put up by Gosforth Urban District Council. It is said that Kenton got its name because it could be 'kenned' or seen from afar.

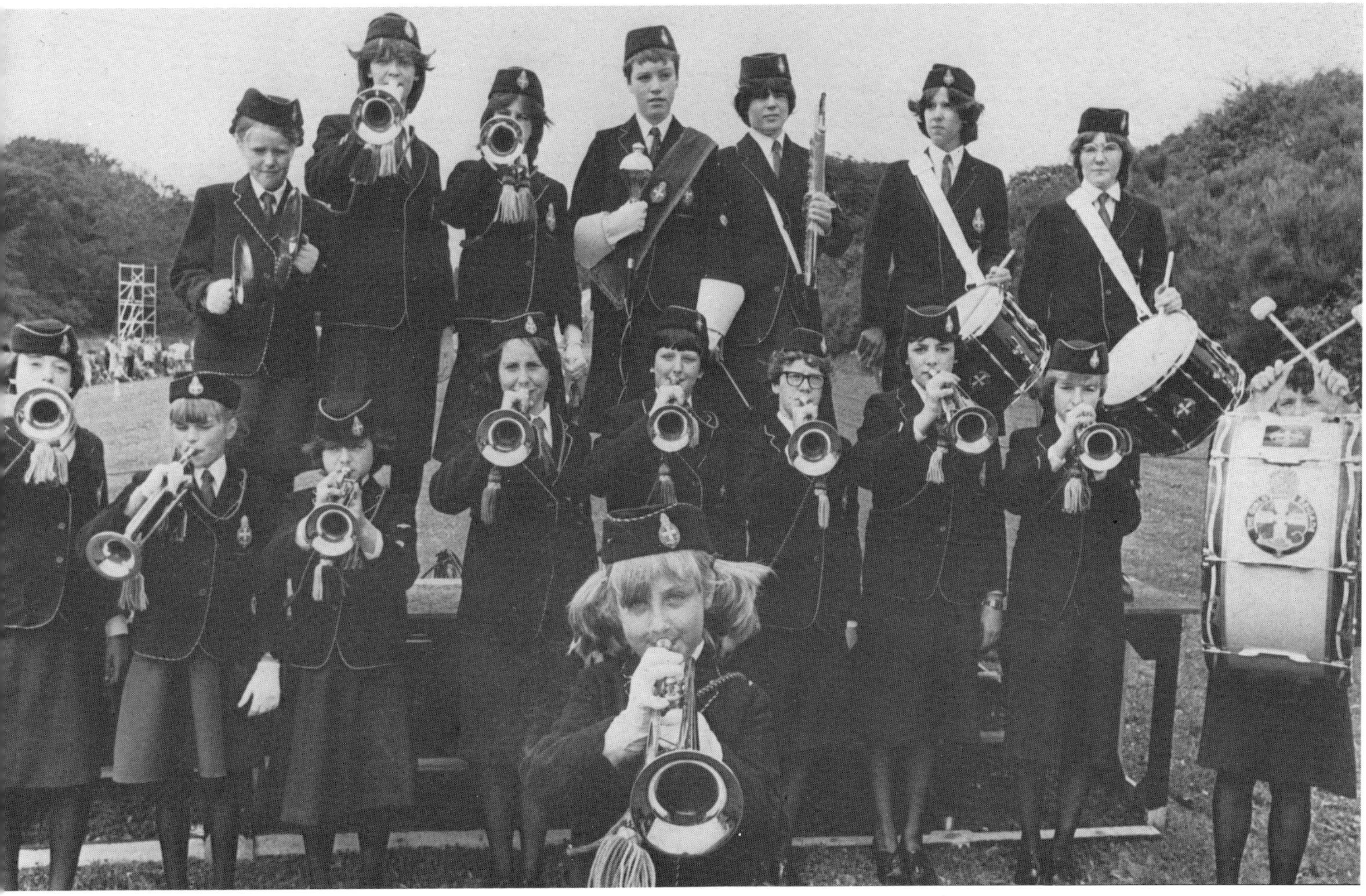

82. Strike up the band! Members of the 1st Newbiggin Girls' Brigade Band, July 1982

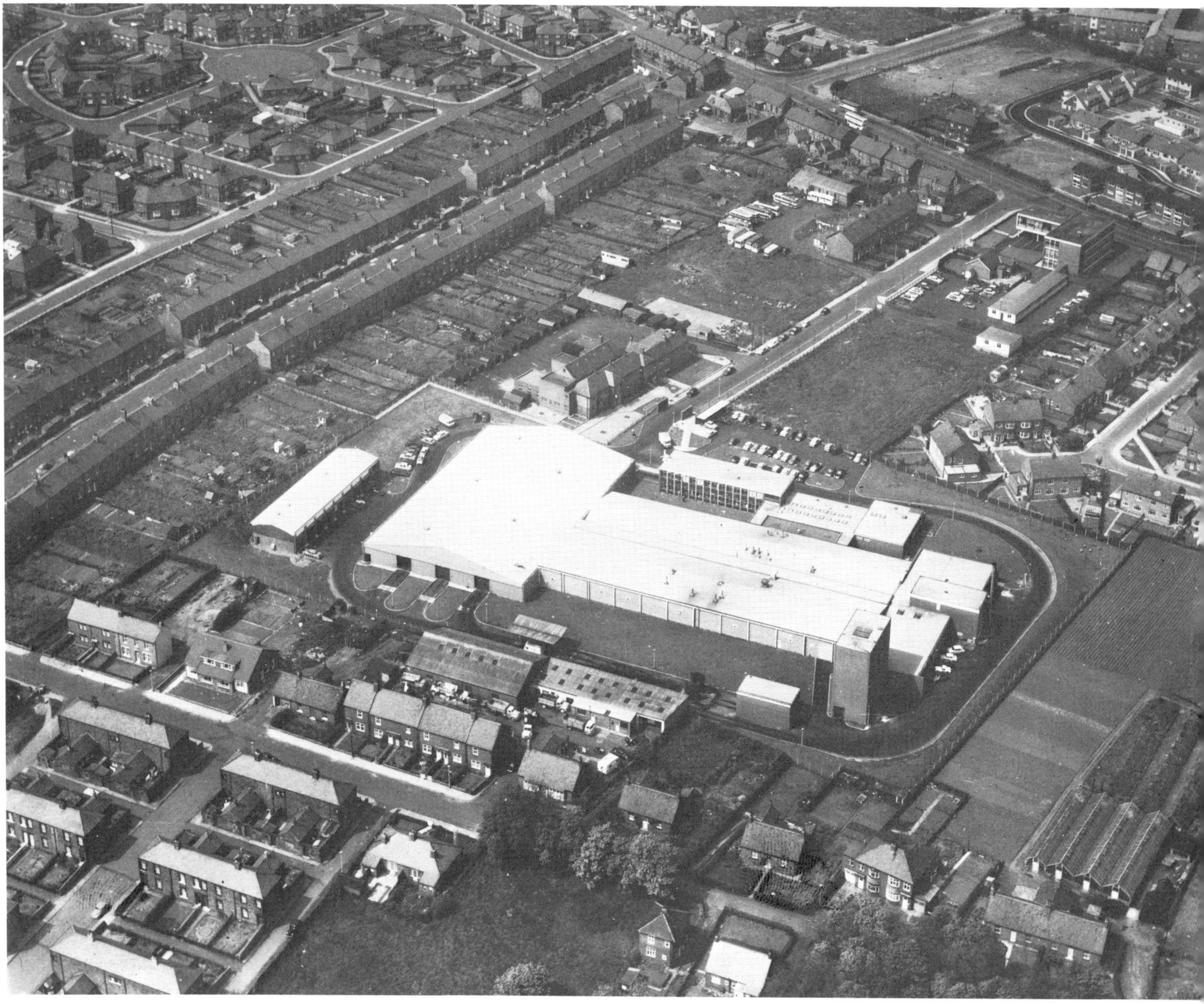

83. Westerhope. At top left is Chipchase Crescent which is off Rogerson Terrace. Running parallel to Rogerson Terrace is Beaumont Terrace.

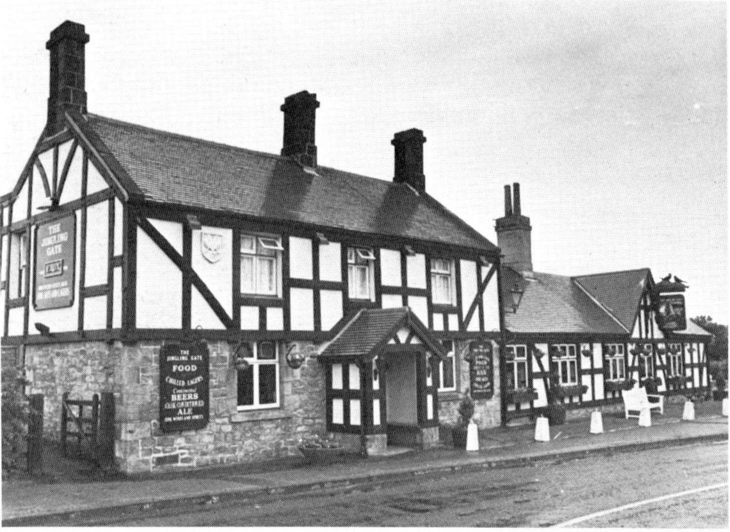

84. The Jingling Gate, Westerhope, with its stunning frontage has long been a popular haunt not only with the locals from the nearby Chapel House and Chapel Park estates, but also with travellers to and from the city.

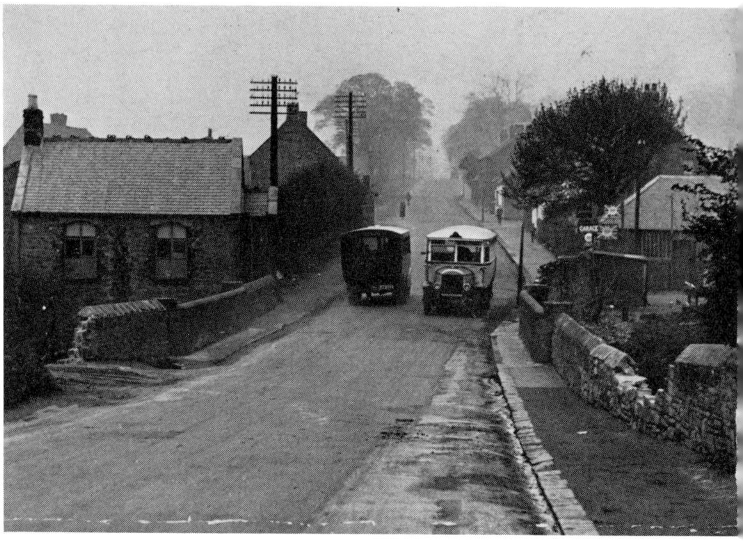

85. *The Dip* at Denton Burn in May 1927.

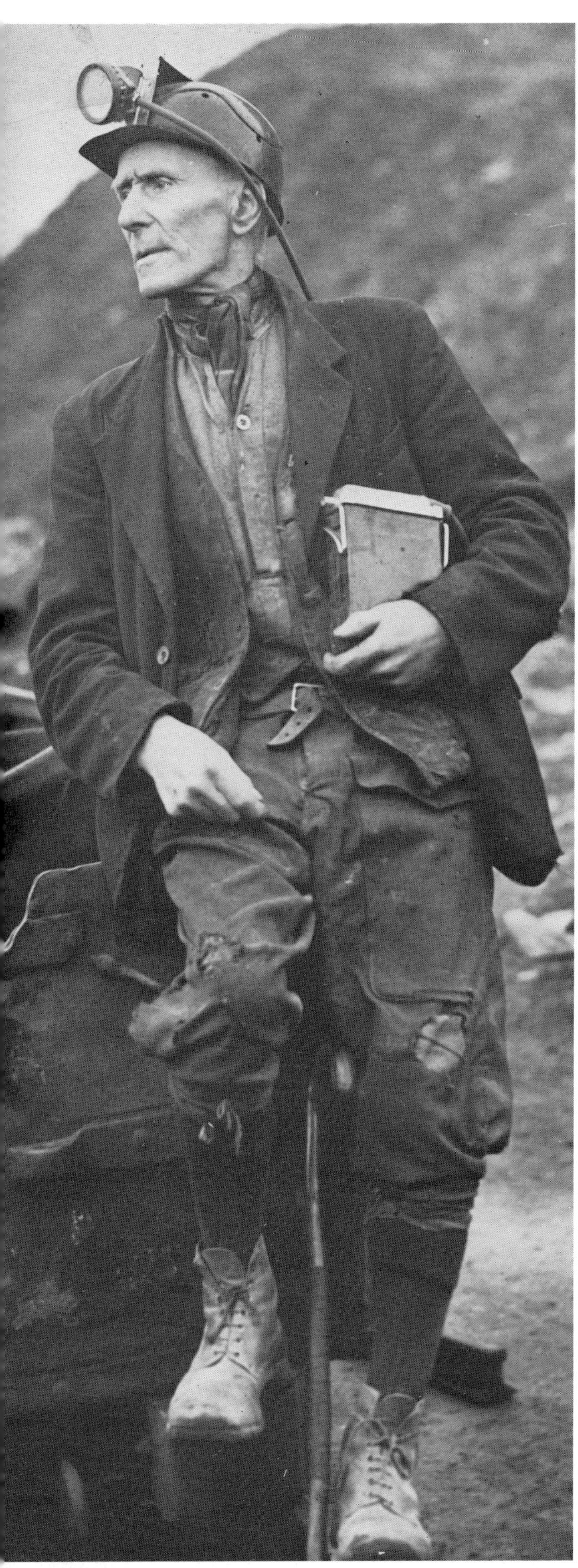

86. A superb study of a miner. This picture of Mr Thomas Brown was taken in December 1949 at the Montague Pit where he had just completed his last shift before retiring after 56 years. Mr Brown lived at Caroline Cottages, Denton Burn.

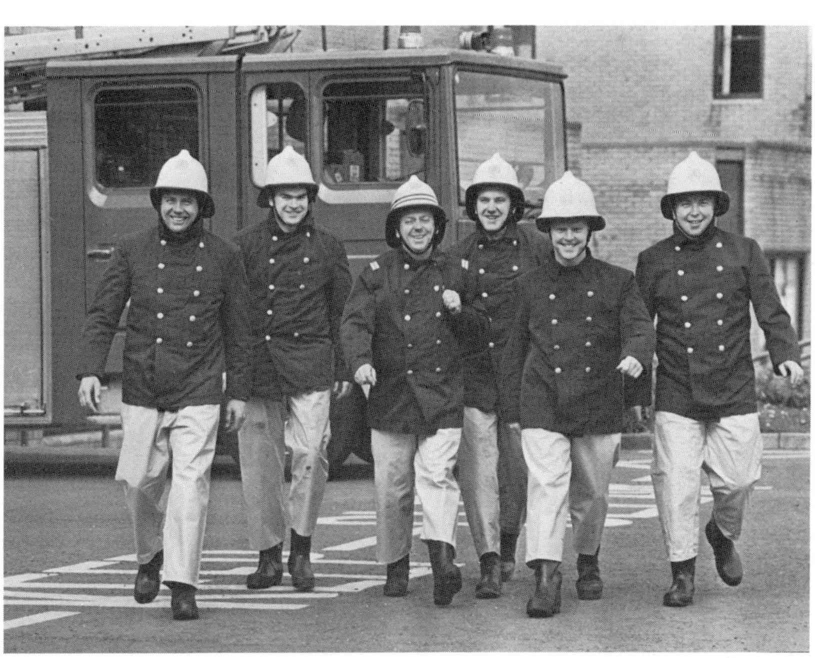

87. The magnificent six in May 1989. Firemen from White Watch at West Denton Fire Station planned to raise money for charity with a sponsored turnout against the clock. The plan was for the six to split into teams of two and use any means available to reach their objectives, one team to London, the second to Dorset, the third to Inverness and John O'Groats. The six were Peter McEwan, Graeme Sharp, Sub Officer Dave Simpson, Neil Turnbull, Peter Mudie and Tony Rochford.

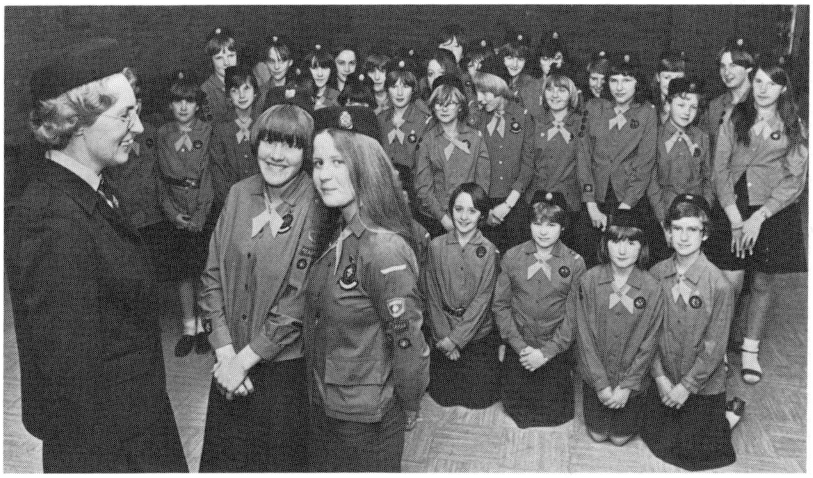

88. County Commissioner Mrs Brenda Parke talks to Helen Younger (*left*) and Helen Lane at the presentation of their Queen's Guide Awards in April 1982. The girls belonged to the 1st Denton (Church of the Holy Spirit) Girl Guide Company.

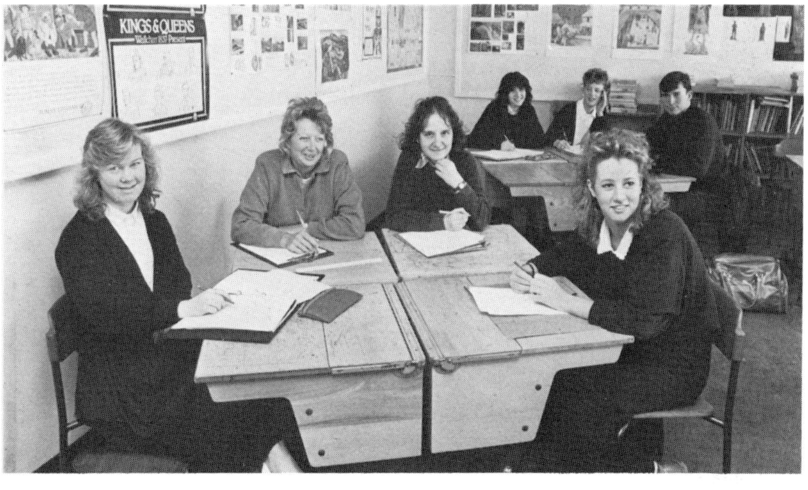

89. *Right:* You're never too old to learn. More than 40 adults were studying alongside sixth formers at Walbottle High towards A-levels and GCSEs. Pictured are Lesley Walsh and Pauline Voase with fellow A-level history students.

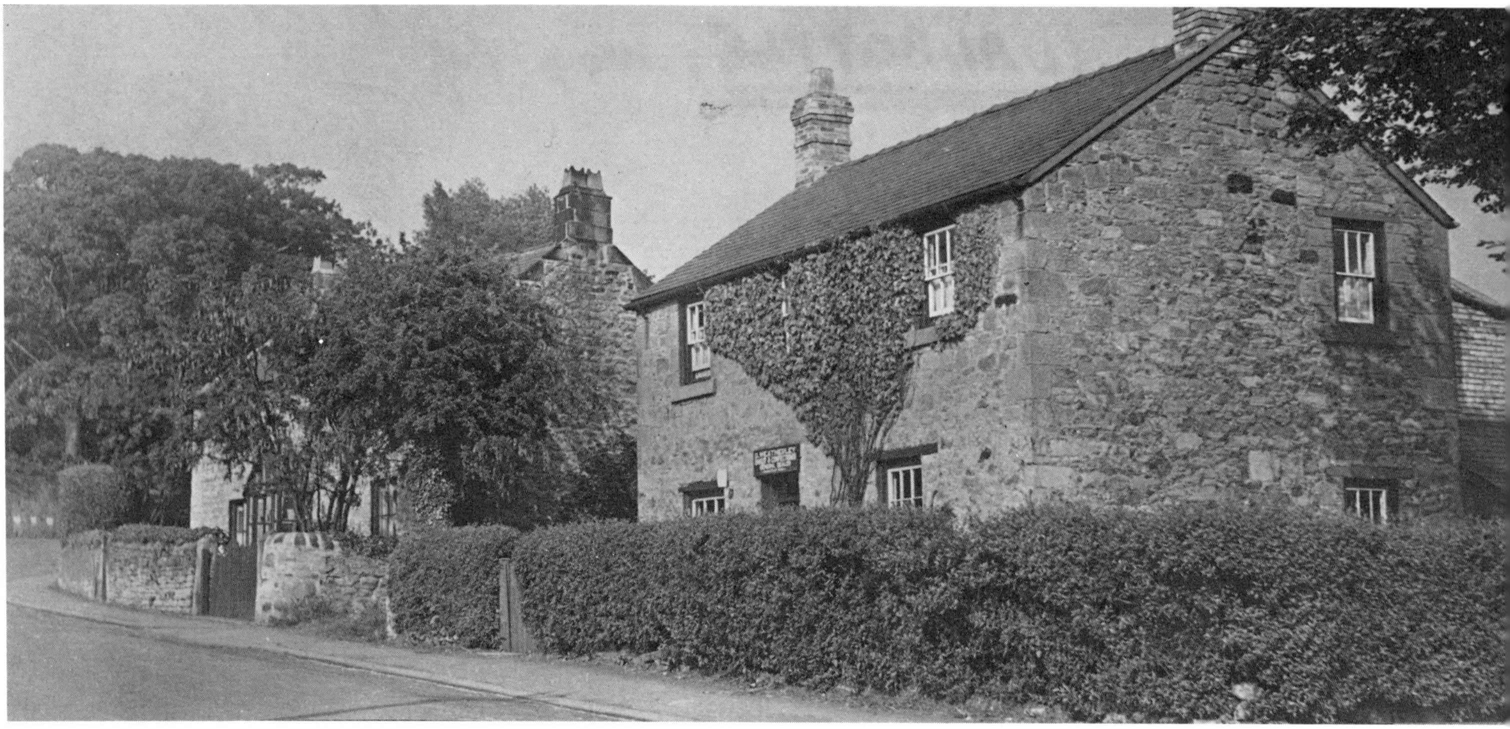

90. Weatherley's shop in Walbottle Village, August 1944, when the announcement was made that the village was to be rebuilt in the '*old world style*'.

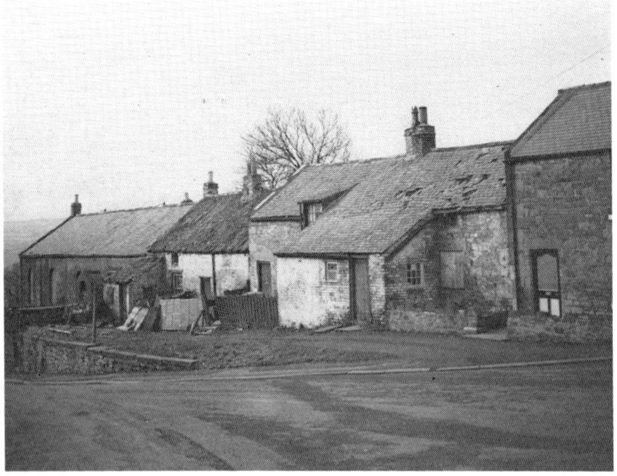

91. School Bank, Walbottle.

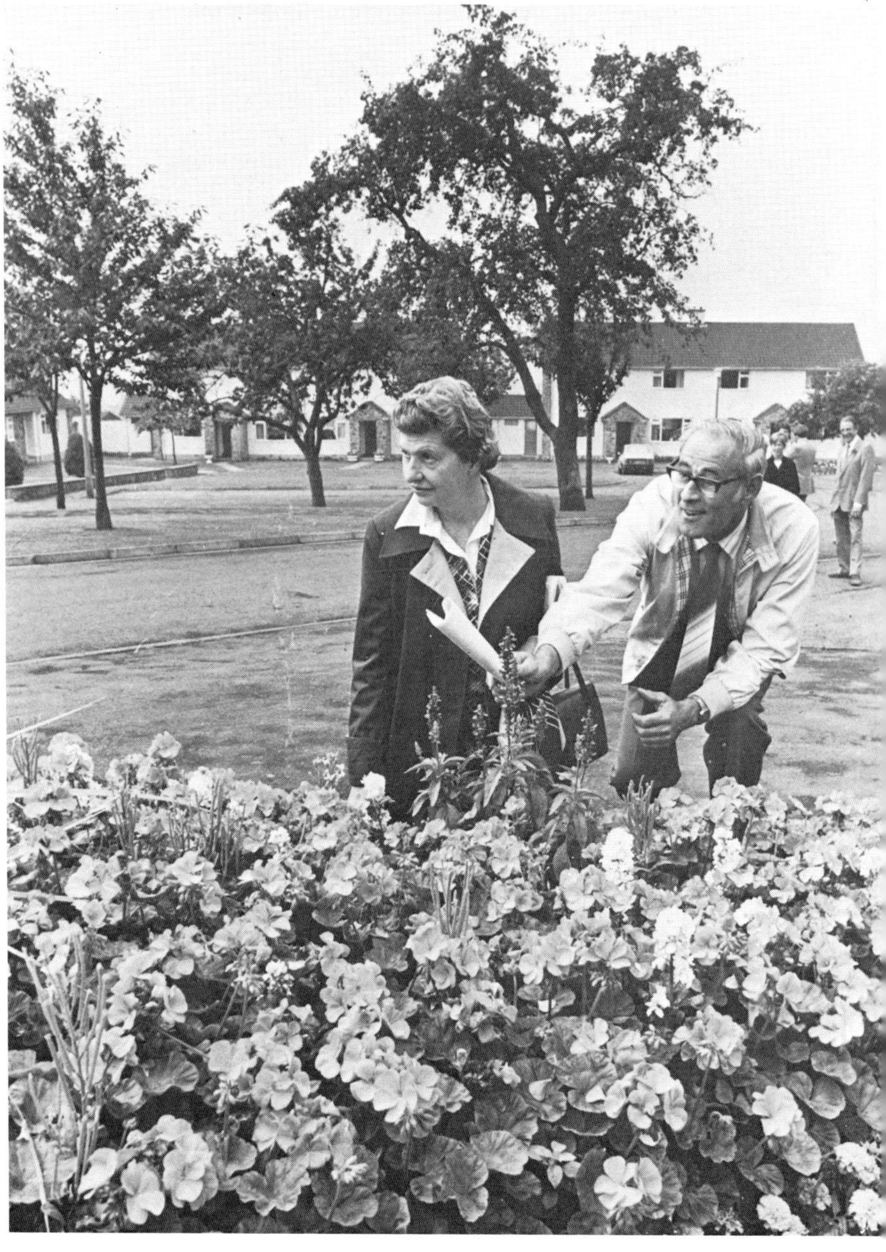

92. *Right:* Walbottle Village was looking its best in August 1982 for the Britain in Bloom contest. The village was one of six finalists in the running for the national title, and judges Mrs Kenneth Clark and Mr Ron Lewis were giving nothing away when questioned by *The Journal*. Said Mrs Clark: 'Walbottle is certainly a very colourful village and there is obviously a great deal of effort by the local people in looking after it.' Mr Lewis, who travelled up from Exmouth to judge, said: 'I'm very impressed with the way Walbottle looks. Obviously the community takes a great pride in their village.'

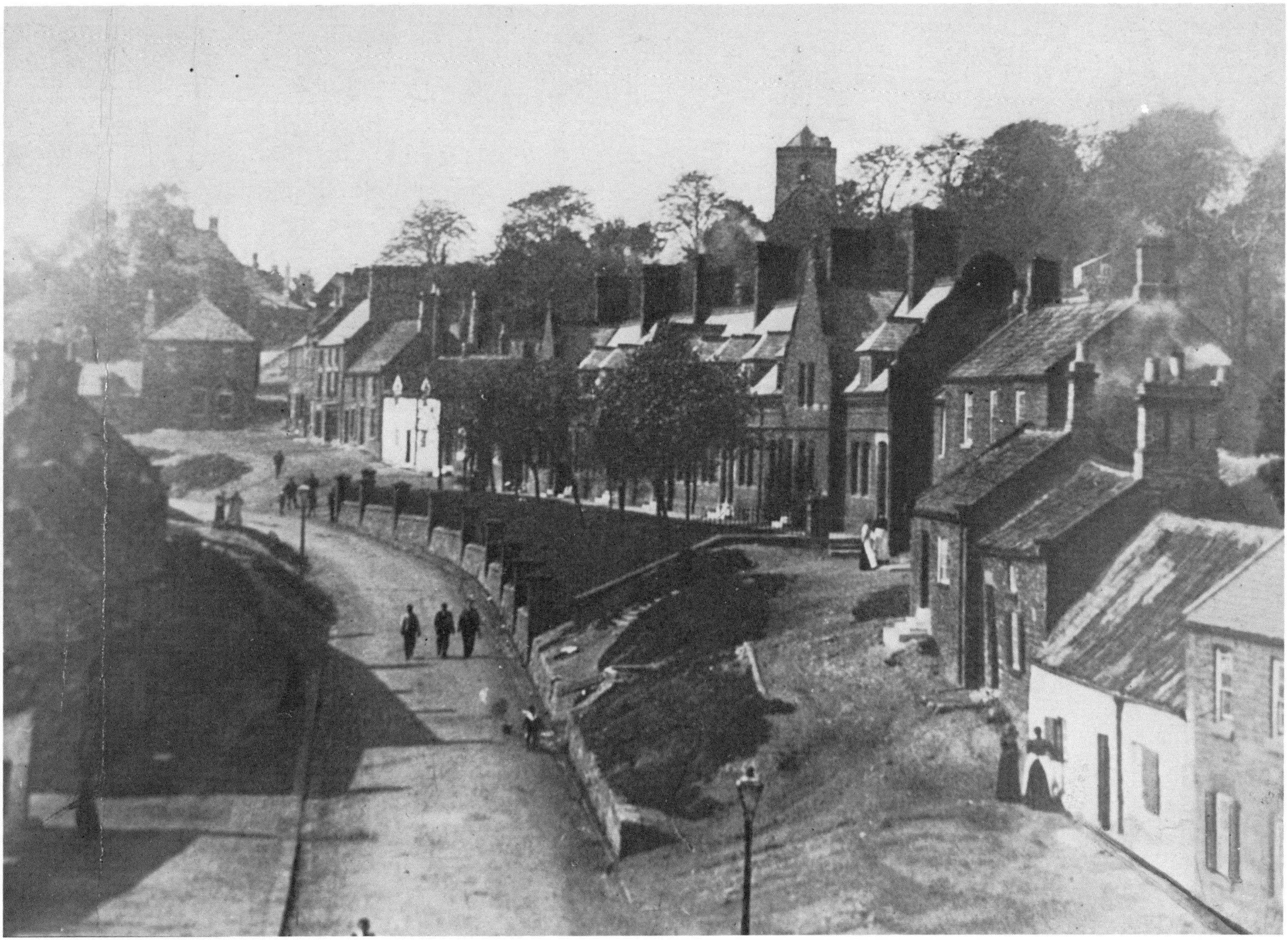

93. Downtown Newburn before the Great War. During the battle of Newburn Ford on 28 August 1640, the Scottish mounted portable cannon on the tower of Newburn church. *Courtesy:* Mrs Hetherington.

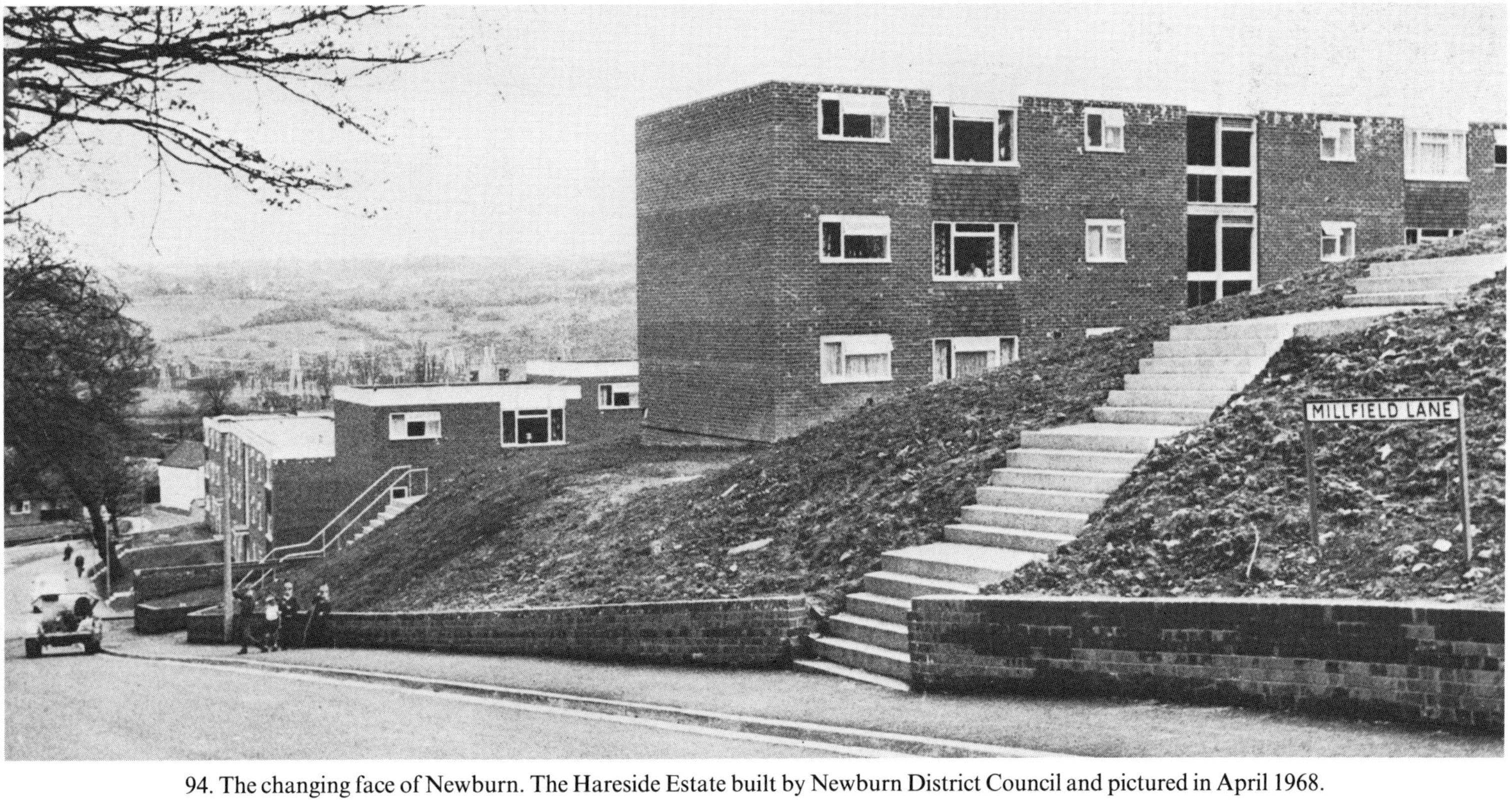

94. The changing face of Newburn. The Hareside Estate built by Newburn District Council and pictured in April 1968.

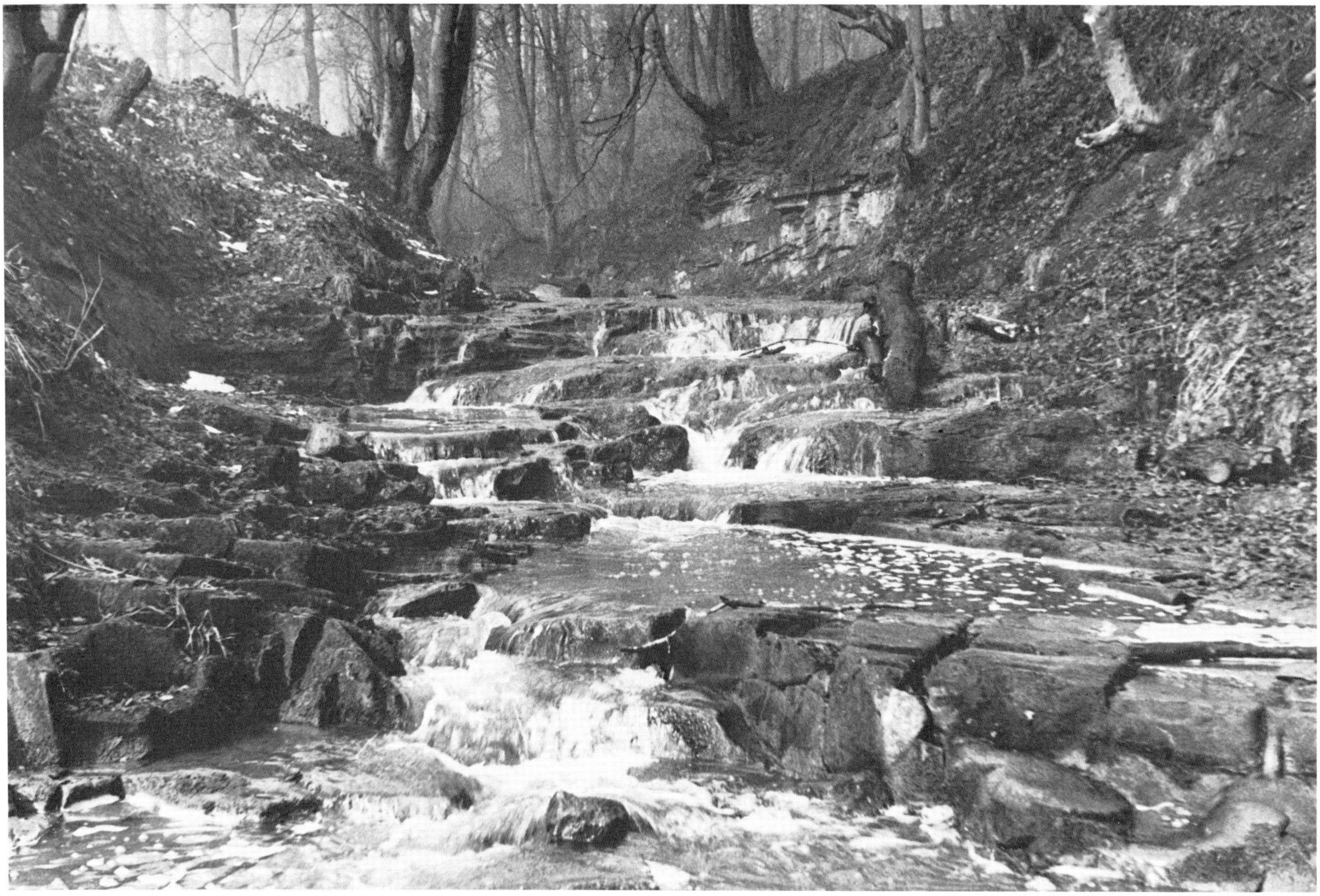

95. Newburn Dene. The photograph is of an unknown date but was published in the *Evening Chronicle* in March 1965 and again in 1982.

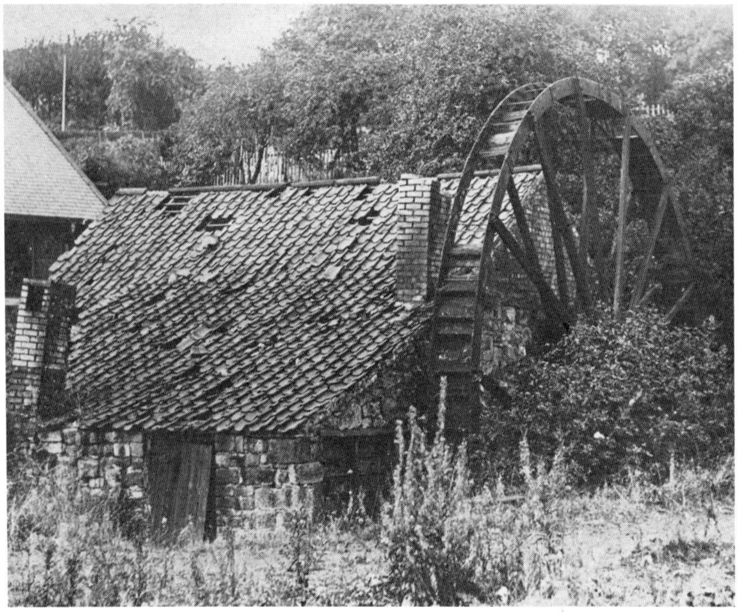

96. The old waterwheel and workshop of John Spencer, of Newburn, where he ground files at the beginning of the nineteenth century. He used to travel to Newcastle on a donkey to sell his files. The photograph dates from September 1933 and was published in the *Sunday Sun* in August 1971.

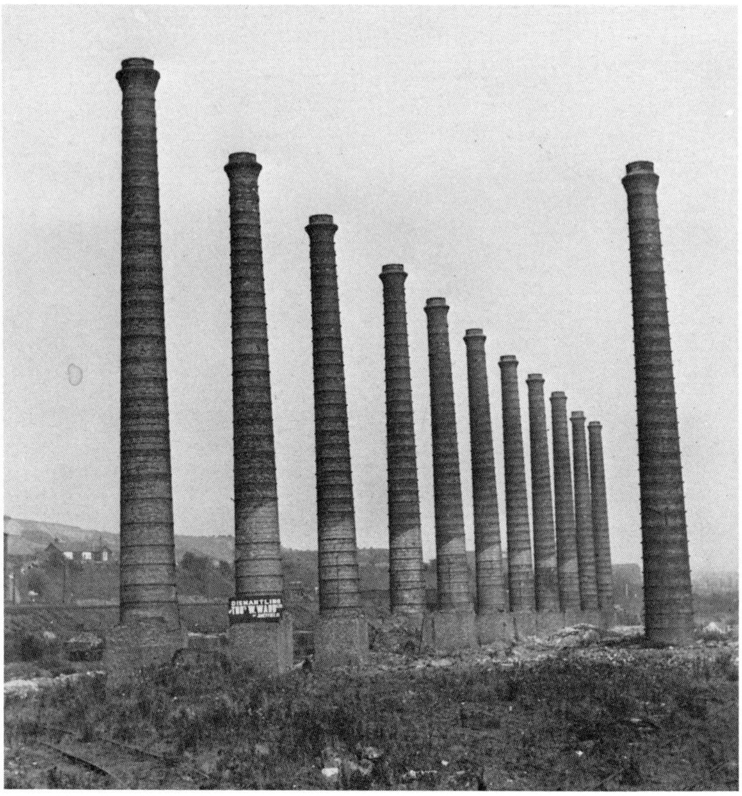

97. *Right:* Tommy Ward strikes again! Not only did T W Ward dismantle the defunct Palmer's yard at Jarrow, they also demolished Newburn steelworks. The picture dates from September 1933 when the first of the eleven chimneys were due to be levelled. The chimneys were 130ft high and each contained around 75,000 bricks.

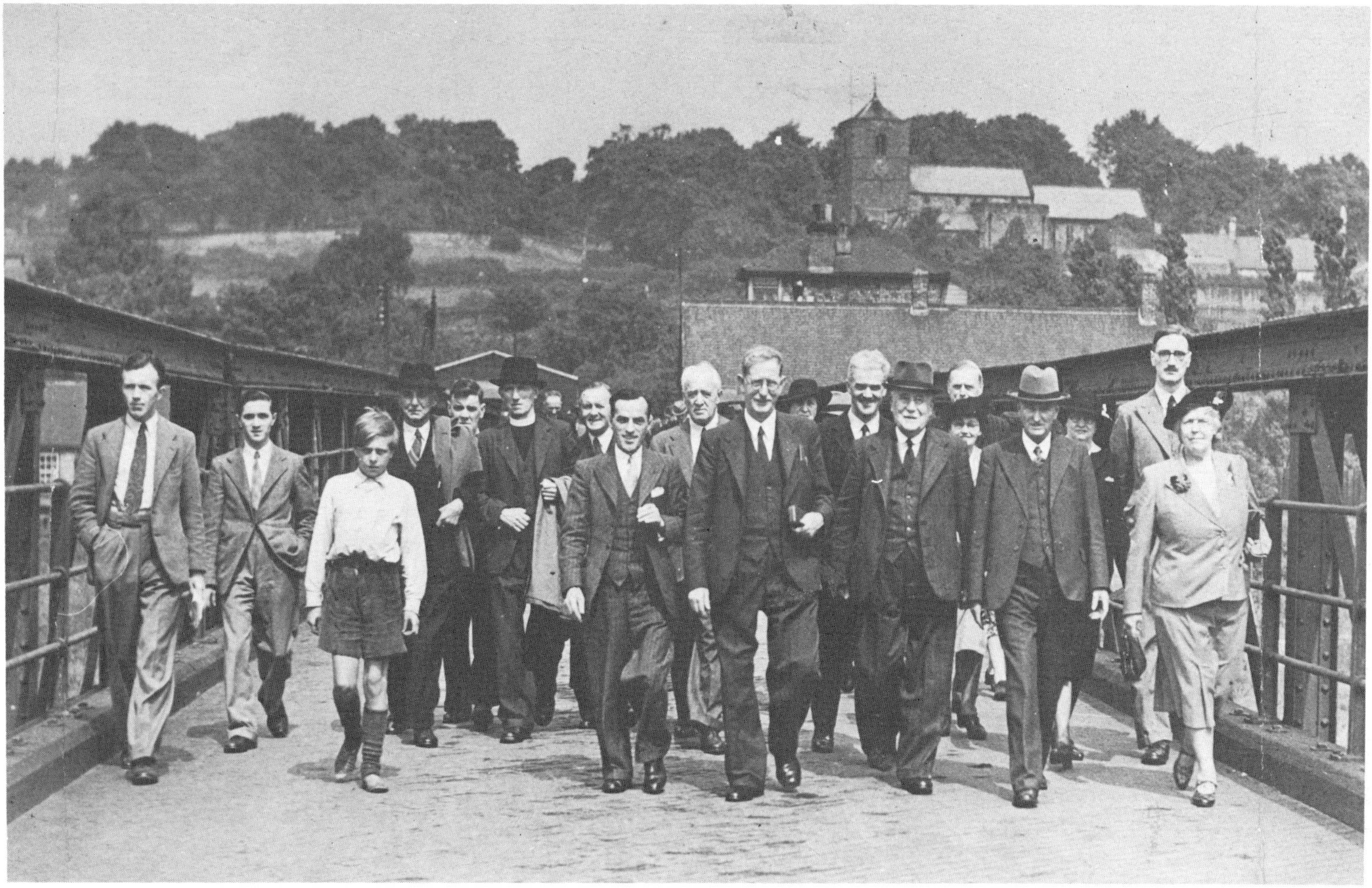

98. August 1947 and Newburn Bridge is freed from tolls. The official party of members of Northumberland County Council and Durham County Council walks over the bridge after it had been freed from tolls – the last Tyne bridge to be freed. On 28 August 1640, Newburn Ford was the site of a battle between Scottish forces under Sir Alexander Leslie and the King's troops commanded by Lord Conway.

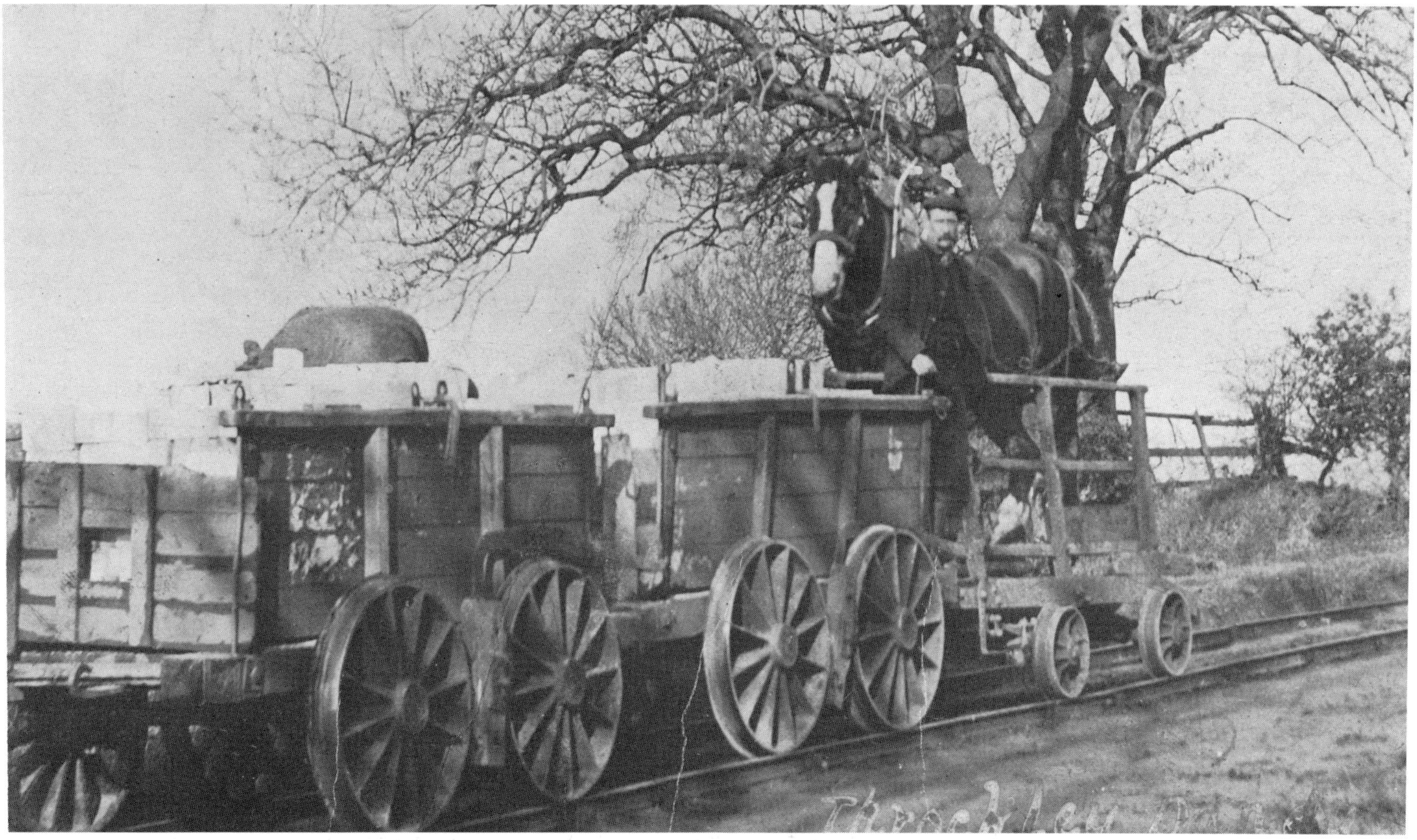

99. This photograph was taken at some time before 1907 and shows Mr Michael Makepeace in charge of the *Throckley Dandy* which transported fire bricks from Throckley Brick Works to Lemington Staithes.

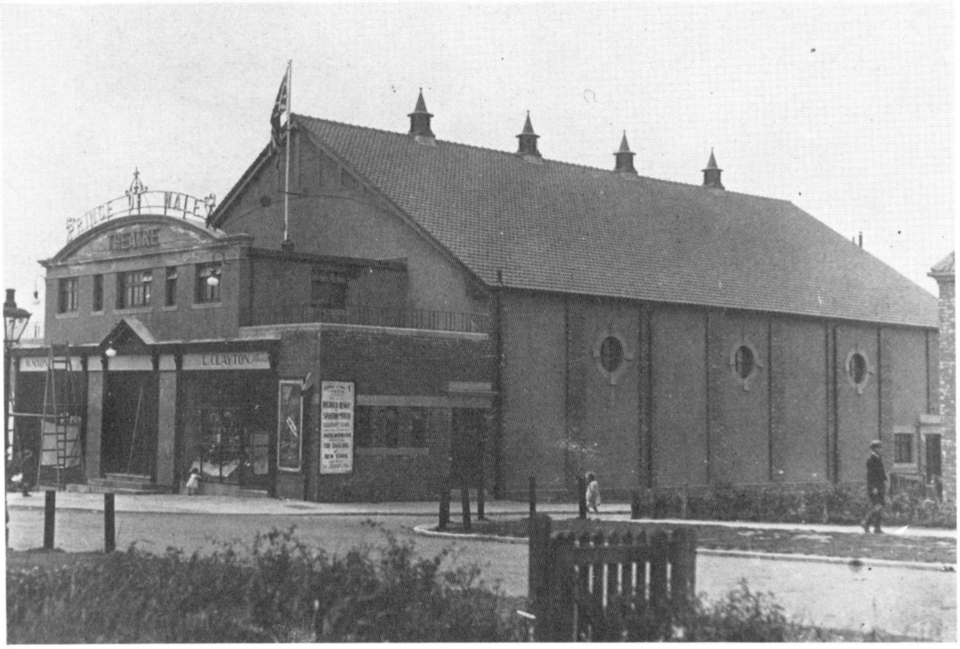

100. The finishing touches are being put to the Prince of Wales Theatre, Lemington, in July 1924 prior to the official opening by Councillor J Grantham.

101. *Right:* In January 1986 it was announced that there were design defects in Newcastle's 544 Unity homes such as these in Centurian Road, Lemington. Unity homes were built using concrete beams for floor and roof supports rather than the more traditional brick and masonry. The fault was caused as the steel within the concrete corroded, leading to cracking and possible collapse.

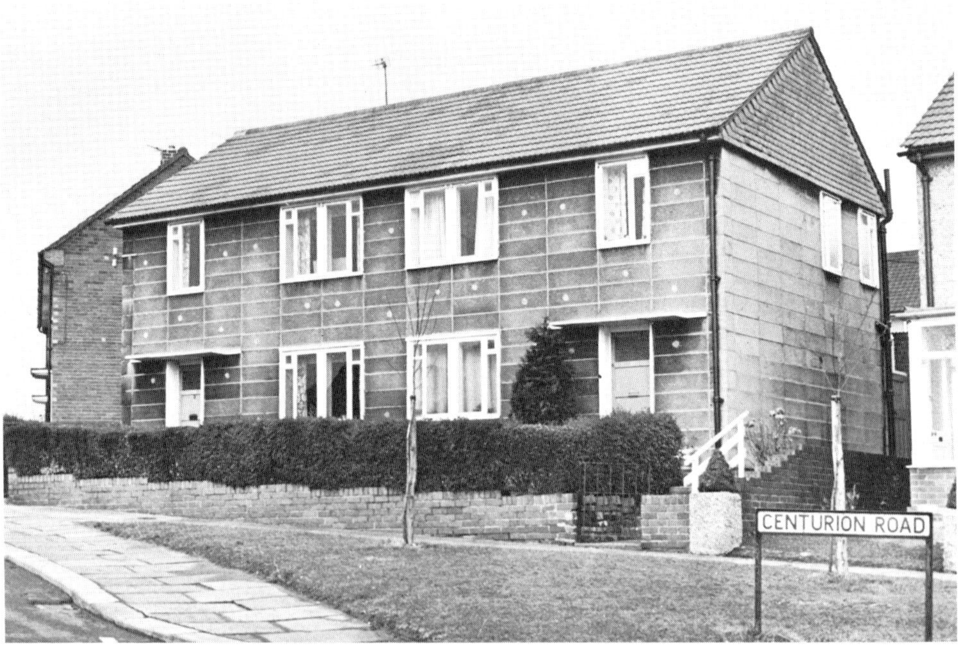

103. *Below right:* In December 1984 experts were called in to Lemington with the discovery of asbestos dumped on two sites.

102. *Below:* Lemington Gut in January 1958. Photograph by P Schaill.

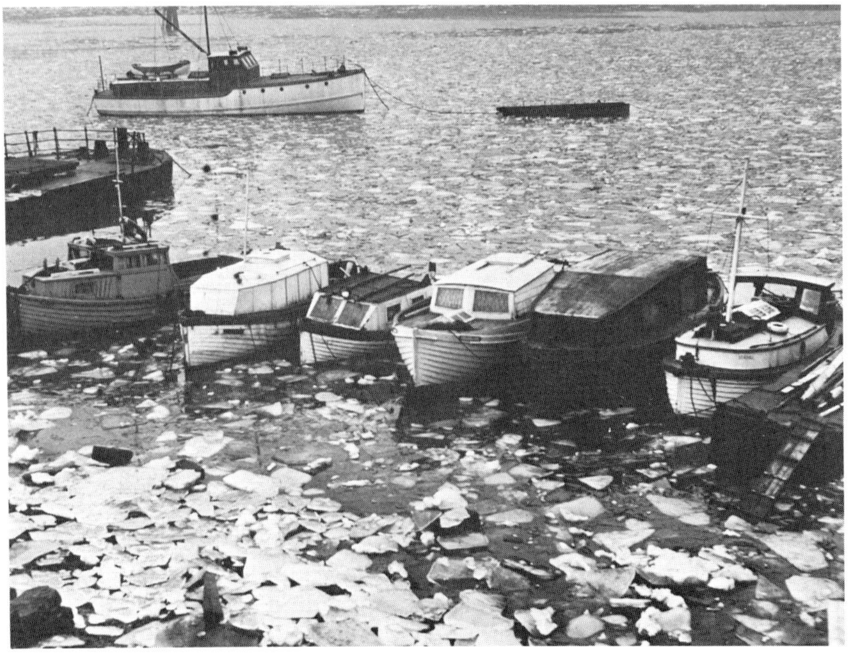

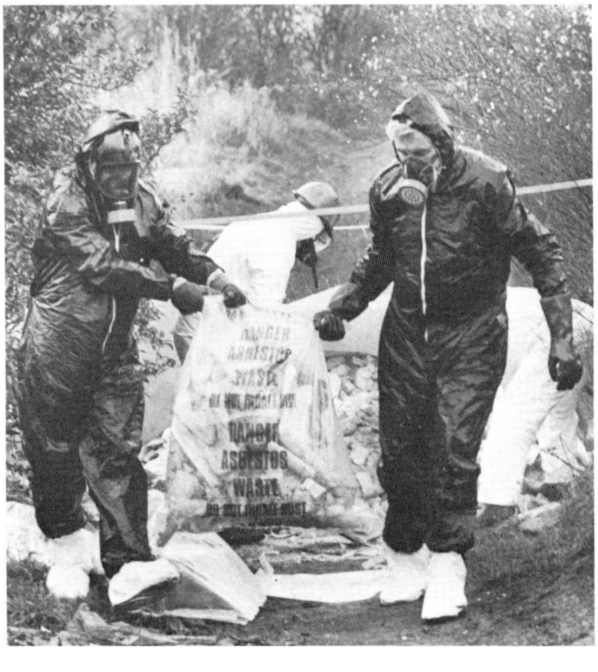

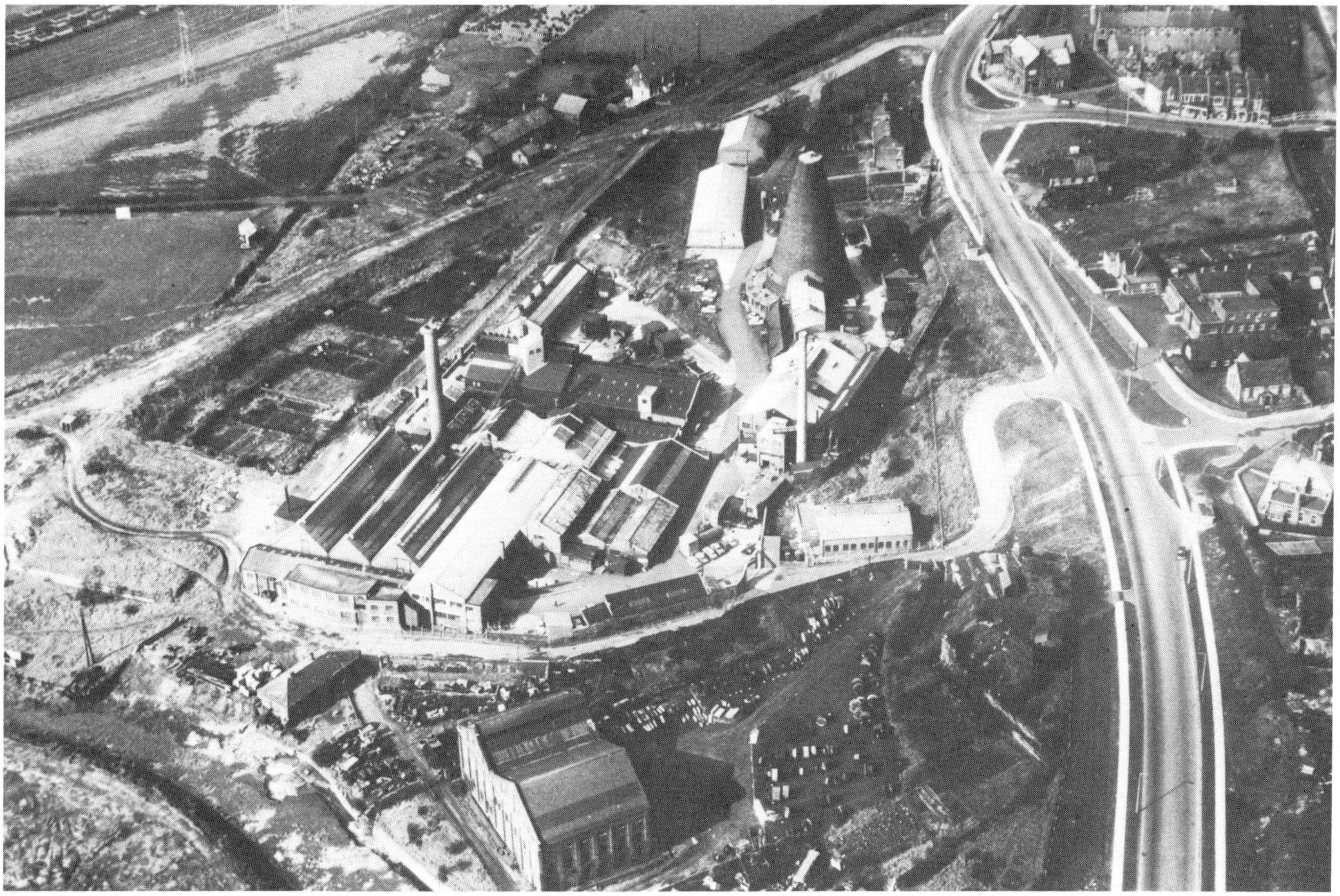

104-106. The Lemington factory of Glass Tubes & Components Ltd as it was c1965, and some of their product range of 1975.

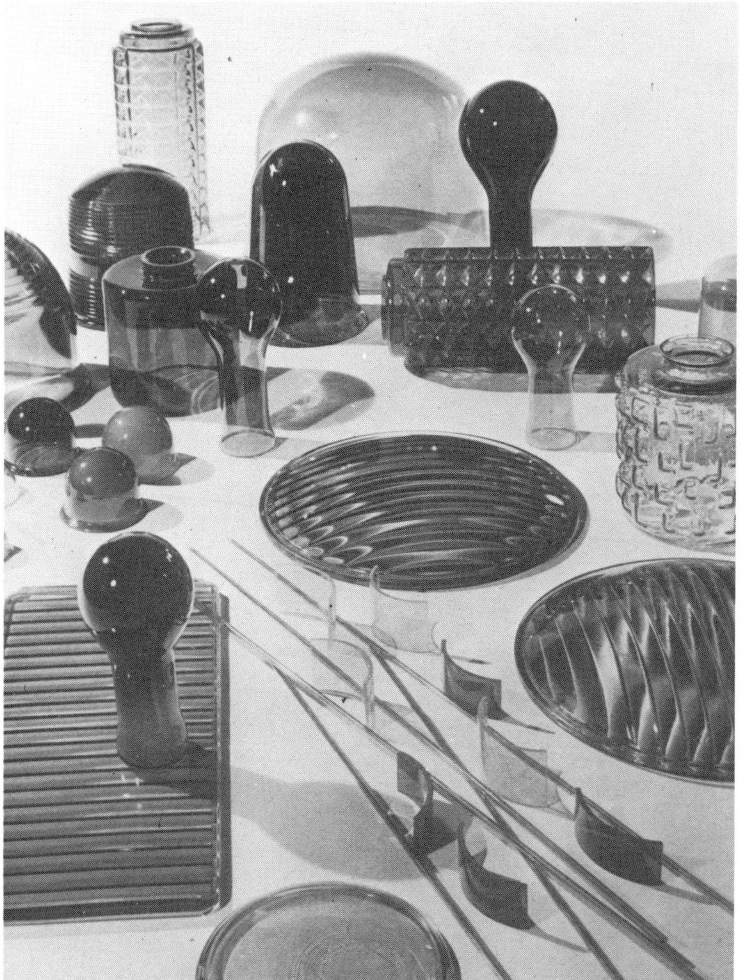

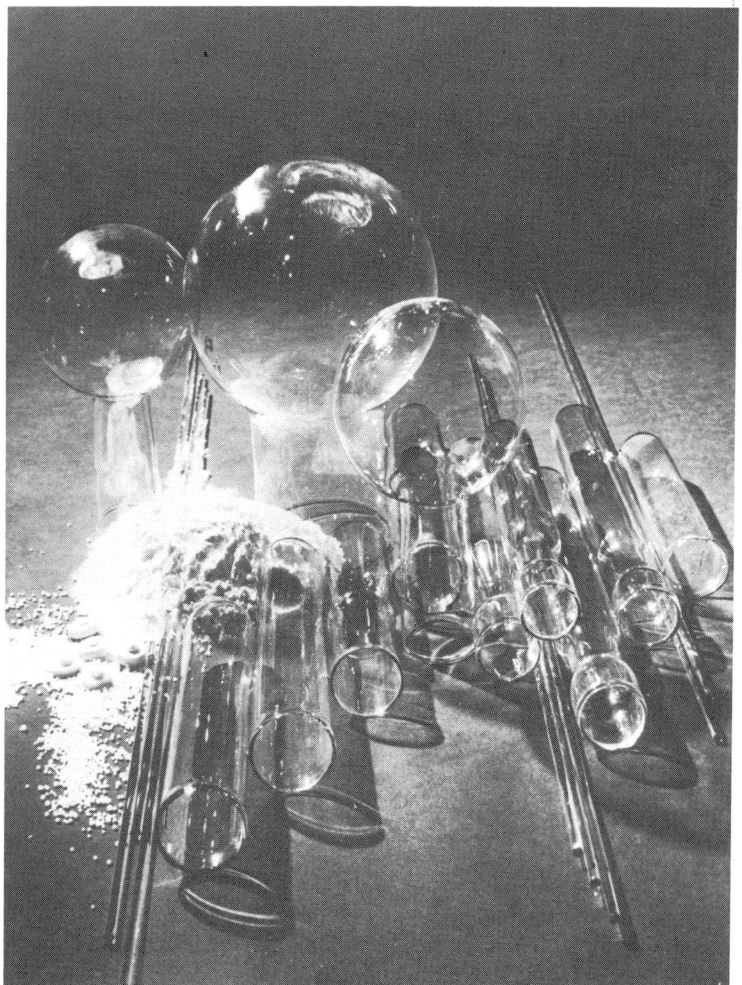

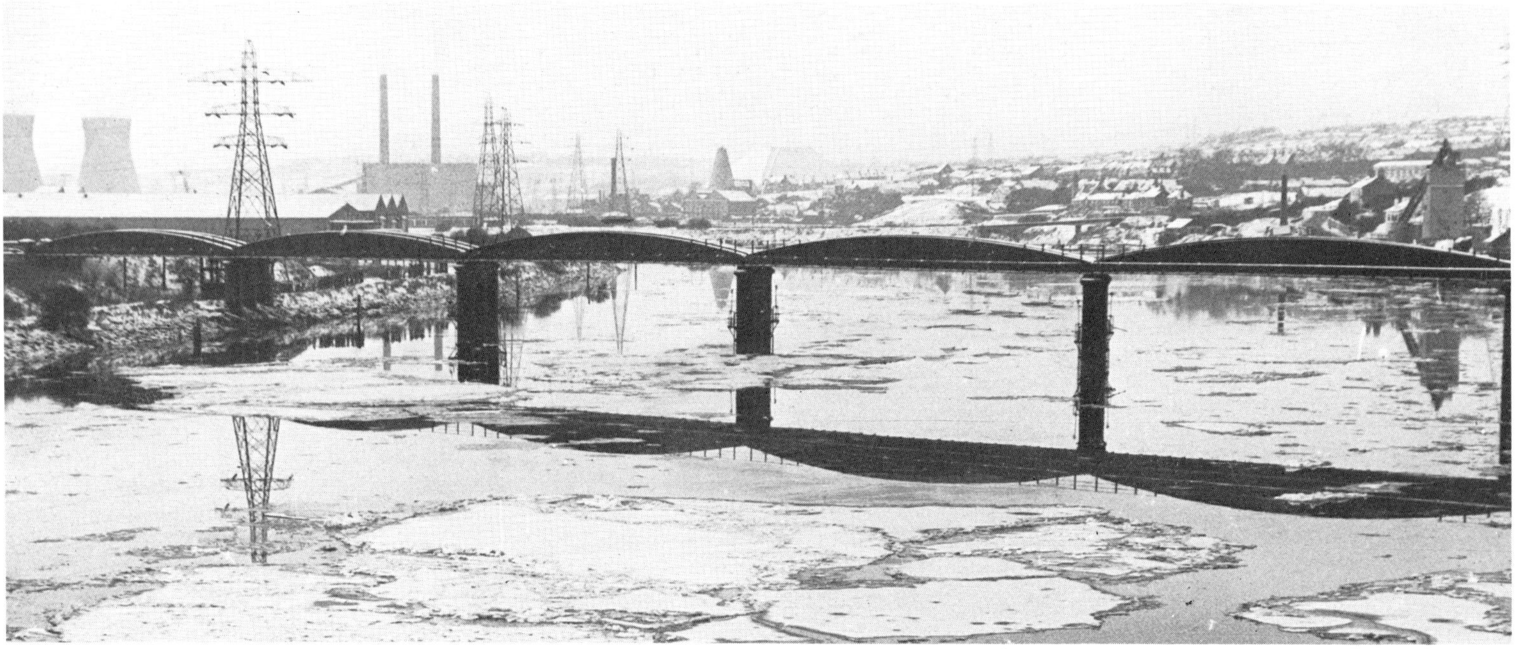

107. The scene from Scotswood Bridge in January 1979, with ice floes moving near the Blaydon railway bridge.

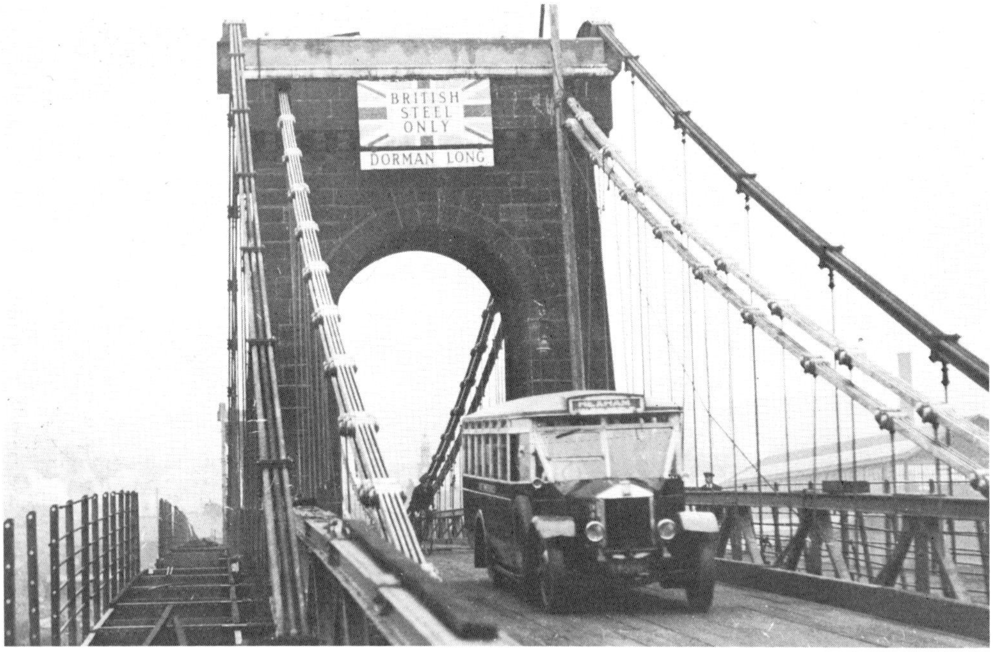

108. *Left:* The Scotswood Bridge after its reopening in May 1931 following widening. The footway on the left has still to be finished. Through the archway is the clock tower of the Ord Arms.

109. The Scotswood Regatta, June 1930.

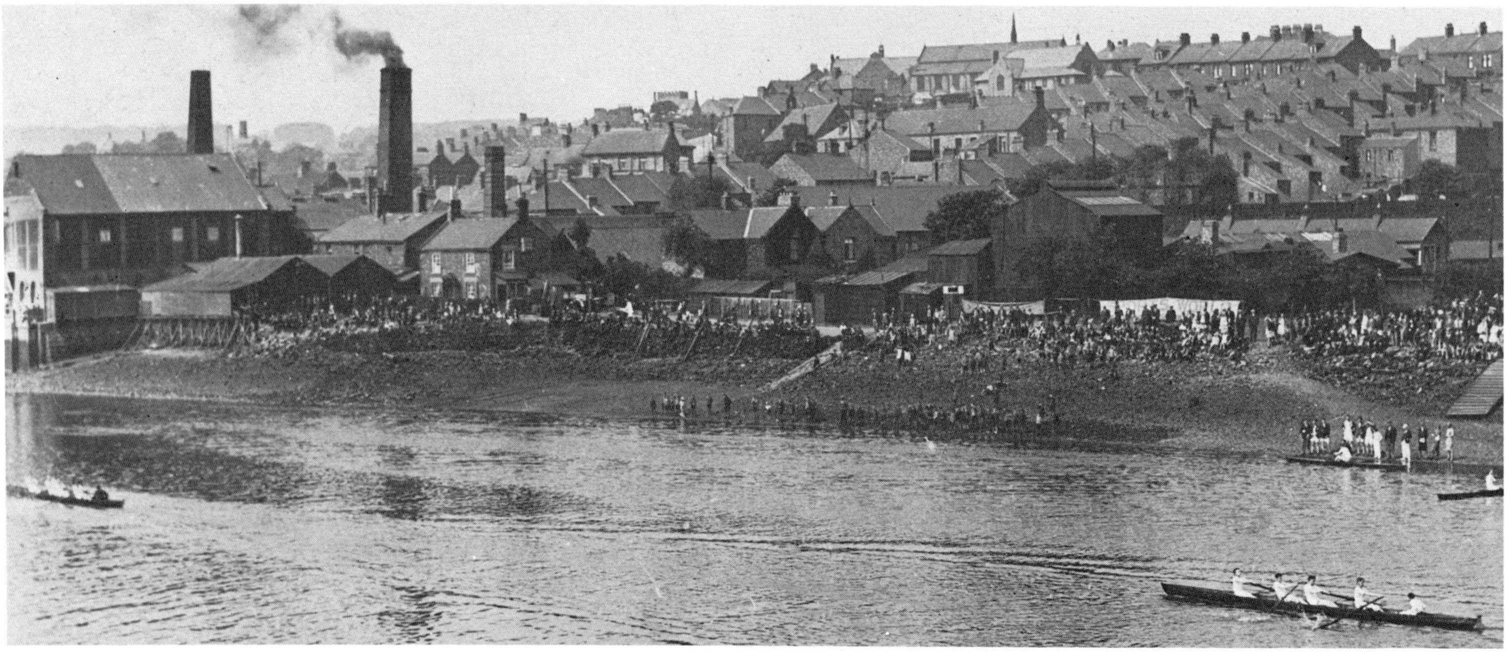

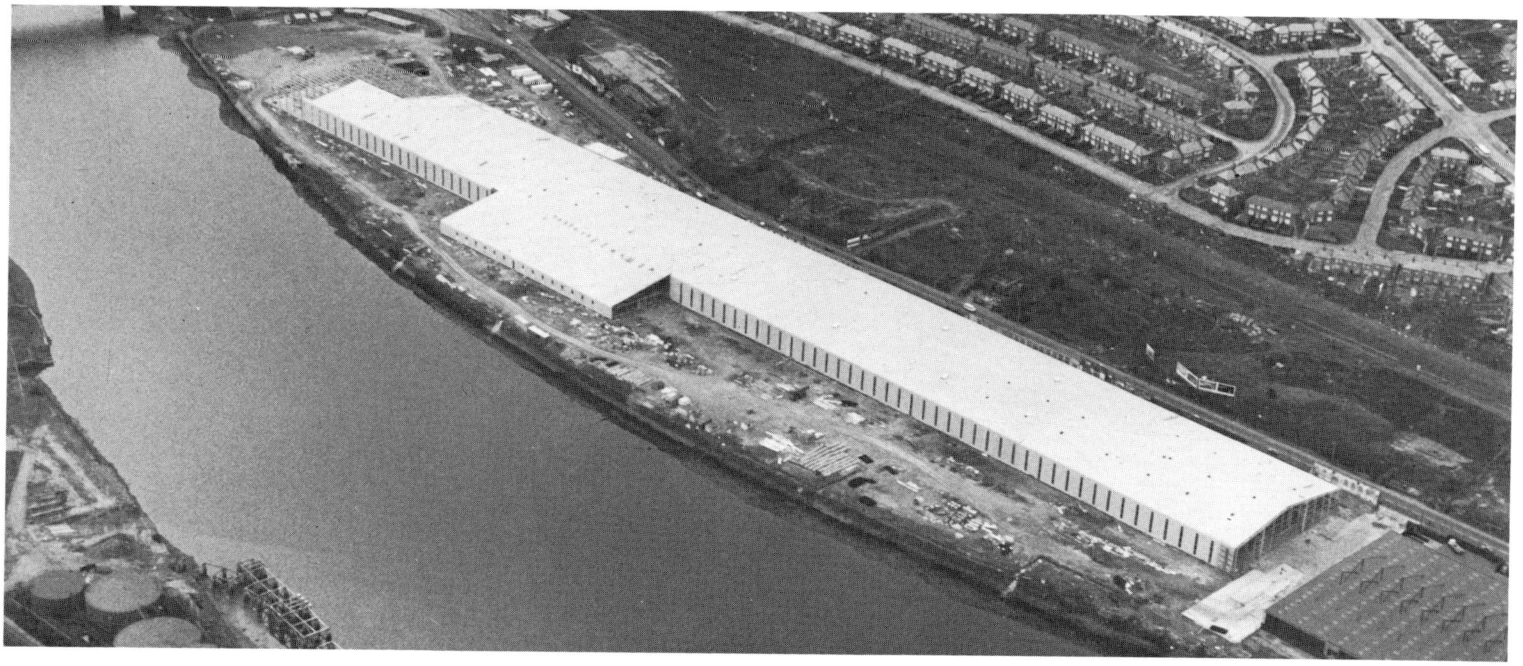

110. Vickers Defence Systems' £7.5 million factory on Scotswood Road nears completion in 1982. Work started on the 546 metre long facility in August 1981. *Courtesy:* Vickers.

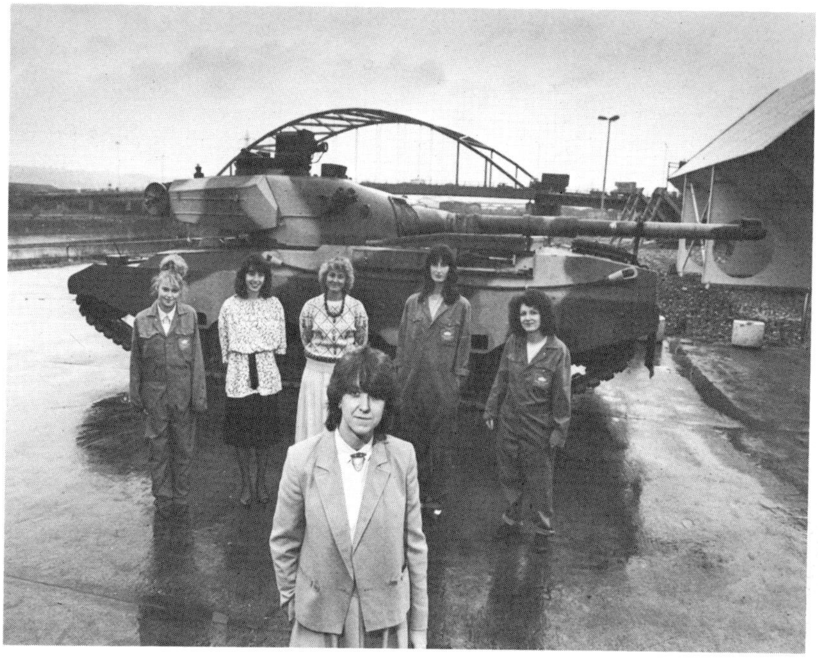

111. *Right:* Equal opportunities in September 1989. Moira Smith, a chief engineer with Vickers Defence Systems, with *left to right:* electronics technical apprentice Joanne Duffy, mechanical engineering undergraduate Sharon Raper, draughtswoman Gillian Rowe and graduate engineers Christine Barron and Judith Wood. In the background is the Vickers MkIII-I battle tank.

112-113. *Below:* From the outside this Vickers Valkyr looked like any other armoured vehicle but inside it was a different story. This particular vehicle had everything that the head of state in a hot spot might need: FM radio, TV, video, Connolly hide seats, cocktail cabinet, French walnut panelling and imperviousness to small-arms fire.

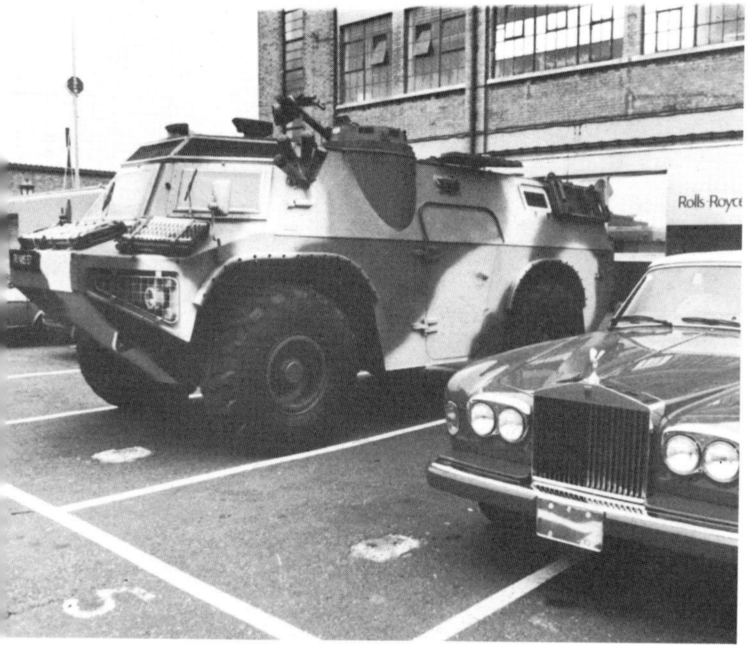

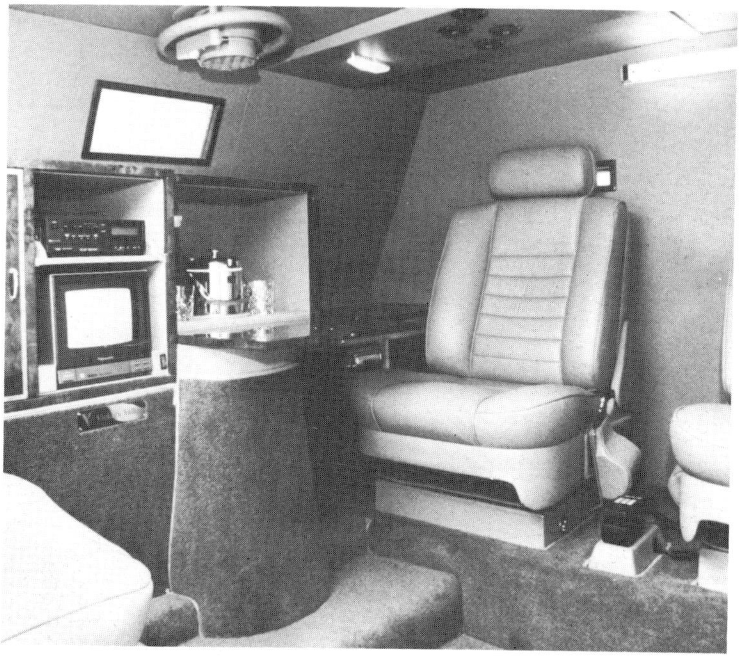

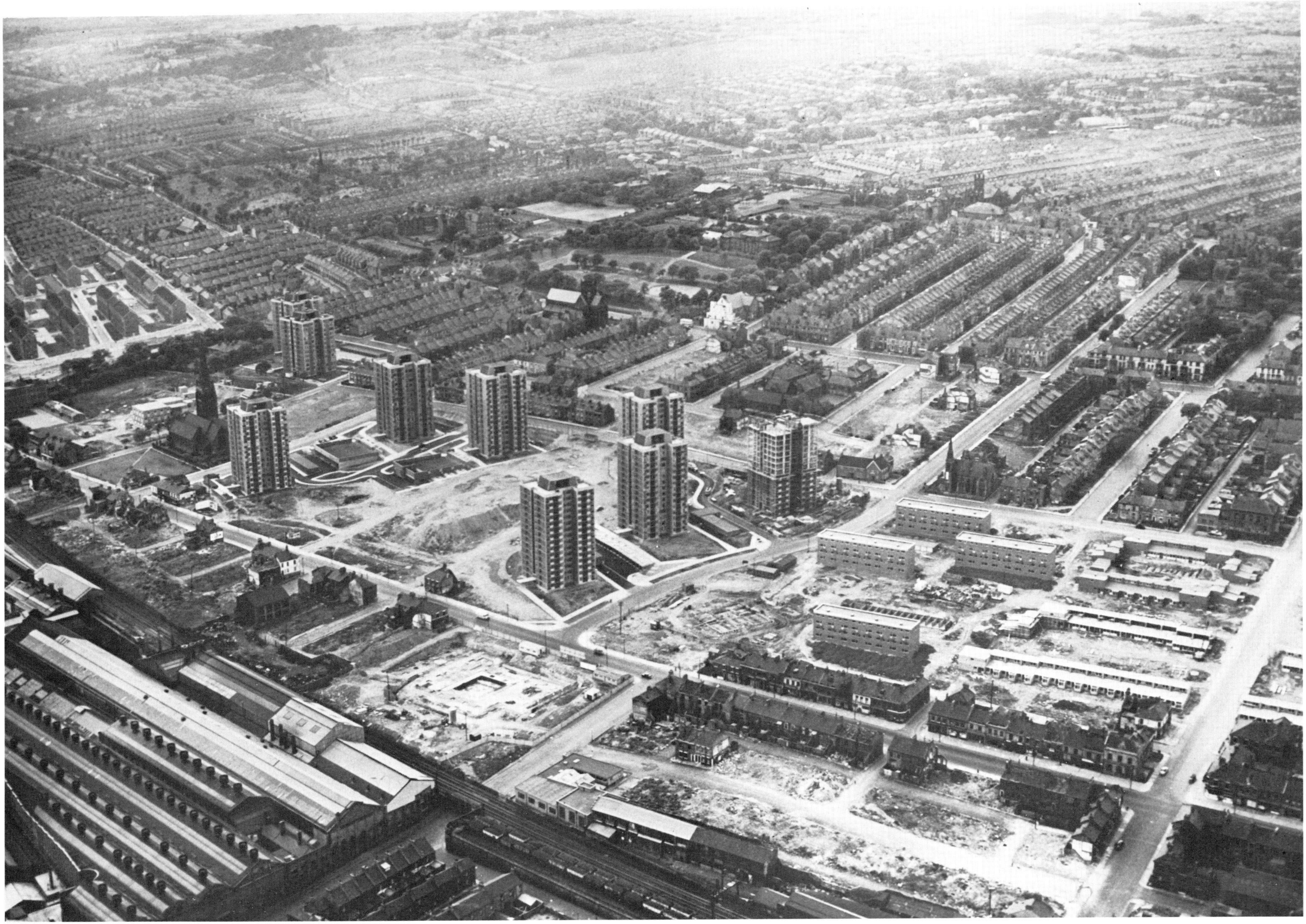

114. The Scotswood Road redevelopment in June 1963, looking from the Cruddas Park area over Elswick Park and St John's Cemetery to Benwell. Scotswood is at the extreme left background.

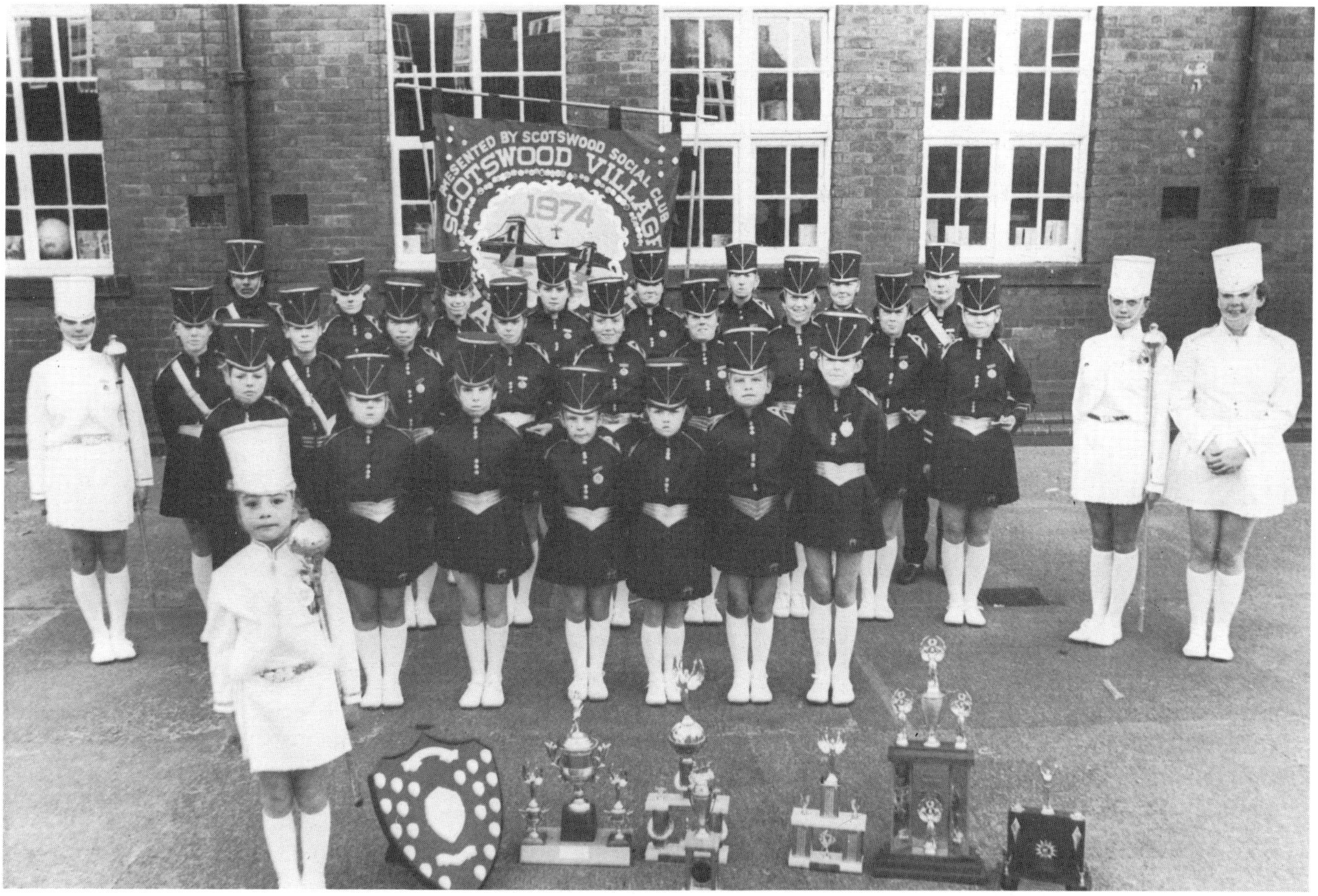

115. The Scotswood Village Starlights junior jazz band was formed in 1974 and within ten years had become UK indoor champions, winners of the Northern jazz band championship and had the world champion mascot in Margaret Davison, of St Margaret's Road. Margaret is pictured in the foreground guarding some of the band's spoils.

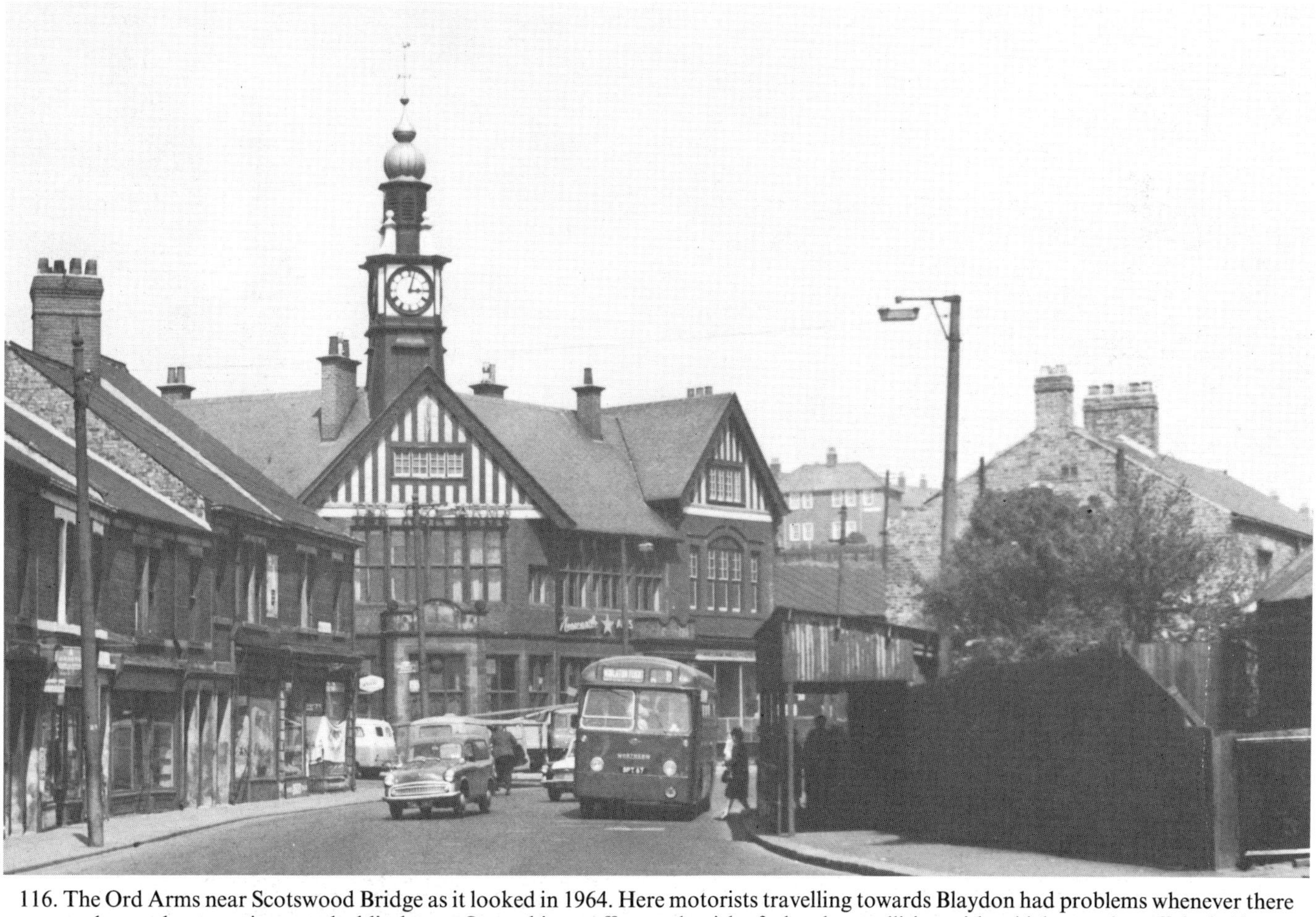

116. The Ord Arms near Scotswood Bridge as it looked in 1964. Here motorists travelling towards Blaydon had problems whenever there was a bus at the stop – it created a blind spot. Overtaking traffic ran the risk of a head-on collision with vehicles coming off the bridge.

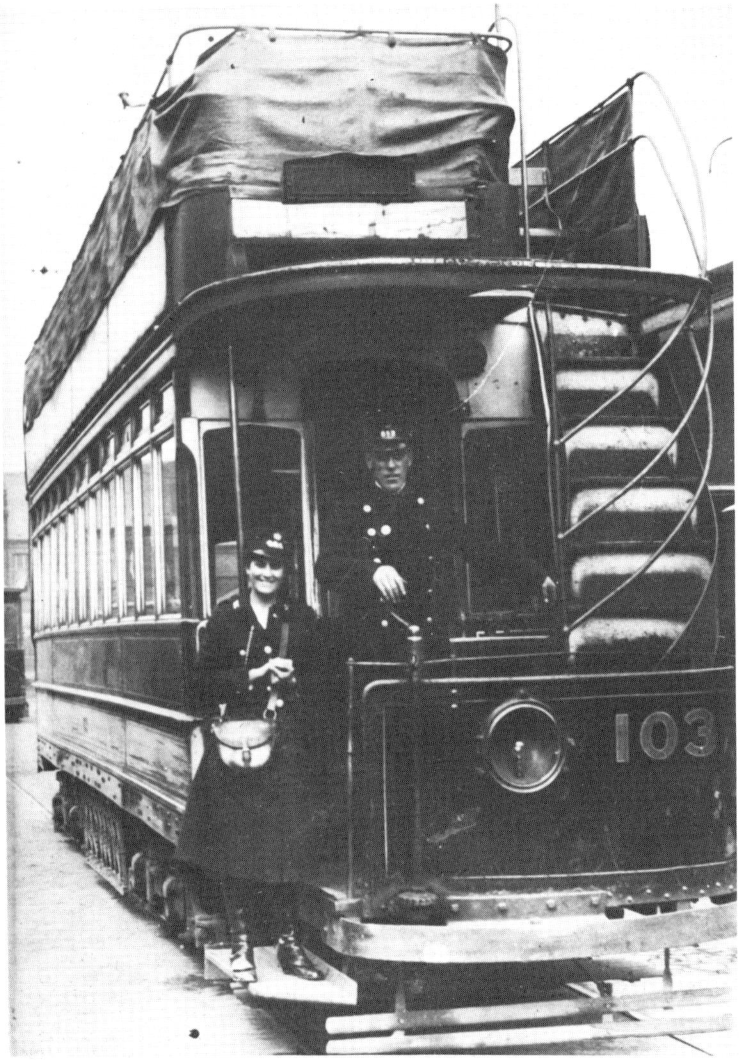

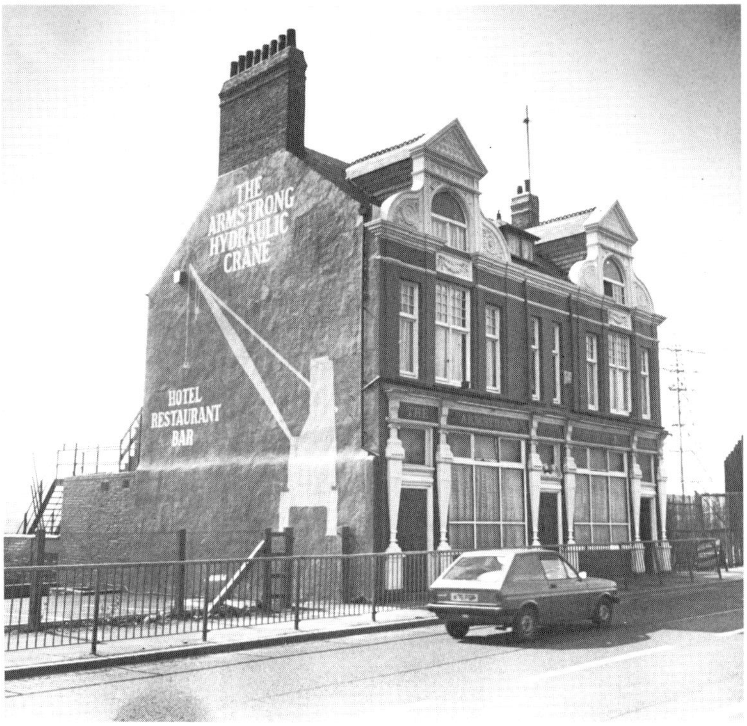

118. The refurbished Armstrong Hydraulic Crane Hotel, Restaurant Bar, three or four months after its reopening in December 1987.

117. *Left:* Love blossomed in 1918 for clippie Hilda Stevens and driver George Taylor as their tram trundled its way backwards and forwards between Scotswood and Heaton. It was indeed love on the right lines; they were married at Heaton Presbyterian Church.

119. A scene along the Scotswood Road in May 1937. In the background is the Duke of Cumberland pub.

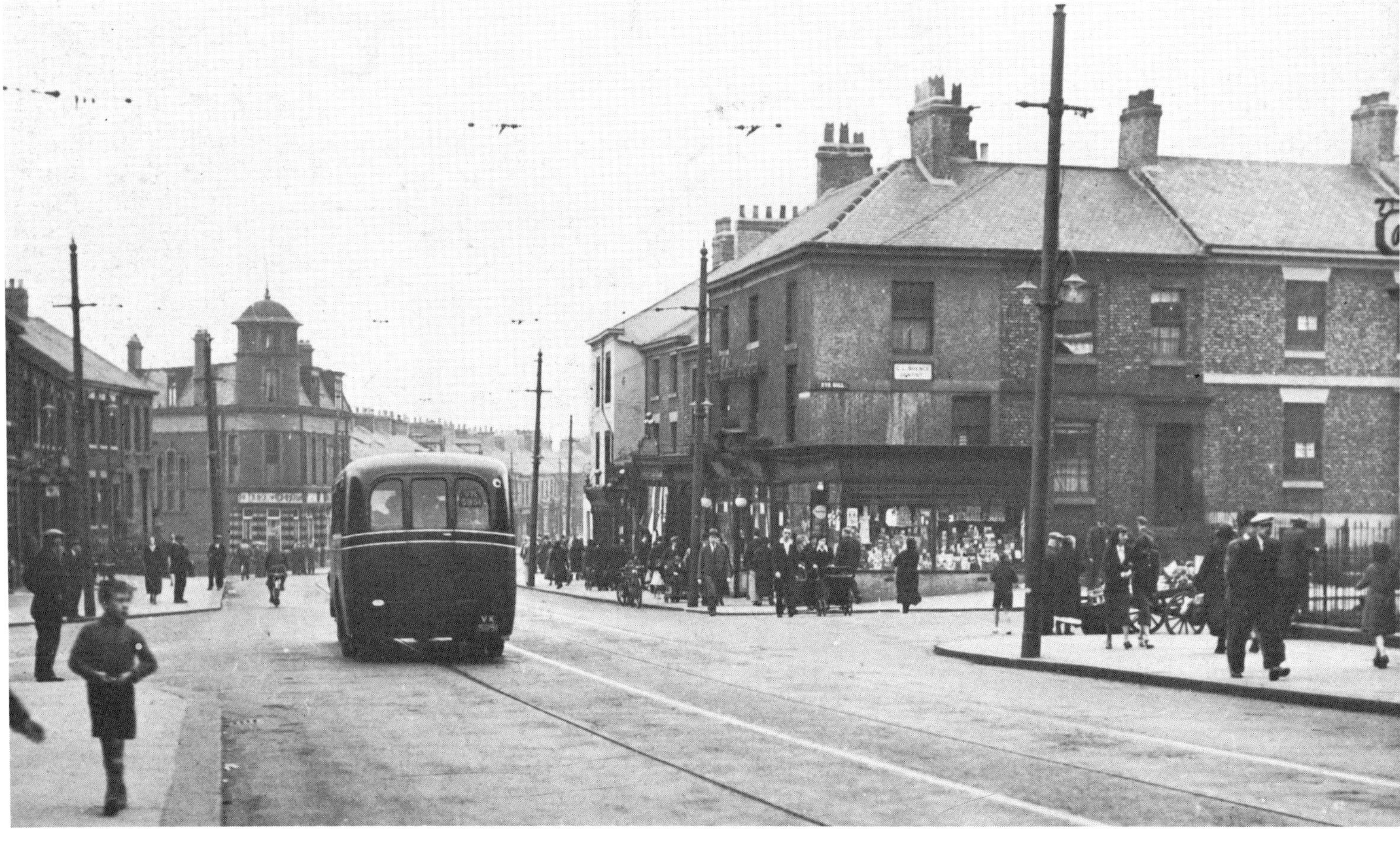

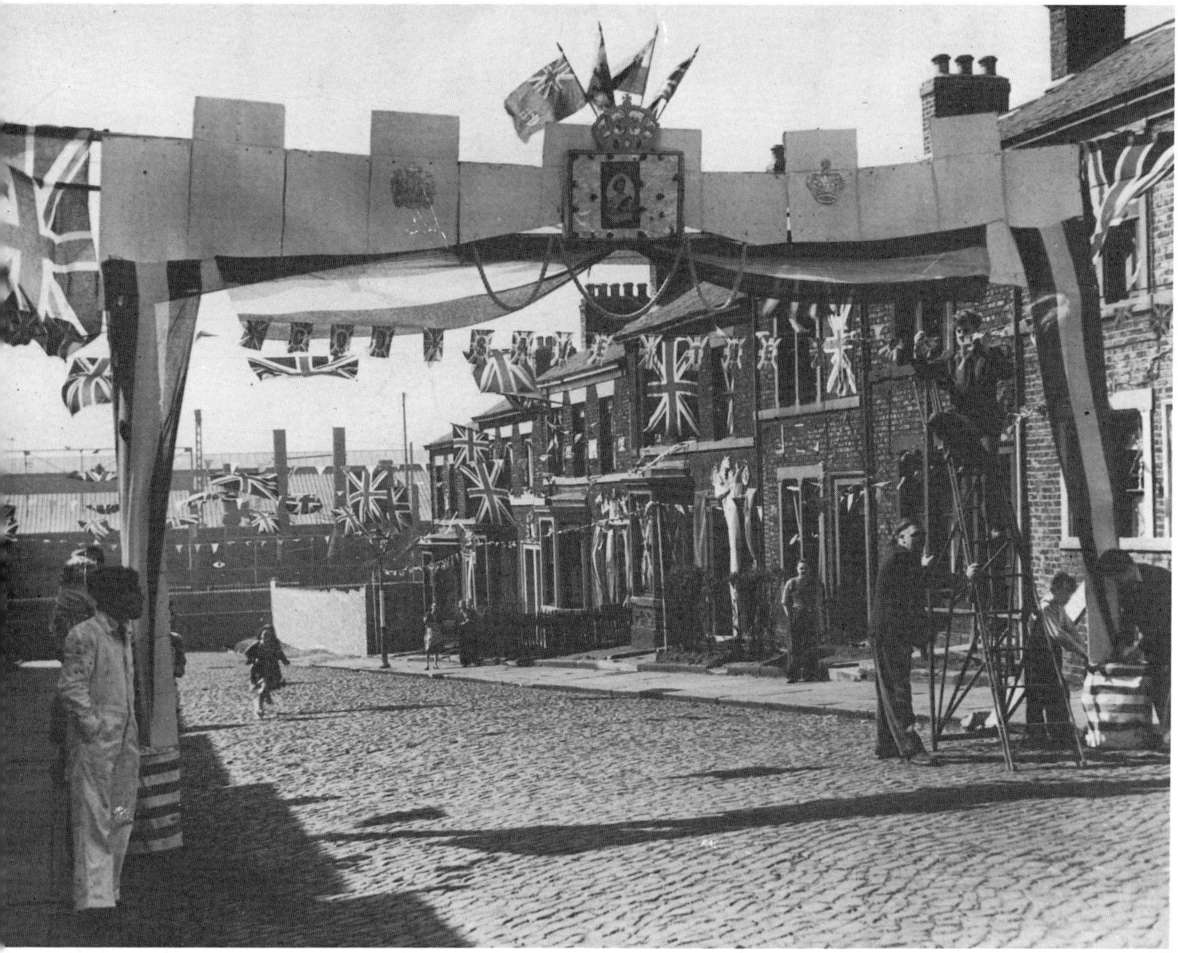

120. Bowman Street, off Scotswood Road, hangs out the bunting as preparations to celebrate the forthcoming Coronation of Queen Elizabeth II near completion.

121. It looked in this September 1959 view of Scotswood Road as though the heavens had opened. But the drought of that year had not come to a dramatic end. A burst water main was to blame for the flood.

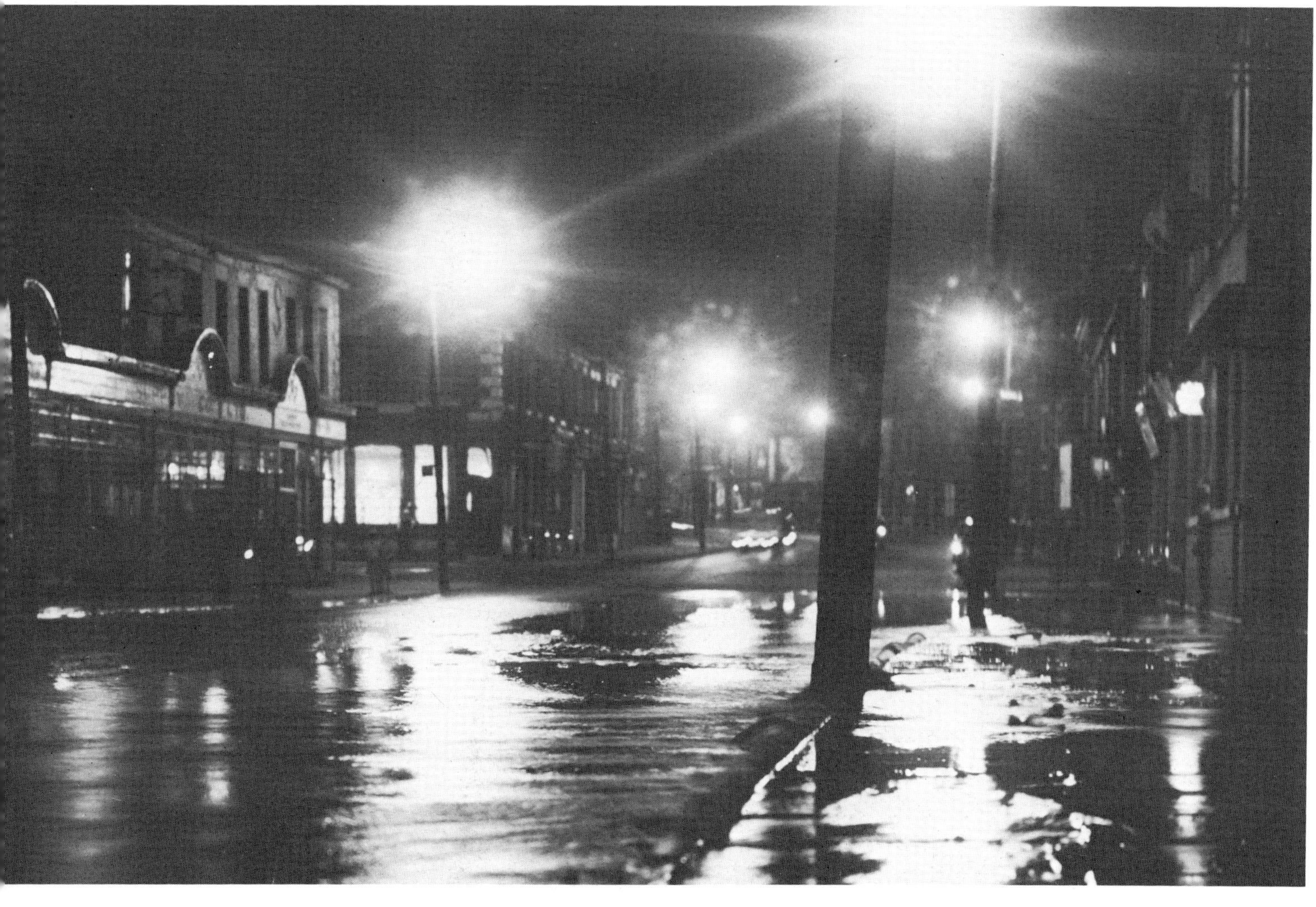

Farewell to the street called NOBLE

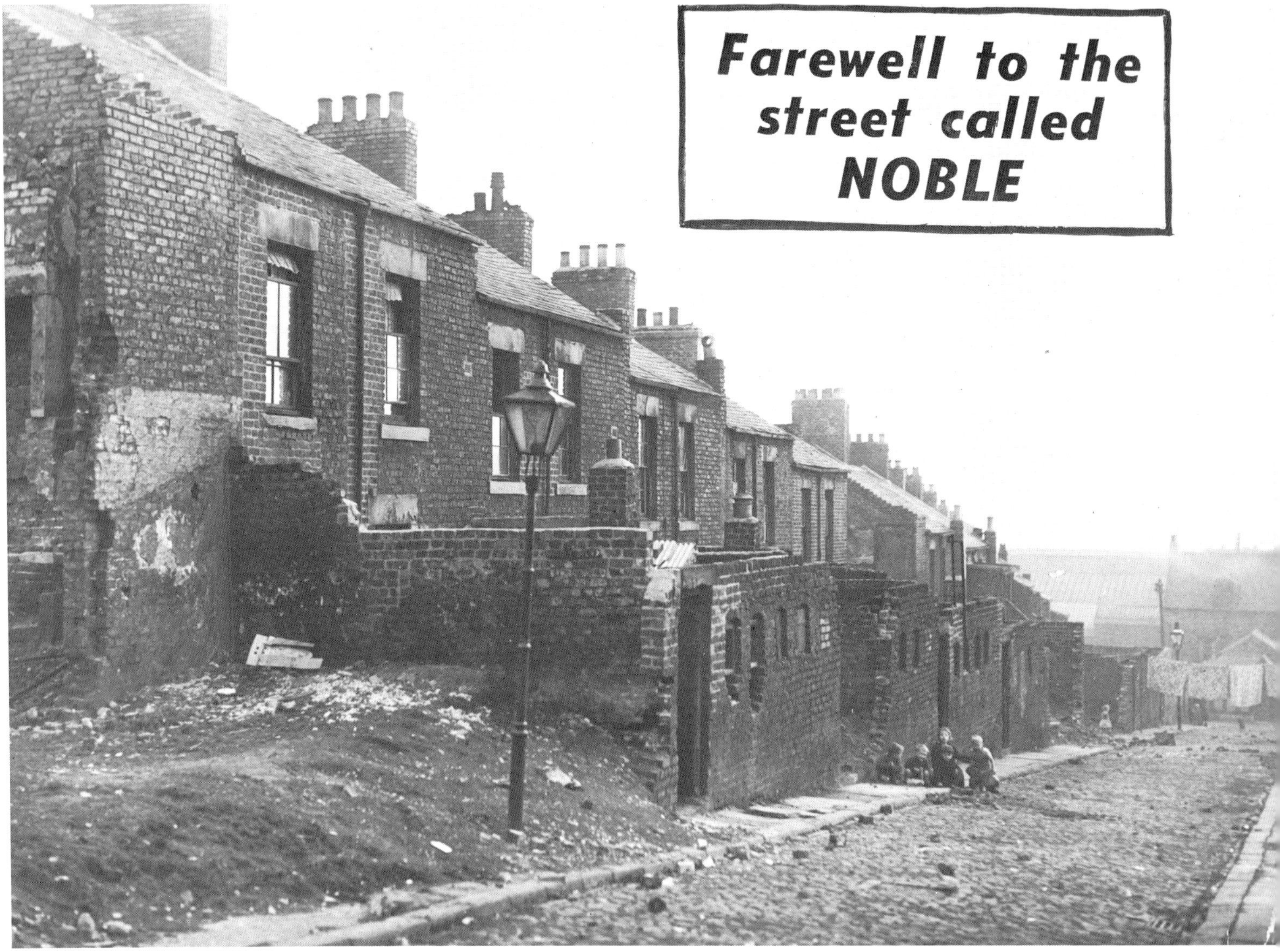

122-124. The end came to Noble Street twice in less than twenty-five years. In November 1955, the 40 families who had endured the slums of the first Noble Street were told that within weeks they would all be rehoused by the council's housing department. Then the demolition men moved in and flattened the area to make way for newer, brighter, modern housing. Sadly, something went terribly wrong, for on 15 August 1978 Noble Street was demolished for a second time. The bright, modern homes had steadily deteriorated through lack of being kept modern – commonly known as penny-pinching – to such an extent that the blocks were known locally as *Alcatraz*.

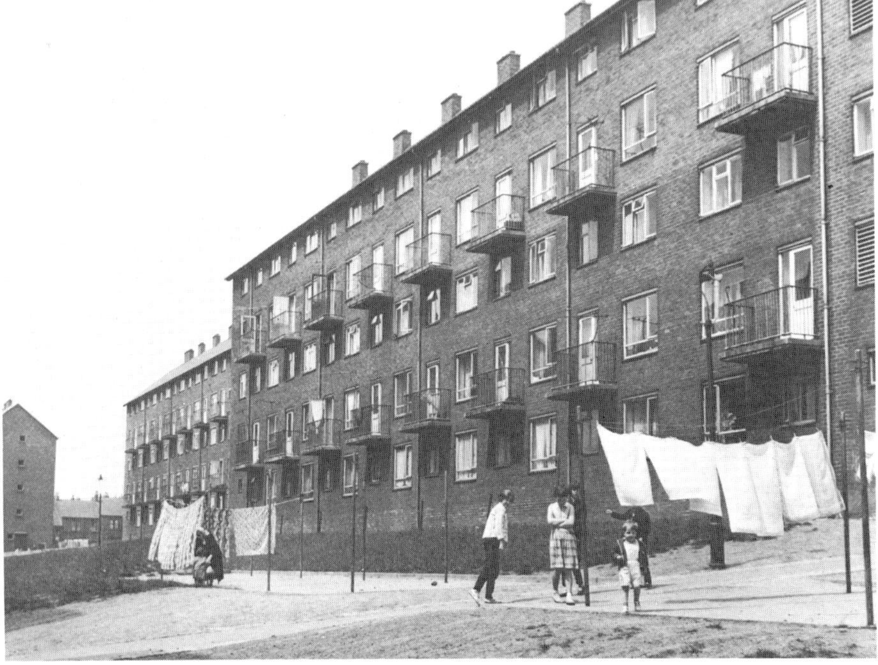

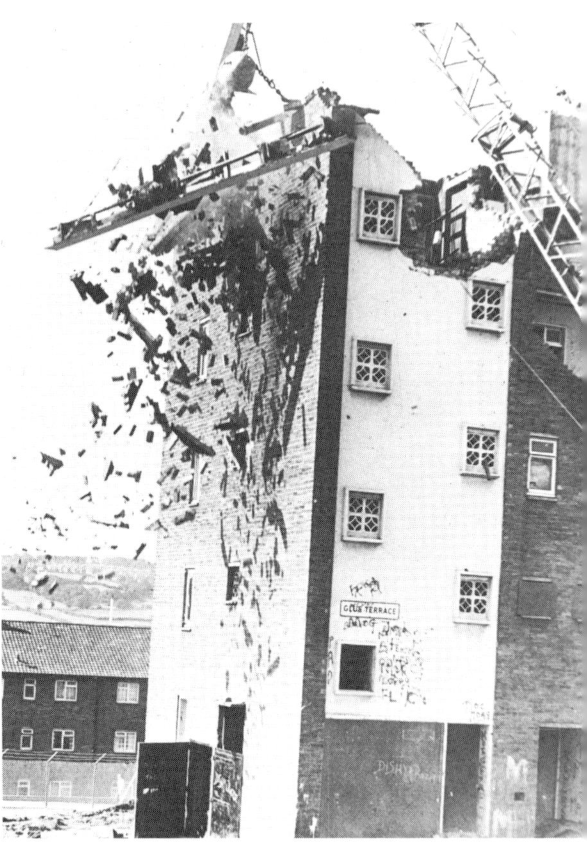

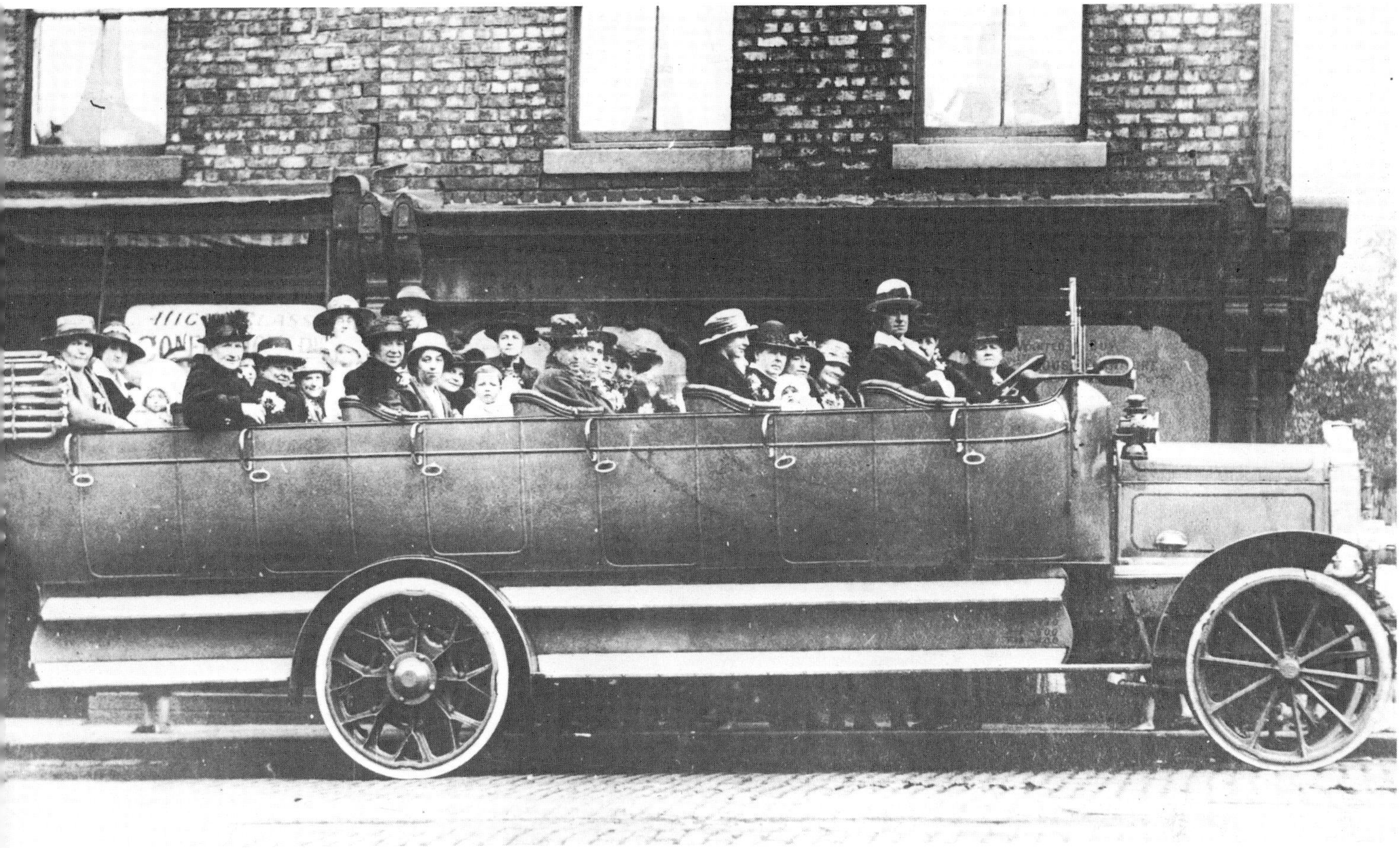

125. A trip to the seaside on a charabanc from Polly Charlton's pub at the bottom of Clumber Street and Scotswood Road.

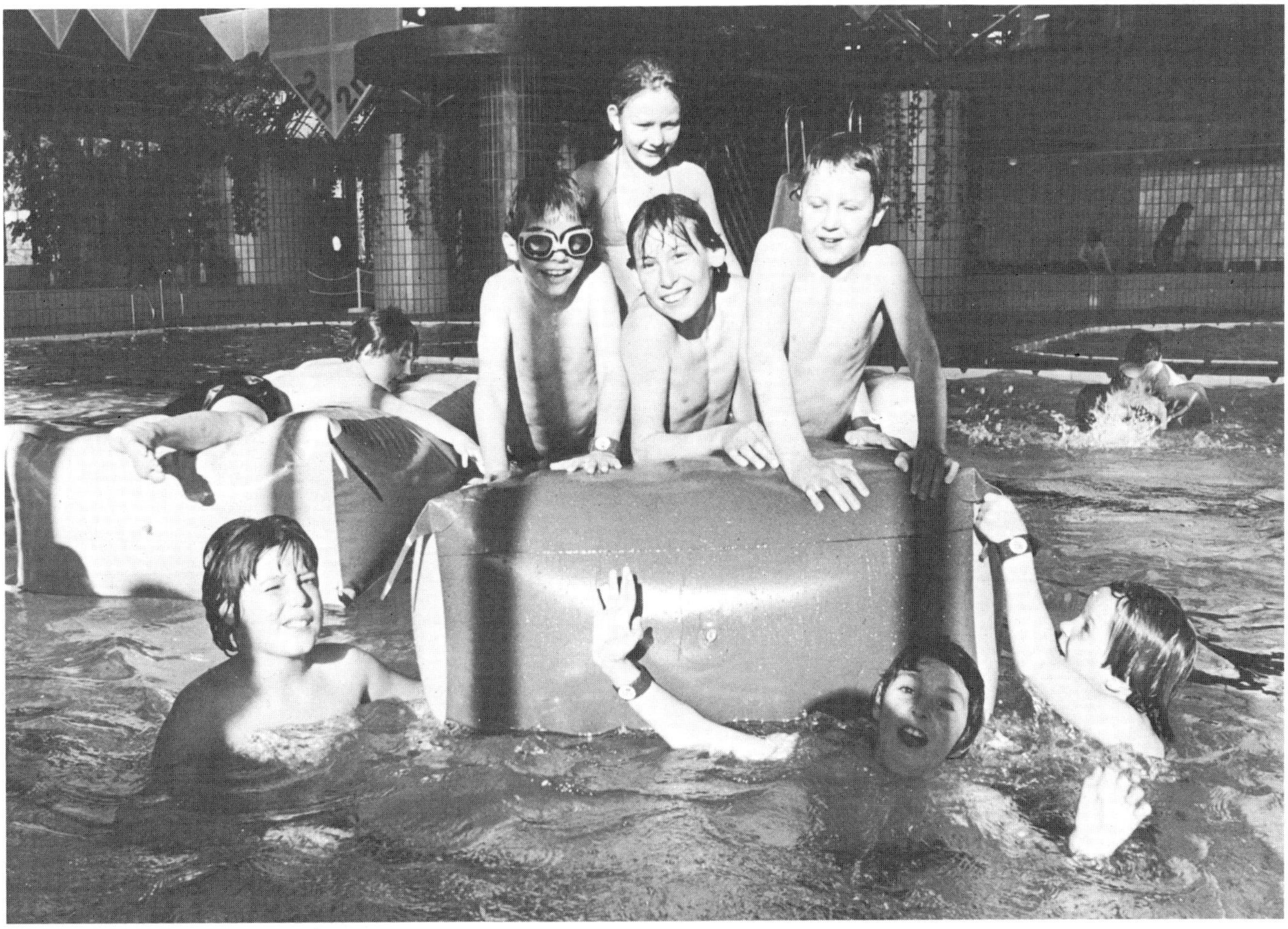

126. Funtime at Elswick Pool in October 1981 with the arrival of inflatables made by the Benwell-based Airspace Project as part of the Community Enterprise Programme.

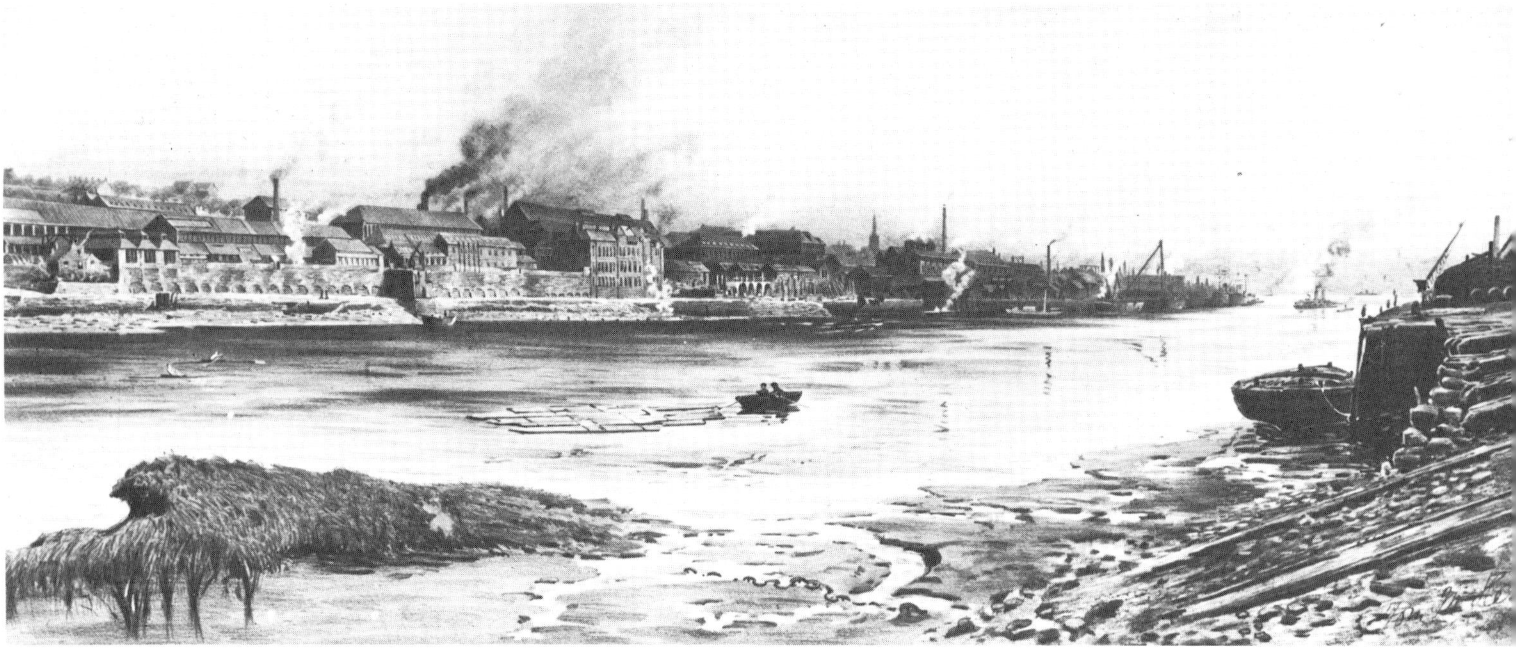

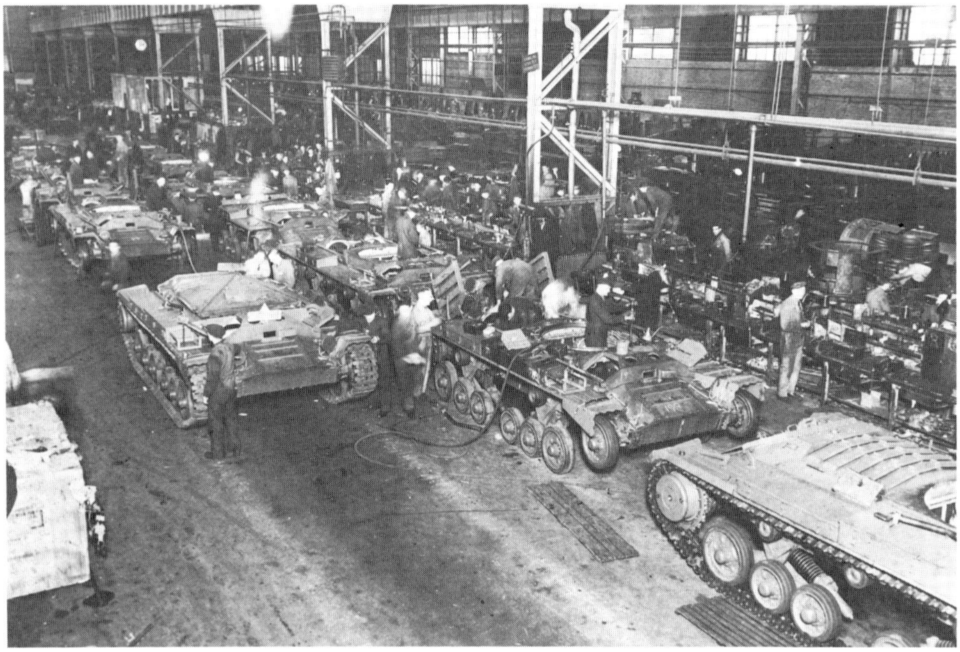

127. Yesterday's Elswick dominated by smoke-belching chimneys. *Courtesy:* Vickers.

128. Tank production at Elswick during the Second World War.

129. September 1947. The repair of steam locomotives was an industry that made a comeback at Elswick with a contract from the War Department.

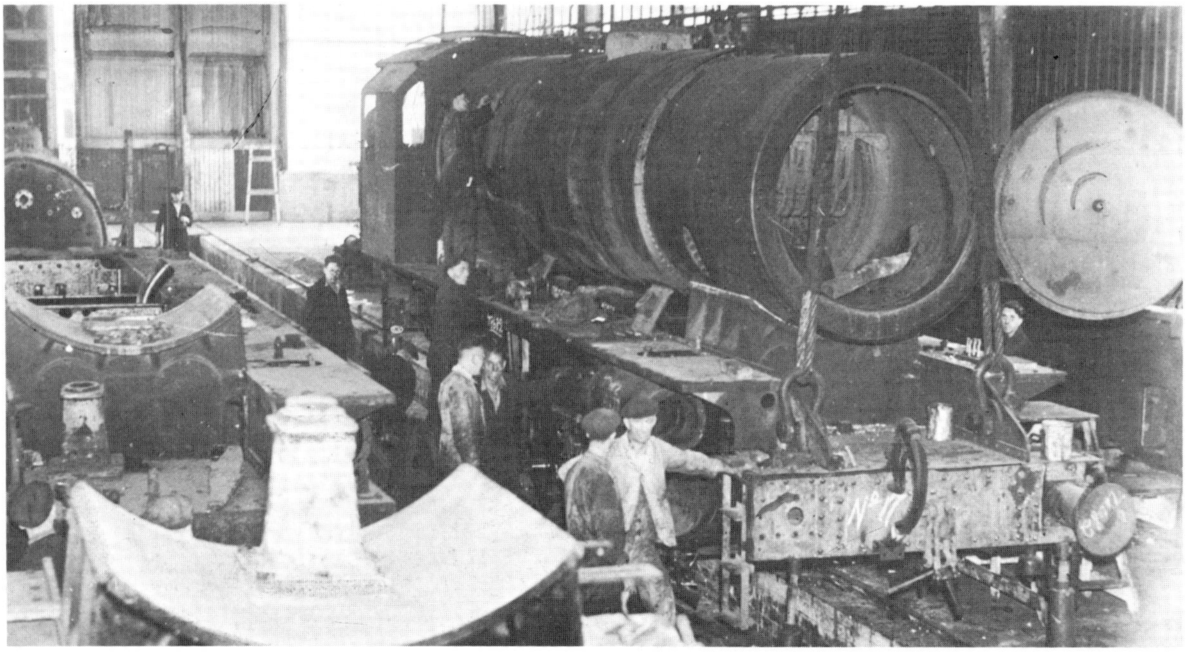

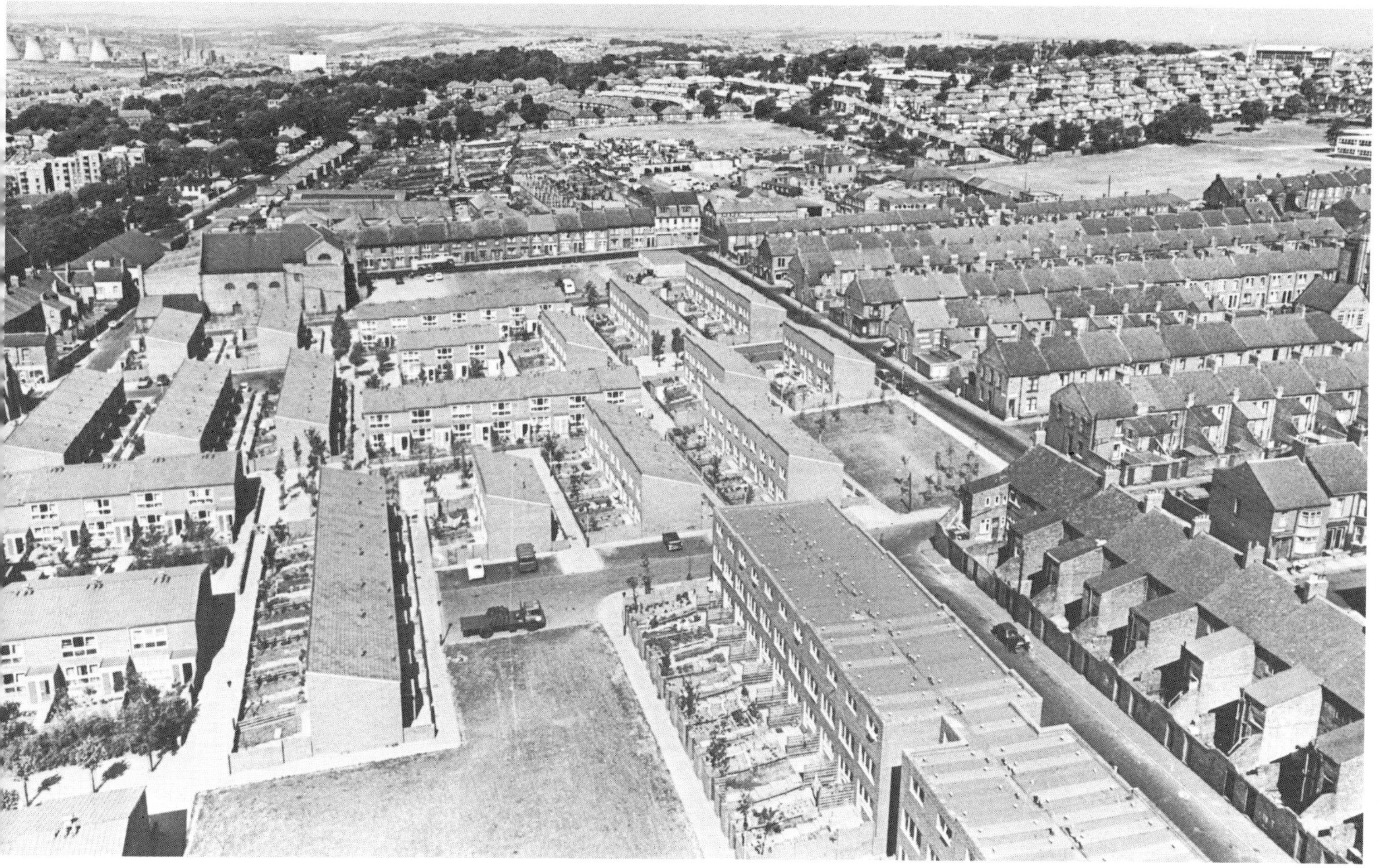

130. The rooftops of Benwell in July 1976.

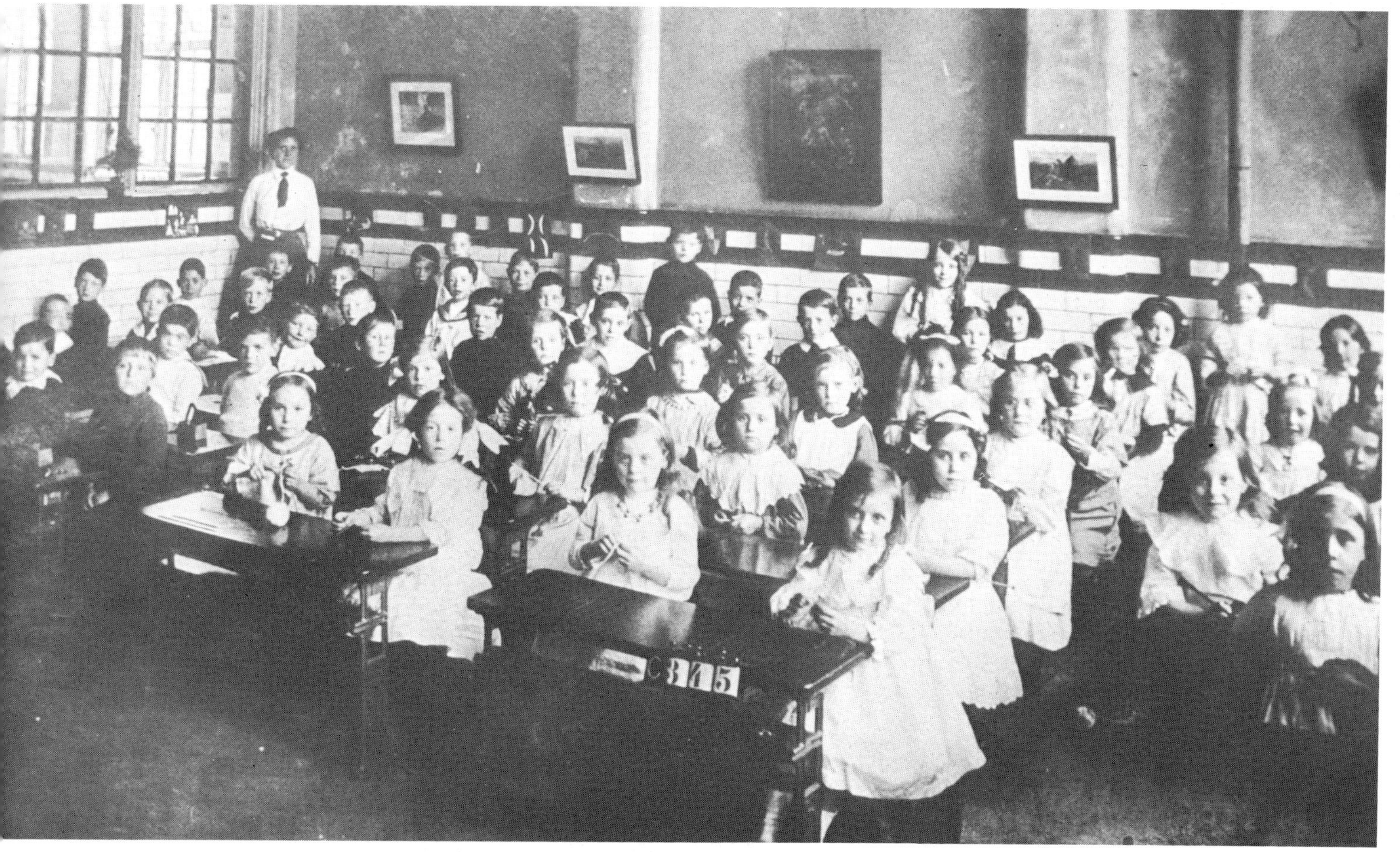

131. These boys and girls attended Atkinson Road Infants' School, Benwell, in the year of Scott's doomed Antarctic expedition and the sinking of the *Titanic*. The teacher's name was Miss Robson.

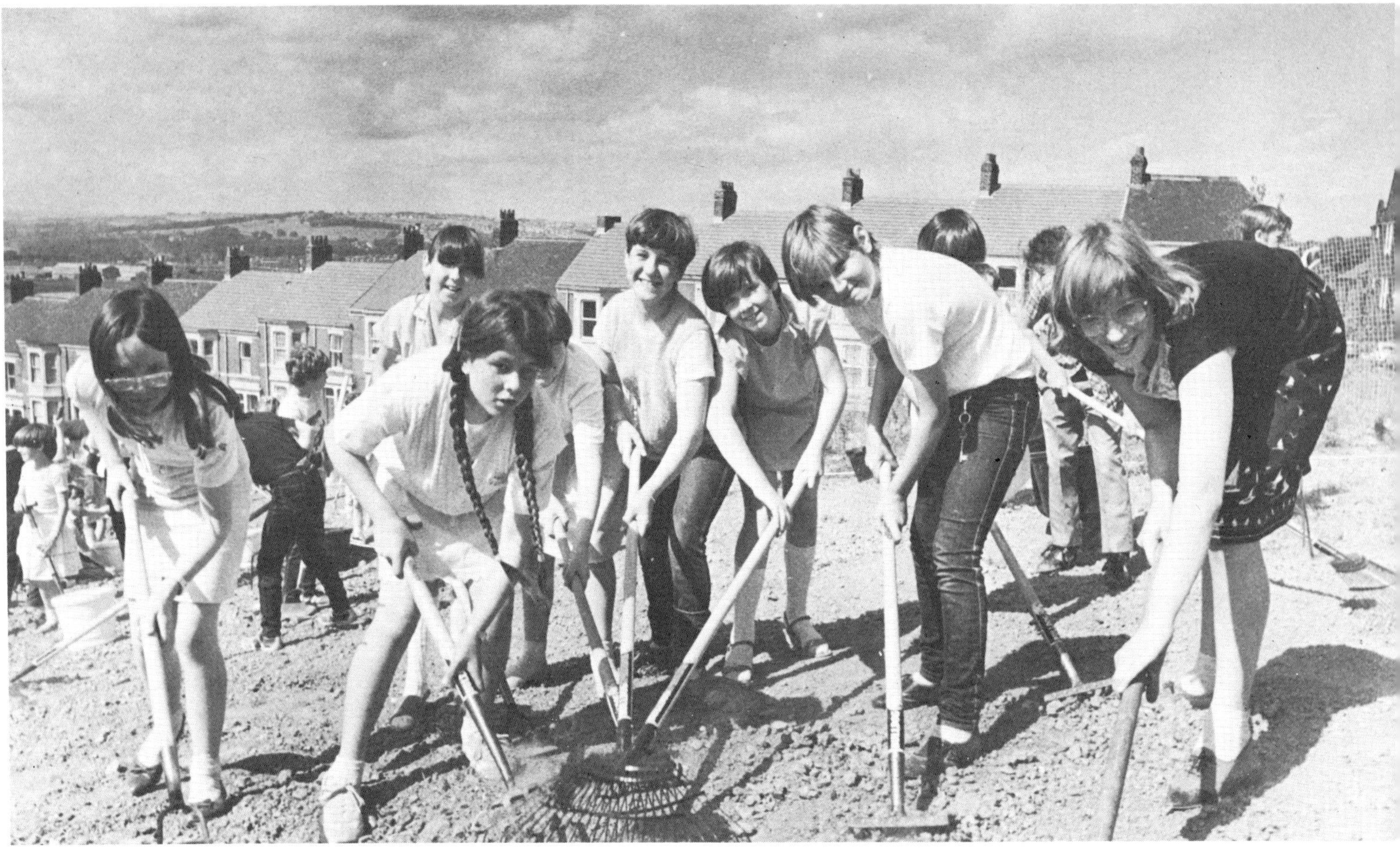

132. Children from South Benwell Primary School plant grass seeds at Benwell Nature Park in July 1983. Mrs Joan McCarthy, the teacher in charge of the project at Joan Street, decided to have a mass seeding of the four acre site to speed up the planting.

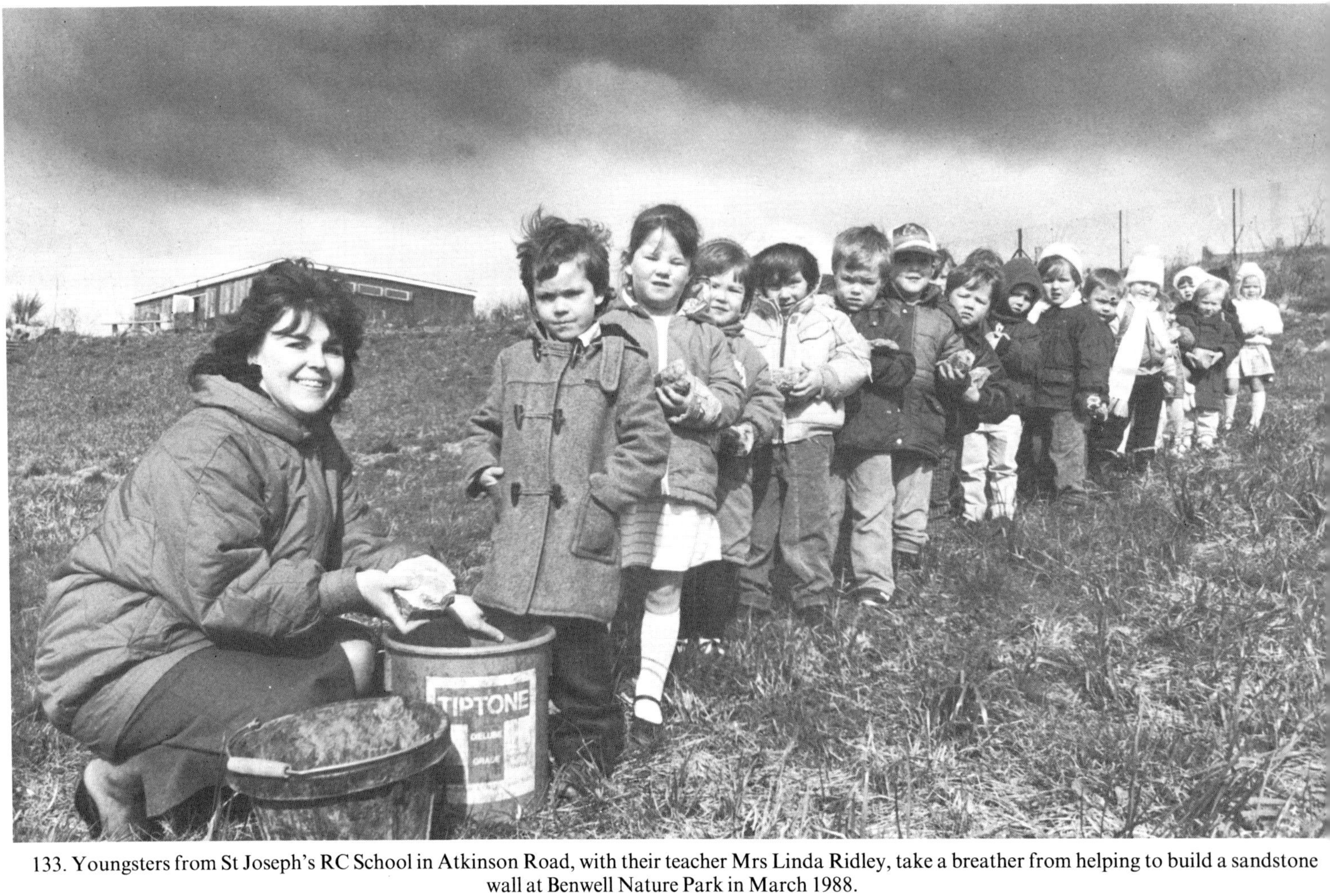

133. Youngsters from St Joseph's RC School in Atkinson Road, with their teacher Mrs Linda Ridley, take a breather from helping to build a sandstone wall at Benwell Nature Park in March 1988.

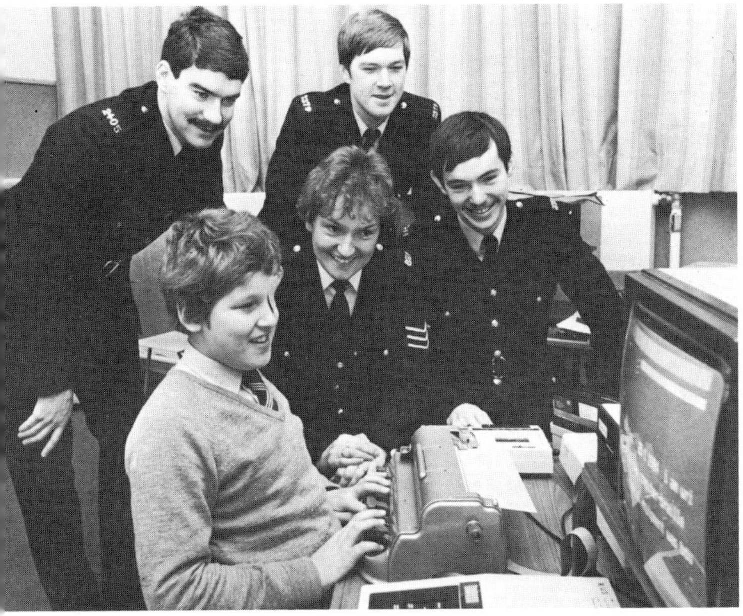

134. New computer equipment that enables parents to read their children's work was installed at Benwell Dene School for the Blind in January 1984 thanks to the fund-raising efforts of recruits at the police training centre in Dishforth. The children do their work in Braille but the print-outs can be in English. Gavin Griffiths operates the equipment with *behind:* PCs Dave Gibson and John Capstaff, and *in front:* Sergeant Carolyn Wilkinson and PC David Lynch.

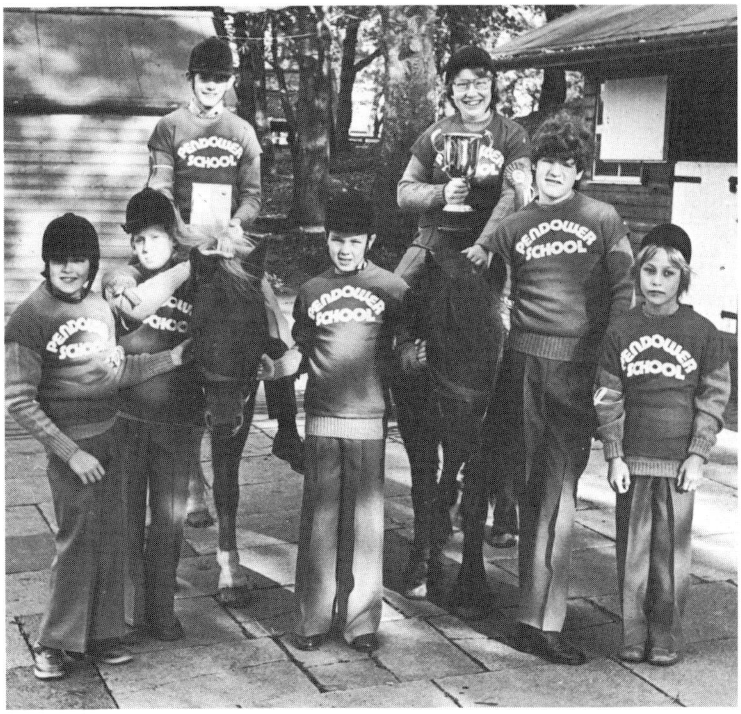

135. Pendower Special School pupils Julie Ellis, Michael Shaw, David Baker, Tony Hildrew, Heather Nicholson, Katrina Hopkinson and David Craggs with the Monzarni Cup won by them at the Spastics Society Gymkhana in 1981.

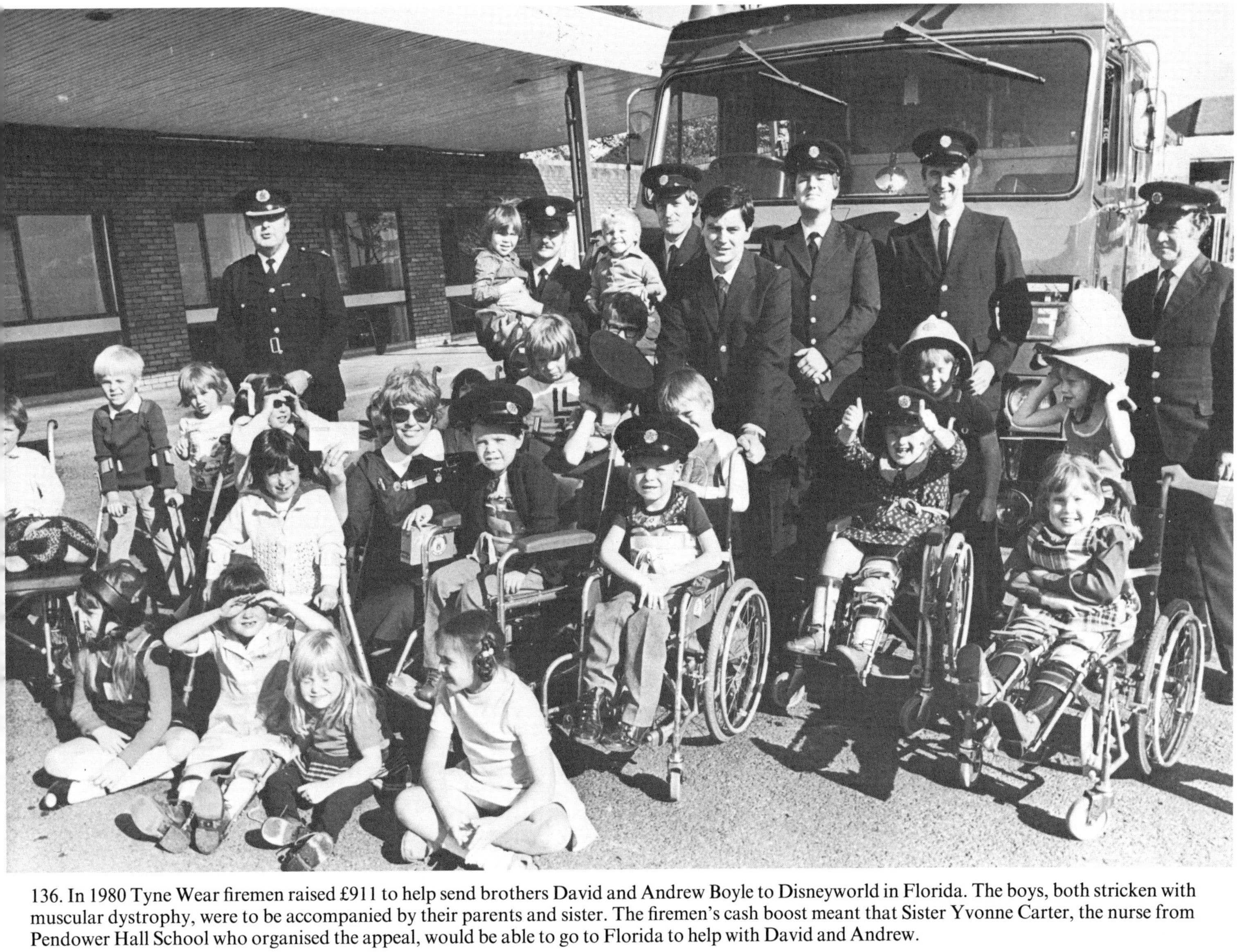

136. In 1980 Tyne Wear firemen raised £911 to help send brothers David and Andrew Boyle to Disneyworld in Florida. The boys, both stricken with muscular dystrophy, were to be accompanied by their parents and sister. The firemen's cash boost meant that Sister Yvonne Carter, the nurse from Pendower Hall School who organised the appeal, would be able to go to Florida to help with David and Andrew.

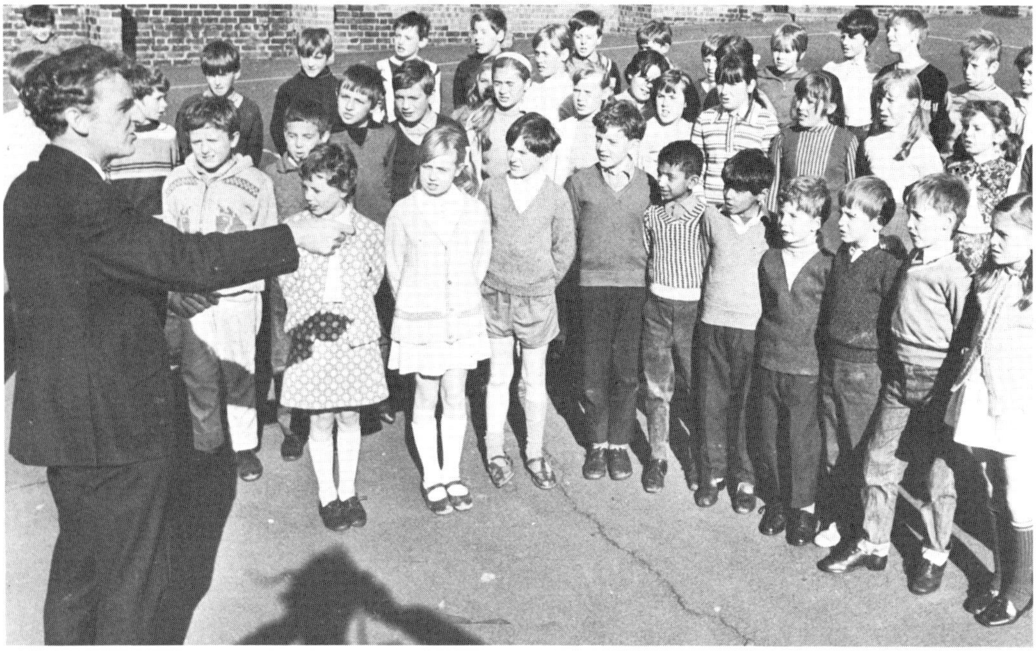

137. Children from Canning Street Primary School were given just a week's notice that they would be leading the singing of *Blaydon Races* at the Newcastle Festival Children's Concert in October 1970.

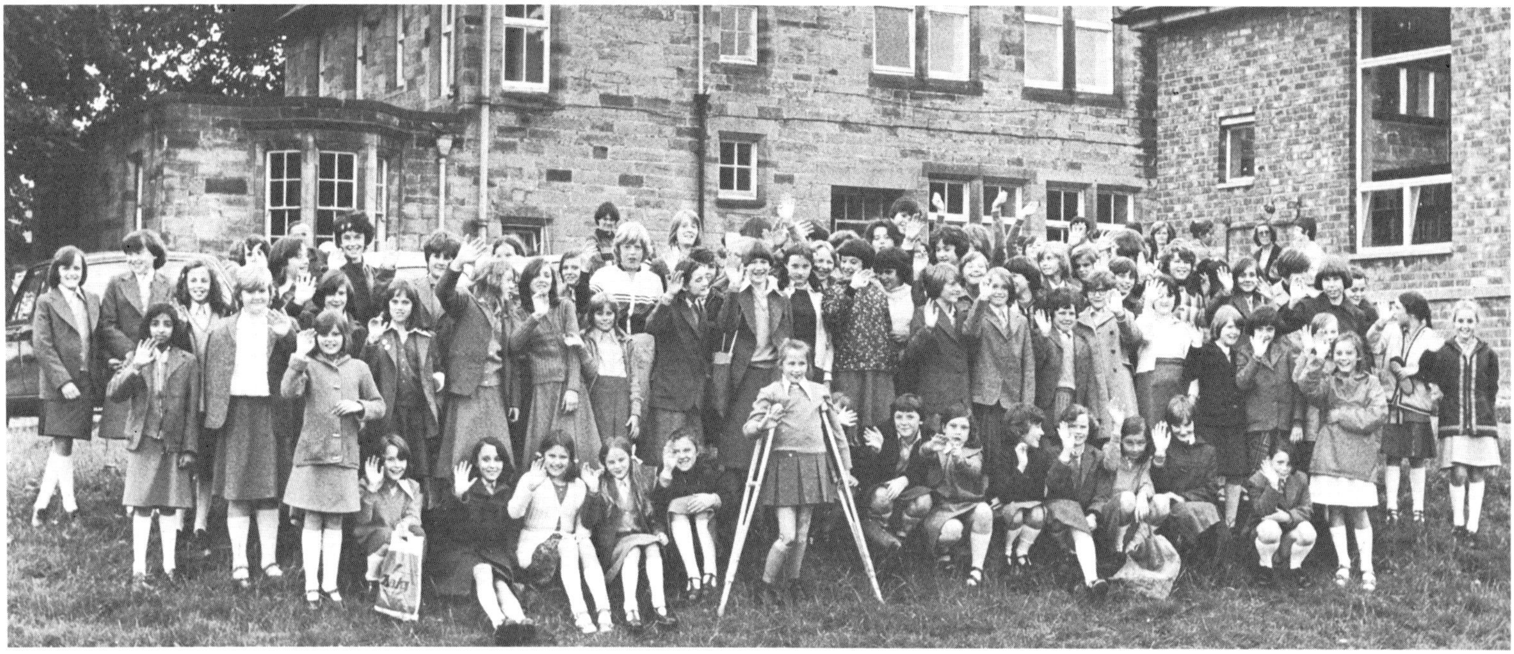

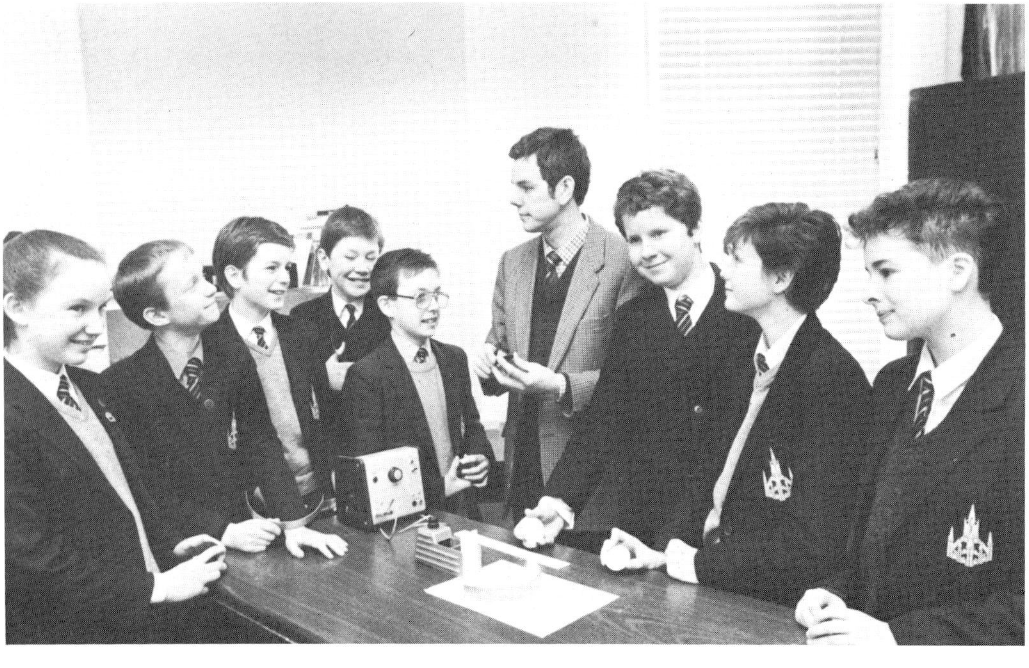

138. *Above:* September 1977 and the girls take possession of the former boys school of St Aloysius in the West End of Newcastle – the boys had moved to St Cuthbert's. As a boys school, St Aloysius won every conceivable trophy that the city put up for football and athletics, and the legendary Billy Cairns, one-time Newcastle United centre forward, was a former pupil. In 1977 St Aloysius was renamed the Sacred Heart Lower School.

139. In 1978 the canons of St Nicholas's Cathedral made a harsh but unavoidable decision that the cathedral school would have to close due to lack of funding. Somehow, ten years later the school was still operating thanks to the efforts of parents, staff and pupils.

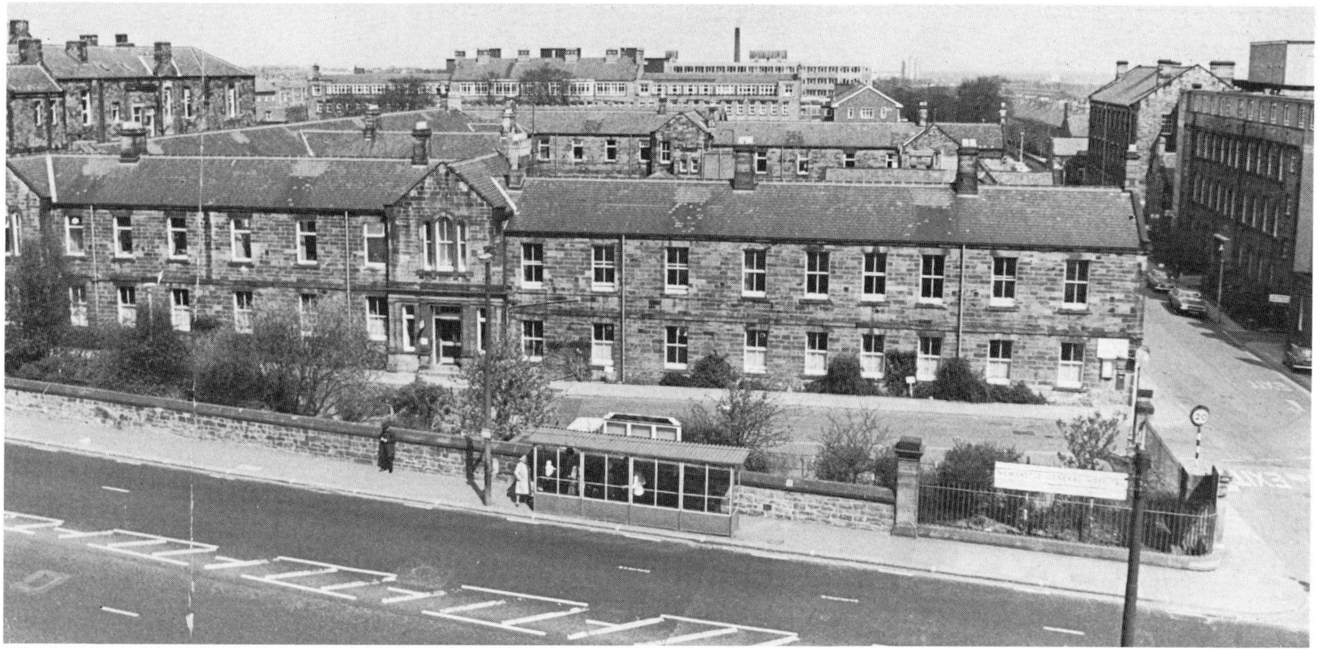

140. Newcastle General Hospital, May 1975.

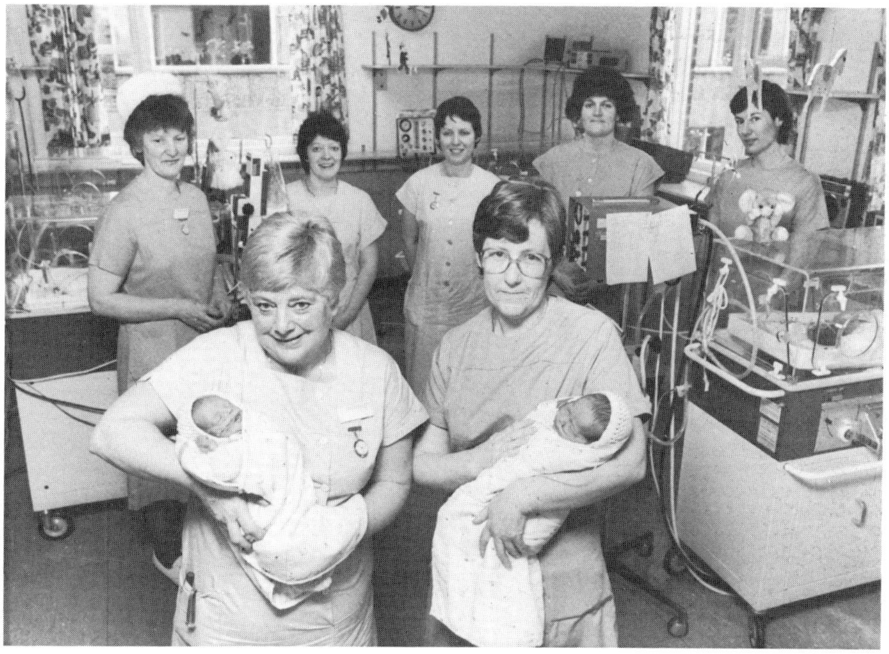

141. *Right:* Auxiliary nurse Jean Hawkins (*left*) and Sister Barbara Watson pictured with babies in the high-dependency unit. Also in the photograph are *left to right:* Nursing Officer Gill Pickering, Enrolled Nurse Sue Tobin, Staff Nurse Kathy Watkins, Staff Midwife Ursula Whiting and Sister Frances Clarke. January 1984.

143. *Below right:* In November 1987 Bucks Fizz singer Mike Nolan returned to Newcastle General to see the opening of a high-dependency unit. Two years previously Nolan and two other members of the group were nursed back to health at the hospital after their coach had been involved in a collision.

142. *Below:* A special double laser on trials at Newcastle General. The money to buy one of these machines was raised in the *Sunday Sun* BEAM appeal. November 1988.

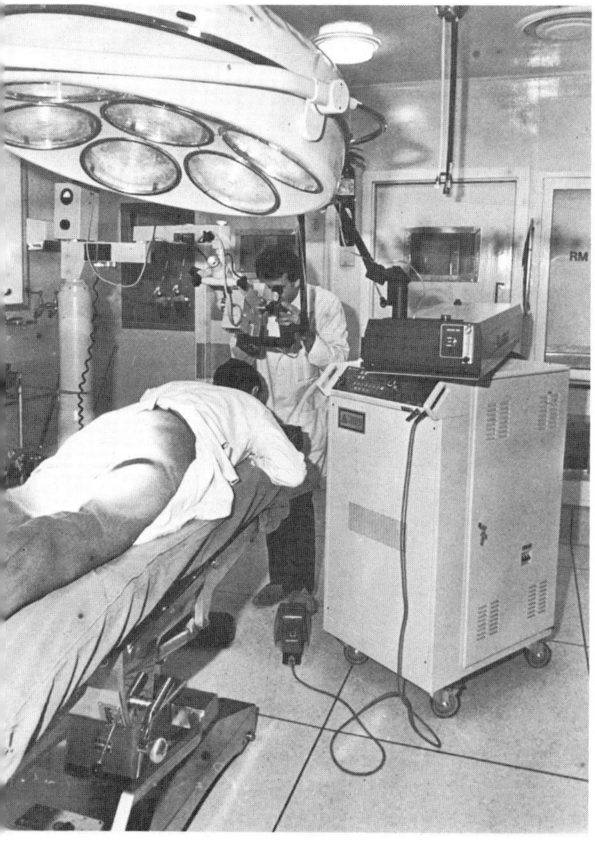

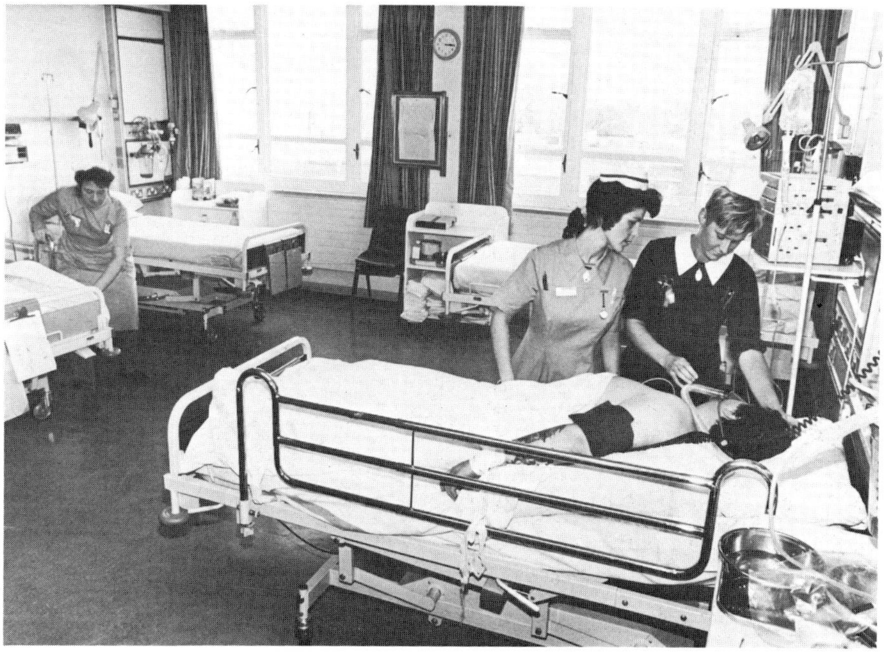

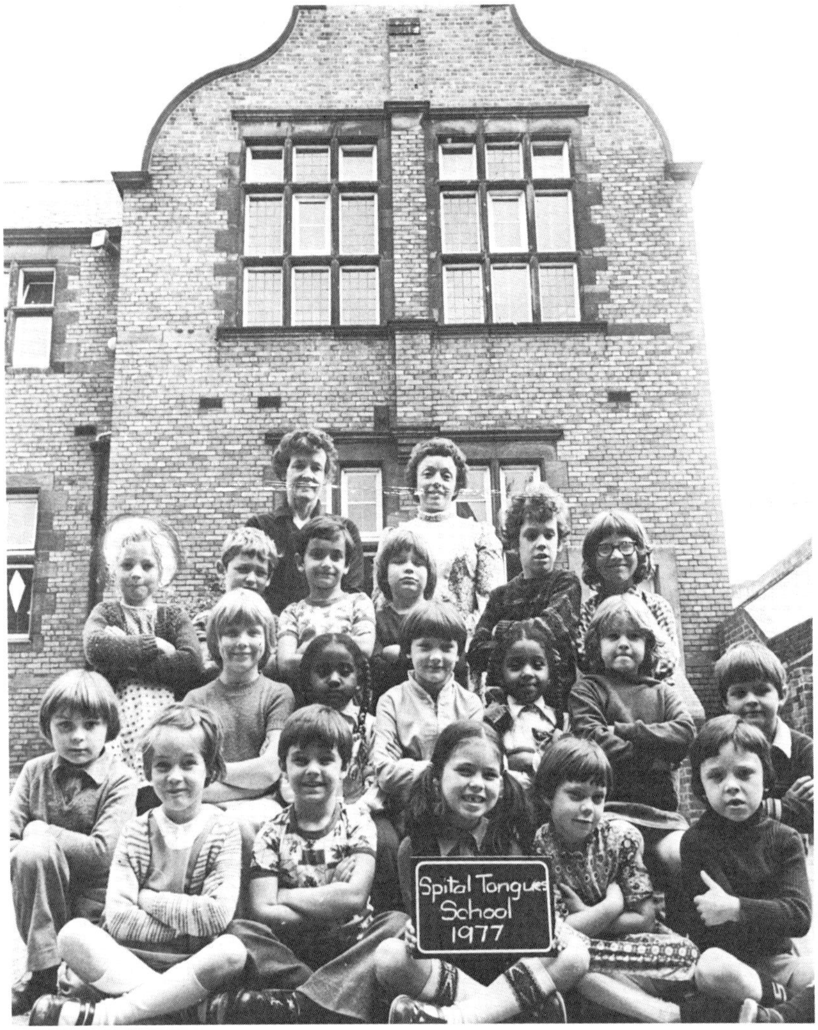

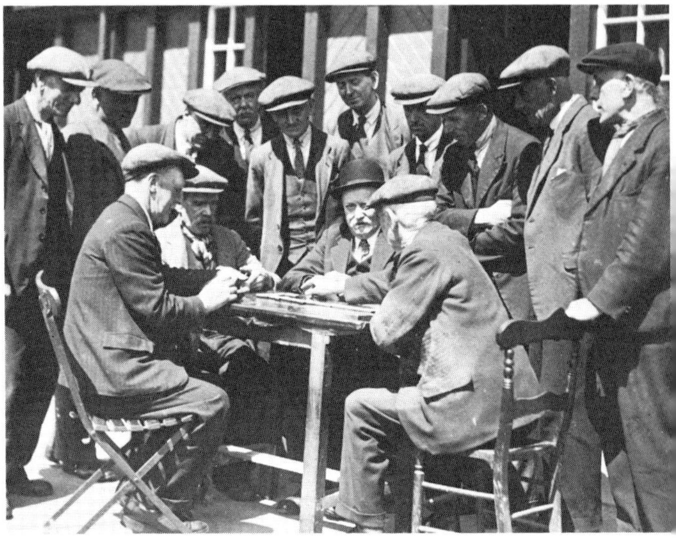

145. Thoughtful moments during an open-air game of dominoes at the old men's shelter in Leazes Park, June 1936.

144. *Left:* A sad momento – the last school photograph at Spital Tongues Infants School which closed in July 1977 just fifteen days short of its 100th birthday. By the late seventies, Spital Tongues, though only a mile from the city centre, had become isolated by motorways, cut off with moorland and lacking a population capable of sustaining the school.

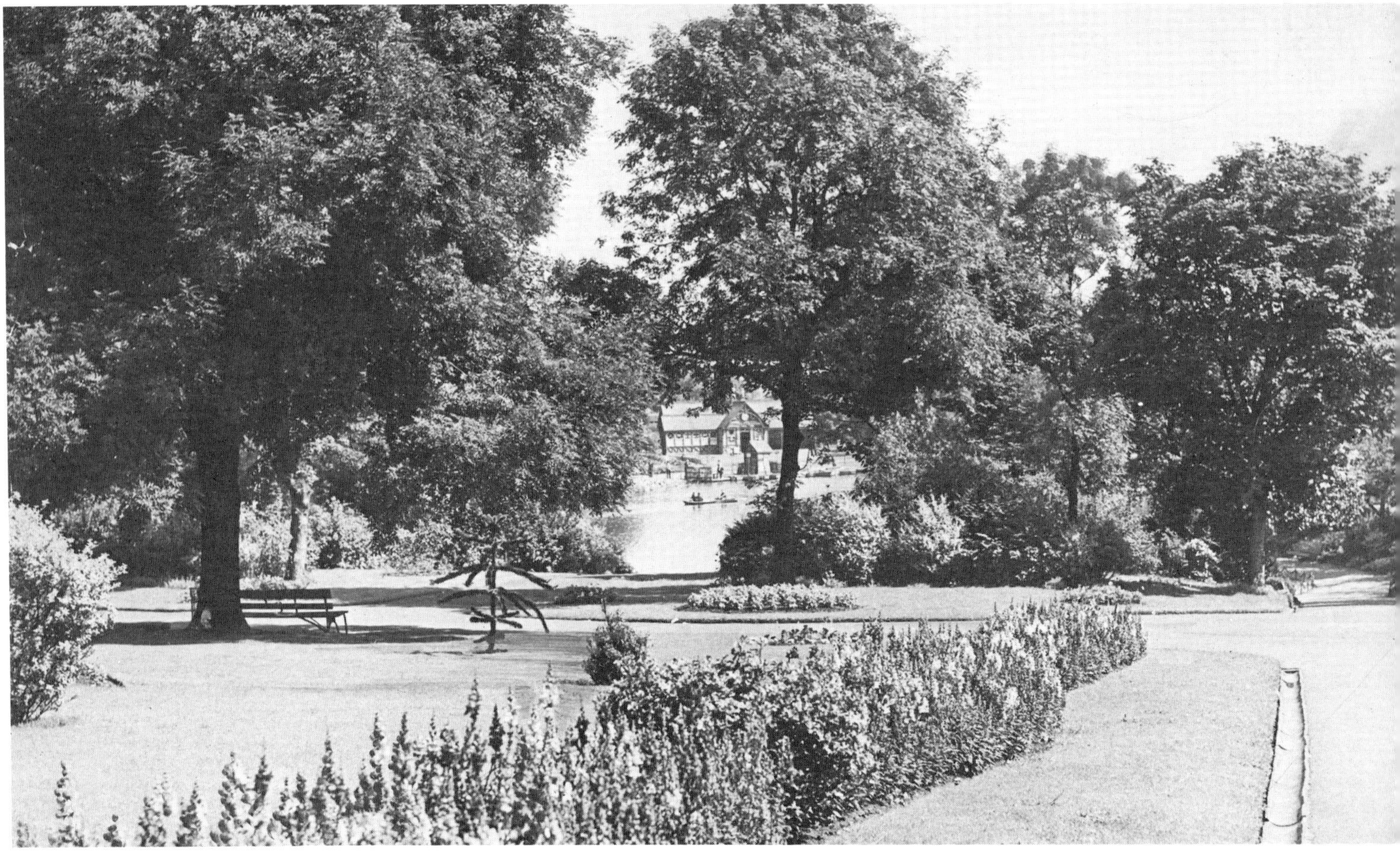

146. This countryside scene, but a few minutes away from one of the busiest roads in Newcastle, was snapped in August 1940 at Leazes Park.

147. From 1,500ft up in the Northumbrian Water airship, an intrepid *Evening Chronicle* photographer turned his camera on the Victoria Infirmary to see how the £30 million extension programme was coming along. The picture was taken in August 1989 but the work at the infirmary is not due to be completed until 1992.

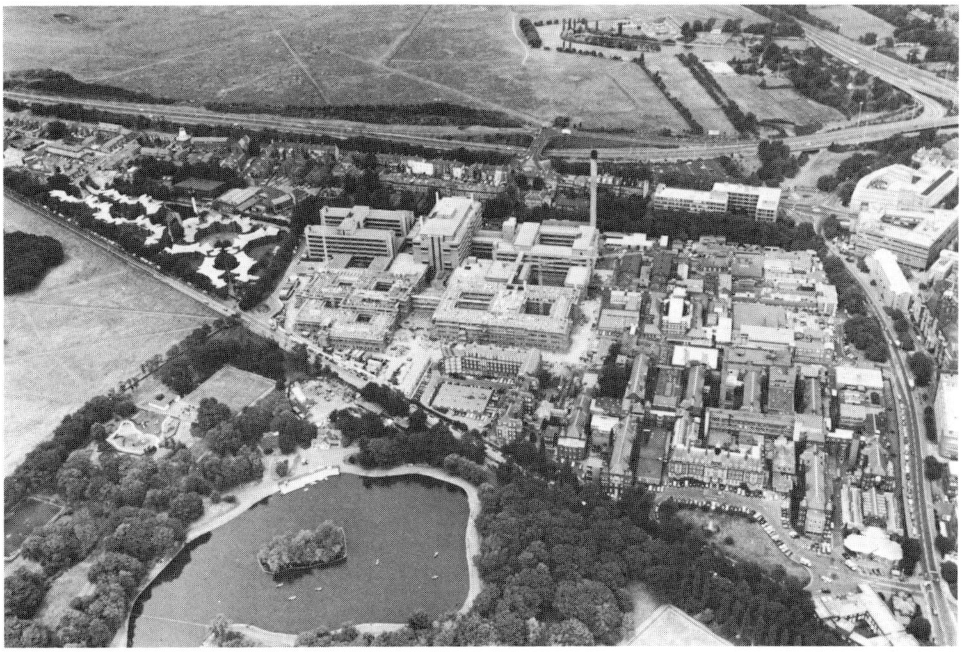

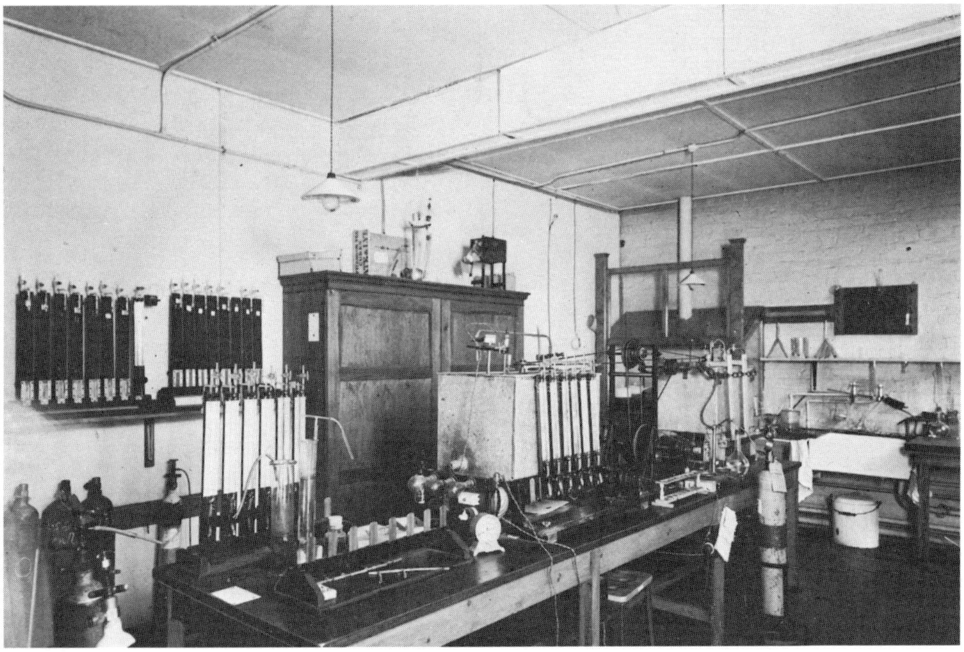

148. *Left:* The cancer research centre at the Royal Victoria Infirmary as it looked in December 1937.

149. *Below left:* Members of the children's cancer research team at the RVI in July 1986. Almost all the jobs are paid for by charity donations.

150. *Below:* Easter in the form of a 3ft chocolate elephant came early for children at the RVI thanks to cricketer Ian Botham and the Makhani Restaurant. Botham was visiting Newcastle raising cash for his chosen cause, leukaemia. March 1989.

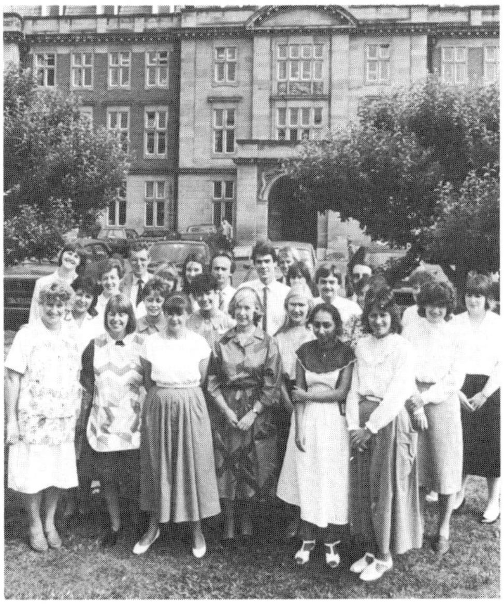

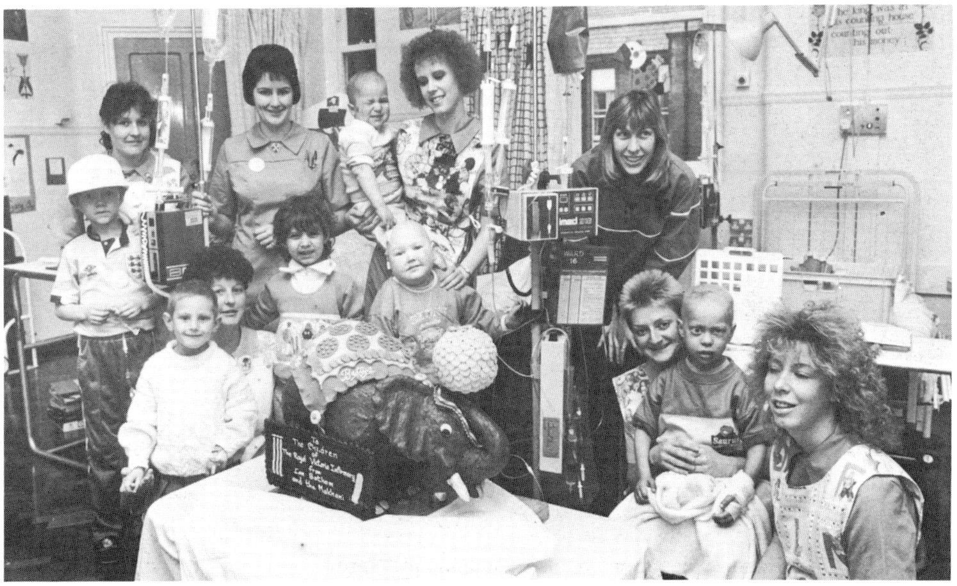

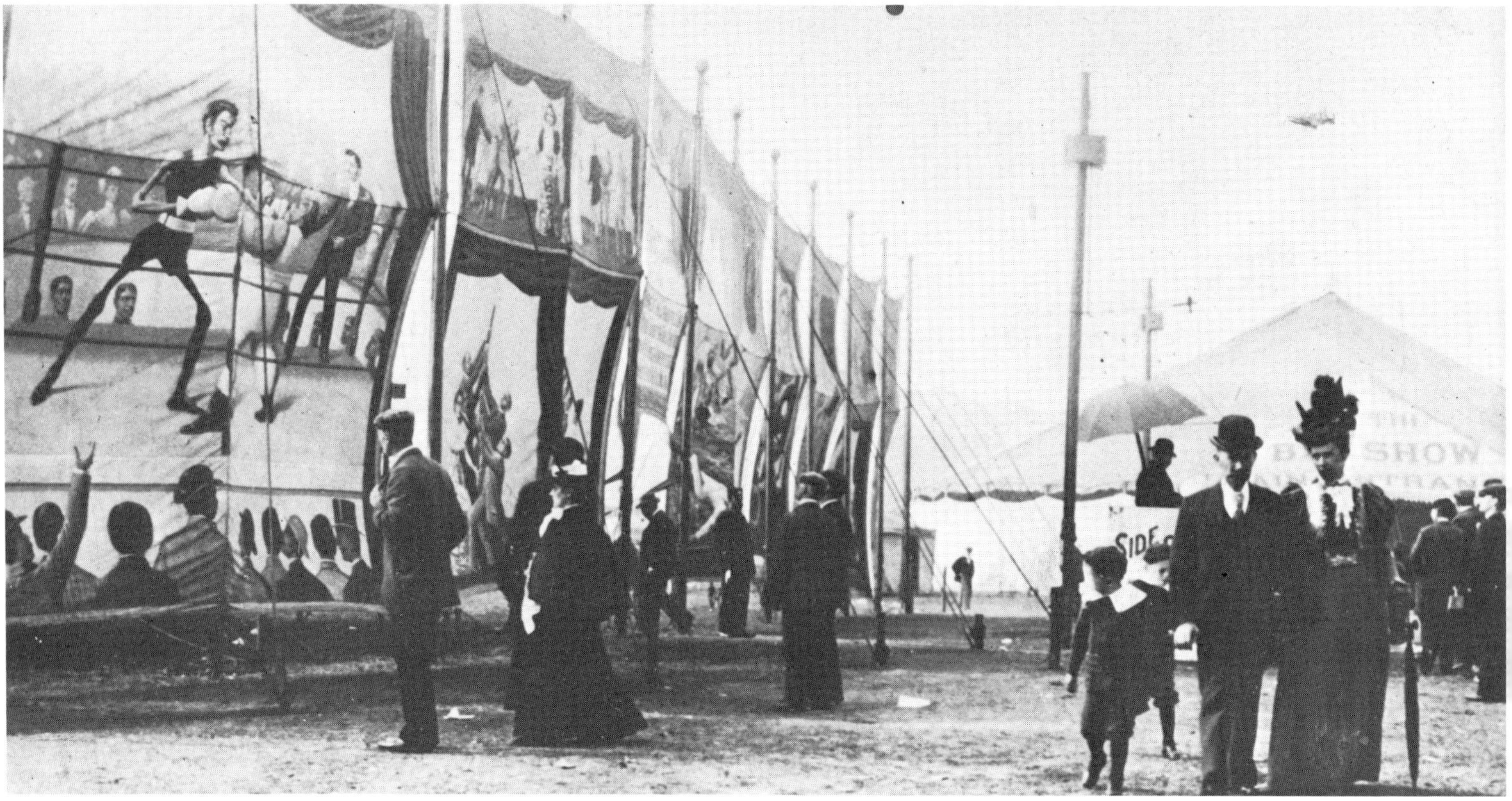

151. June and July 1898 must have been remarkable months for the Town Moor. No sooner had the Temperance Festival ended than show people were at work preparing for the arrival of Barnum & Bailey's circus.

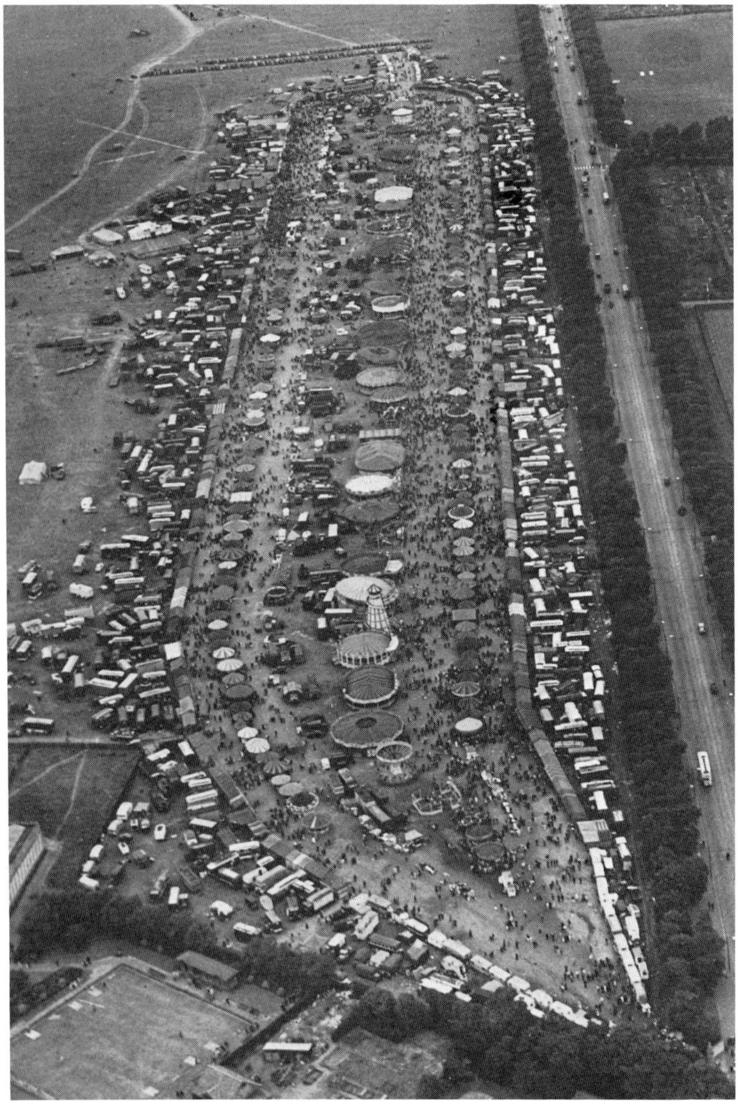

152. Britain's greatest fair looked like a mere model through the lens of D McStea's camera in June 1952 when he took this view of the show.

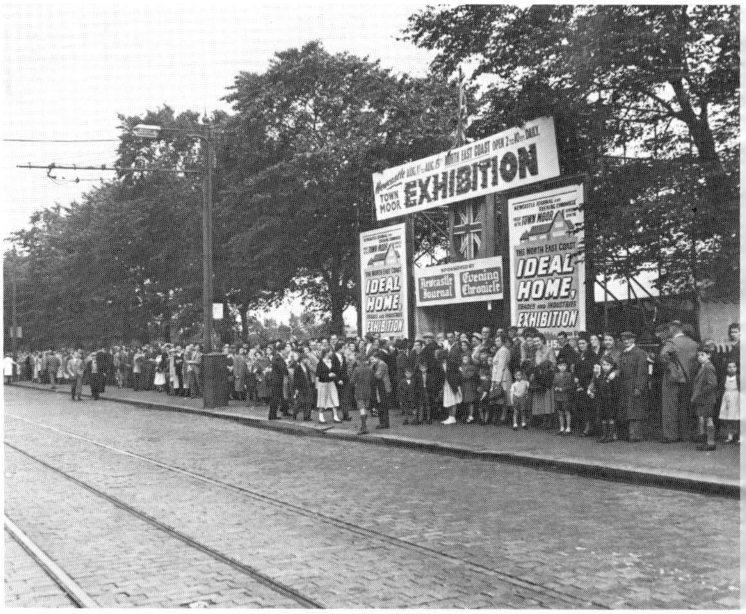

153. Crowds gather for the Ideal Home Exhibition held on Town Moor in August 1953. Photograph by P Schaill.

157. *Opposite page, bottom:* Fun in the snow on the slopes of Town Moor in January 1984.

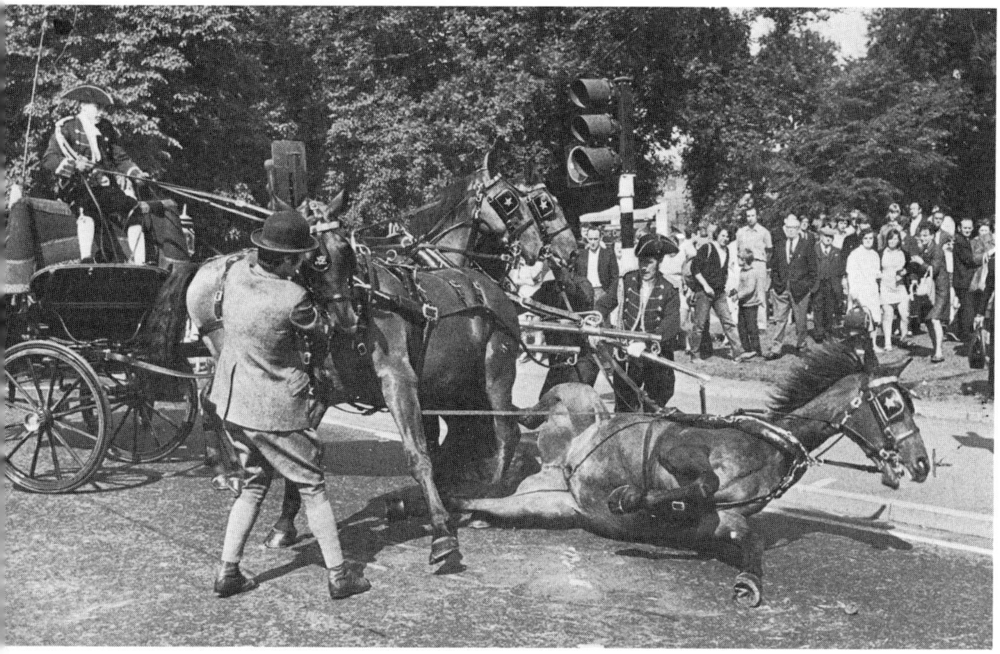

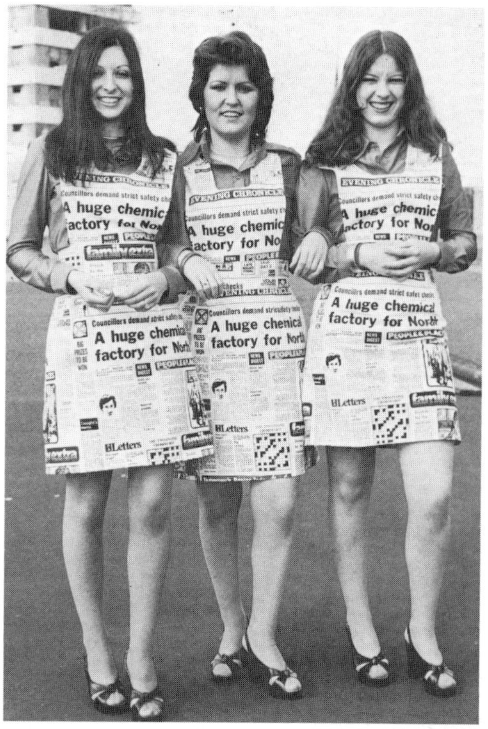

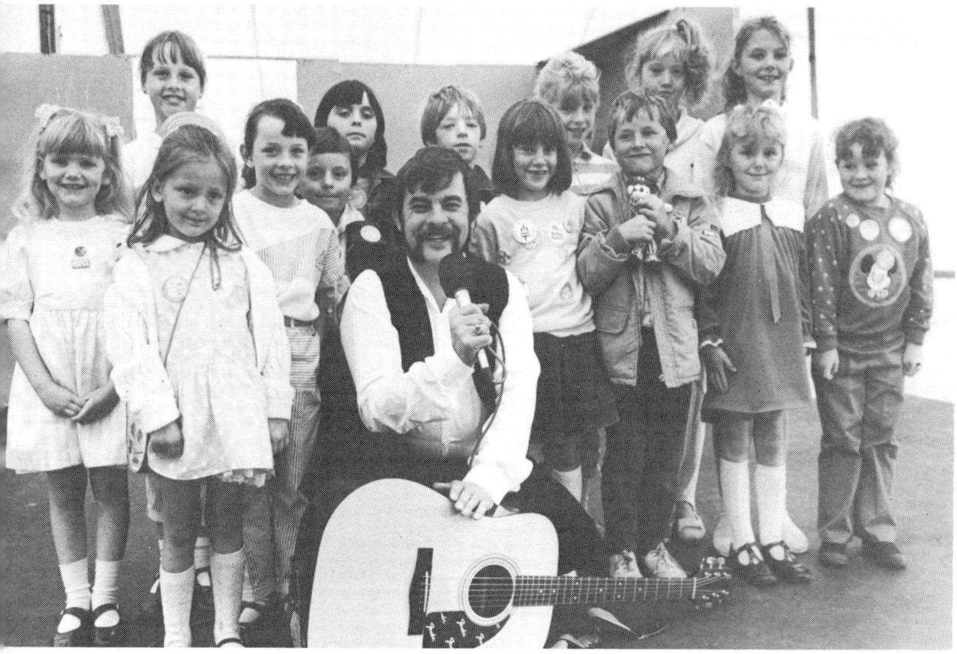

155. Wearing their specially designed *Evening Chronicle* printed pinafore dresses, June, Lyndia and Denise, the *Evening Chronicle Personality Girls*, were on duty throughout the 1974 Summer Exhibition.

154. *Top left:* Disaster struck during the opening ceremony for the 1971 Tyneside Summer Exhibition. At the start of the Lord Mayor's coach ride, one of the horses slipped and fell.

156. *Left:* The children were the stars of the show at the 1987 Tyneside Summer Exhibition. A dozen youngsters lined up to take part in the *Evening Chronicle* sponsored Children's Showcase, hosted by Little Billy Fane. Children who wanted to take part in the show were asked to turn up on the day, so Billy knew only at the last moment how many acts there were.

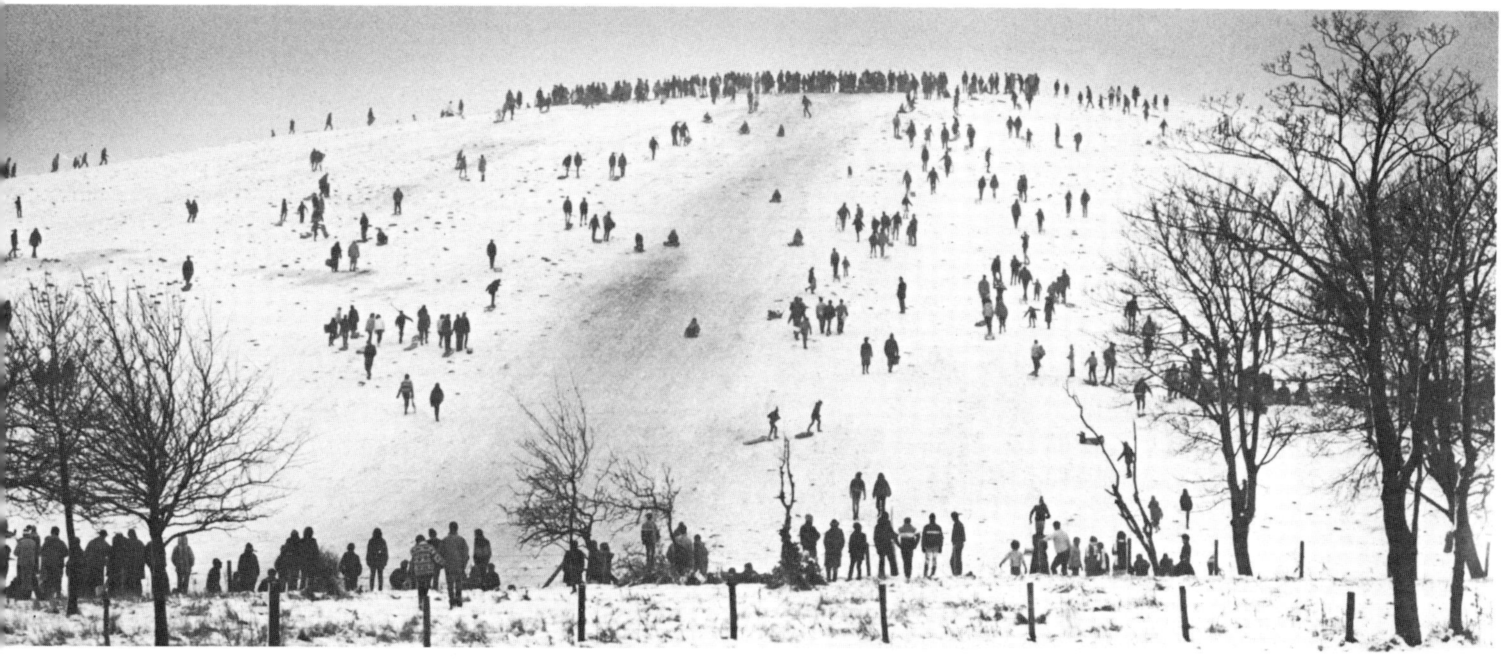

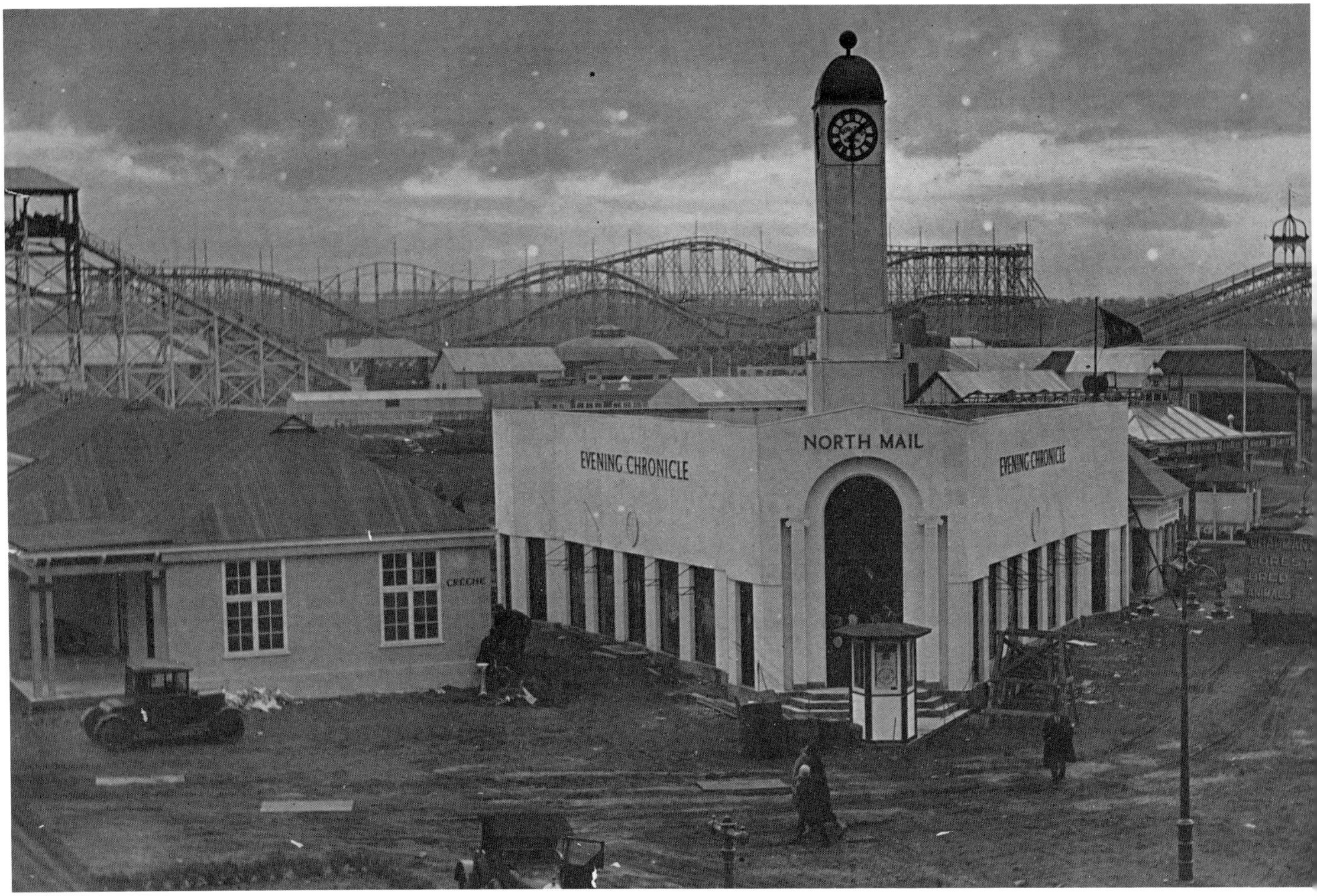

158. The finishing touches are being put to the *Evening Chronicle* pavilion with its clock tower at the North-East Coast Exhibition site.

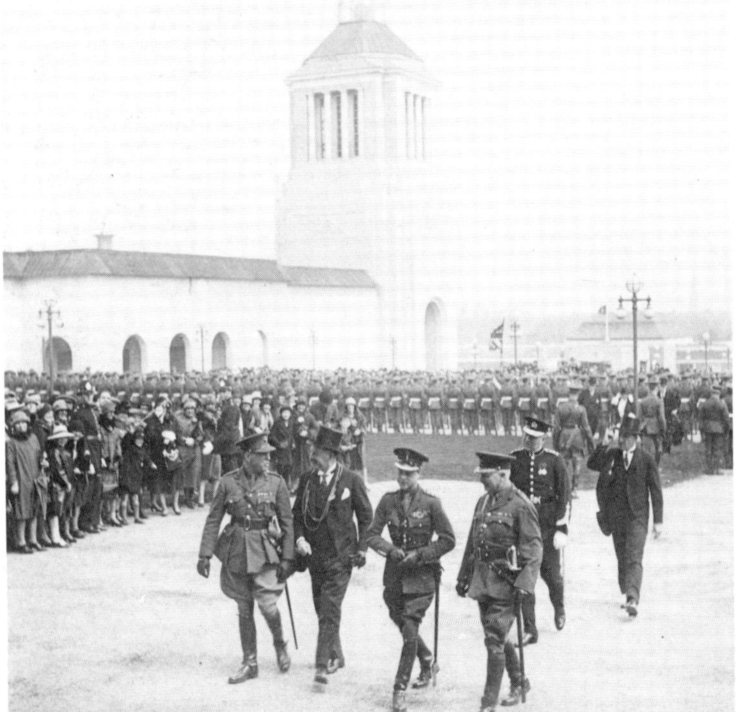

159. HRH The Prince of Wales (later the Duke of Windsor) opened the exhibition on 14 May 1929. The idea for the North-East Coast Exhibition was proposed in 1925 in an attempt to show Britain – and the world – that the North-East was still an industrial powerhouse. The site chosen for the Exhibition was that which had been used for the Exhibition of 1887.

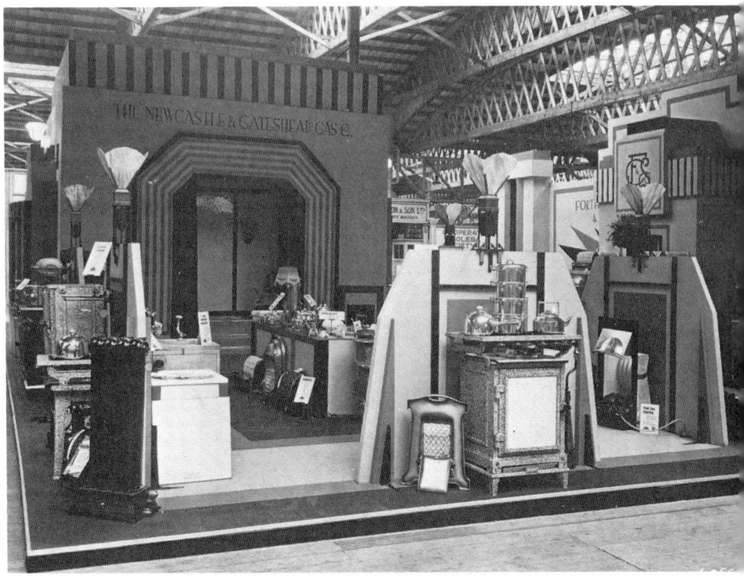

160. The stand of the Newcastle & Gateshead Gas Co features the very latest in household appliances then – museum pieces now. There were a number of exhibition halls. The Palace of Engineering housed the cream of Tyneside's heavy engineering industries; Swan Hunter, Parsons Turbines, Vickers Armstrong, Reyrolle and Clarke Chapman. The Palace of Industries housed the lighter manufacturing firms; carpets, clothing, food processing, pharmaceuticals and so on. When the exhibition finally closed on 26 October 1929, over 4,300,000 visitors had passed through the turnstiles resulting in a profit of around £7,000.

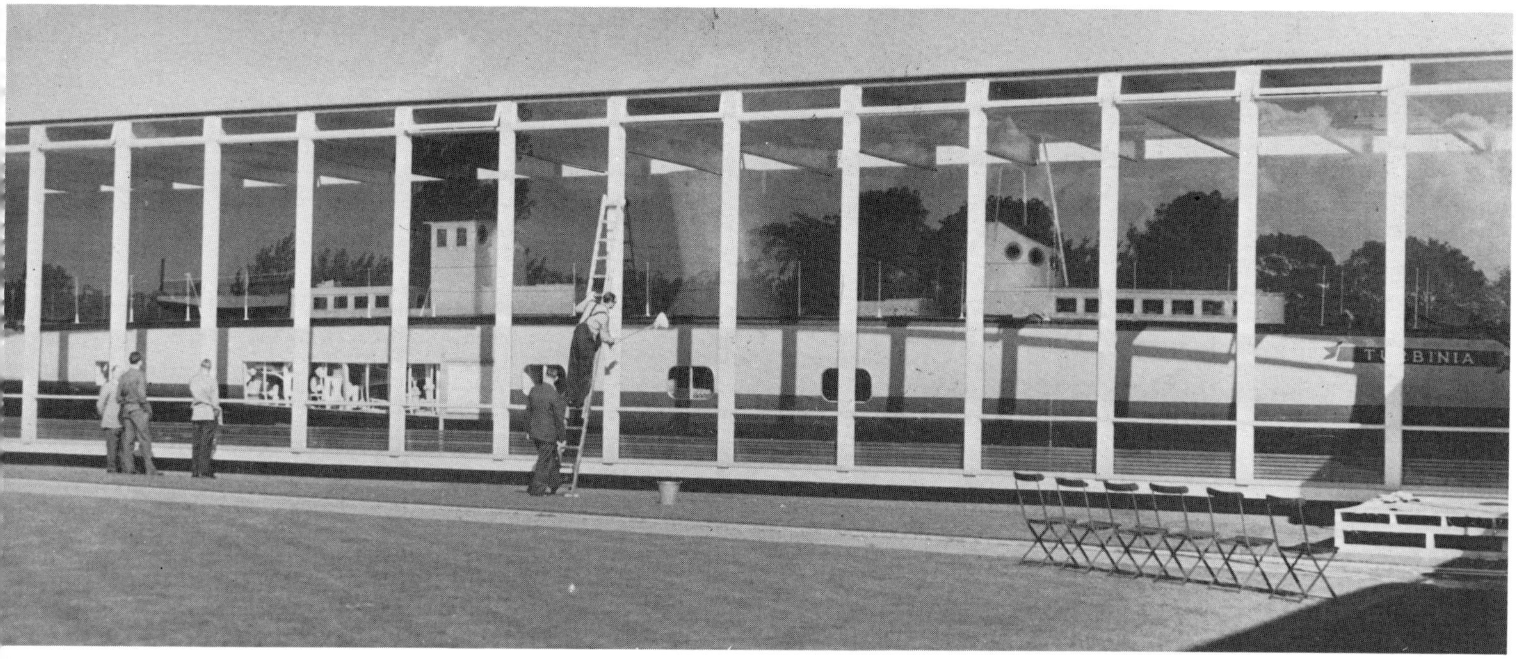

161. The Museum of Science & Engineering was eventually housed in the former NE Coast Exhibition's Palace of Arts. *Above:* C A Parsons' revolutionary steam turbine powered vessel *Turbinia*. September 1961.

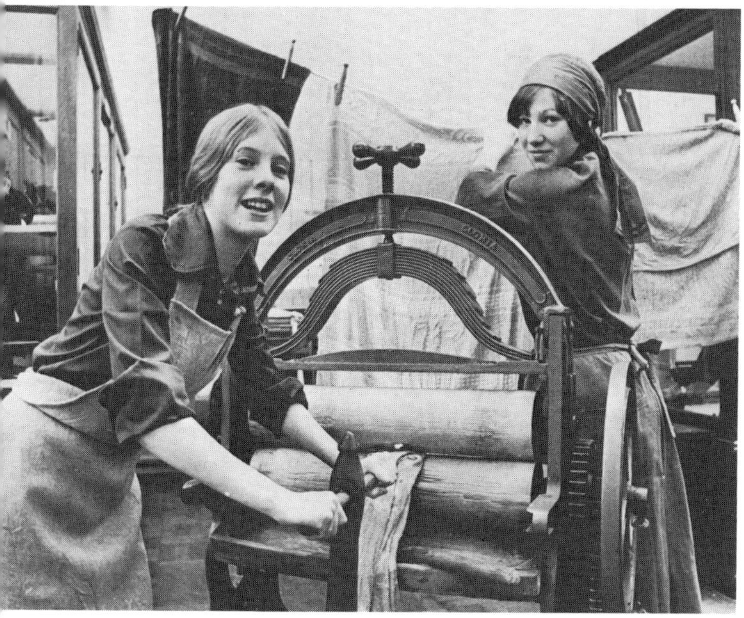

162. Cramlington High School pupils Gwen Armstrong and Beverley Taylor try their hand at doing the washing 1900 style, learning the secrets of the mangle, poss stick and dolly tub. It was all part of a special open day at the domestic science section of the Museum of Science & Engineering. The open day was organised by Mrs Ruth Smith, assistant to the curator, and timed for the half-term holidays. October 1973.

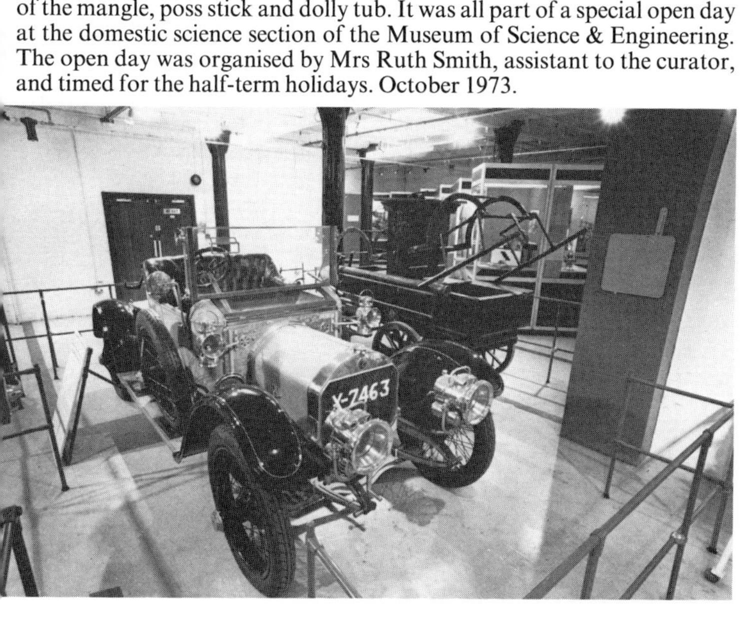

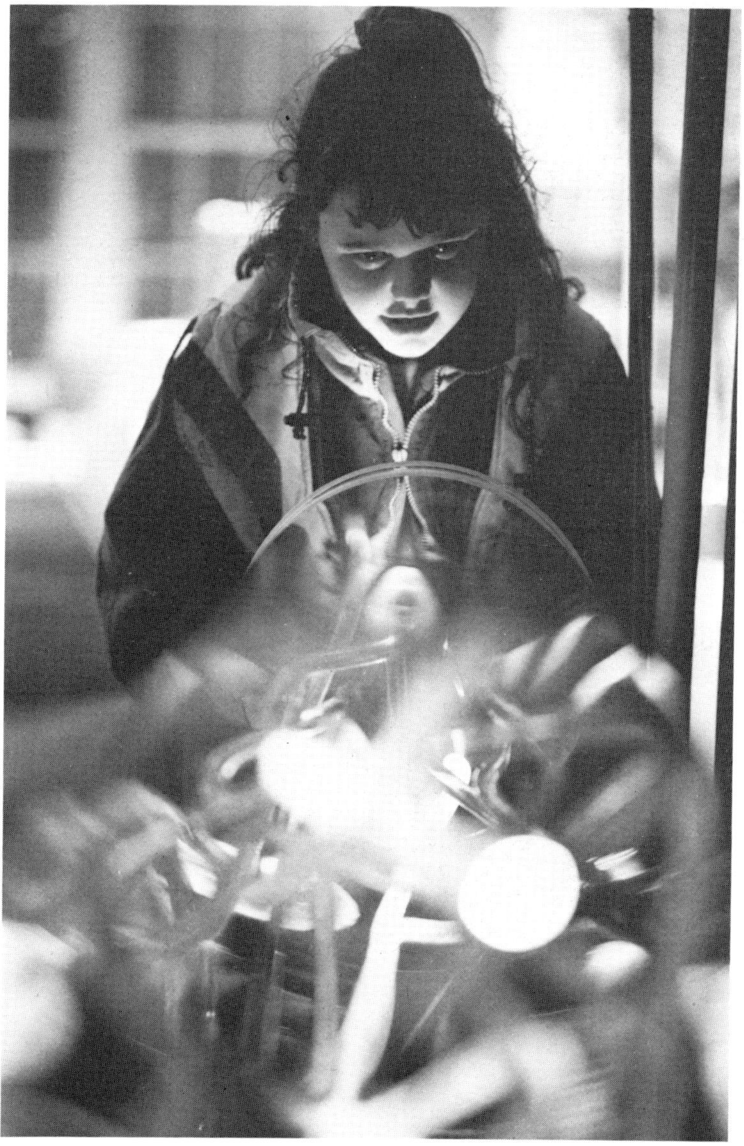

163-164. The museum features static displays and 'hands-on' exhibits. *Above:* Photographer Paul Dodds took this picture of a youngster taking part in a practical science display that uses fibre-optics. January 1990.

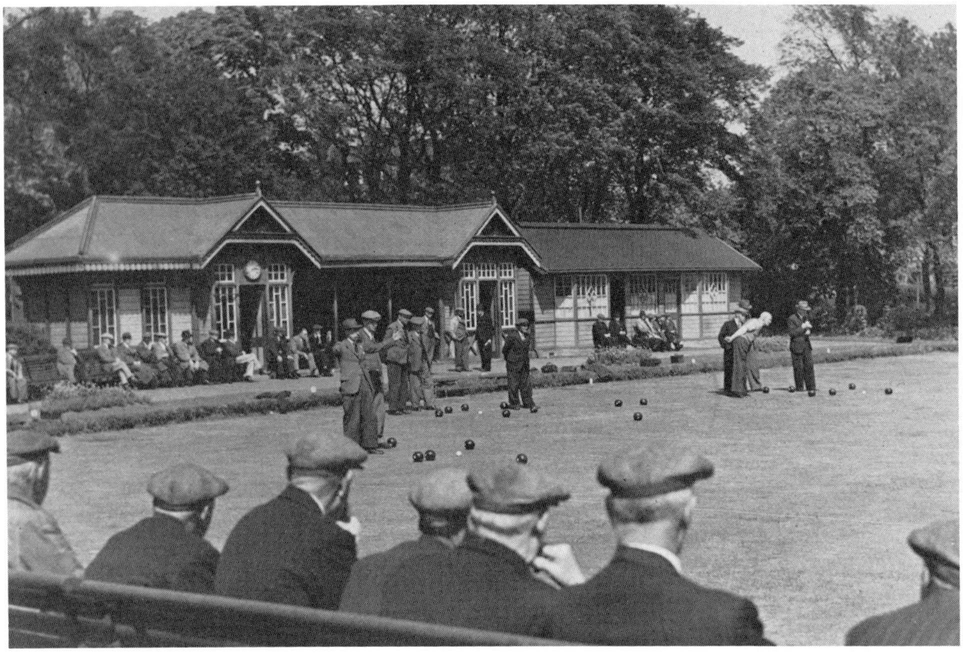

165. Flashback to May 1948 and a game of bowls in the picturesque Brandling Park.

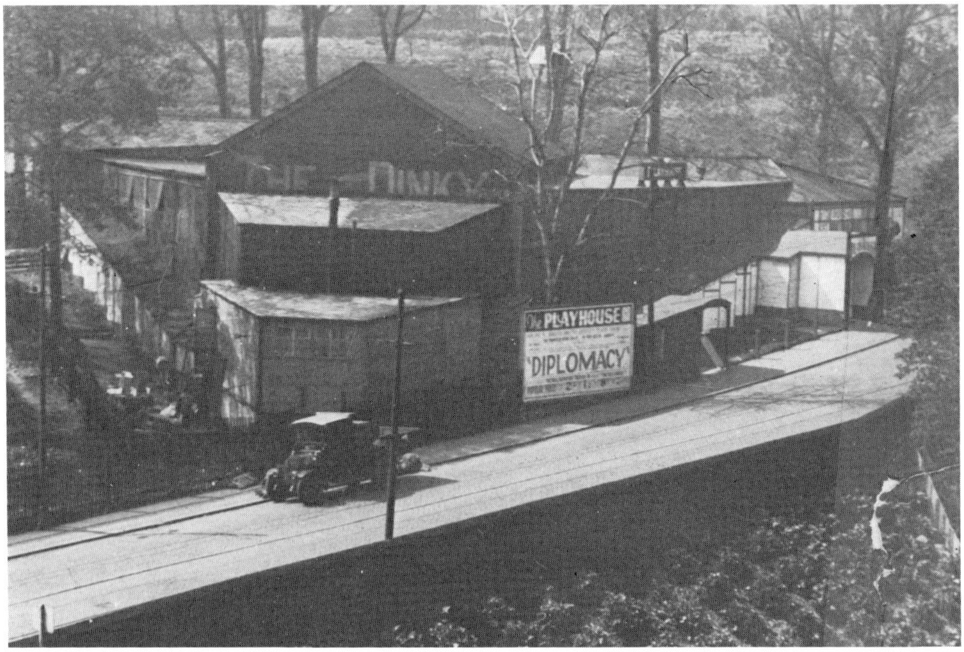

166. The Dinky Theatre at Jesmond was built on the site later occupied by the Playhouse. *Courtesy:* Gordon Hilton.

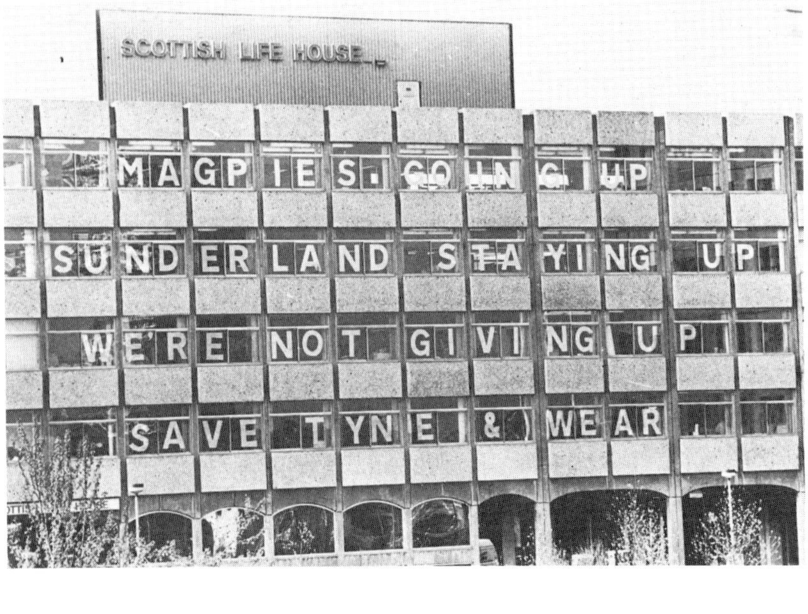

167. In May 1984, NALGO members at the doomed Tyne Wear County Council's offices in Archbold Terrace, Jesmond, made their feelings known. Since the middle of March, the giant letters had spelt out the message that the council should be saved from the axe. The messages came down at one point after solicitors acting for the owners of the building – Scottish Life Assurance – warned the council that they were in breach of their leasing contract. However, even though the letters went back up the council still came down.

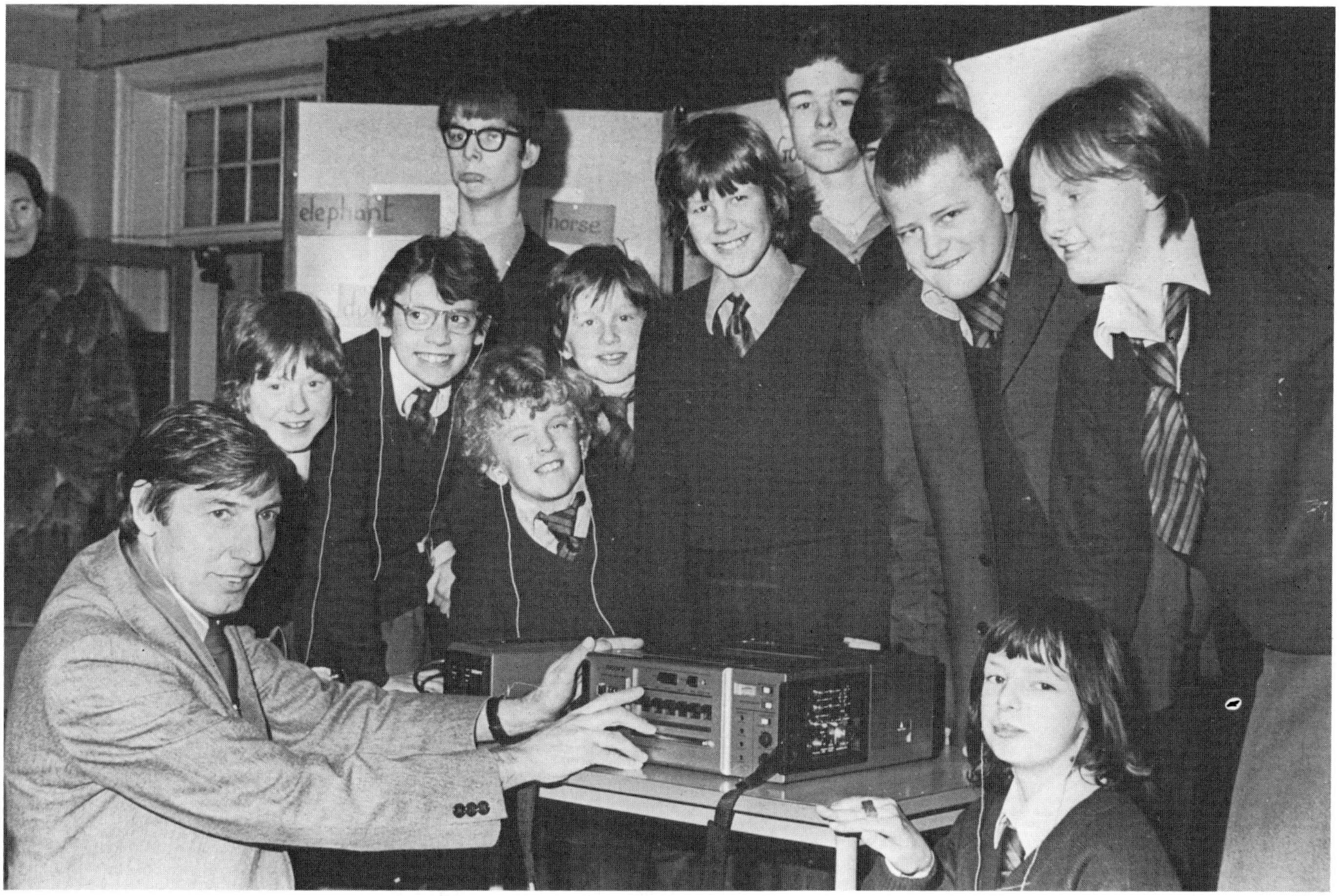

168. In 1981 the Newcastle Lions Club made a good start to the year by presenting a £2,000 video recorder to the Northern Counties School for the Deaf. Mr Dennis Leech, president of the Lions, is seen at the school with some of the children.

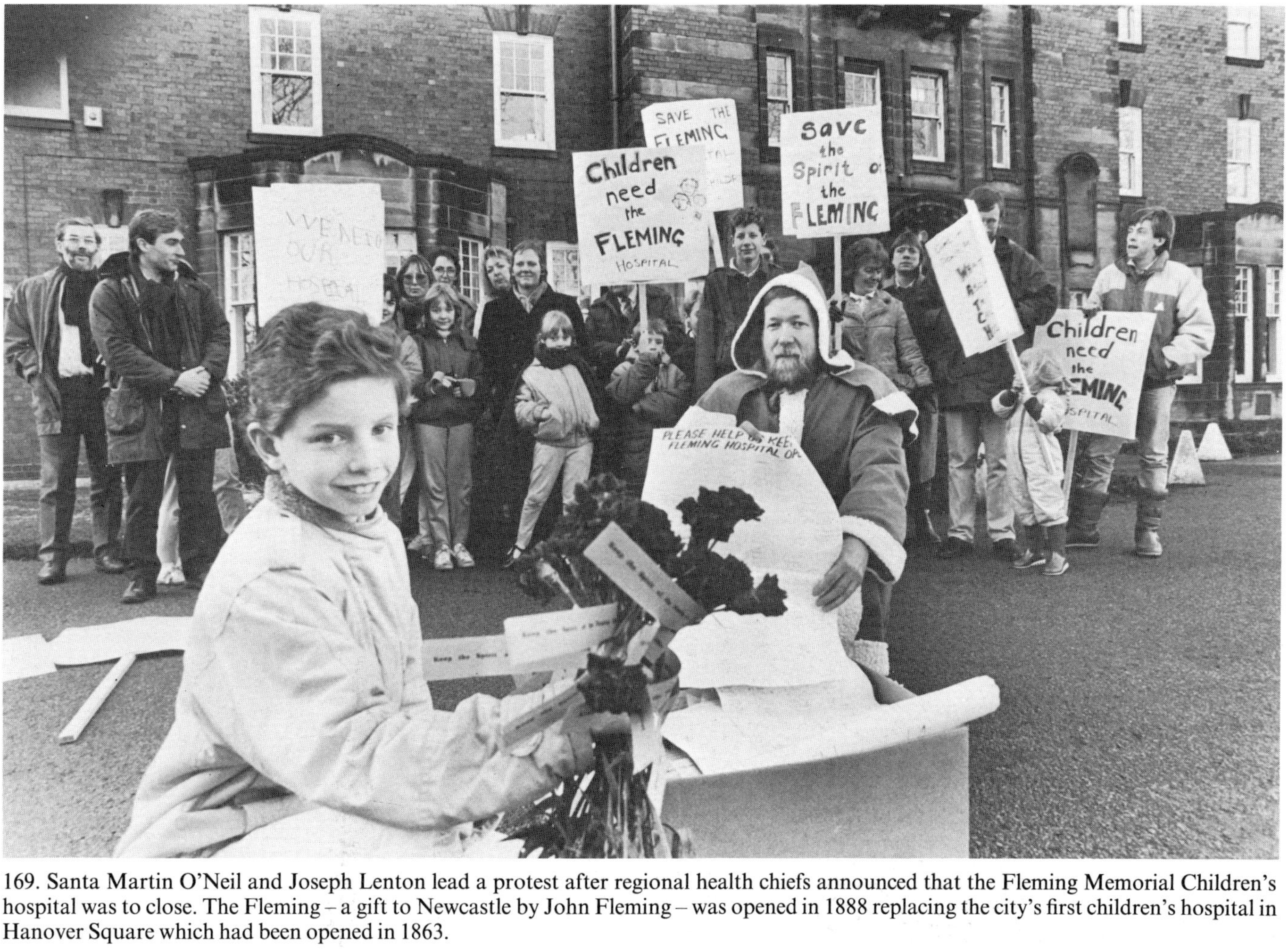

169. Santa Martin O'Neil and Joseph Lenton lead a protest after regional health chiefs announced that the Fleming Memorial Children's hospital was to close. The Fleming – a gift to Newcastle by John Fleming – was opened in 1888 replacing the city's first children's hospital in Hanover Square which had been opened in 1863.

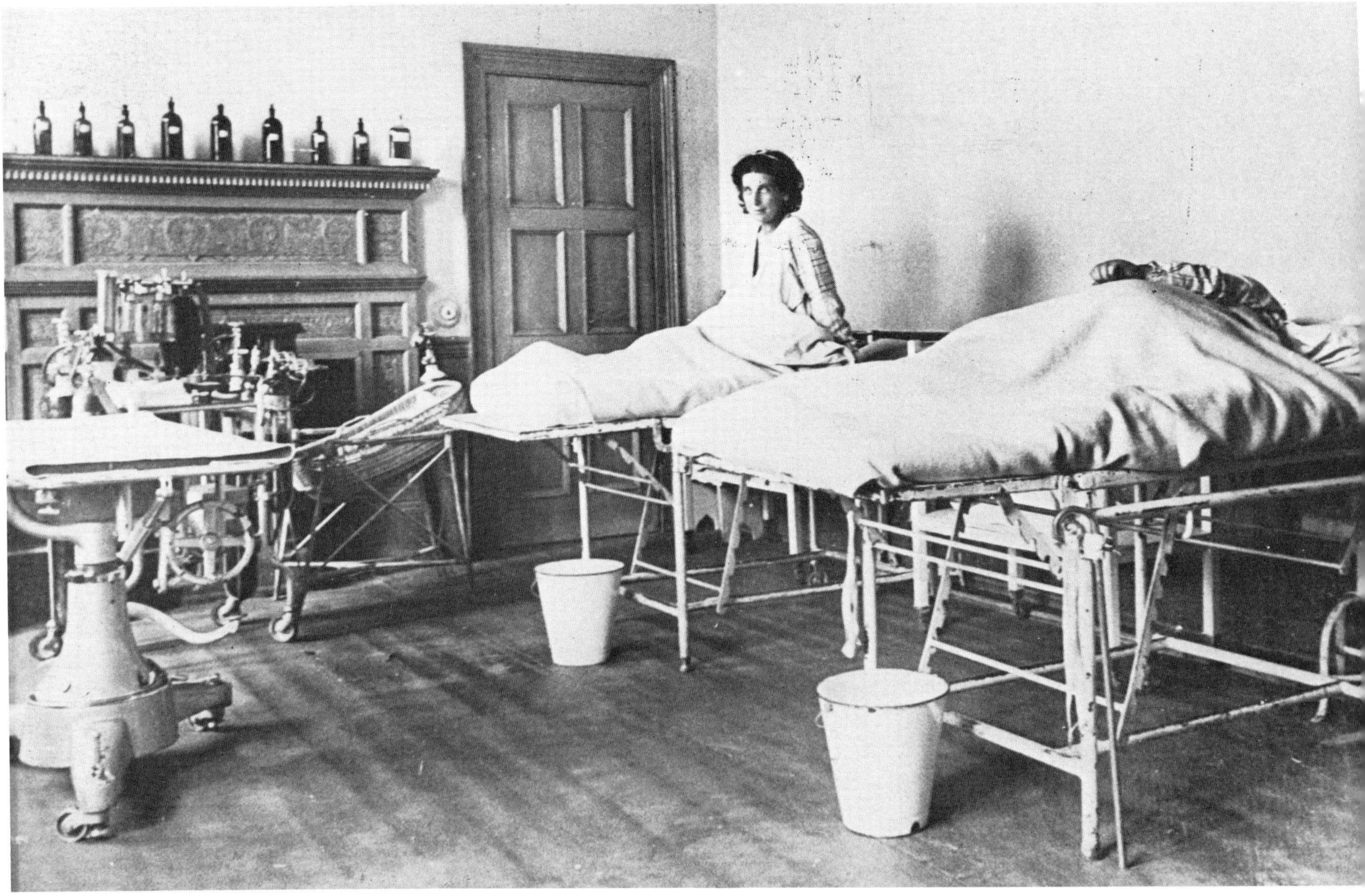

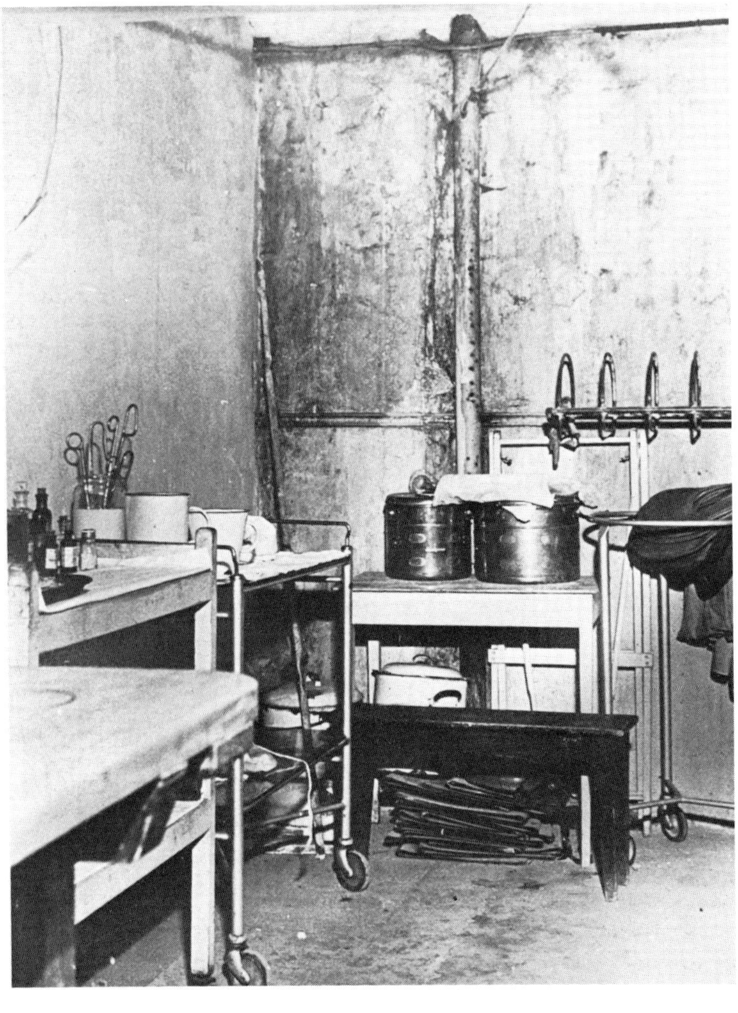

170-172. The old and the new at the Princess Mary Maternity Hospital. The old pictures date from about 1940, the modern day labour ward from August 1980.

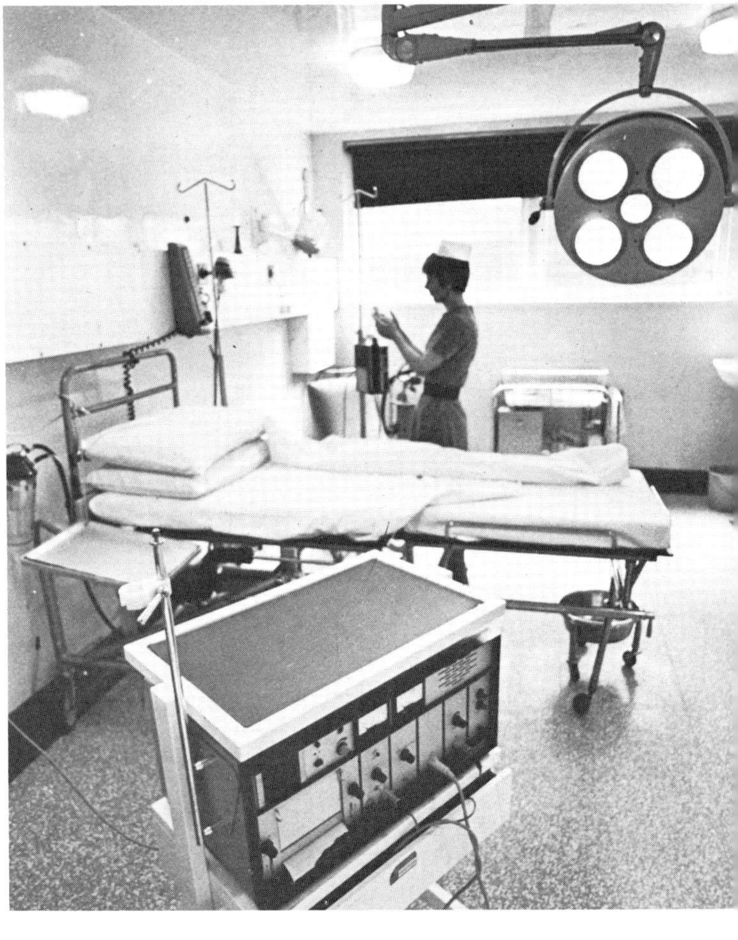

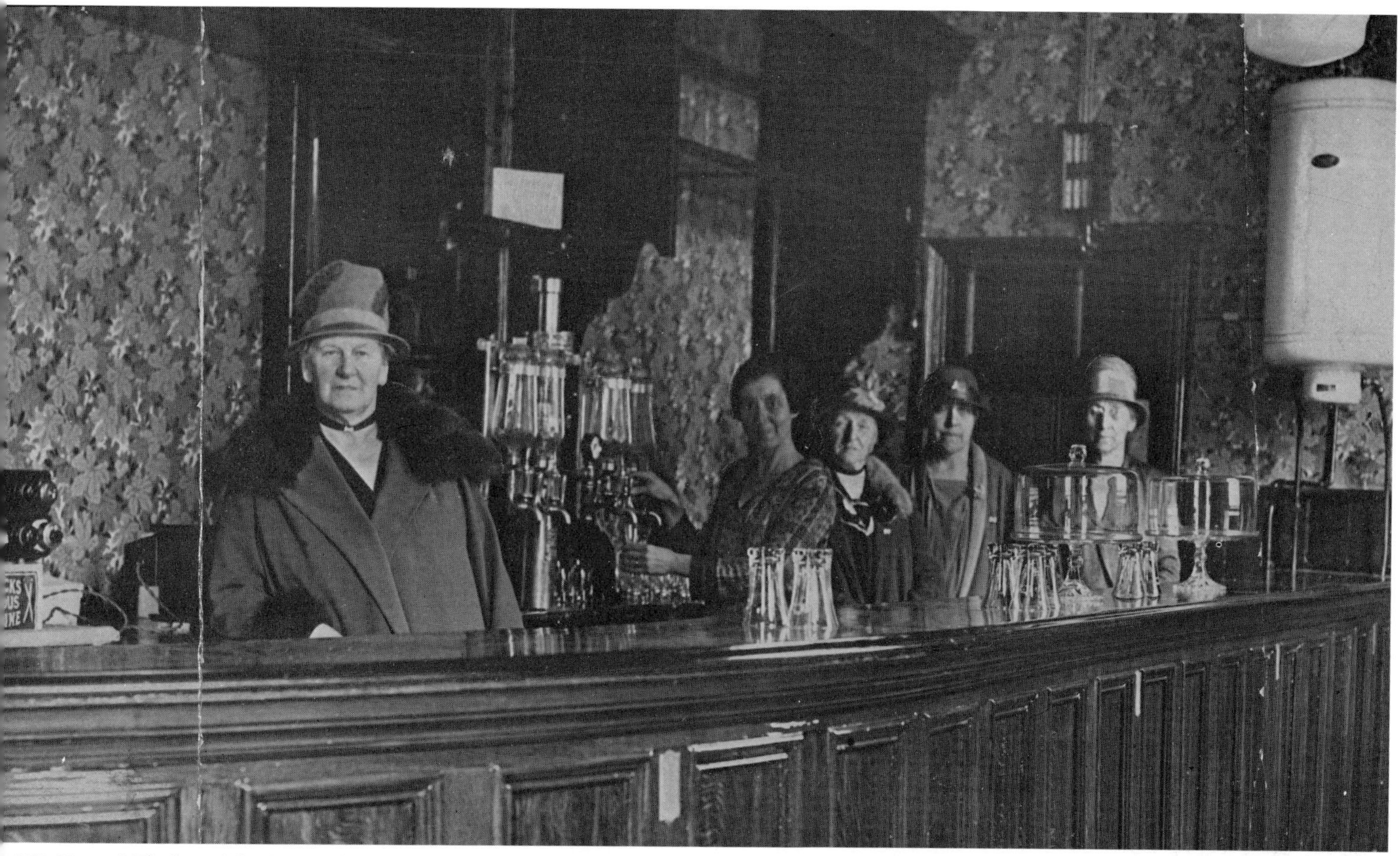

173. Tea up? The bar of the General Wolfe in Canada Street, Shieldfield, was Newcastle's dry public house. The photograph dates from September 1928 and was published in the *Evening Chronicle* in September 1970.

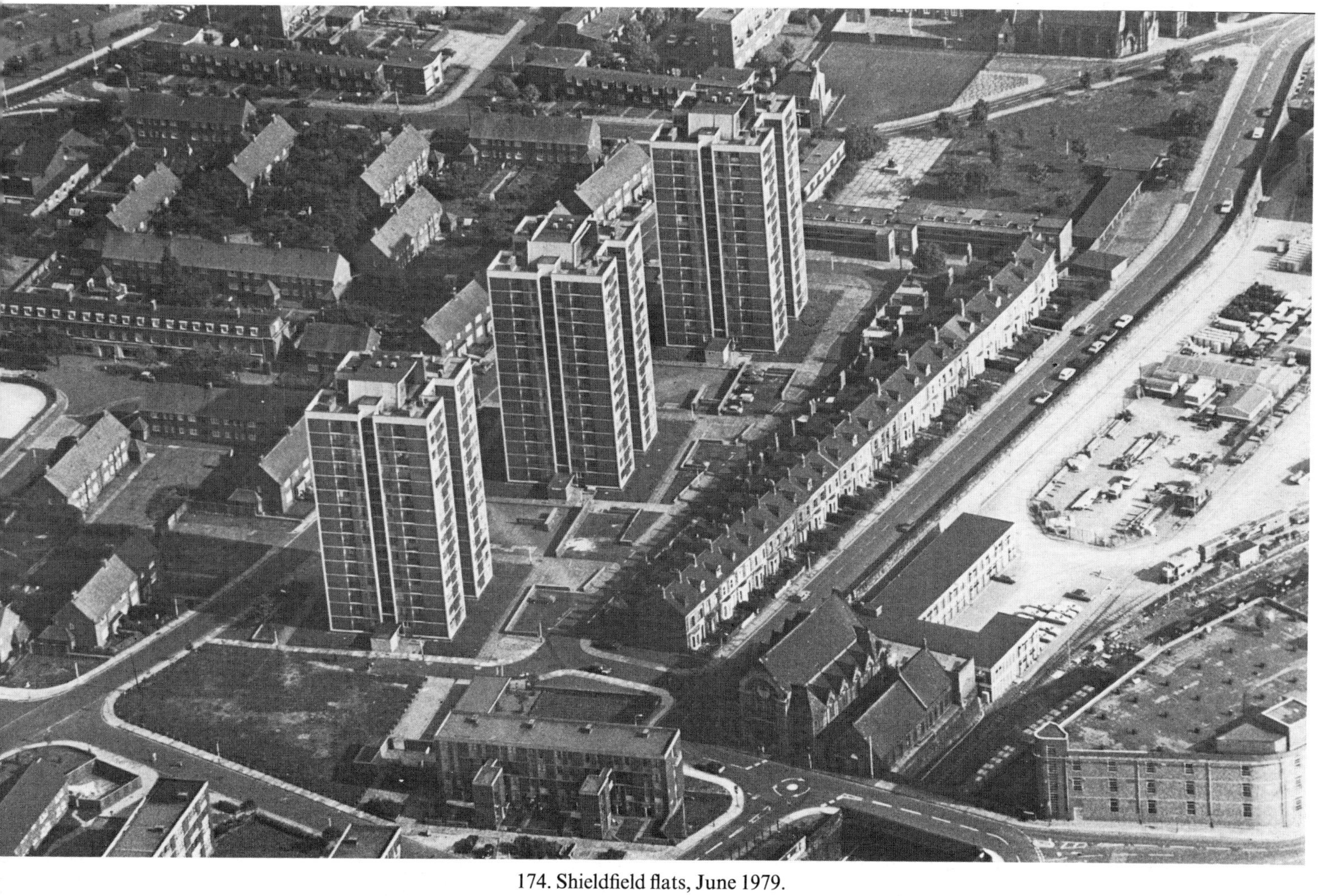

174. Shieldfield flats, June 1979.

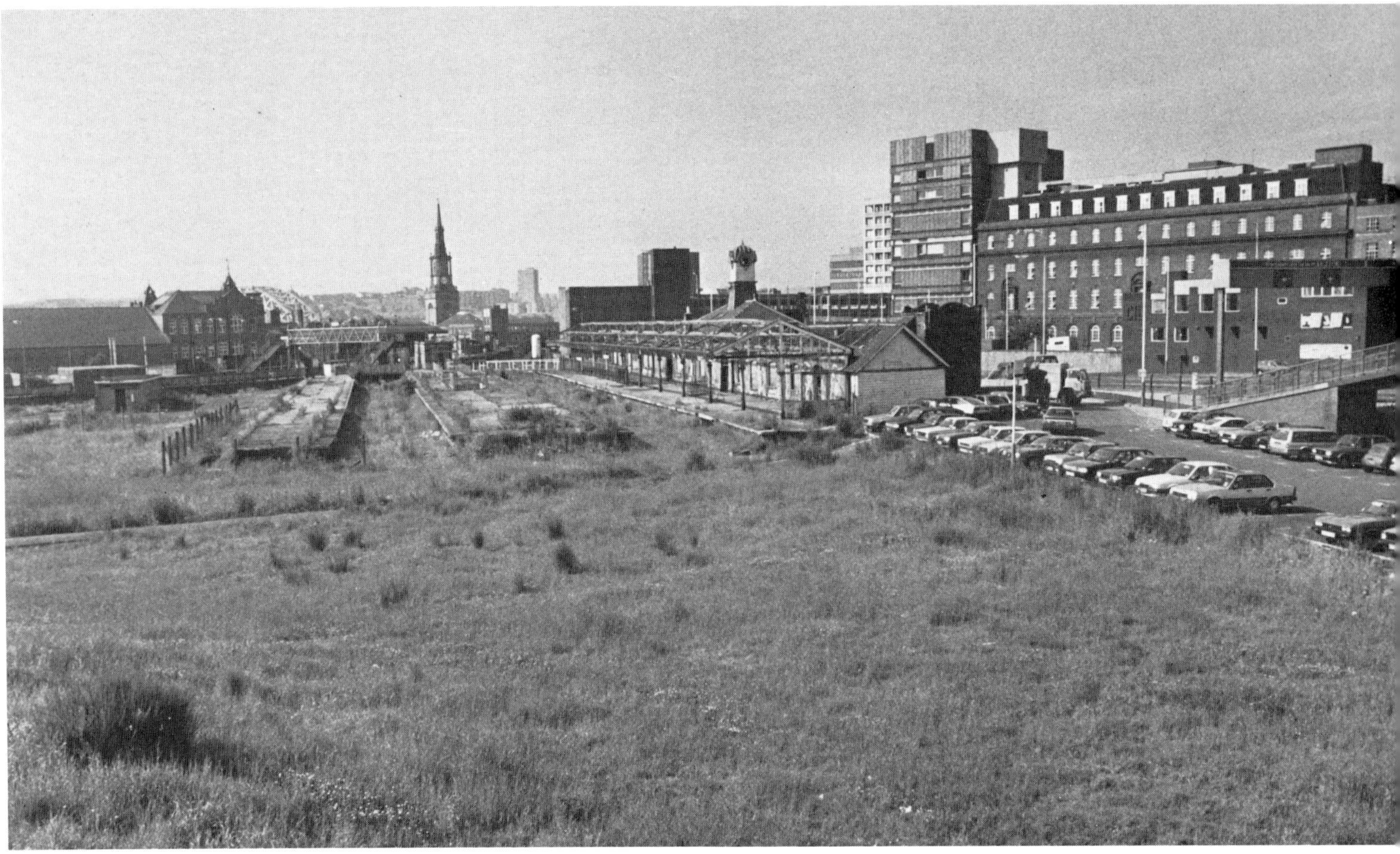

175. It's hard to believe that this desolate area was once a busy railway junction. The mortal remains of Manors Station.

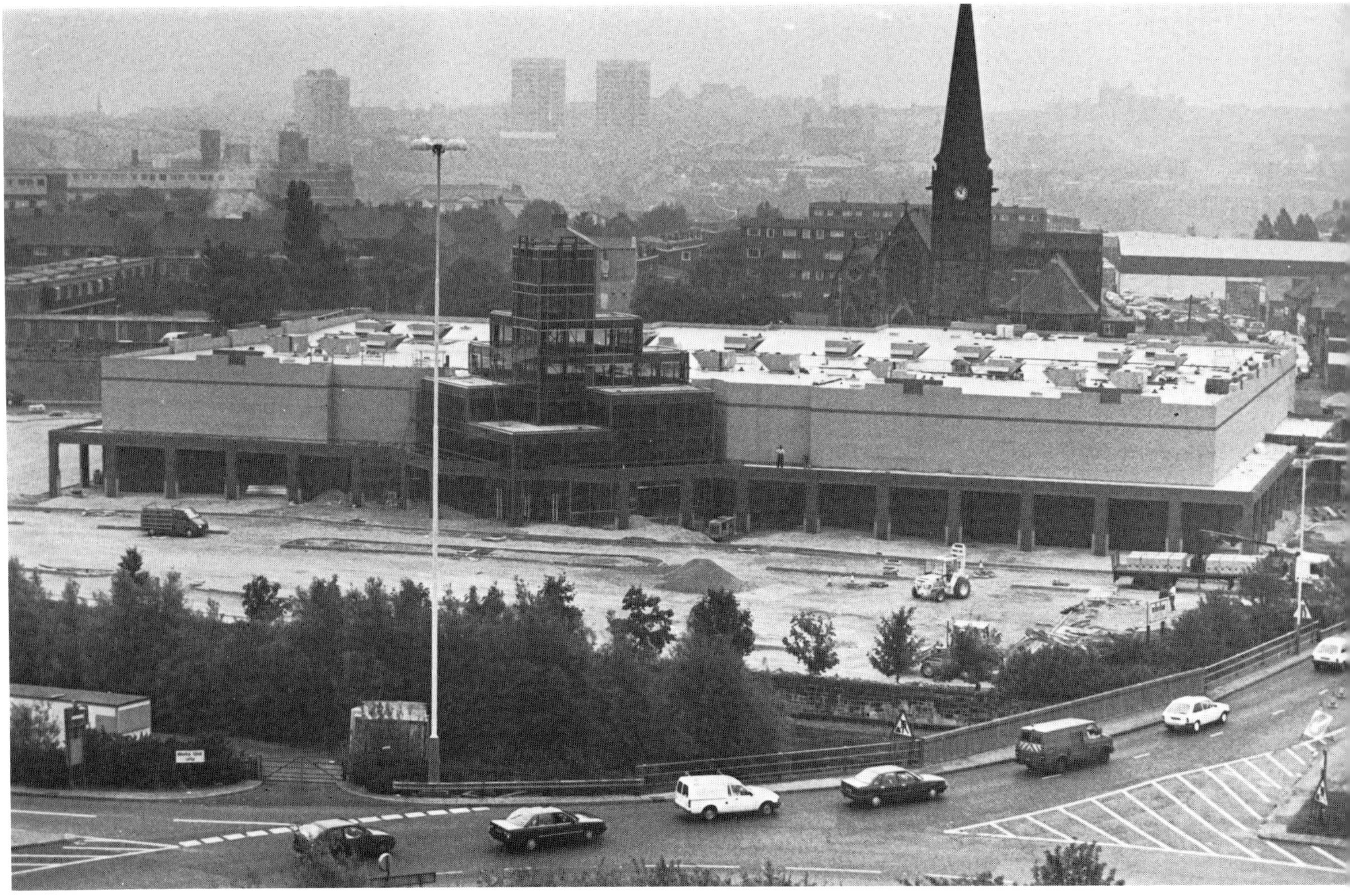

176. Warner Brothers complex under construction in 1989.

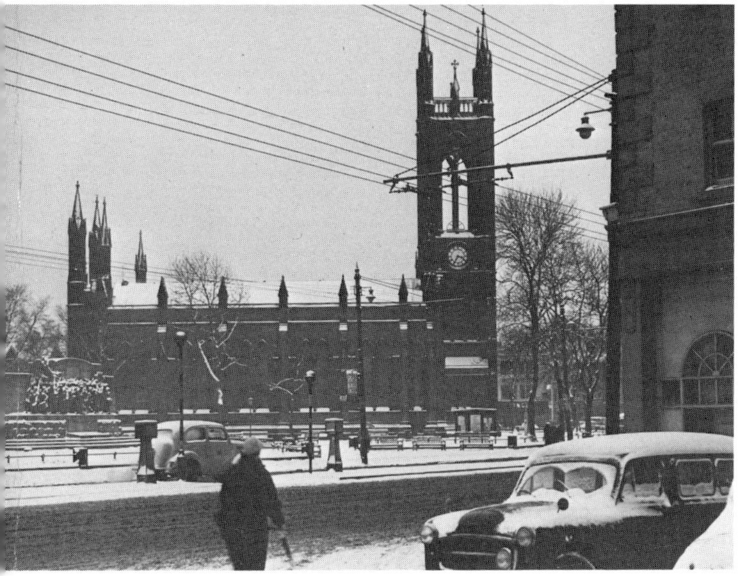

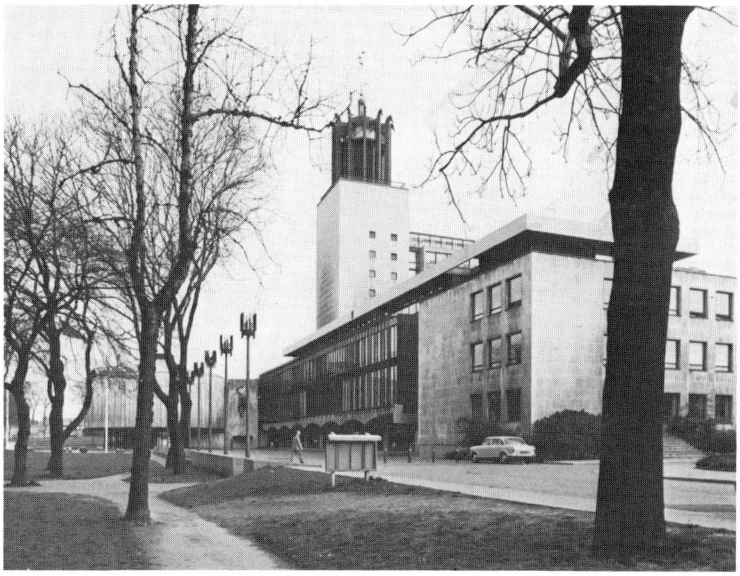

178. Newcastle Civic Centre, April 1977. *Courtesy:* Crown Copyright.

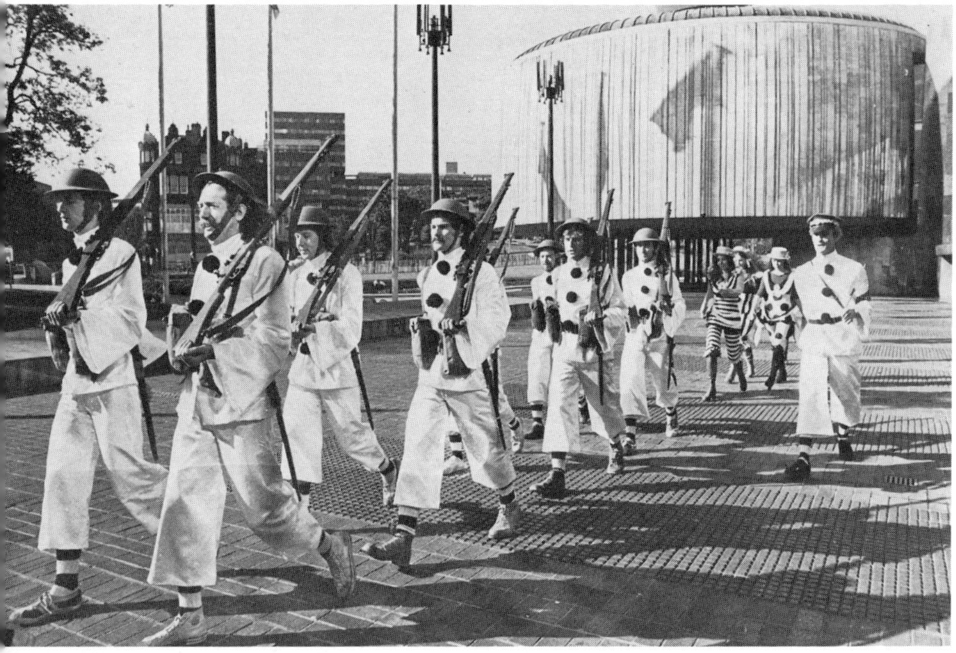

177. *Top left:* Snow and slush around St Thomas the Martyr's church, Barras Bridge, January 1958.

179. *Left:* 'Get fell in you 'orrible lot!' A few eyebrows were raised as this squad marched through Newcastle in September 1972 to publicise the staging of Joan Littlewood's play *'Oh, What a Lovely War'* at the University Theatre. It was a full turn-out by the cast, who marched and sang from the theatre to the bottom of Northumberland Street, put on a mini-show, then marched and sang all the way back again.

180. *Below:* 7 March 1990 and police link arms to hold back poll tax protesters.

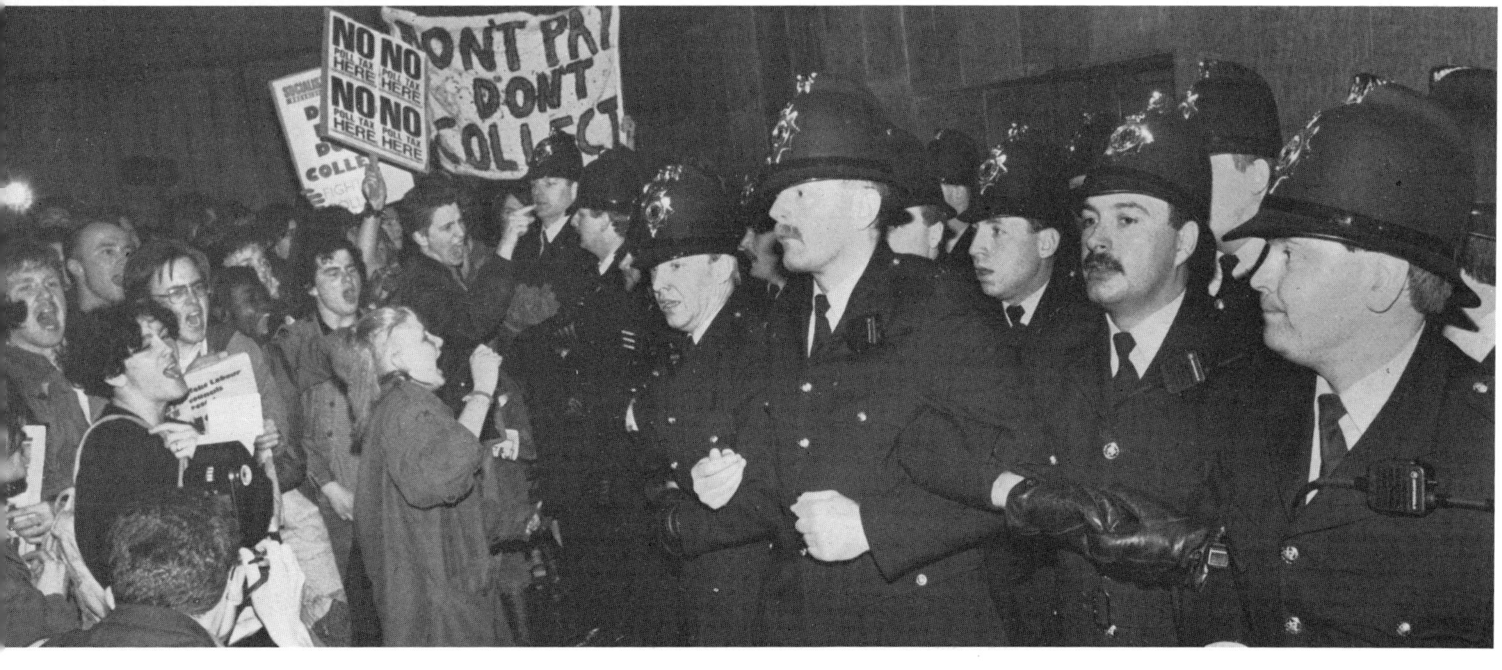

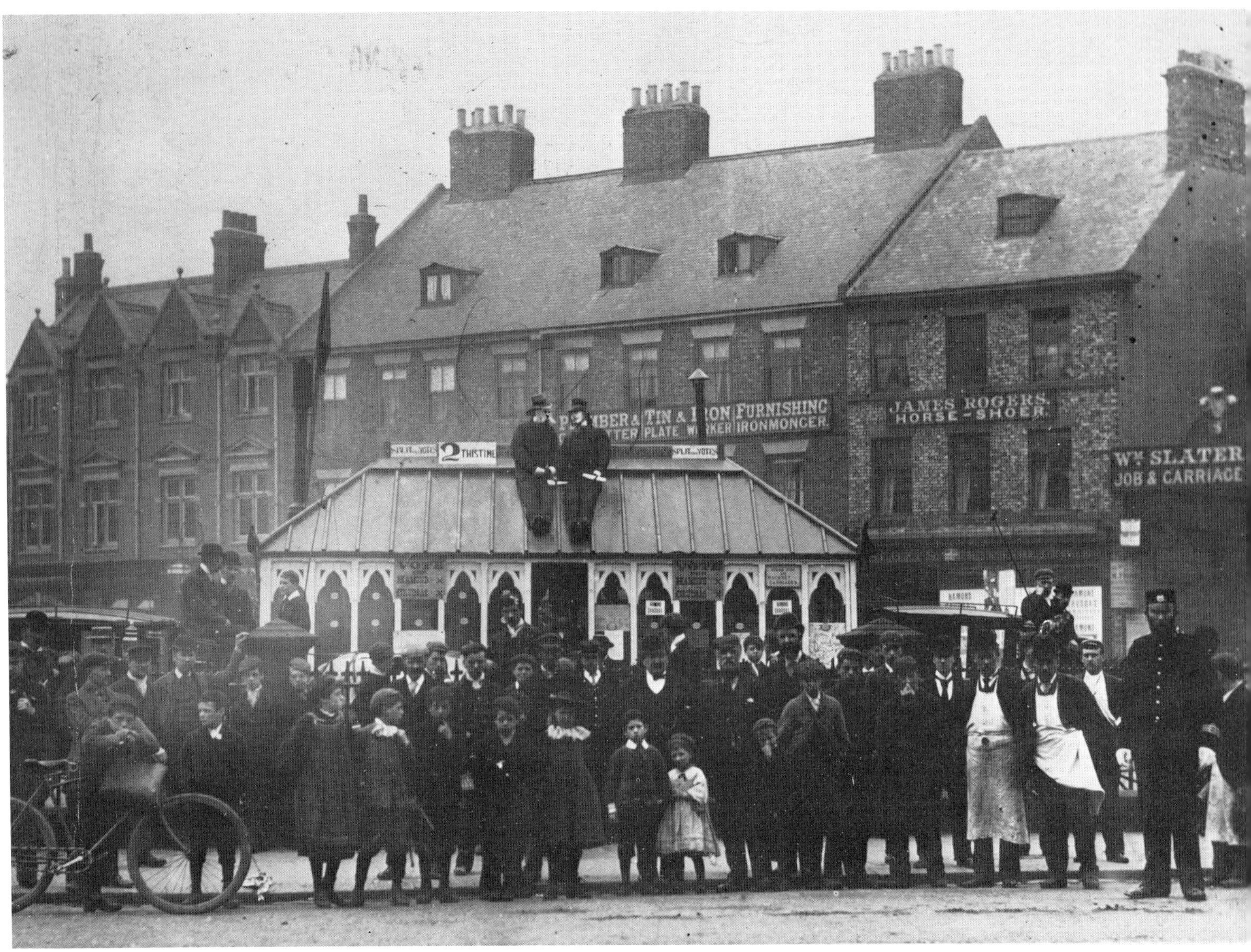

181. Political protestations of an earlier generation. An election is in the offing and the two effigies of politicians on top of the drivers' shelter are arousing a keen interest – or is it the cameraman? Just behind the shelter is the building that became the Haymarket Cinema. *Courtesy:* Miss Margaret Rogers.

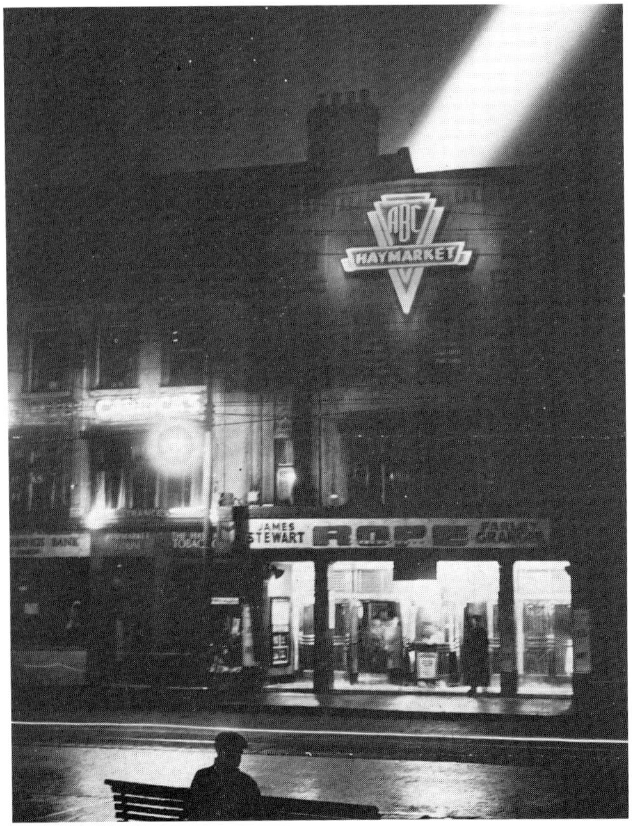

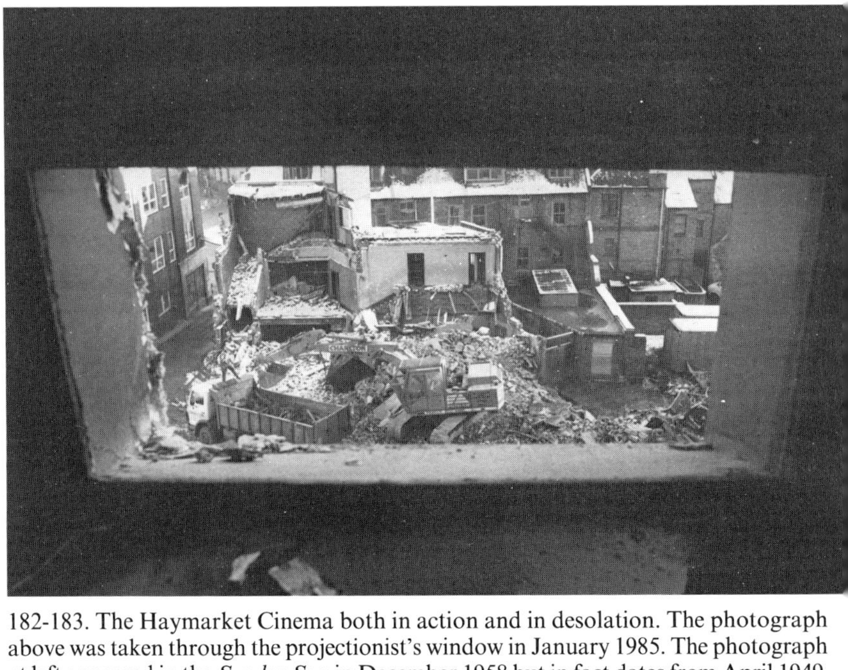

182-183. The Haymarket Cinema both in action and in desolation. The photograph above was taken through the projectionist's window in January 1985. The photograph at left appeared in the *Sunday Sun* in December 1958 but in fact dates from April 1949.

184. This view of Northumberland Street, looking north, was taken in May 1910, the flags and bunting celebrating the Coronation of King George V. As can be seen, the tramway standards used to be sited down the middle of the street.

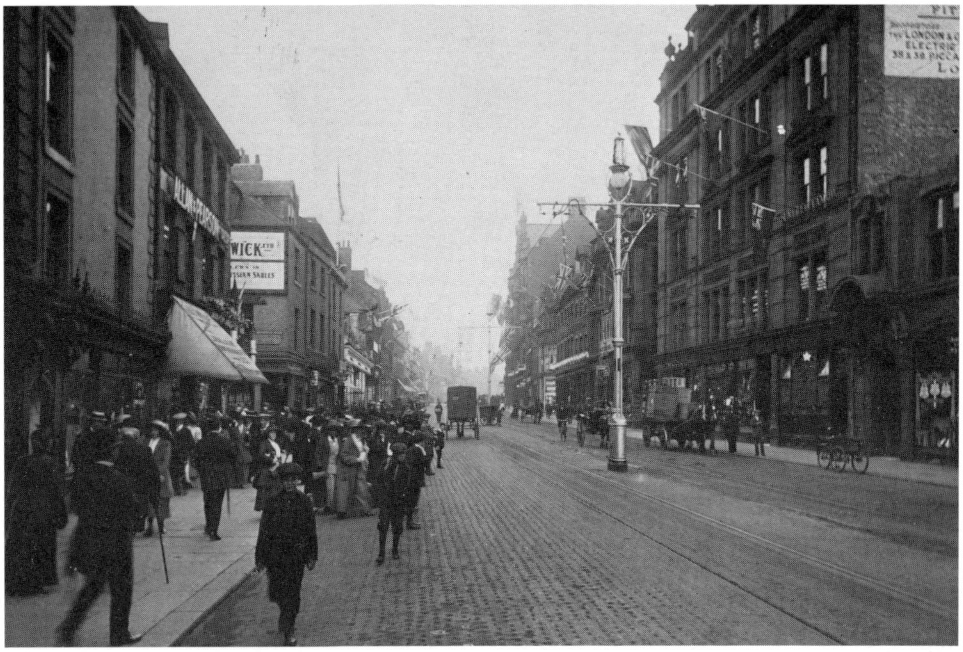

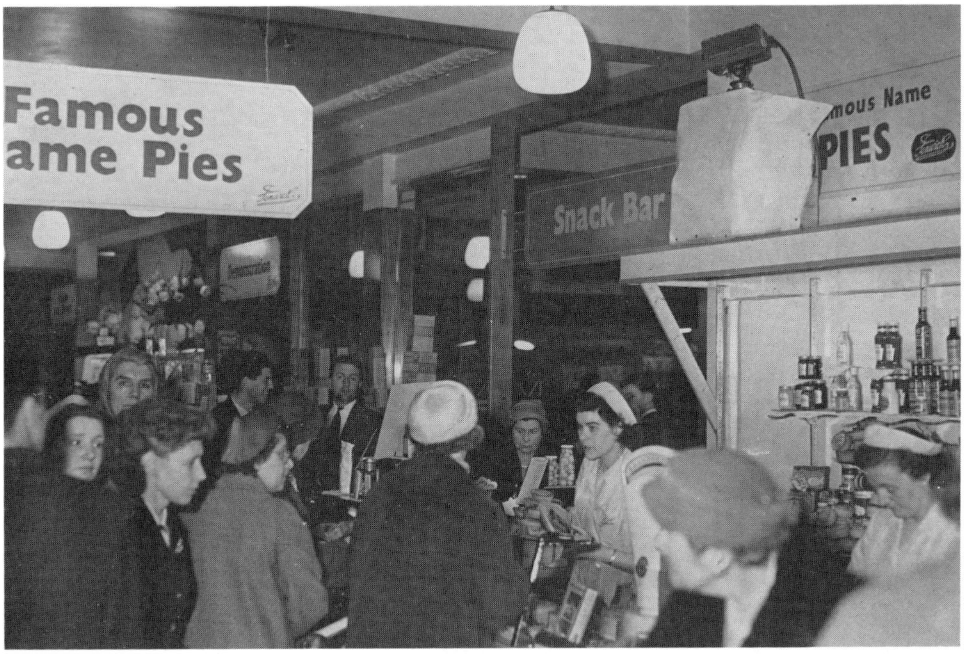

185. The spy on the pie. Conspicuously placed above the heads of shoppers and assistants in Fenwick's, Northumberland Street, in April 1959 was a television camera. The cable led back to a viewing room where twenty or so shop and store executives were taking part in a study that included monitoring the flow of customers and the way they were served.

186. Fenwick's is ready for the Christmas rush. November 1962.

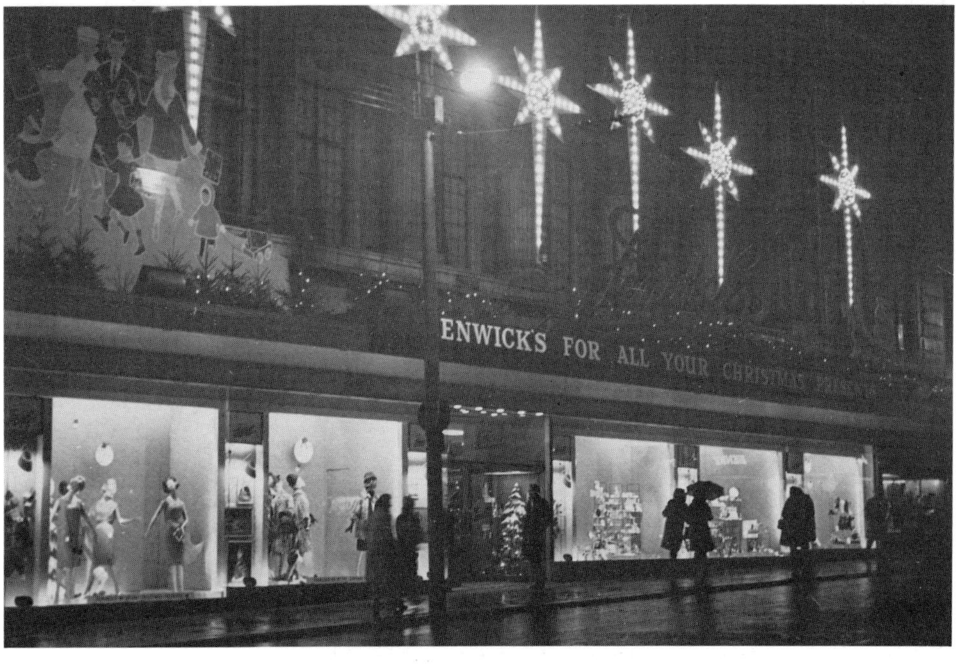

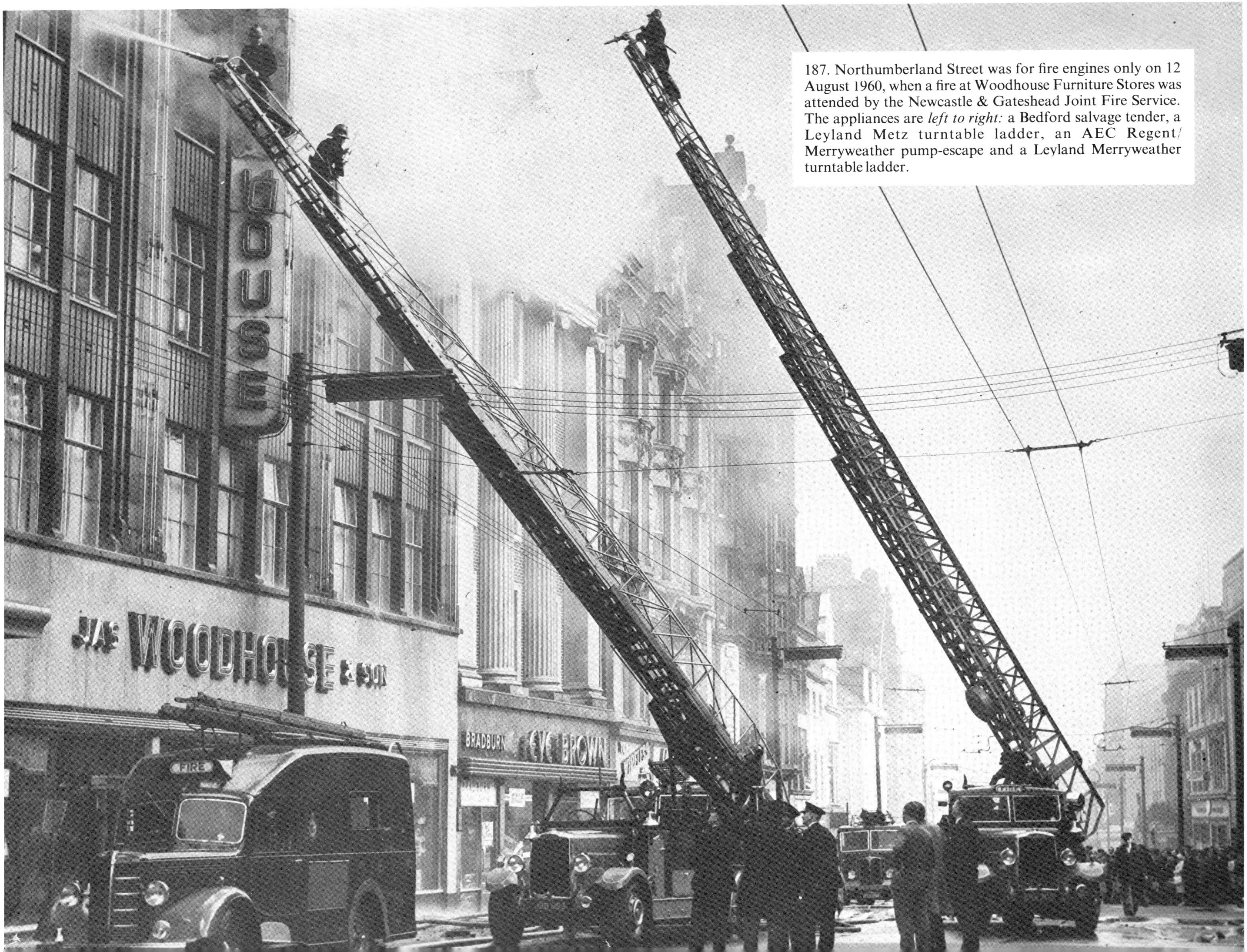

187. Northumberland Street was for fire engines only on 12 August 1960, when a fire at Woodhouse Furniture Stores was attended by the Newcastle & Gateshead Joint Fire Service. The appliances are *left to right:* a Bedford salvage tender, a Leyland Metz turntable ladder, an AEC Regent/ Merryweather pump-escape and a Leyland Merryweather turntable ladder.

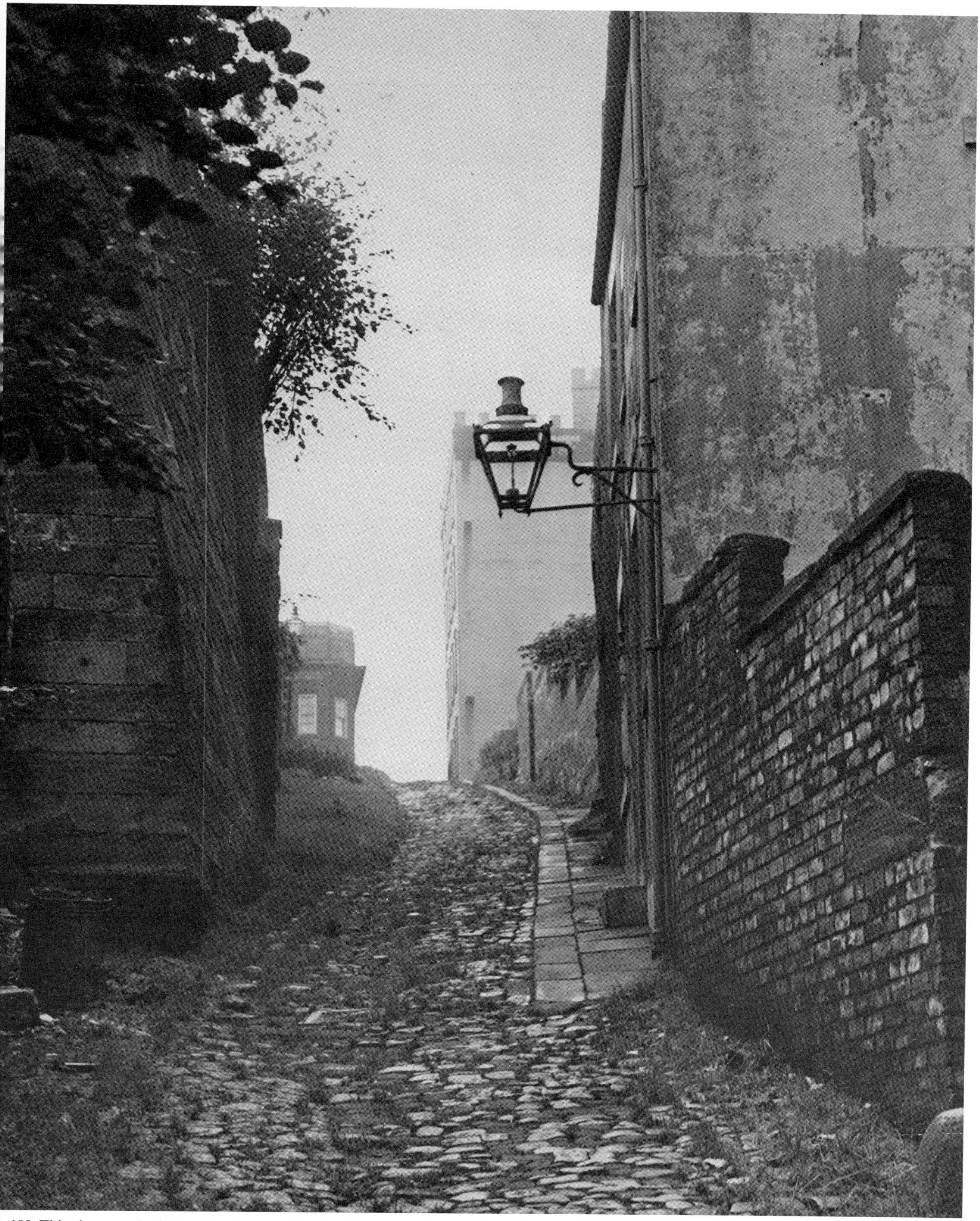

188. This photograph of Silver Street featured in Alan Haydock's *Evening Chronicle* series on the histories of Tyneside highways and byways in October 1953. As far back as the Middle Ages pilgrims passing up Pilgrim Street on their way to Our Lady's Chapel in Jesmond were at the mercy of thieves, rogues and coiners who frequented the area. The name *silver* derives from the fact that this was where Jews traded in silver plate and silverware, and there is a reference dating from 1700 to "Silver Street, alias Jew Gate."

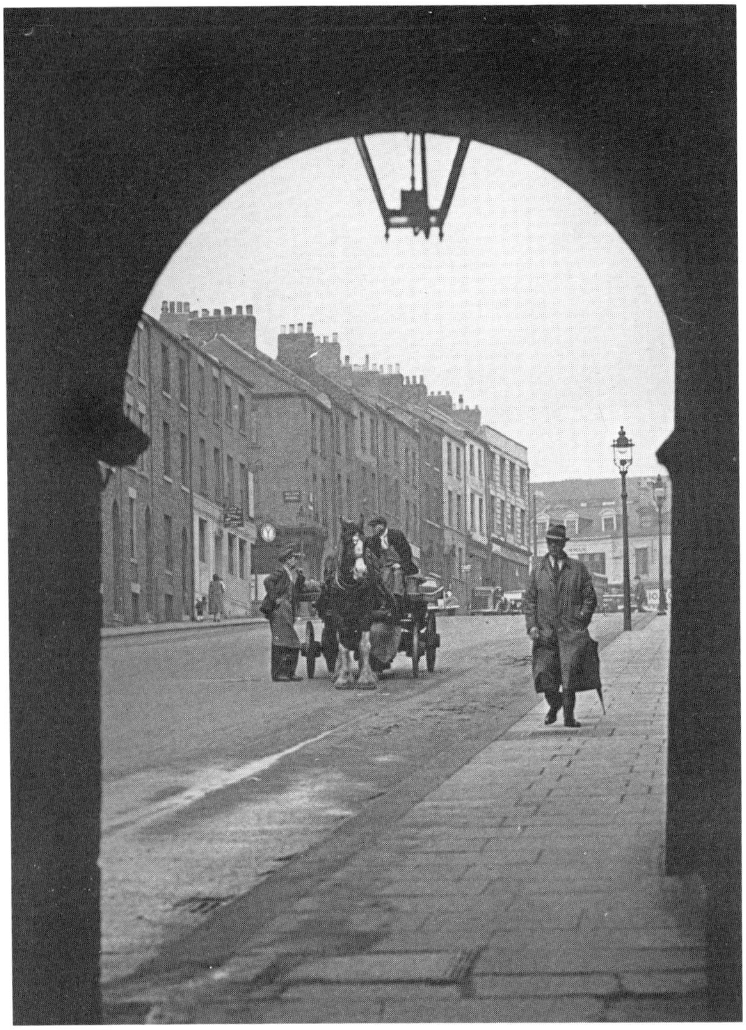

189. An interesting view of Trafalgar Street dating from July 1939.

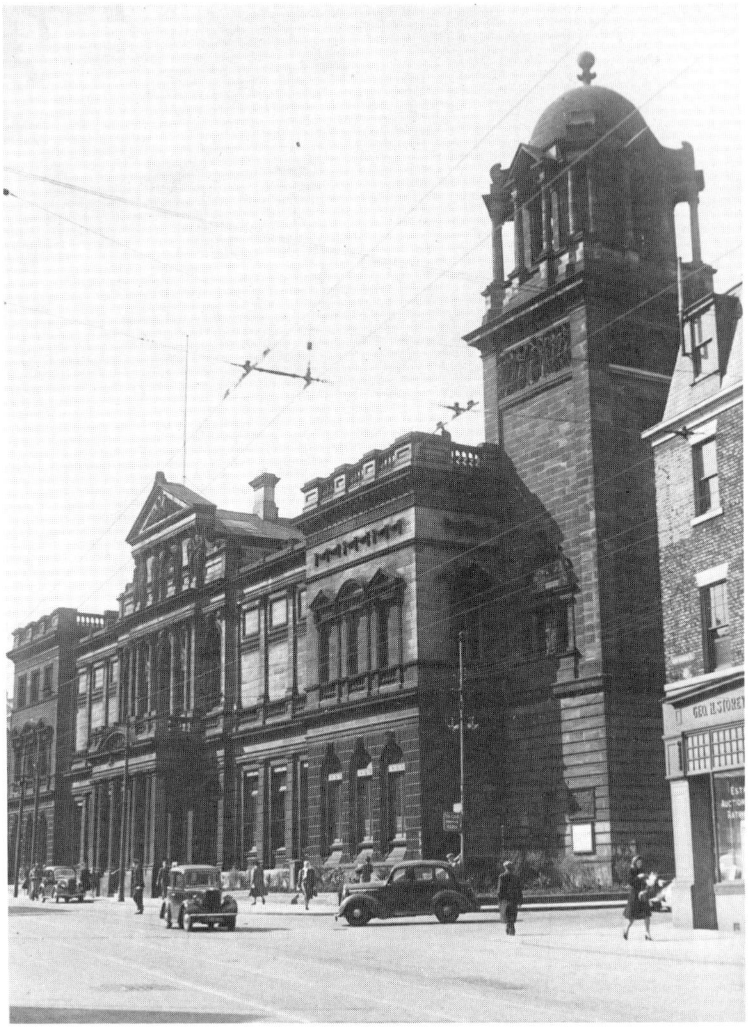

190. The Central Library, New Bridge Street, as it looked in April 1948.

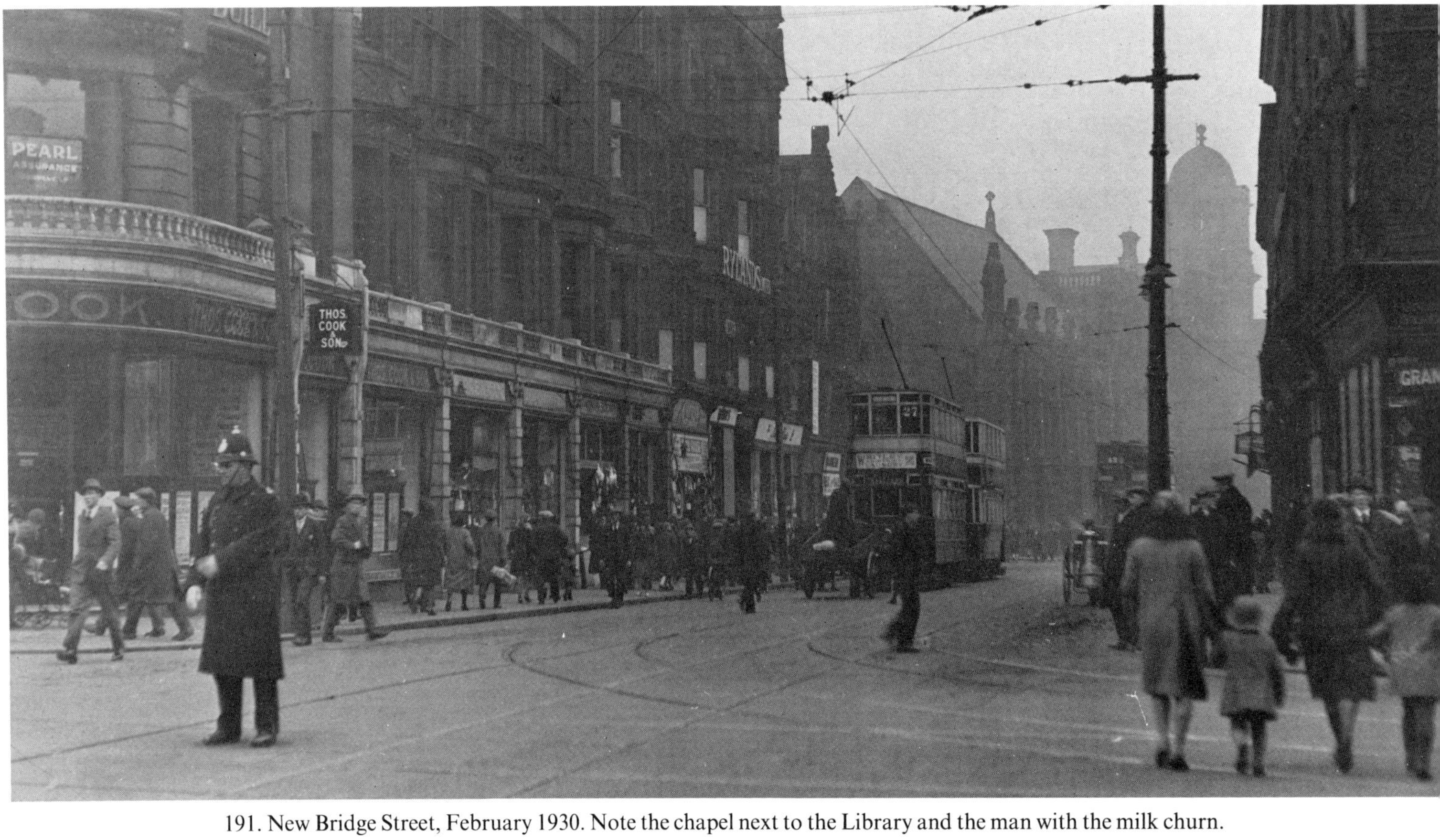

191. New Bridge Street, February 1930. Note the chapel next to the Library and the man with the milk churn.

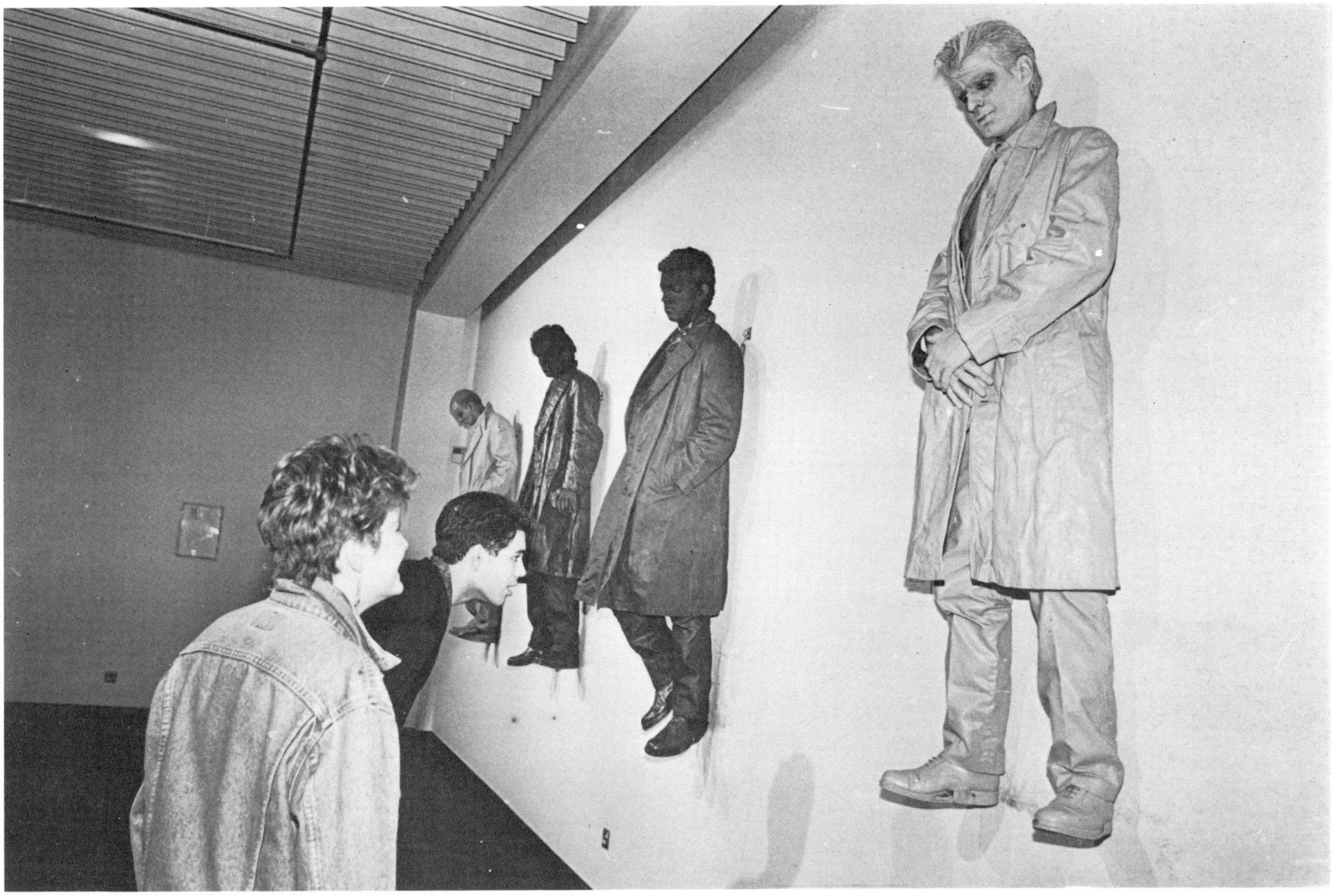

192. Probably one of the most unusual assignments that David Whestone was sent to cover was at the Laing Art Gallery in March 1986. The sight that greeted our intrepid reporter was of four men; two sprayed head to foot in brown dye and two in grey, who were giving a performance called Living Paintings.

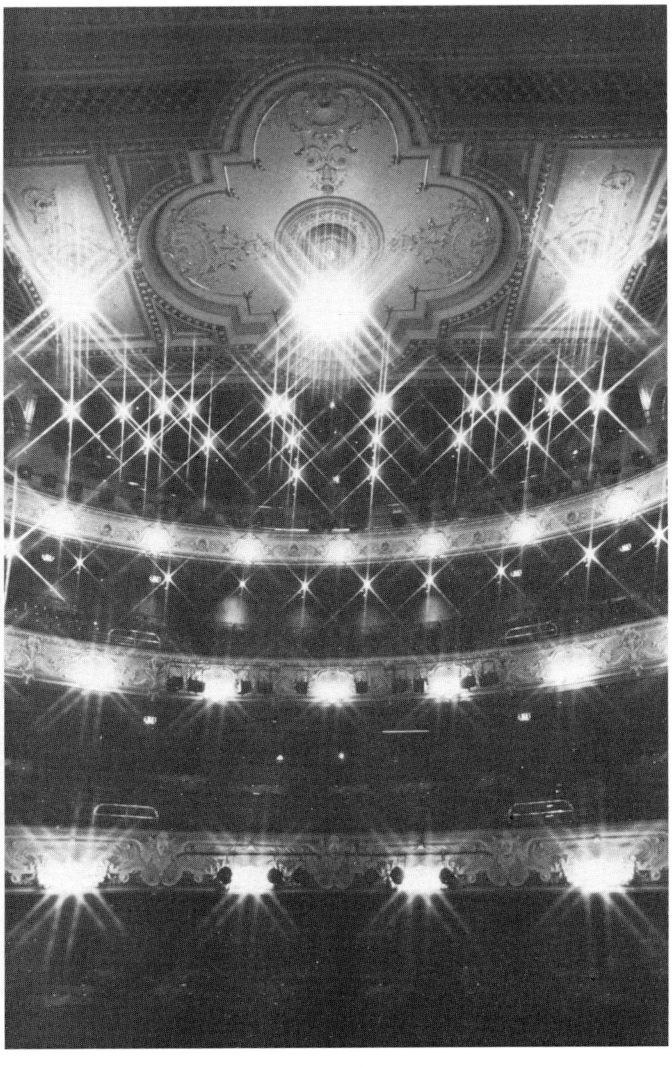

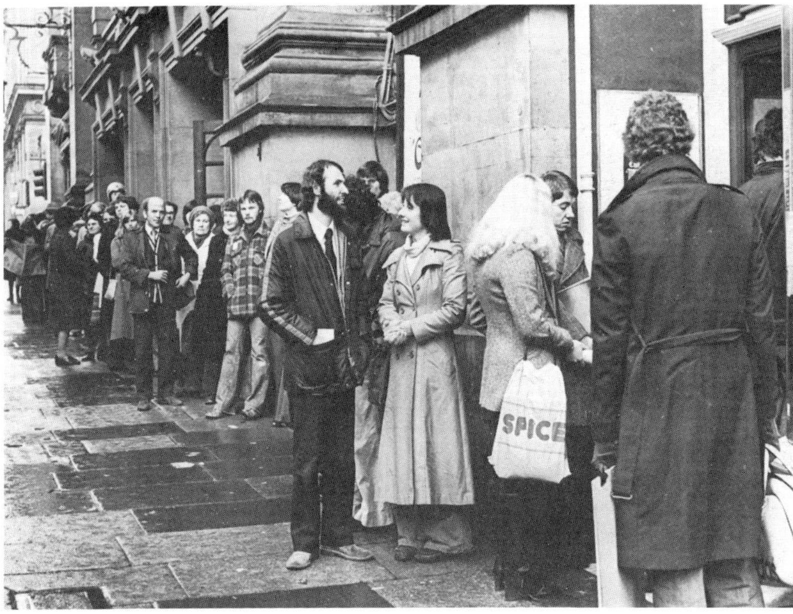

194. In December 1977 hundreds of Northerners queued in freezing weather for tickets to see the Royal Shakespeare Company. In the first week of selling, ticket sales hit the £24,000 mark, all the more remarkable for the RSC's visit was still three months away.

193. *Left:* The revamped four circles and refurbished ceiling at the Theatre Royal. January 1988.

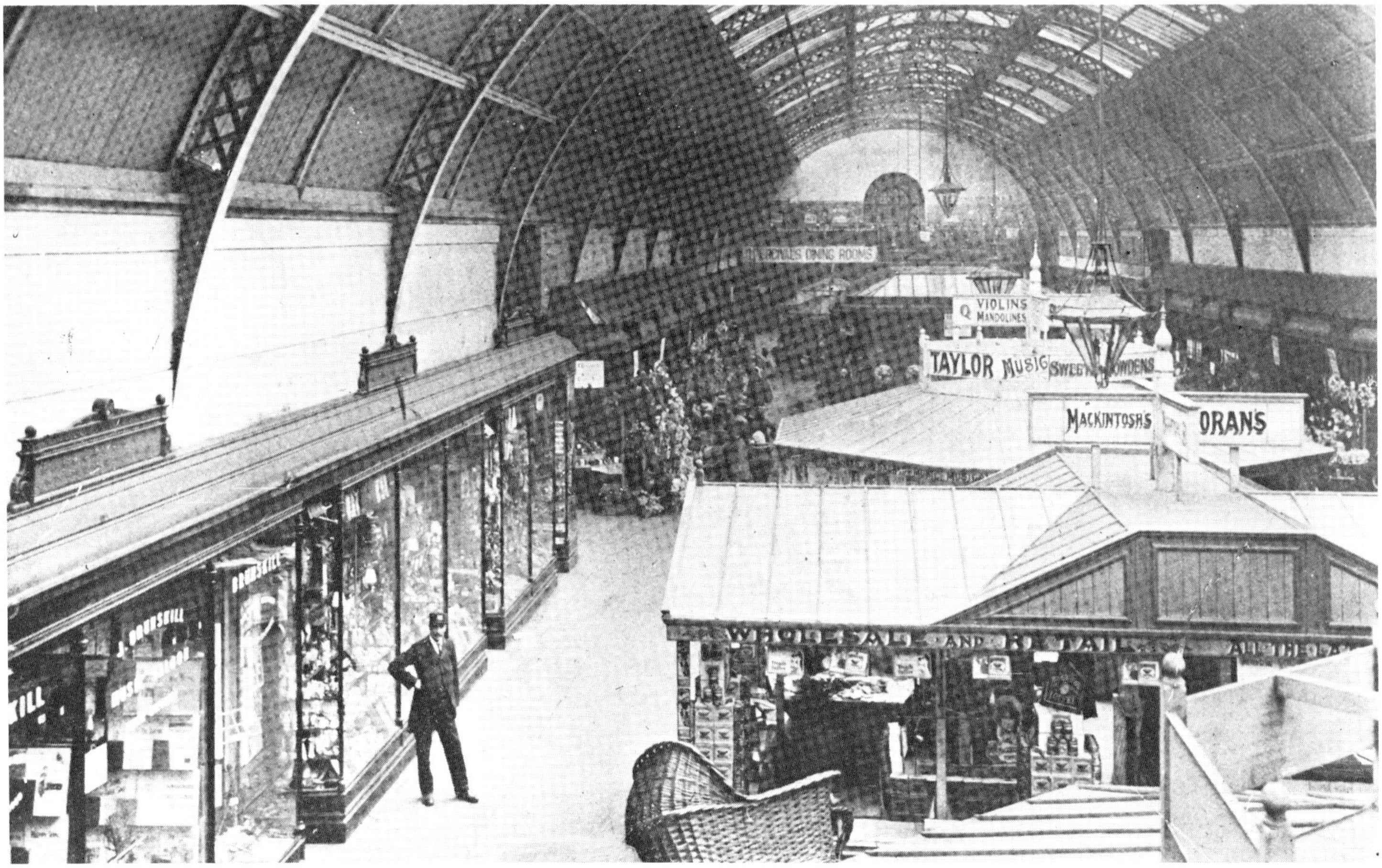

195-196. Grainger Market at the turn of the century and *below* in 1960 when *Evening Chronicle* photographer Lawrie Wilson popped in to snap this typical day to day shot.

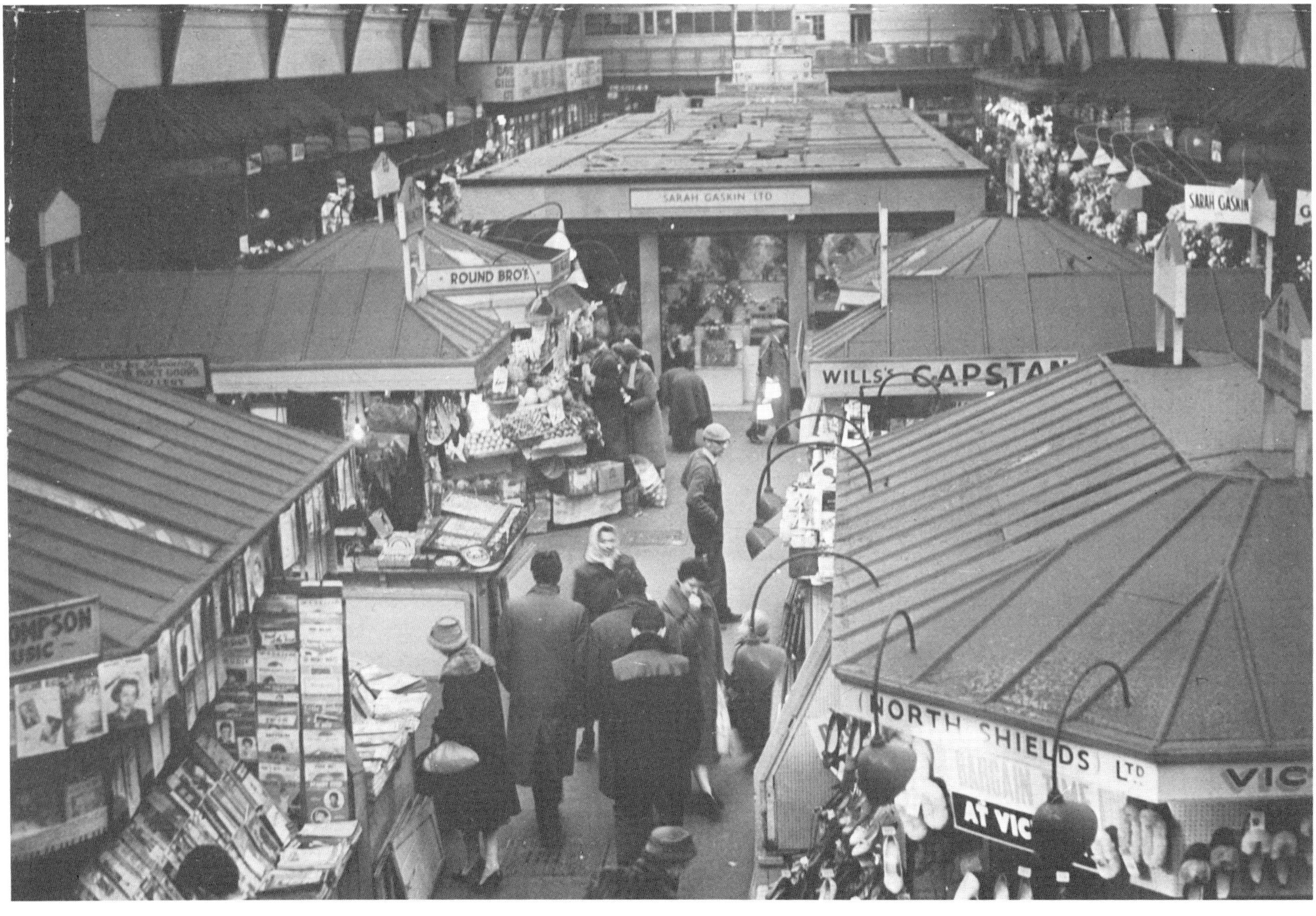

197. Binns as it looked in September 1953.

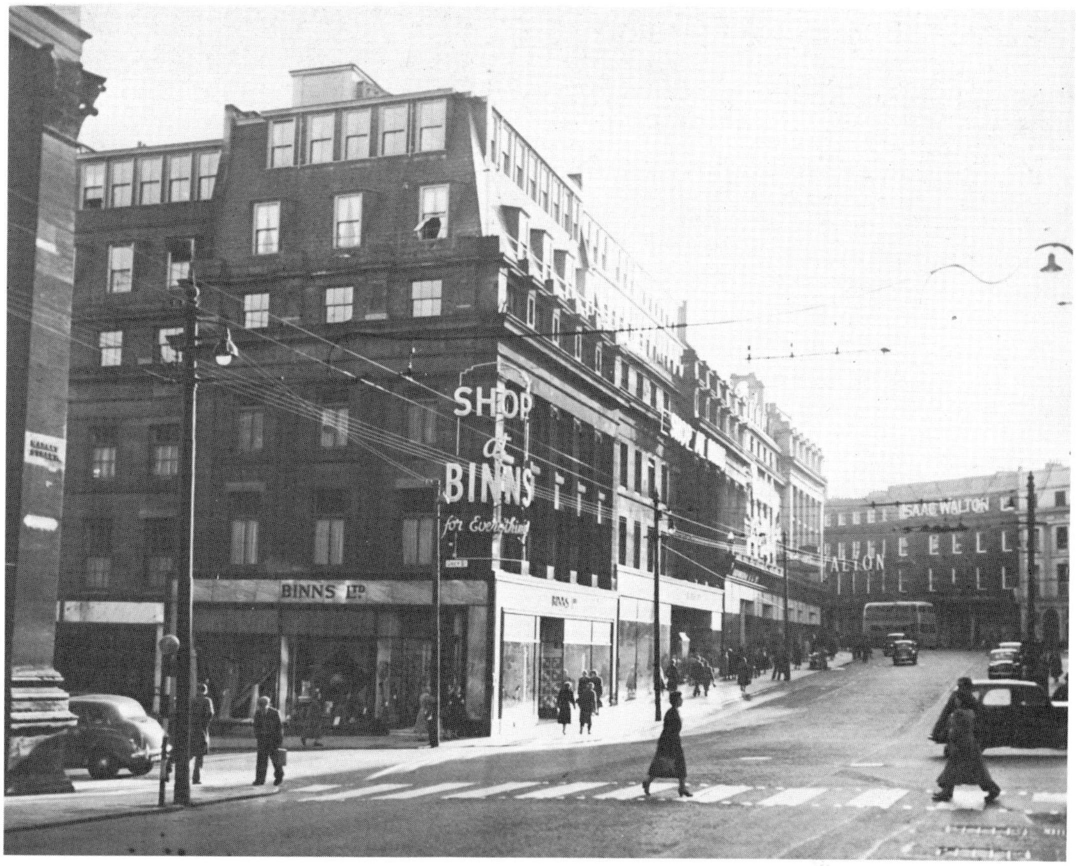

198. It was all go-go-go at Bainbridge's store in Market Street in October 1976, when more than 1,000 staff helped move goods to the new premises in the Eldon Square development. In the day-long trek, delivery vans, shopping trolleys and cardboard boxes were pressed into service.

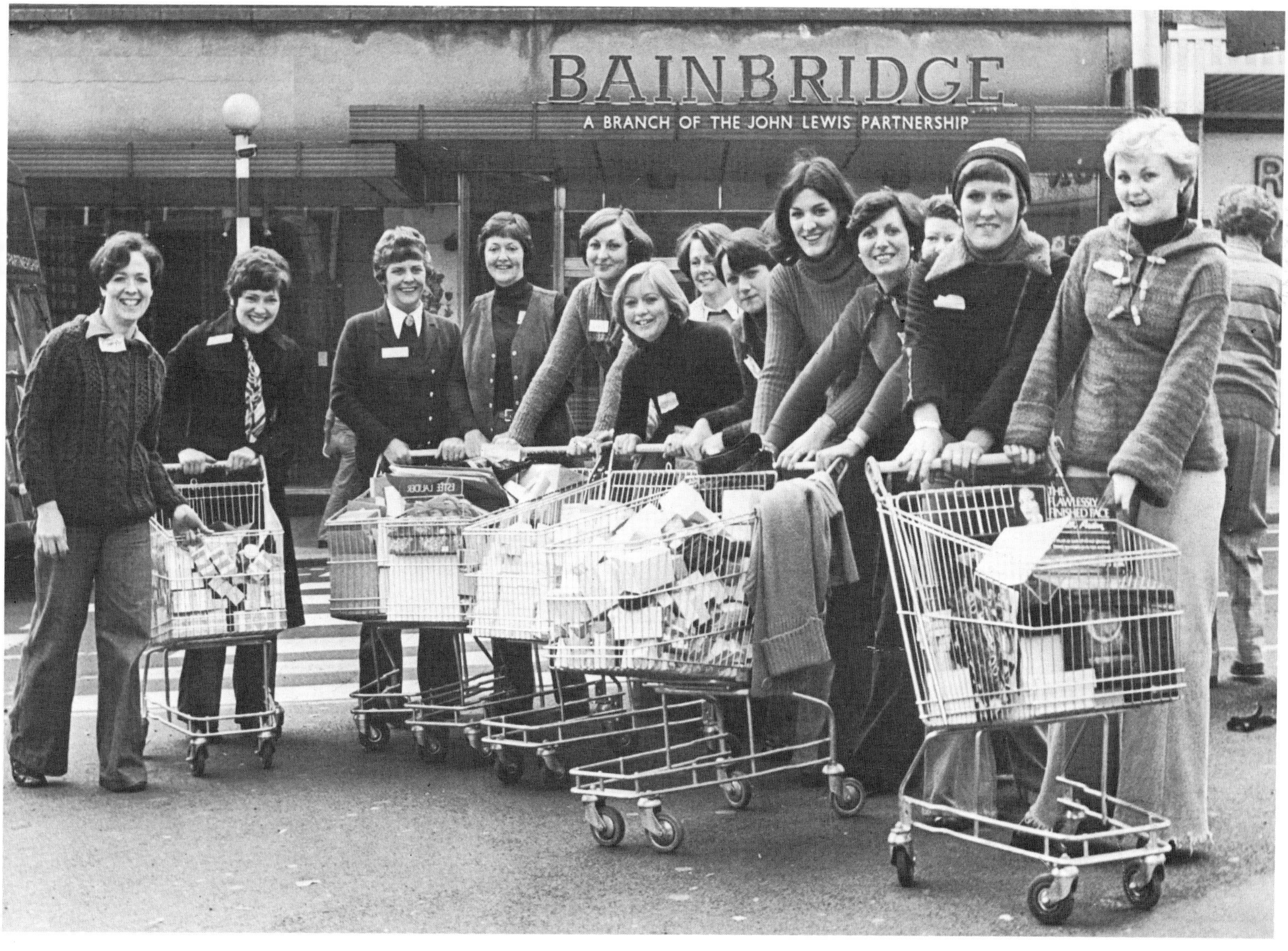

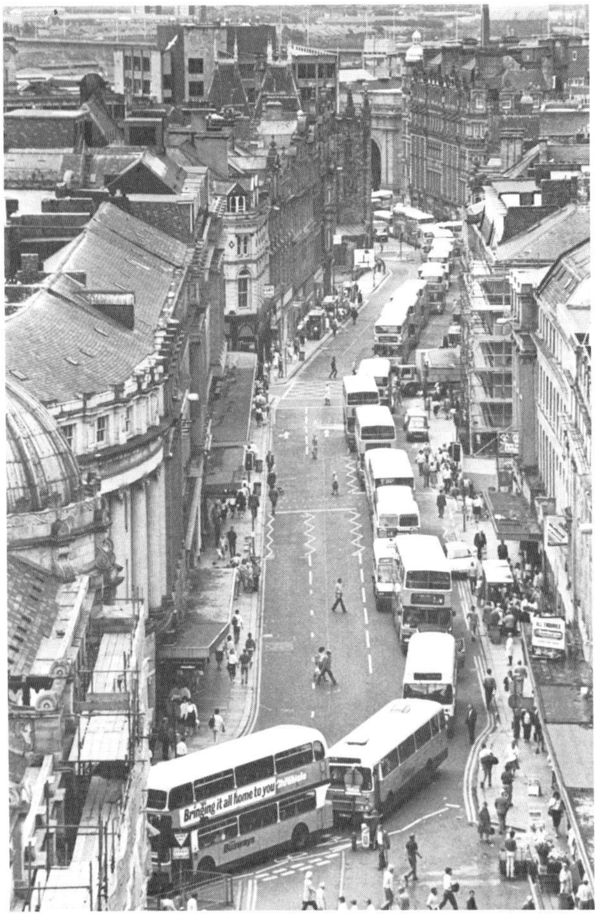

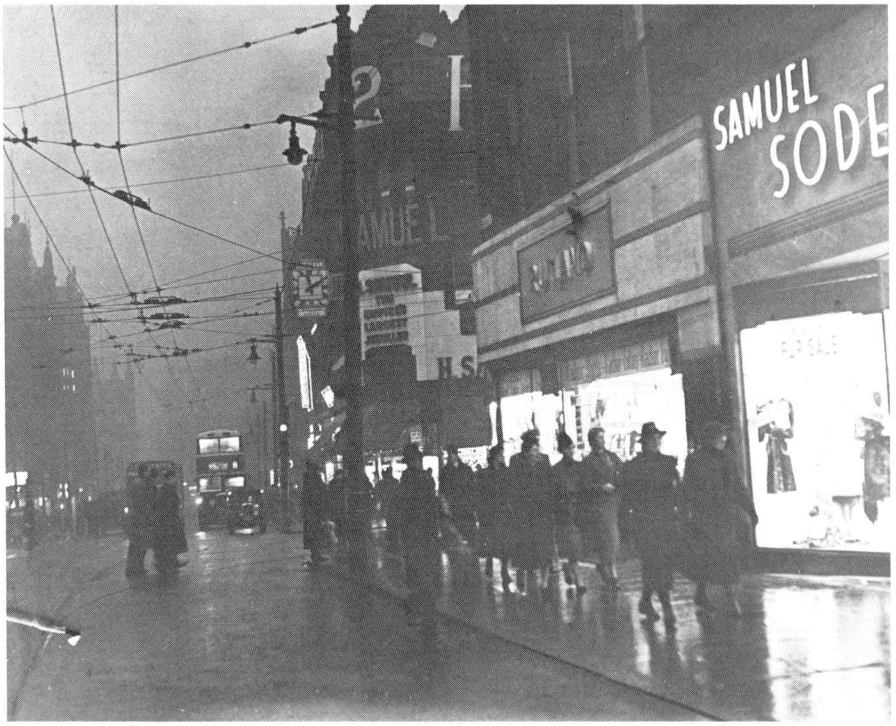

200. Grainger Street on 19 January 1939. If you want to know the time, look at H Samuel's clock. It's the afternoon and this is a fog 'black-out'.

199. *Left:* Journal photographer Paul Dodds climbed Grey's Monument to capture this scene of buses packed bumper to bumper in Grainger Street in the traffic chaos caused by the start of the 1988 Kellogg's Tour of Britain Cycle Race. The city was brought to a virtual standstill for about three hours.

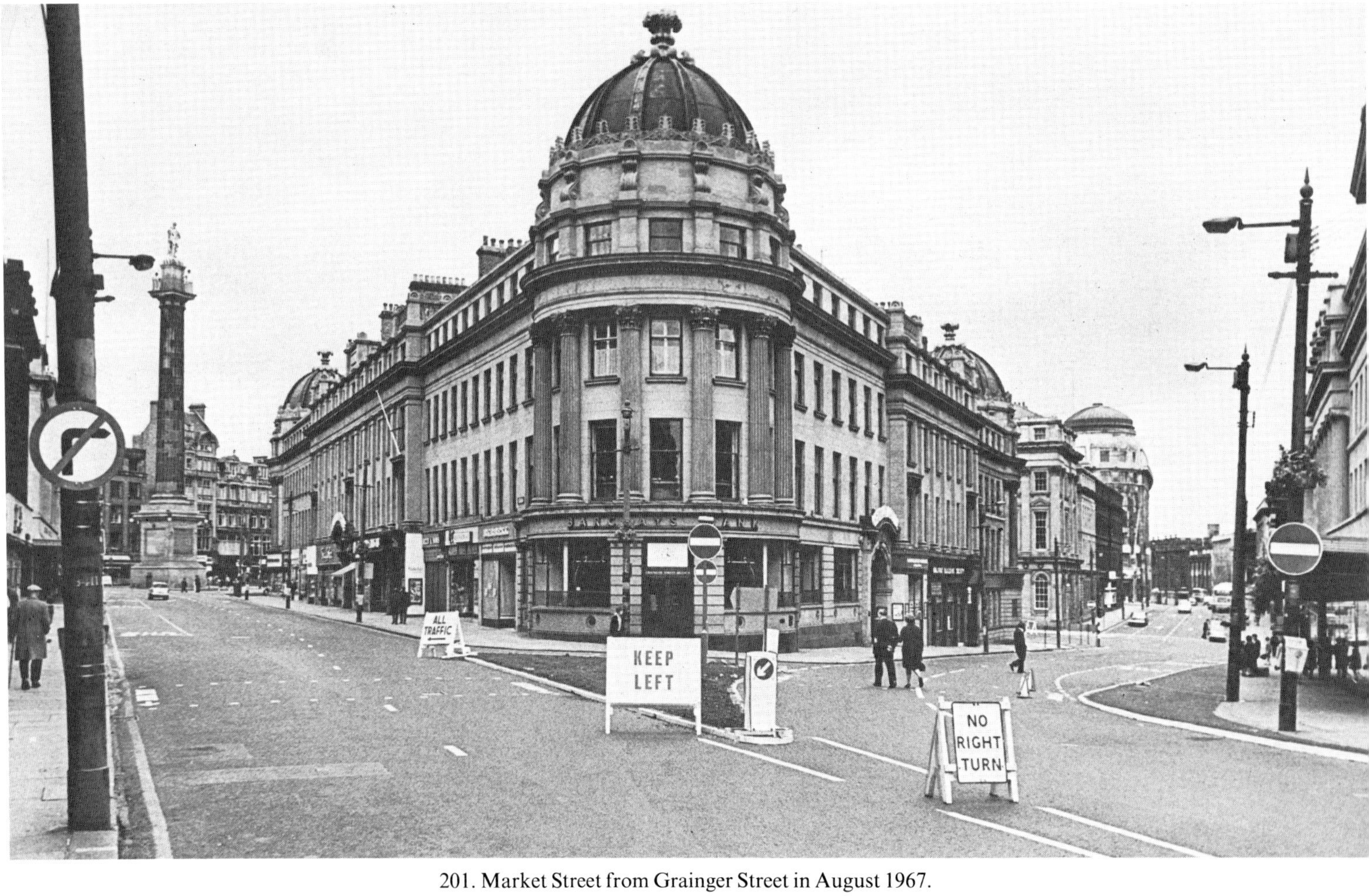

201. Market Street from Grainger Street in August 1967.

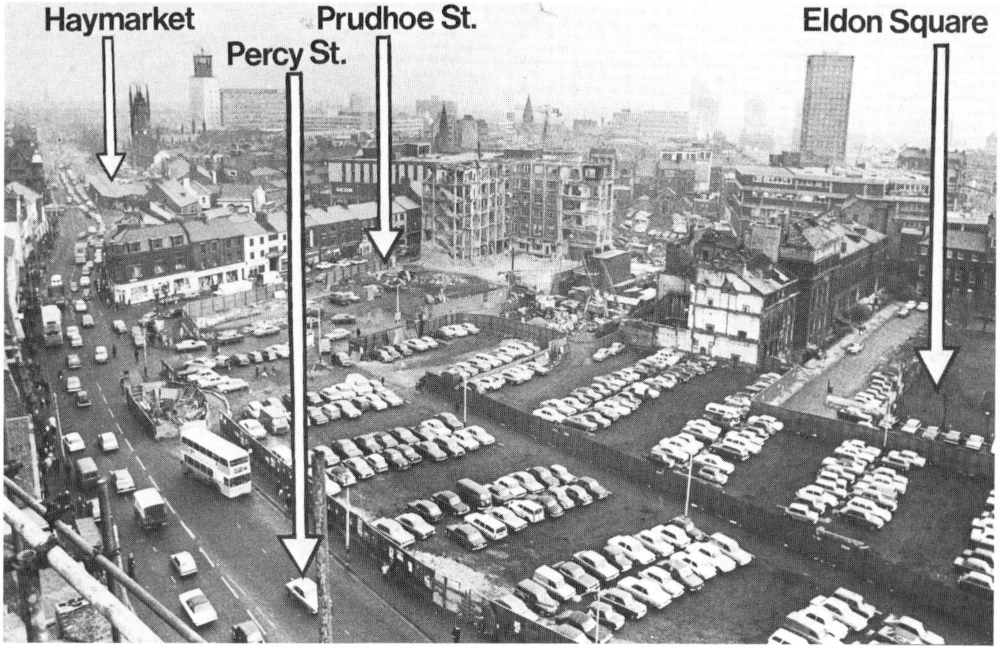

202. This picture was published in the *Evening Chronicle* in December 1972, showing the site of the Eldon Square shopping centre development just three or four days before the first builders began work. Work on the shopping centre was bad news for motorists. At a stroke, parking on Prudhoe Street, Eldon Square and 'Park Place' disappeared, soon to be followed by Prudhoe Street East.

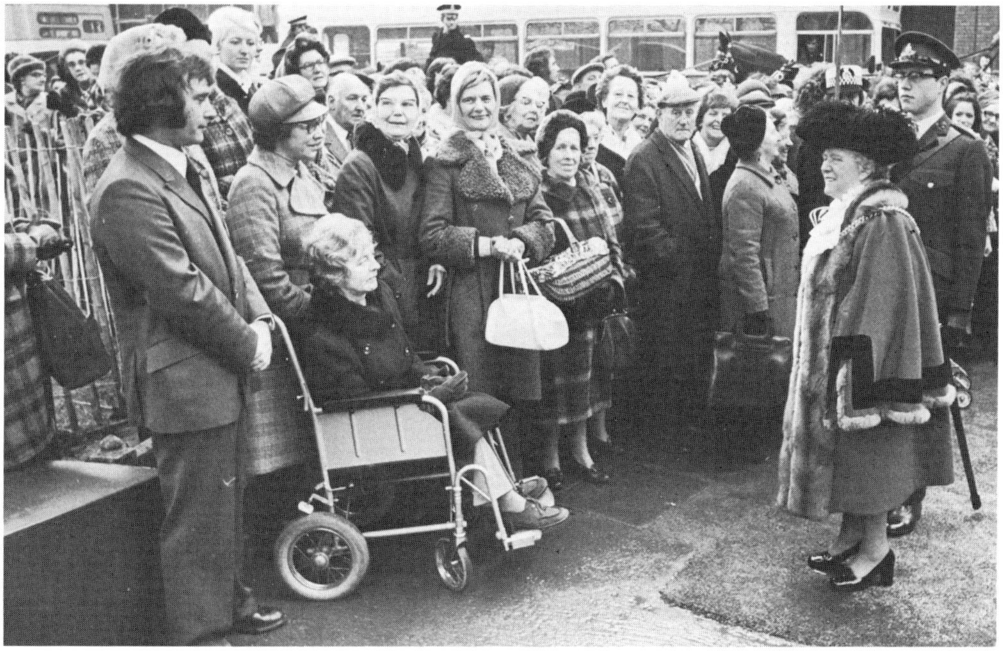

203. The Lord Mayor, Councillor Iris Steedman has a word with some of the large crowd at the official opening of Eldon Square in March 1976.

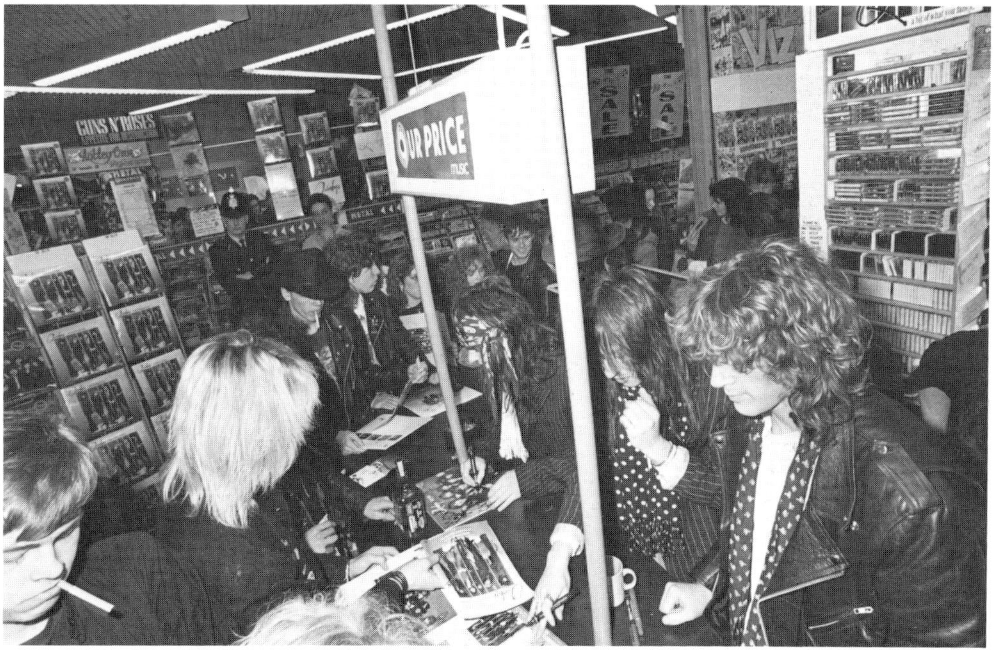

204. Eldon Square, February 1990. Local band, the Quireboys, meet their fans at Our Price.

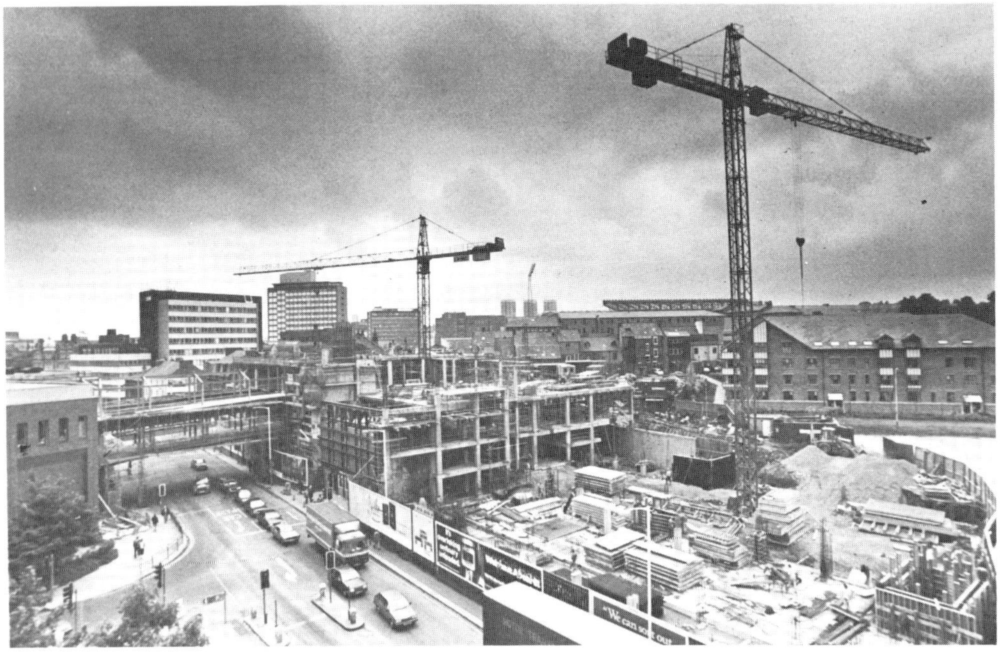

205. July 1988. Another sign of enterprise on Tyneside as a bridge is erected over Percy Street to link a new shopping development on the site of the old Handysides Arcade with the well-established Eldon Square centre. The photograph was taken from the top of the multi-storey car park.

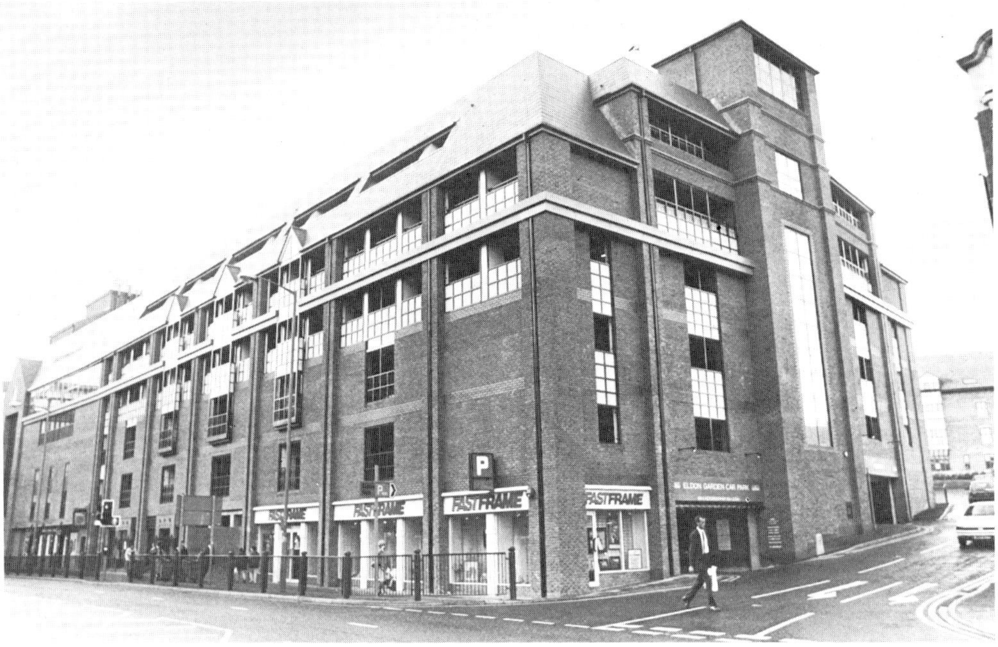

206. Eldon Gardens in October 1989.

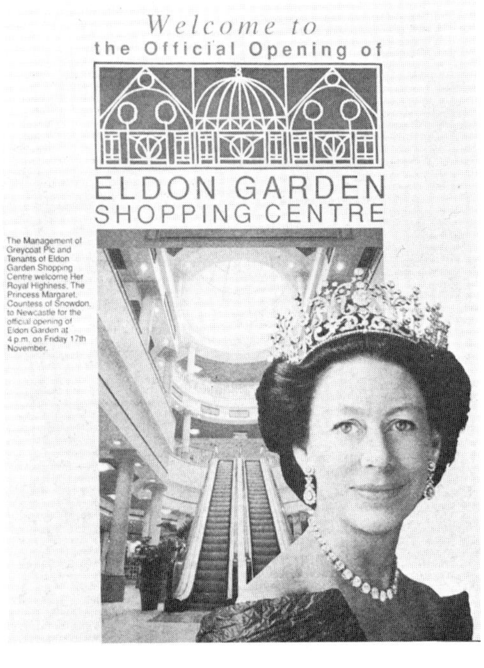
Welcome to
the Official Opening of
ELDON GARDEN
SHOPPING CENTRE

The Management of Greycoat Plc and Tenants of Eldon Garden Shopping Centre welcome Her Royal Highness, The Princess Margaret, Countess of Snowdon, to Newcastle for the official opening of Eldon Garden at 4 p.m. on Friday 17th November.

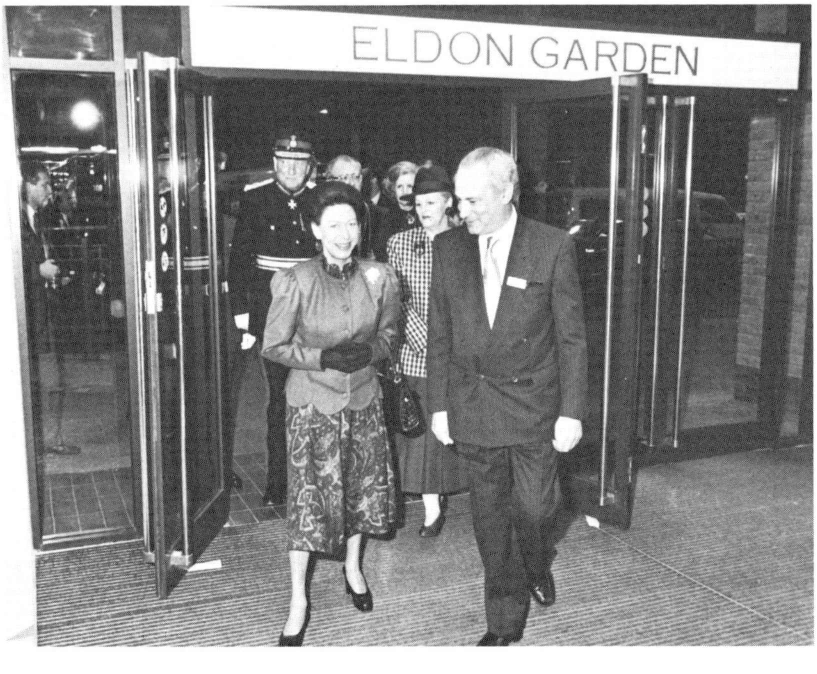

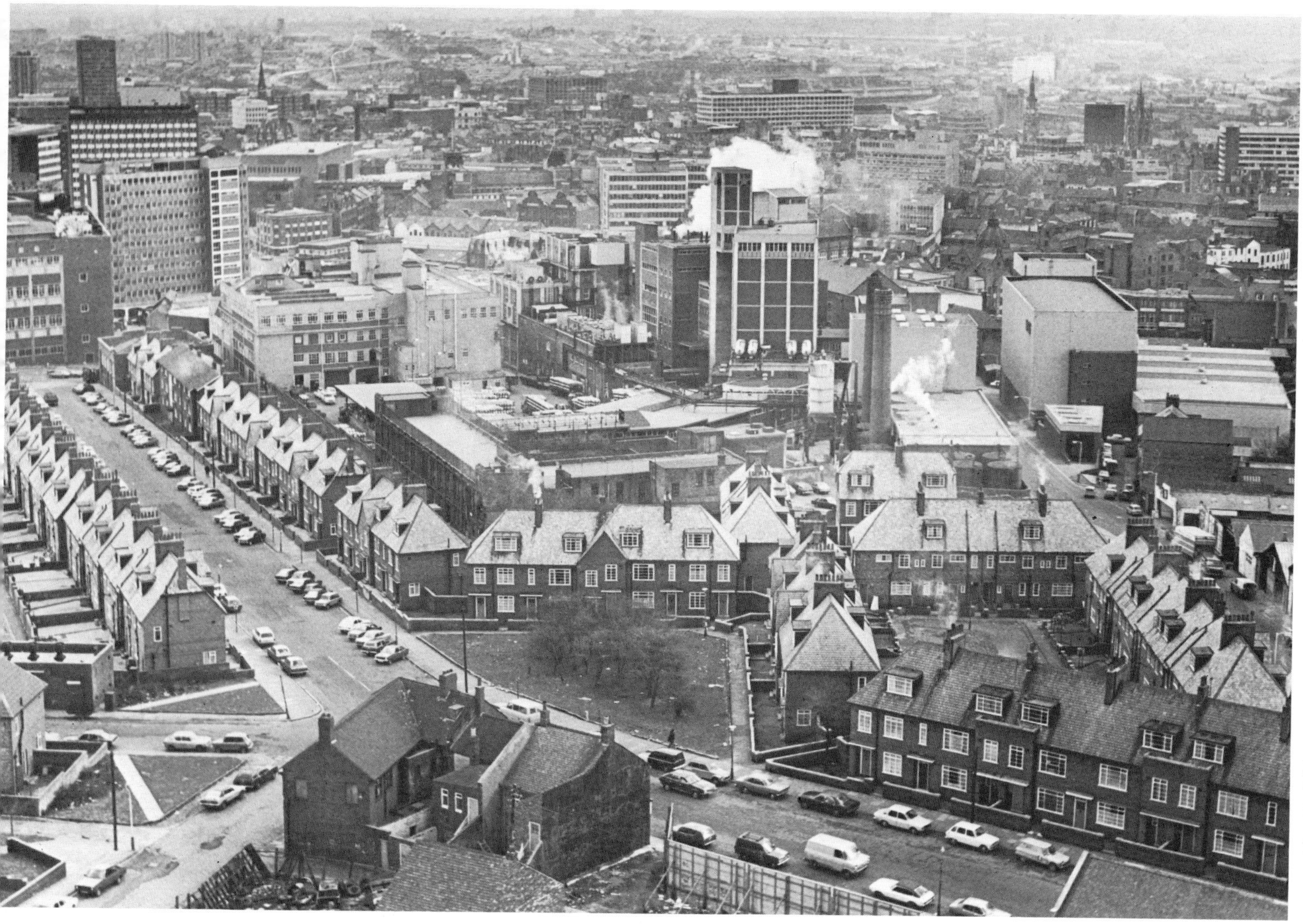

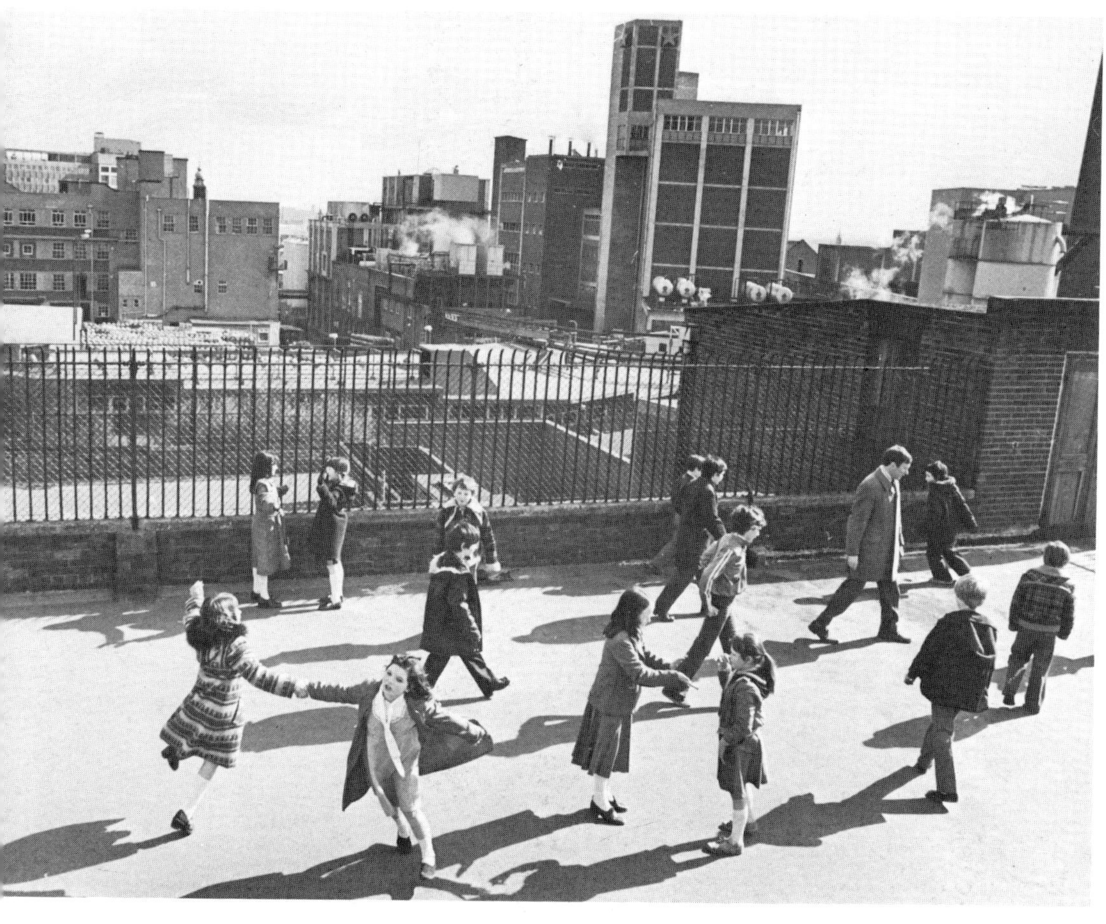

209. Scottish and Newcastle Breweries in April 1979 when a £10 million expansion scheme was announced.

210. In April 1979 it was announced that St Mary's Infant and Junior School, at the heart of the area of the proposed S and N development, would become virtually surrounded by brewery buildings. The idea might have sounded totally dotty but it was nothing new. Fifty years earlier one of S and N's predecessors had embarked on an expansion programme that encroached on St Cuthbert's Grammar School in Bath Lane. However, the school moved out to the then open countryside of Benwell Hill.

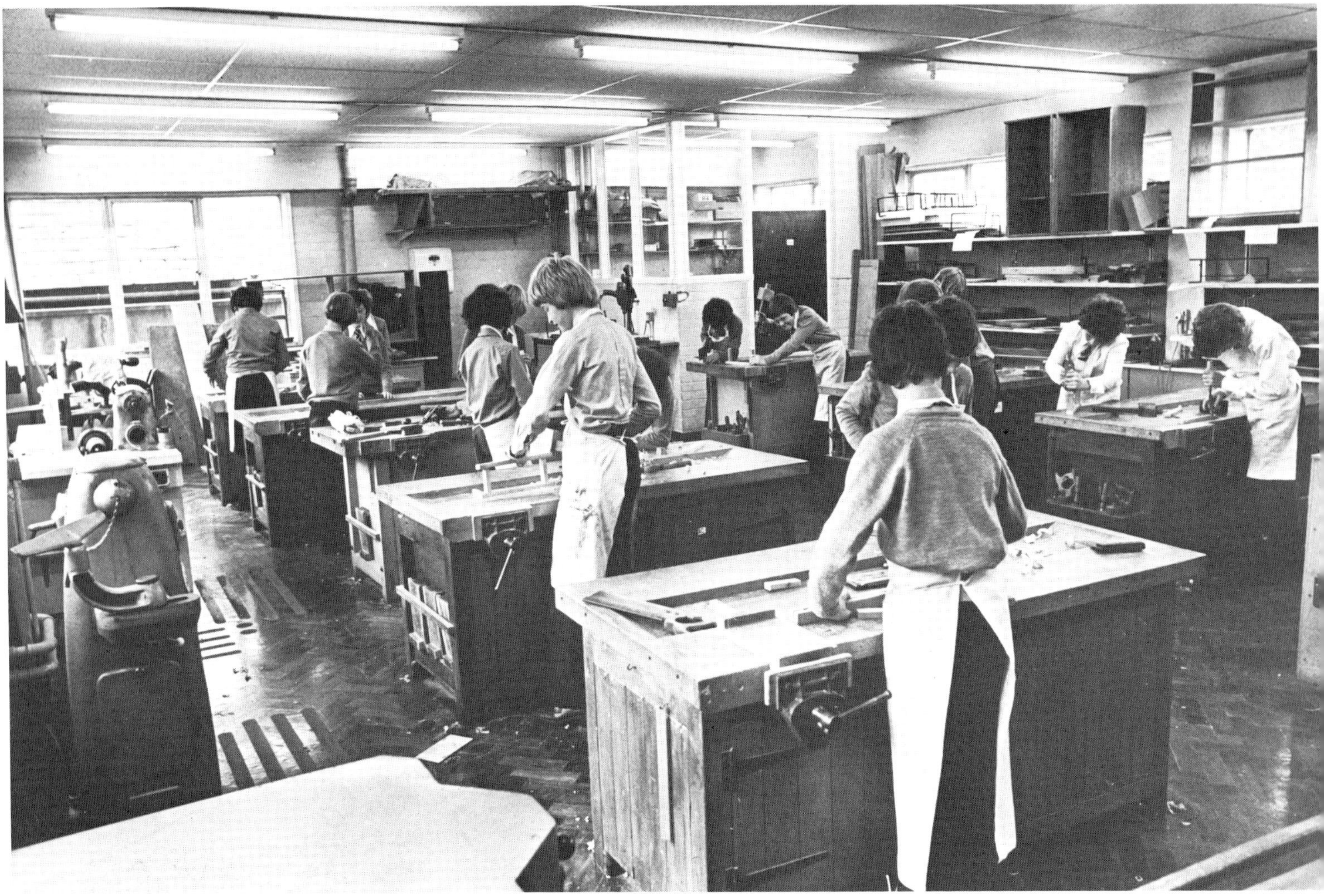

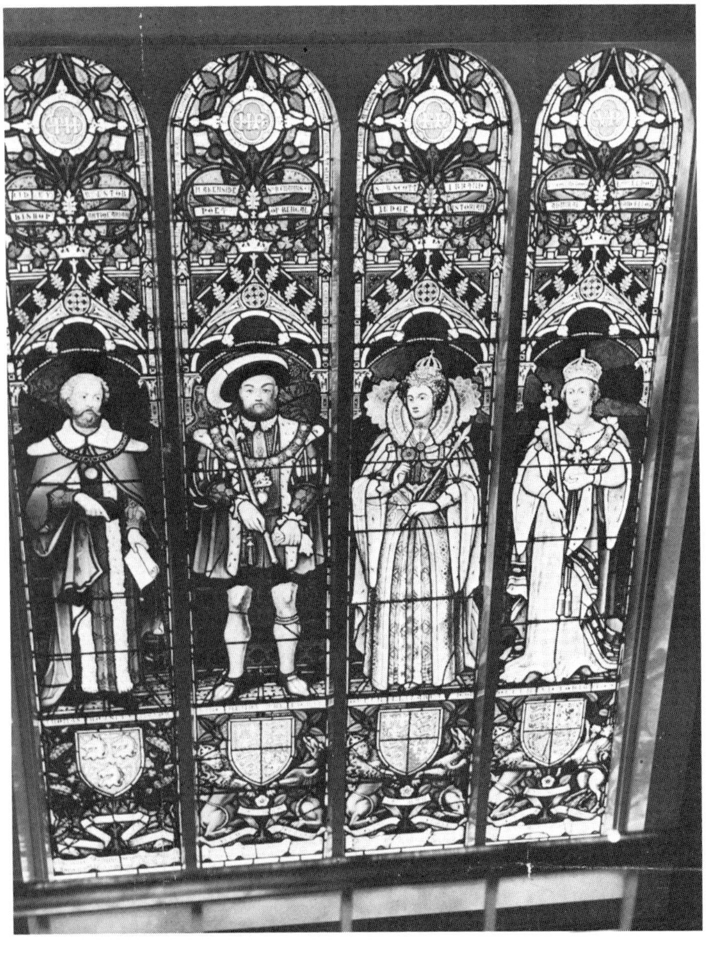

211. Budding DIY at the Royal Grammar School? During its long history, the RGS has had several homes. From its founding up until 1607 the school was housed in St Nicholas' Churchyard, when it was then moved to the Virgin Mary Hospital. The school moved again in 1844 for a five-year sojourn at Forth House before taking up residence in Charlotte Square in 1848. In 1870 the school moved yet again, this time to Rye Hill where it stayed until 1906 when Eskdale Terrace became its home.

212. *Left:* The stained-glass window transferred in 1956 to the RGS from Rutherford High School for Girls which was once the RGS building. It depicts RGS founder Thomas Horsley, Henry VIII, Elizabeth I, who granted the school its charter, and Queen Victoria.

213. The main hall at the RGS.

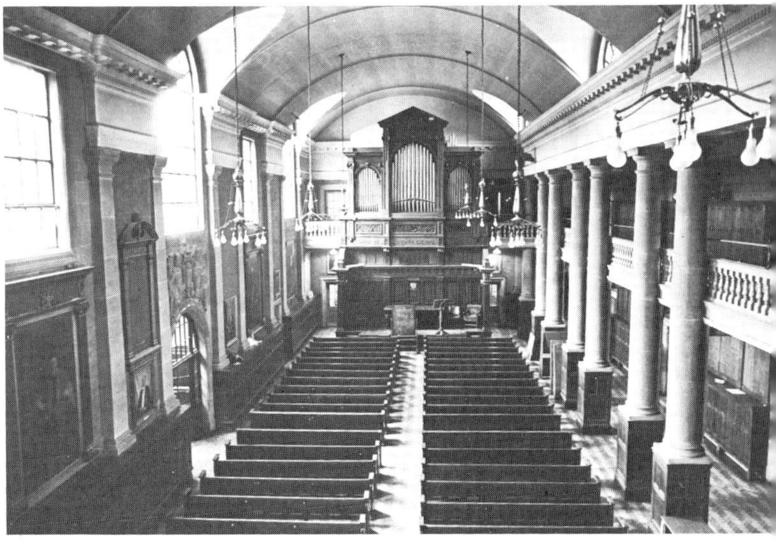

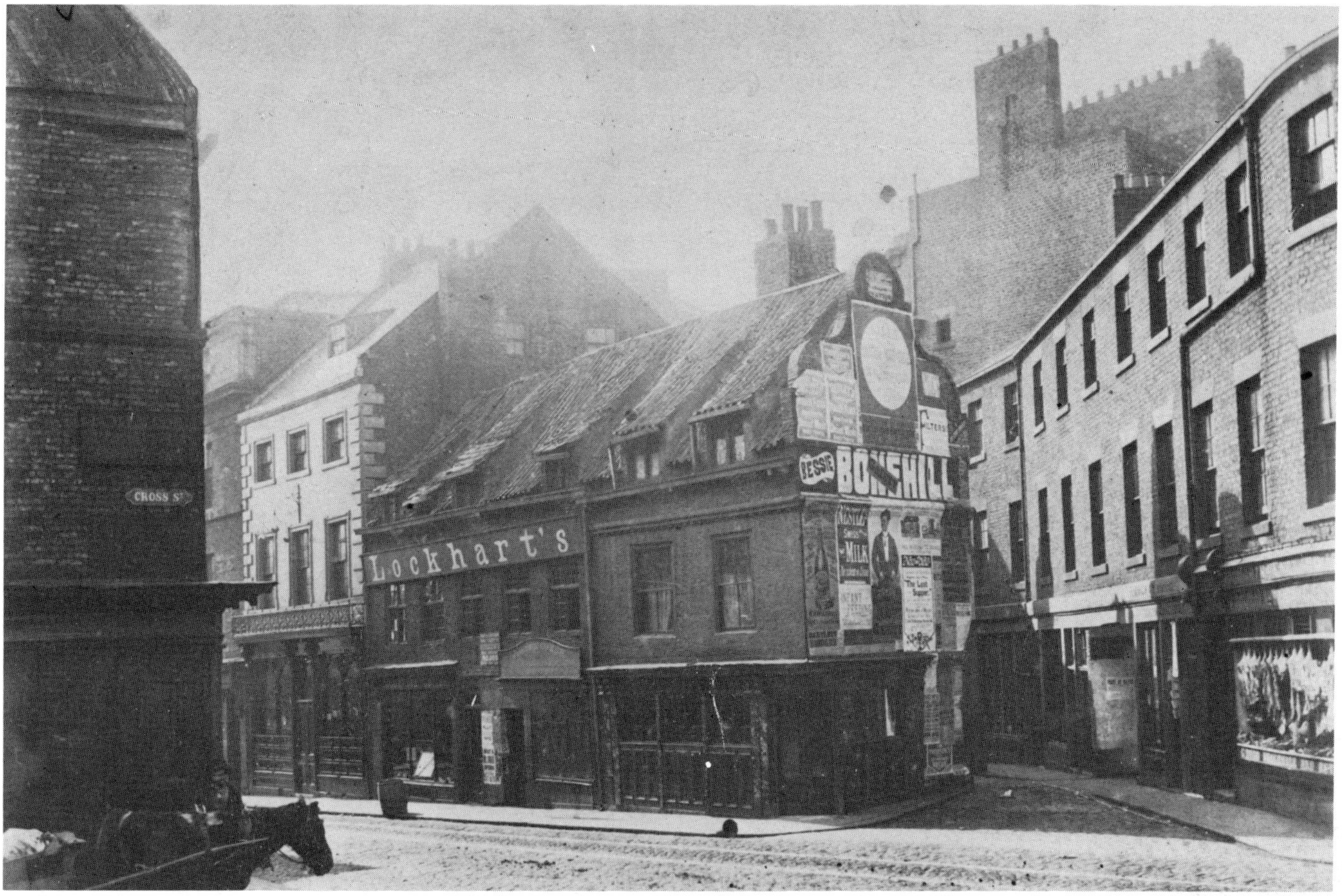

214. The original Lockhart's Cocoa Rooms pictured when they first opened in Westgate Road in 1891.

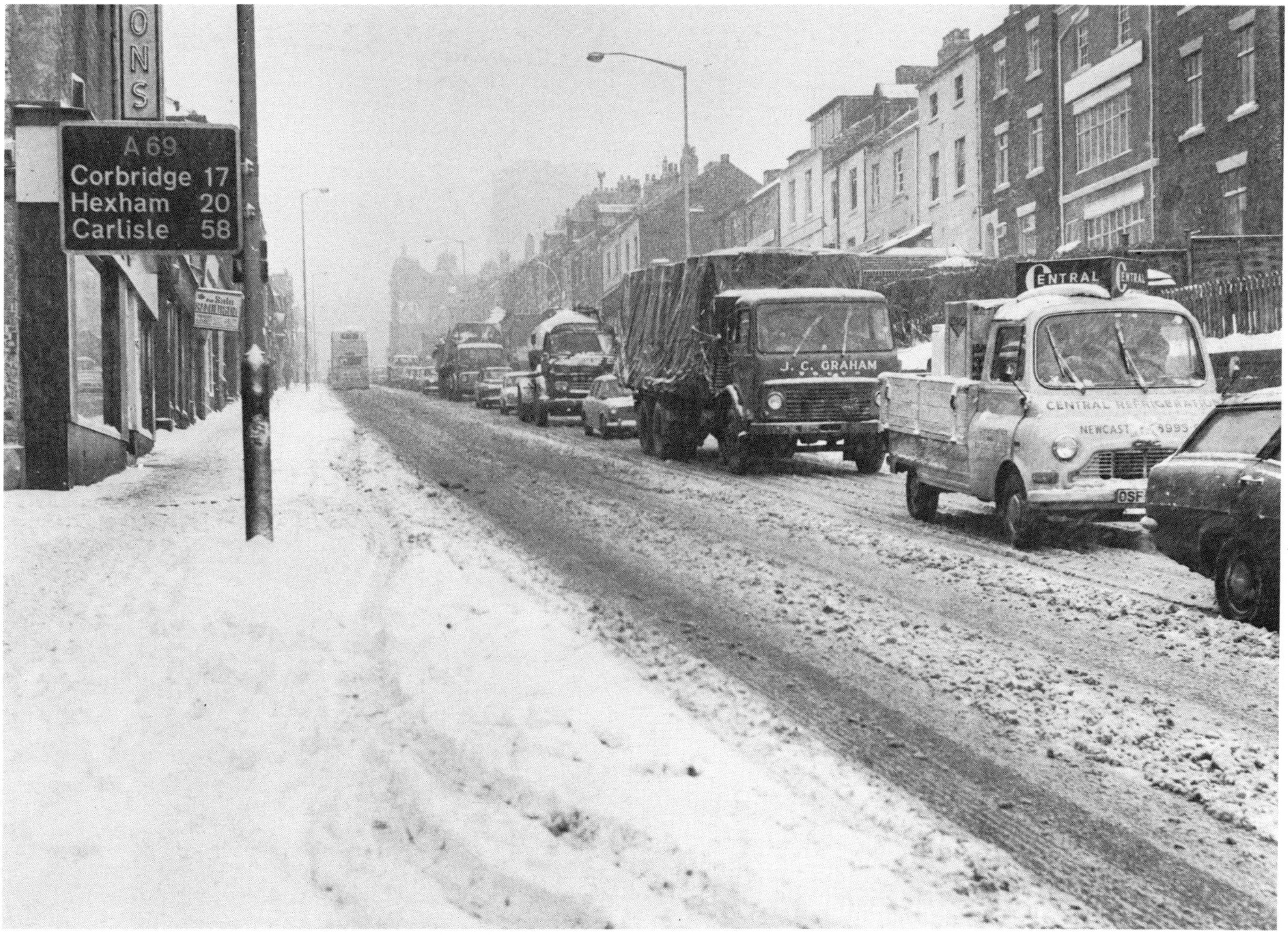

215. Snow in February 1970 brings a nose-to-tail traffic jam in Westgate Road.

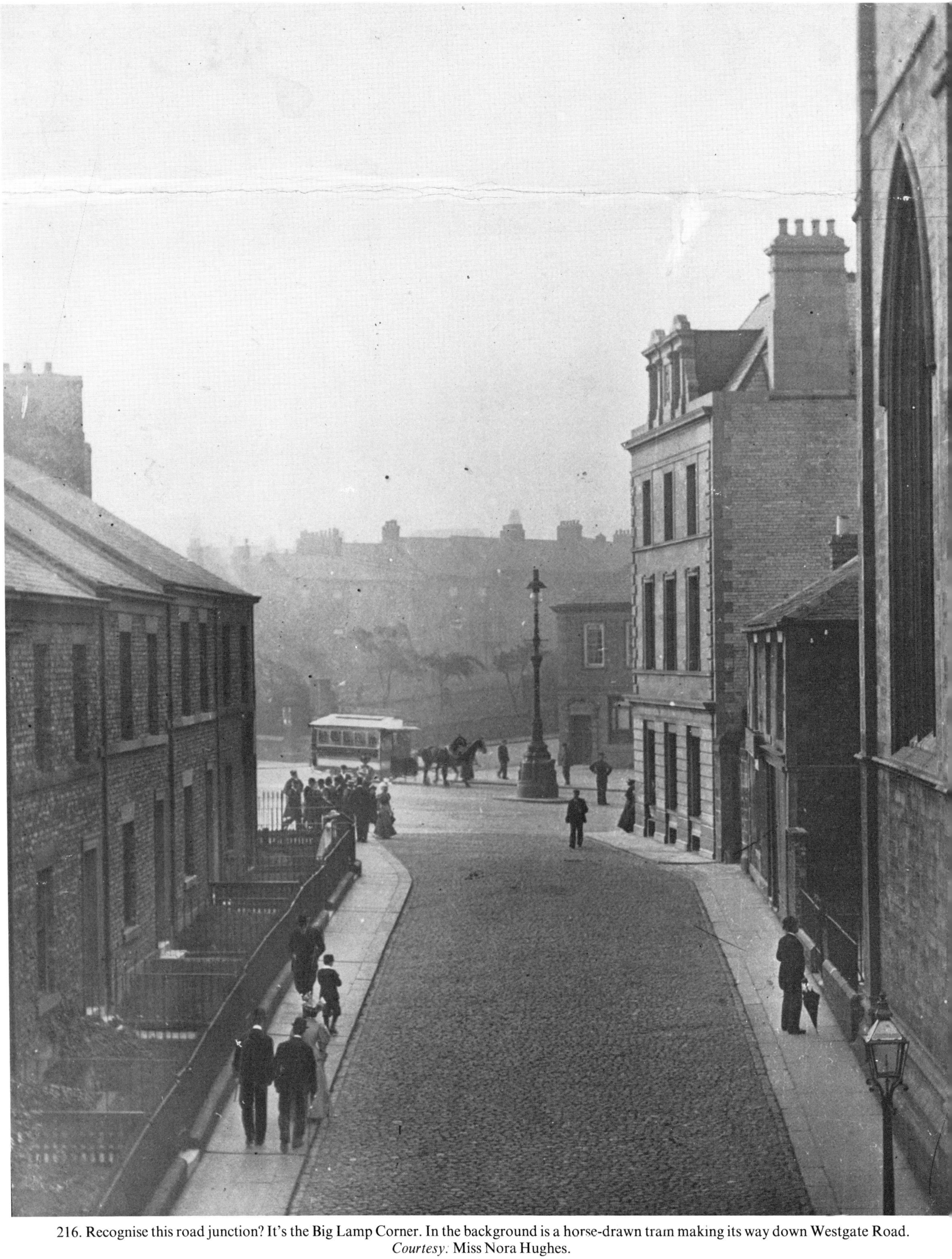

216. Recognise this road junction? It's the Big Lamp Corner. In the background is a horse-drawn tram making its way down Westgate Road.
Courtesy: Miss Nora Hughes.

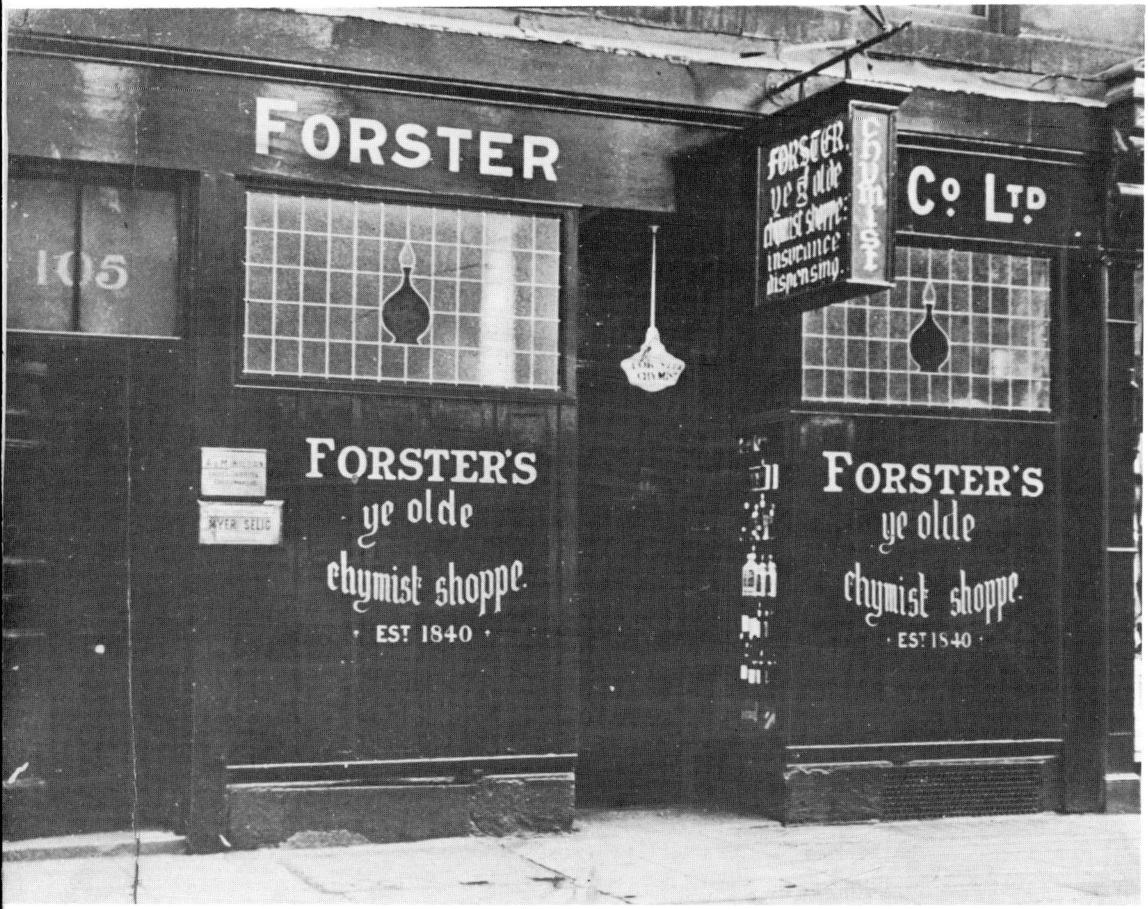

217. Forster's chemists shop in Clayton Street in December 1931 was in the news because the shutters had remained up for more than sixty years. The shop, known locally as *Dirty Dicks*, finally closed its doors in 1972. It holds the unique record of being the only shop in Britain never to have taken its shutters down in over 100 years.

218. Farnons were 111-years-old in 1978 but definitely kept their shutters down. As part of the store's celebrations, members of staff dressed in costumes depicting the various generations served by Farnons, ranging from the elegance of Edwardian England to the 'flappers' of the Charleston era and lots more besides. Here, our 'flappers' get ready to Charleston their way in to Farnon's shopping festival.

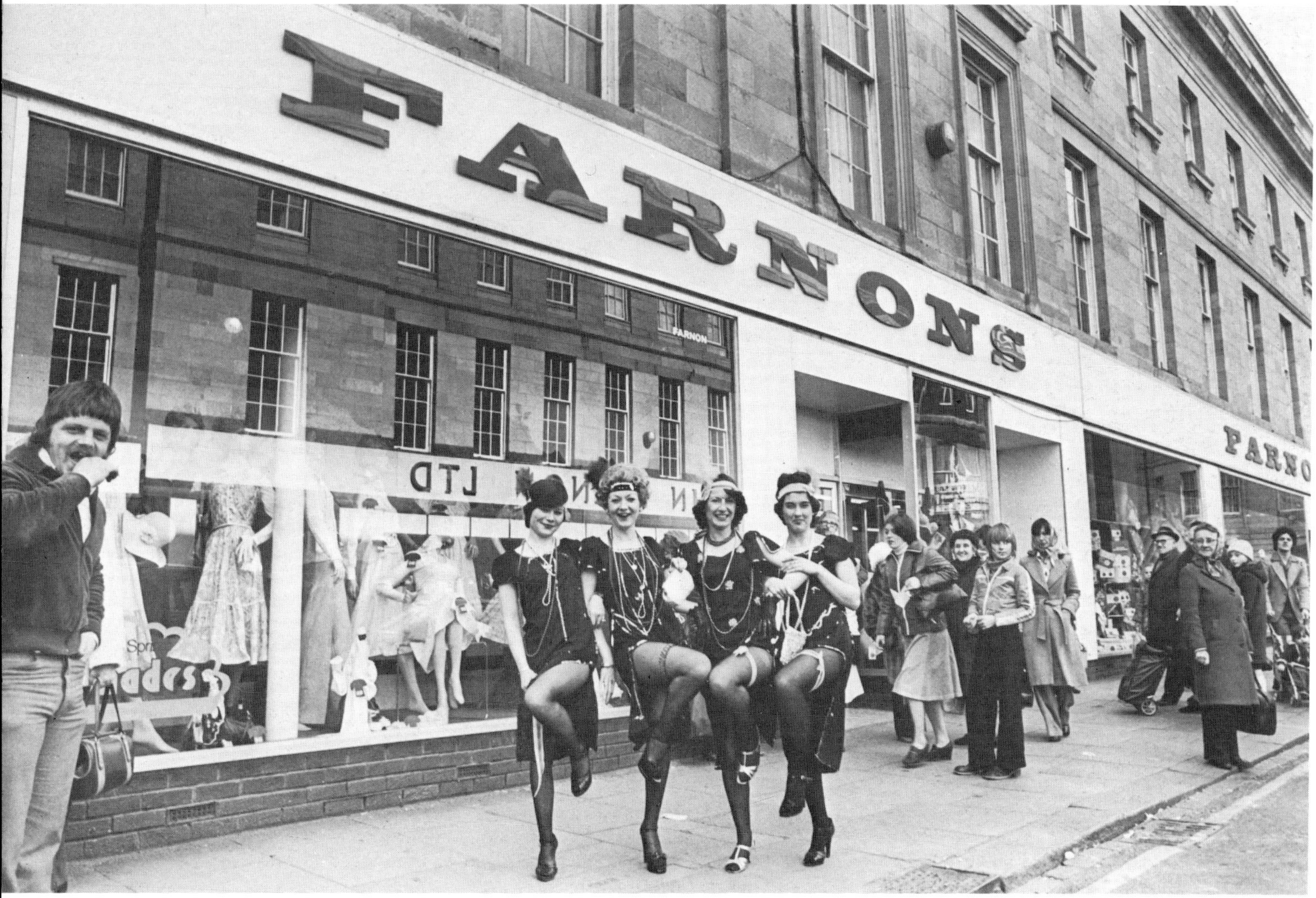

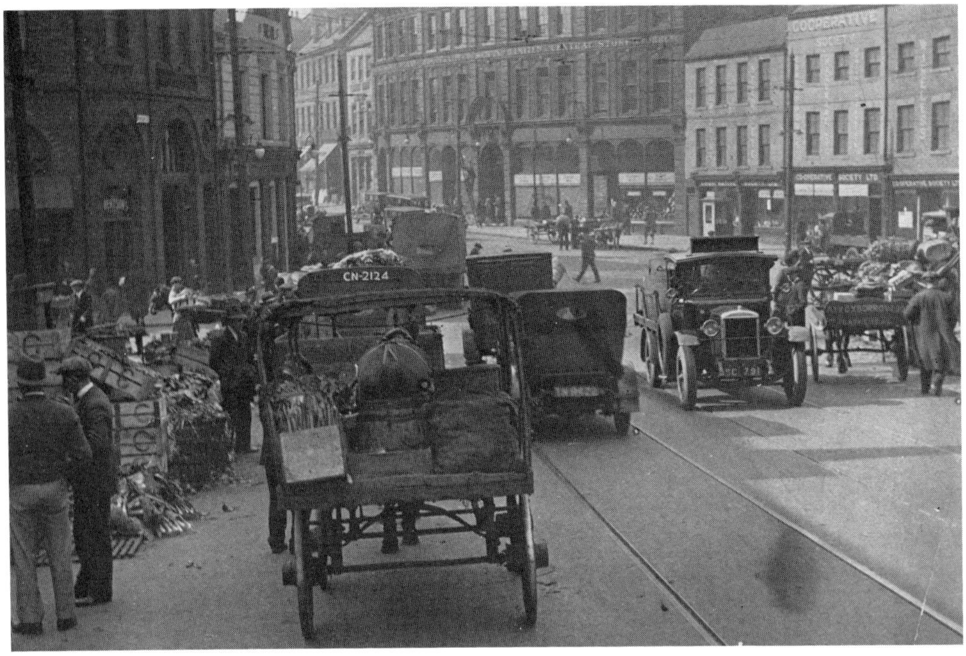

219. This photograph dates from May 1930 and shows the traffic problem created by the vegetable market in Newgate Street as produce was set out on the roadside.

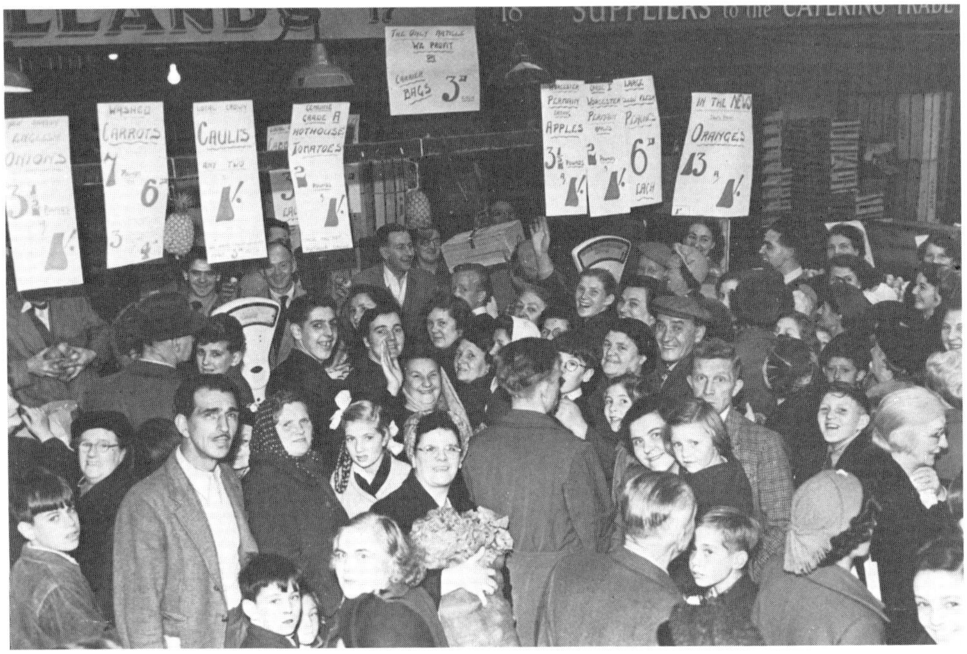

220. Congestion of a different kind as bargain-hunters queue in the Green Market in September 1953.

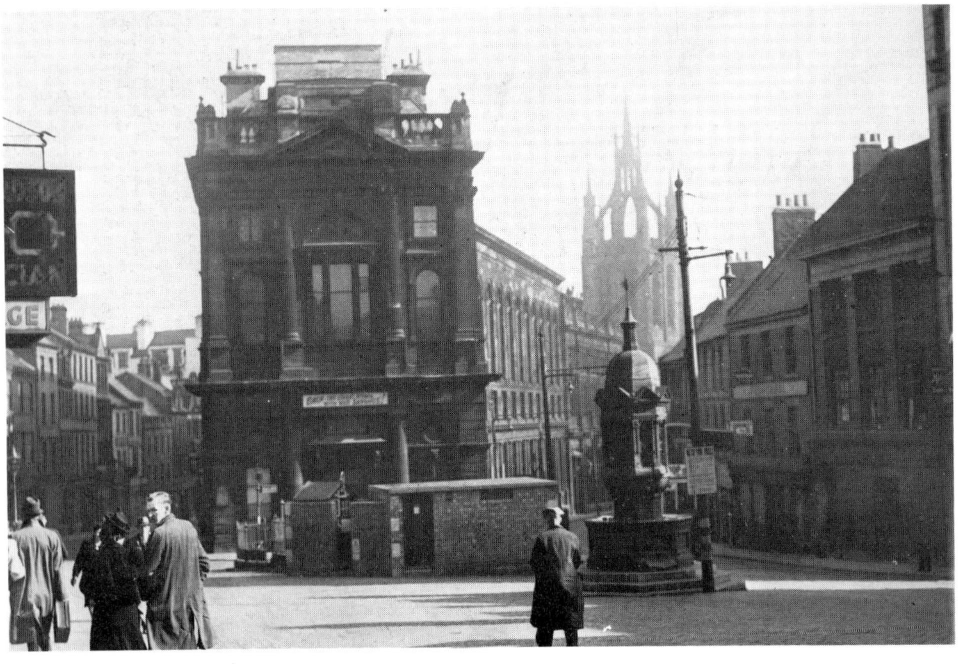

221. Newcastle Town Hall as seen from Bigg Market in April 1945. In July 1939 it was announced that the town hall tower might be demolished if Britain found herself at war. This was because it was felt that the tower might cause casualties if it collapsed as the result of an air raid. The town hall was eventually demolished in 1973.

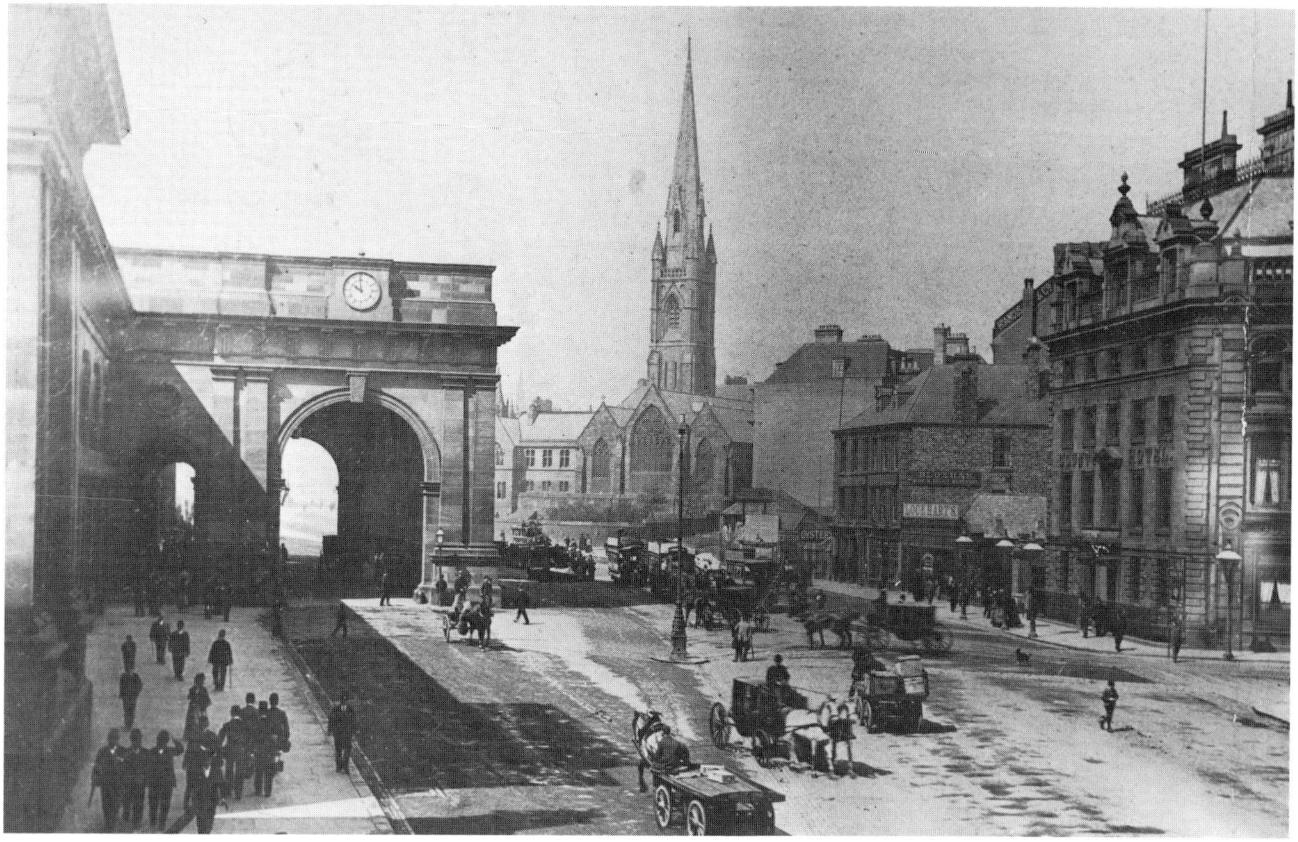

222. Outside the Central Station at some time before the introduction of electric trams in 1901.

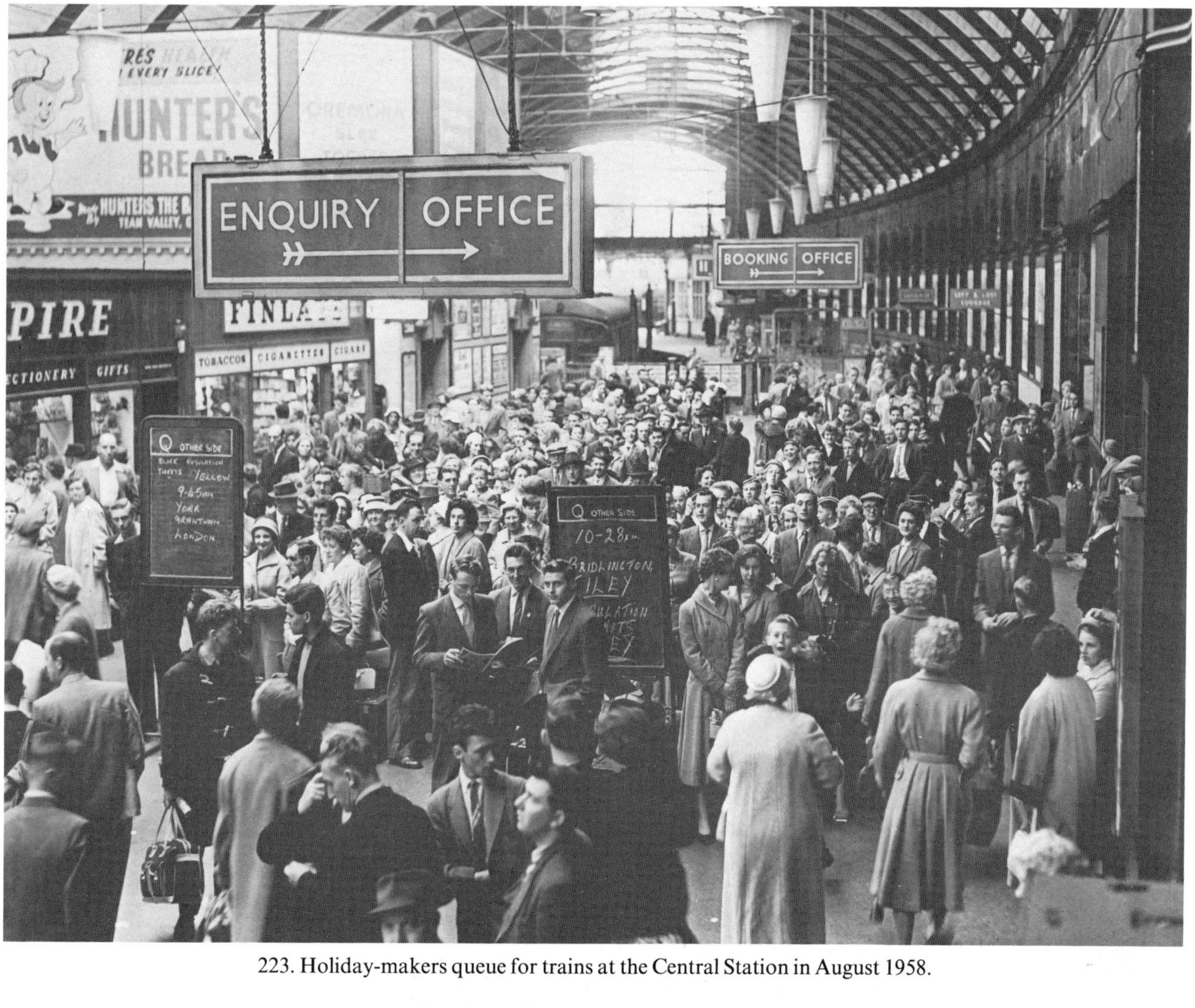

223. Holiday-makers queue for trains at the Central Station in August 1958.

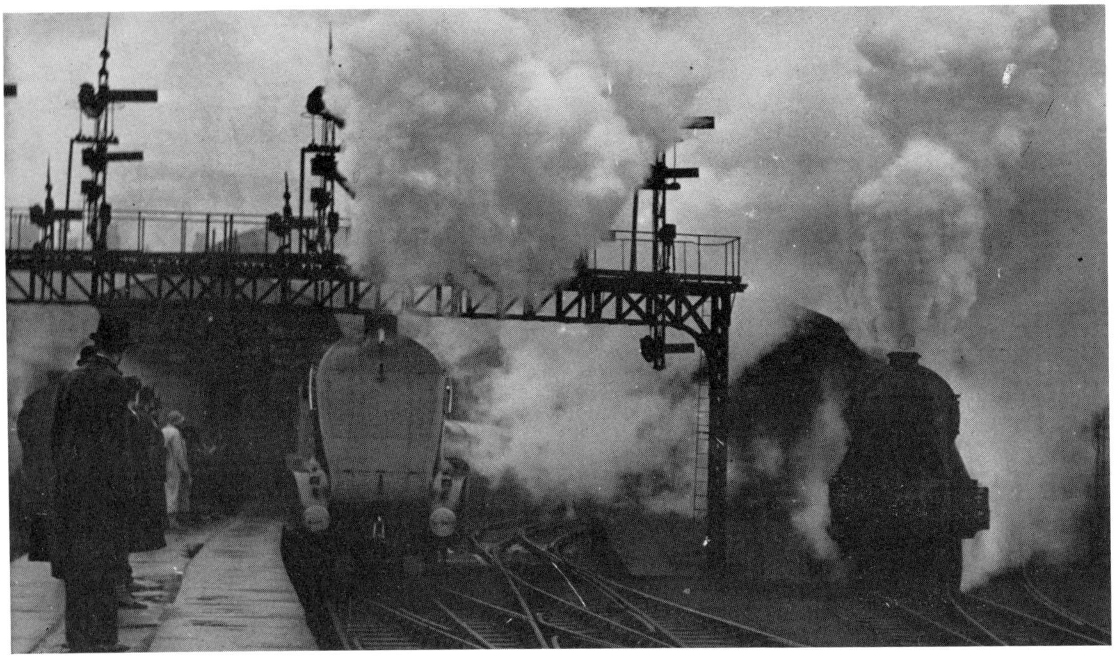

224. January 1936 and the latest LNER streamlined locomotive, *Silver Fox*, draws out of the Central Station for its run to London. On the right is the Liverpool express which started its run at the same time.

225. On test at the Central Station in January 1959 was the *Deltic*, a 3,300 horse power prototype diesel-electric locomotive for use on the East Coast main line. Twenty-two of the locomotives were ordered from English Electric to replace 55 steam locomotives – *Silver Fox's* days were numbered. The tests at Newcastle were to check on the clearance between the locomotive and the platforms. *Deltic* was presented to the Science Museum, London, in April 1963 and was placed on permanent display sporting its distinctive blue and light grey livery.

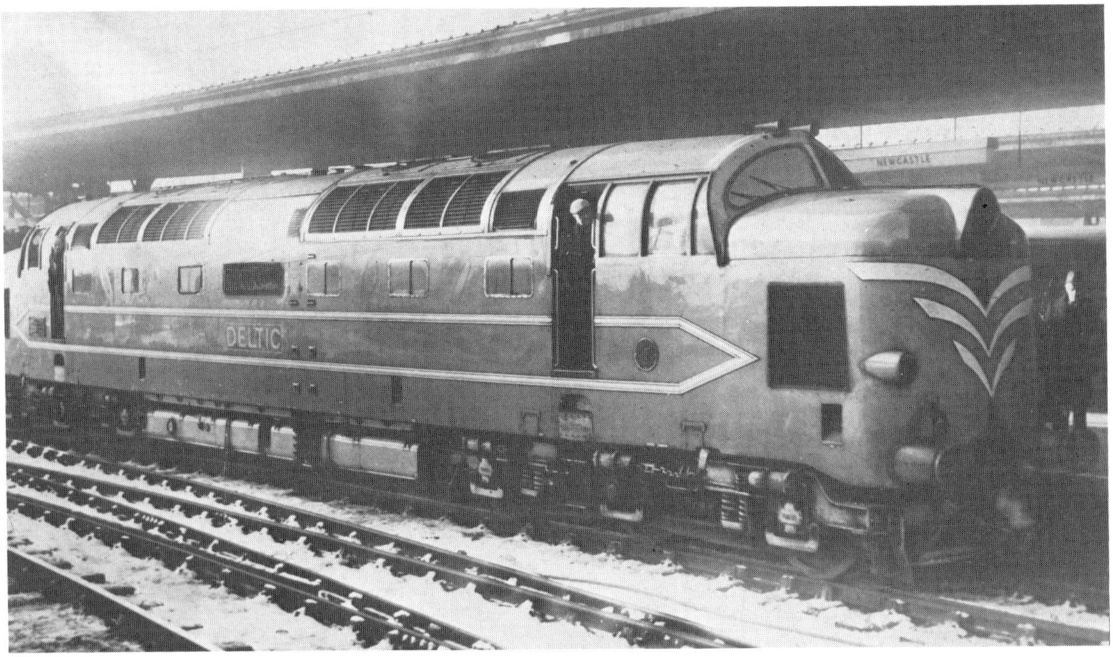

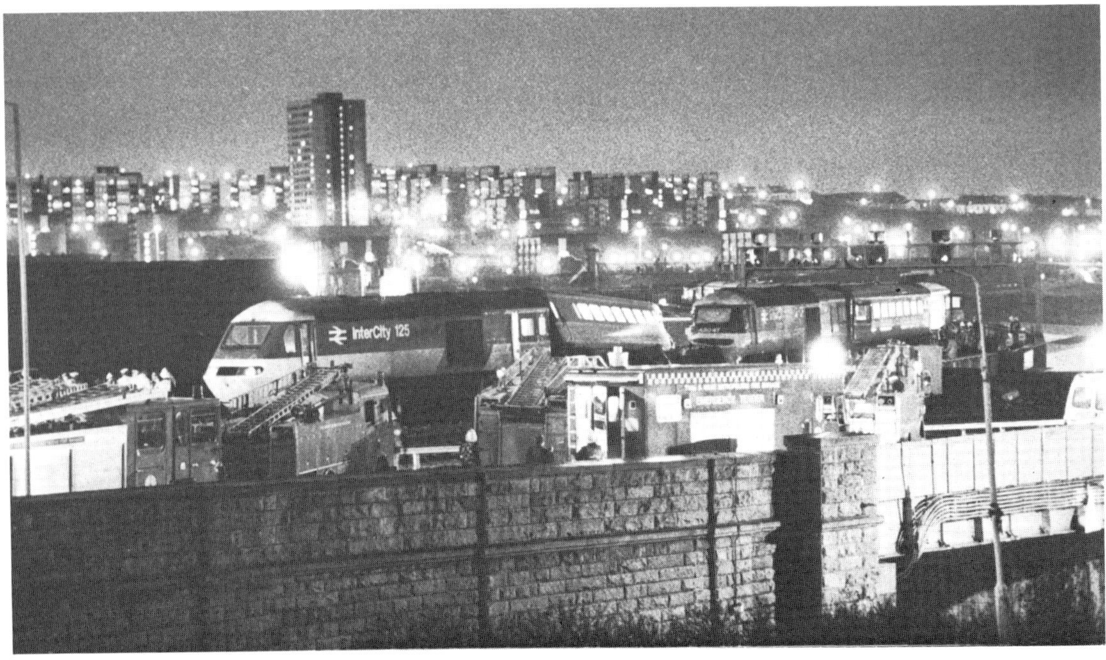

226. Thirteen people were injured and hundreds more were led to safety from the King Edward Bridge when two Inter-City 125 trains collided. The main East Coast line was blocked by the accident and services were diverted over the High Level Bridge.

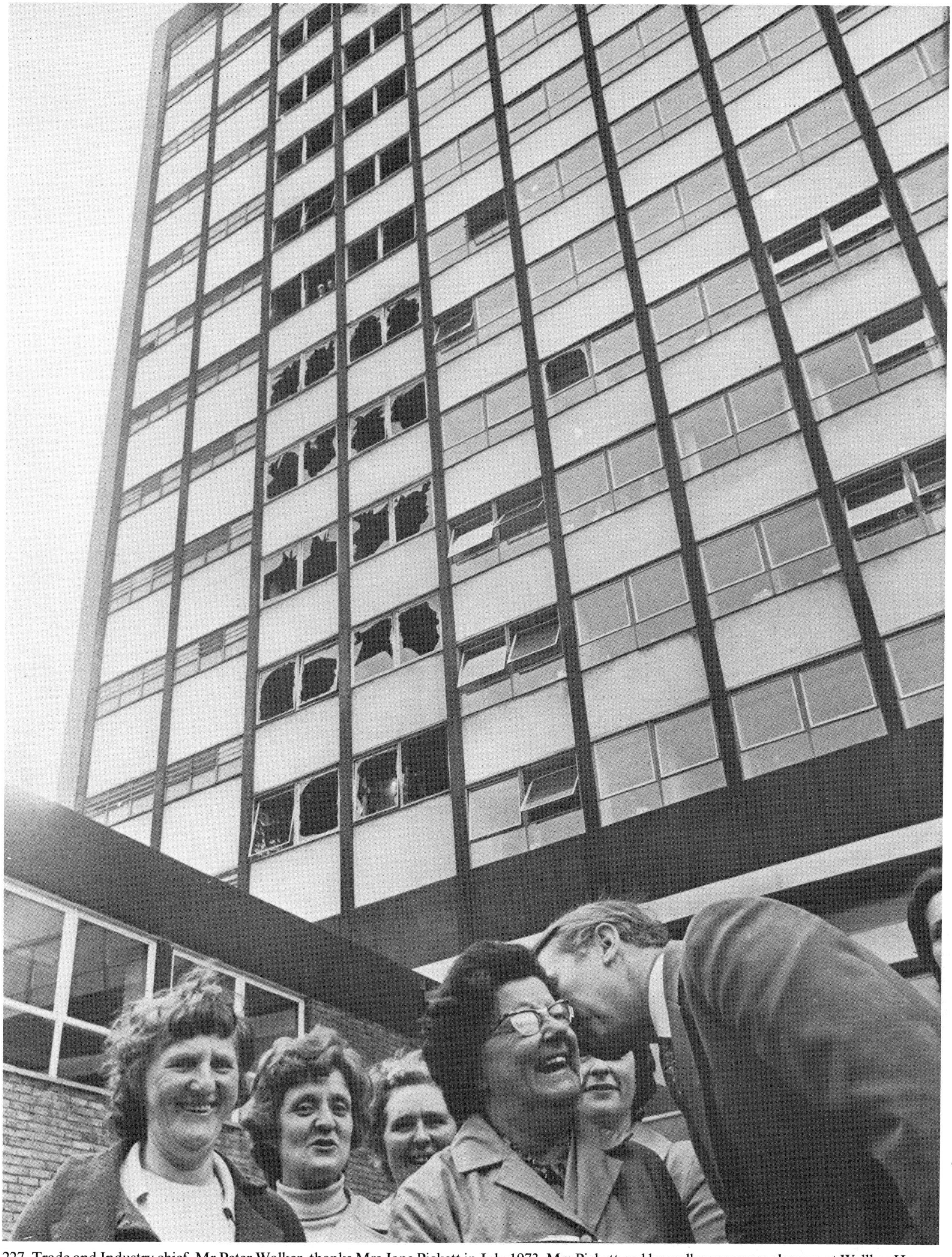

227. Trade and Industry chief, Mr Peter Walker, thanks Mrs Jane Pickett in July 1973. Mrs Pickett and her colleagues were cleaners at Wellbar House, and if they had not diligently locked all the fire doors one Friday night, then the building would have been gutted in an ensuing fire. Thanks to their efforts the fire was confined to the lift shaft of the 13-storey building.

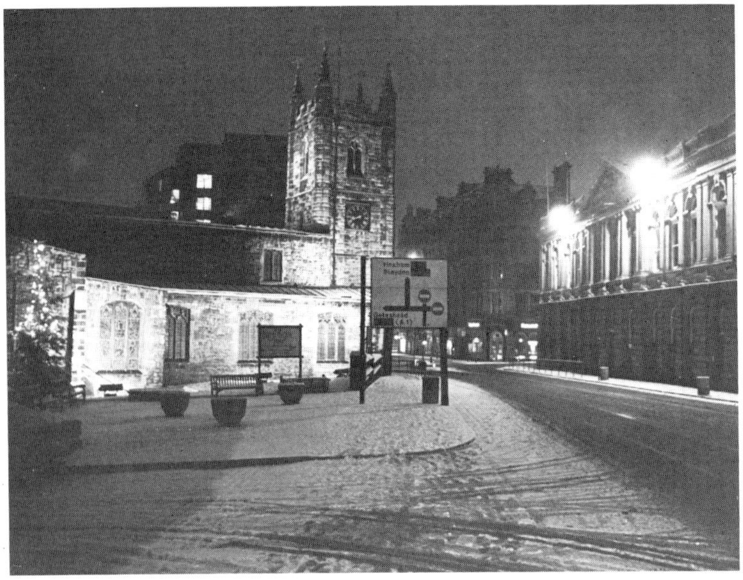

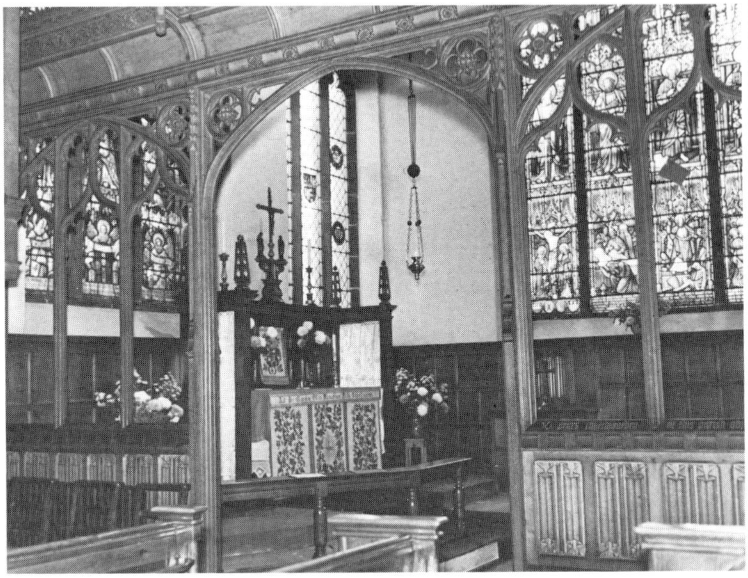

229. The Sacrament Chapel in St John's Church, October 1954.

228. *Top left:* A floodlit St John's Church, January 1986.

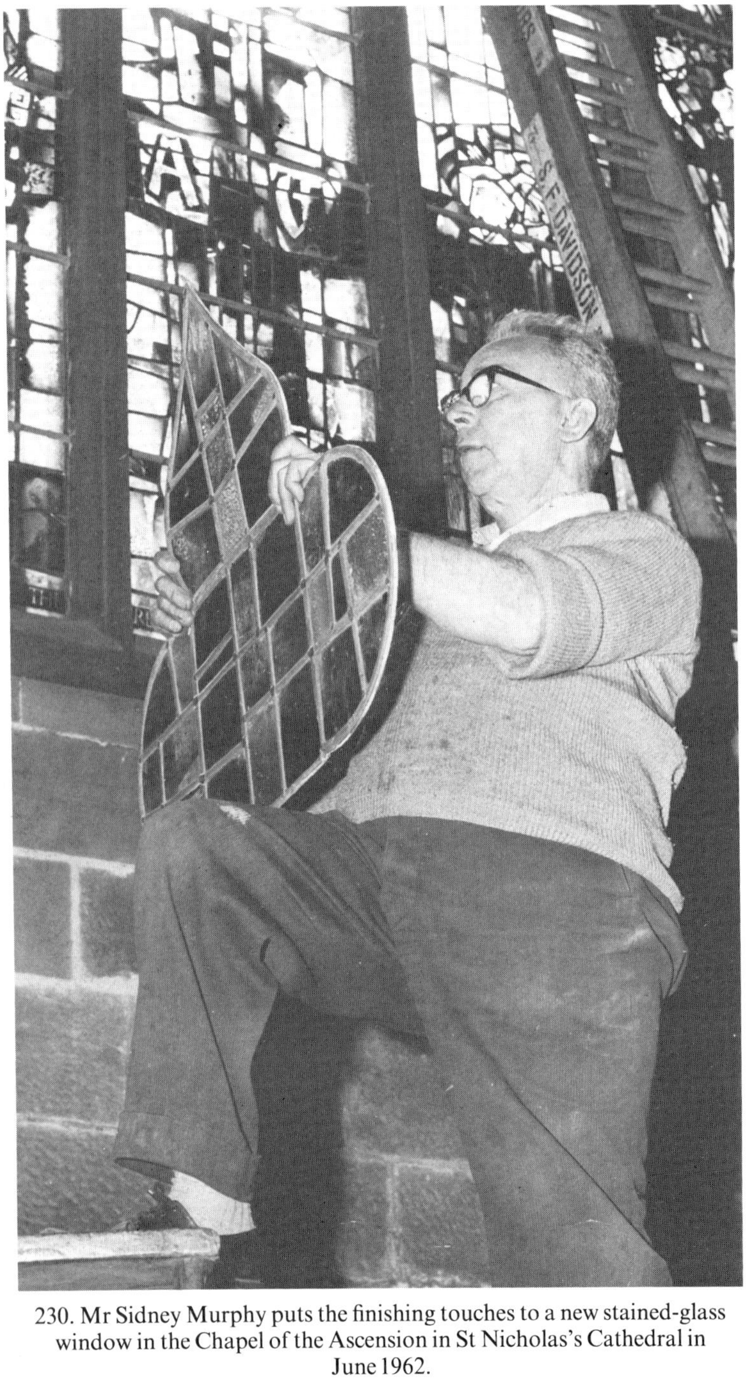

230. Mr Sidney Murphy puts the finishing touches to a new stained-glass window in the Chapel of the Ascension in St Nicholas's Cathedral in June 1962.

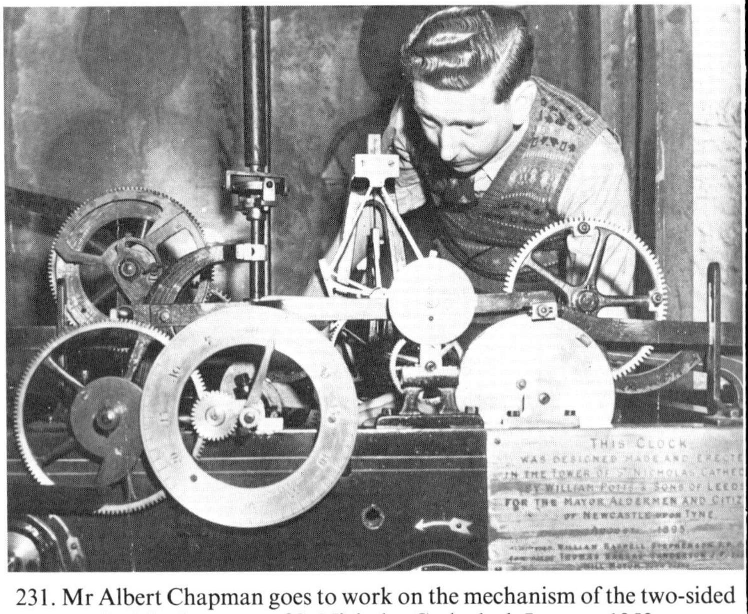

231. Mr Albert Chapman goes to work on the mechanism of the two-sided clock in the tower of St Nicholas Cathedral, January 1953.

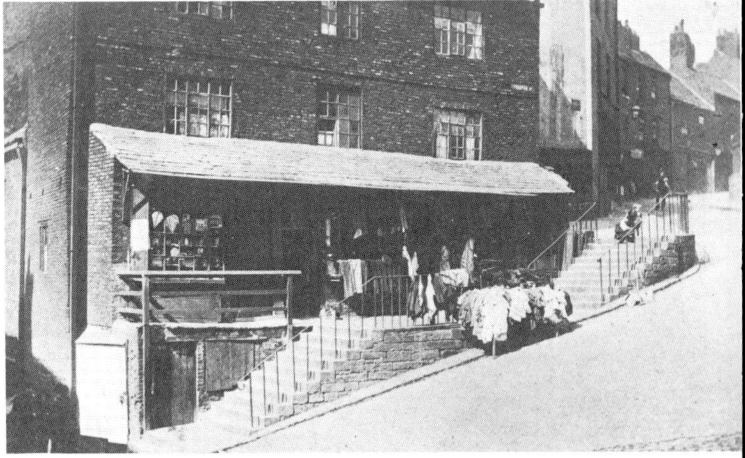

232. The bottom of Pilgrim Street in 1886.

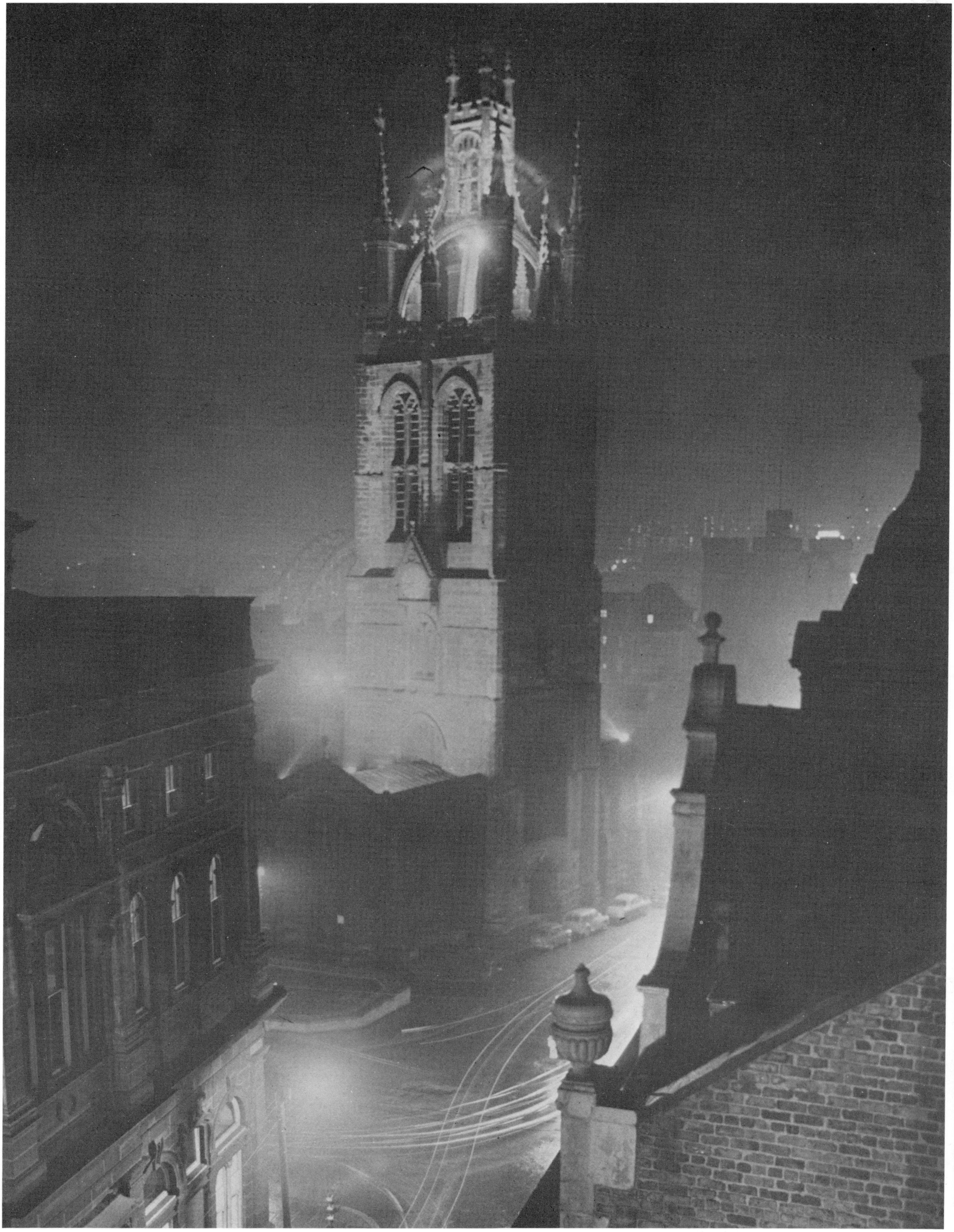

233. St Nicholas's Cathedral, November 1966.

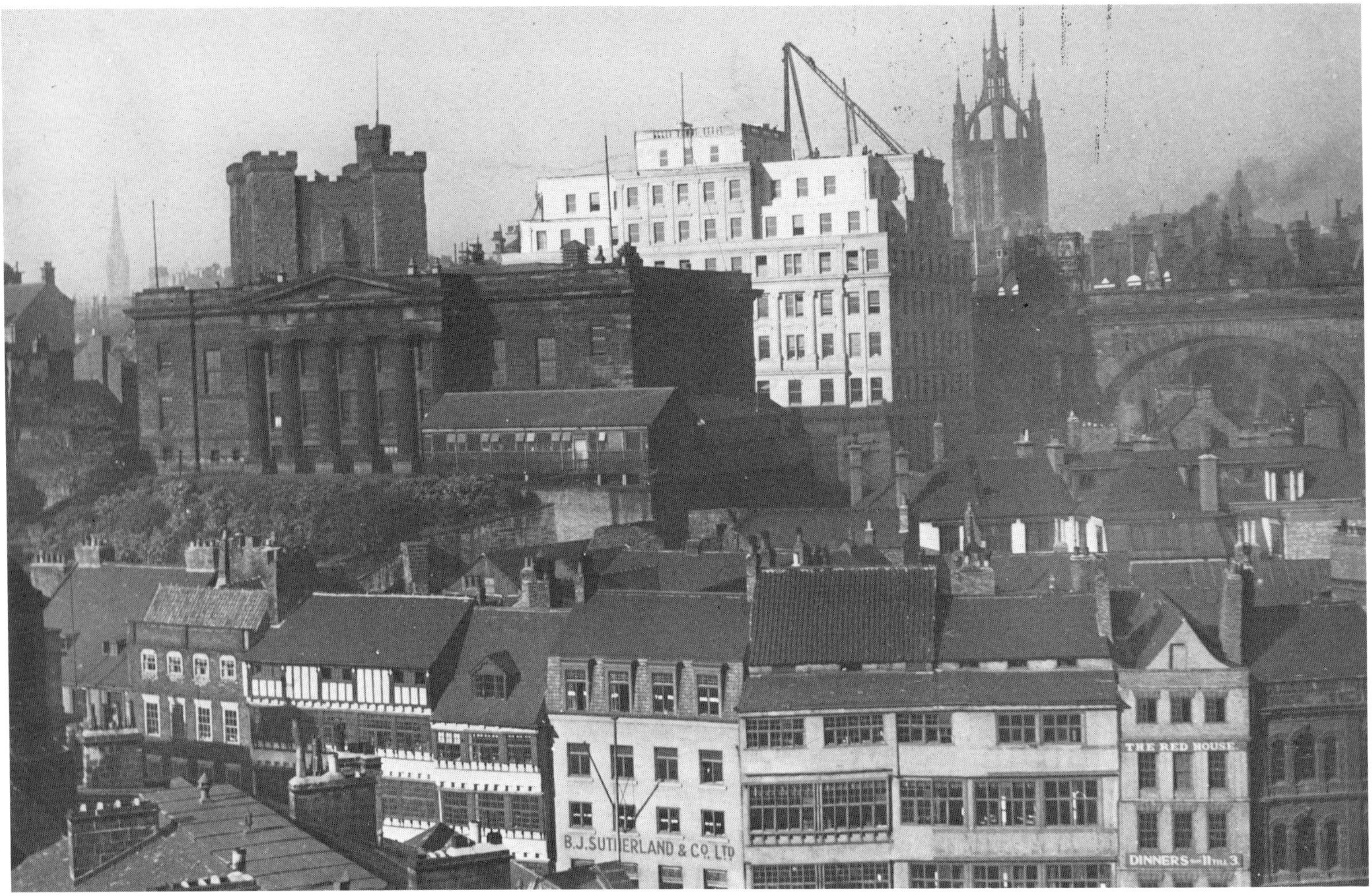

234. Newcastle landmarks in October 1934. The Old Castle, the Moot Hall, the County Council buildings, St Nicholas's Cathedral and, in the foreground, Bessie Surtees' house on the Sandhill.

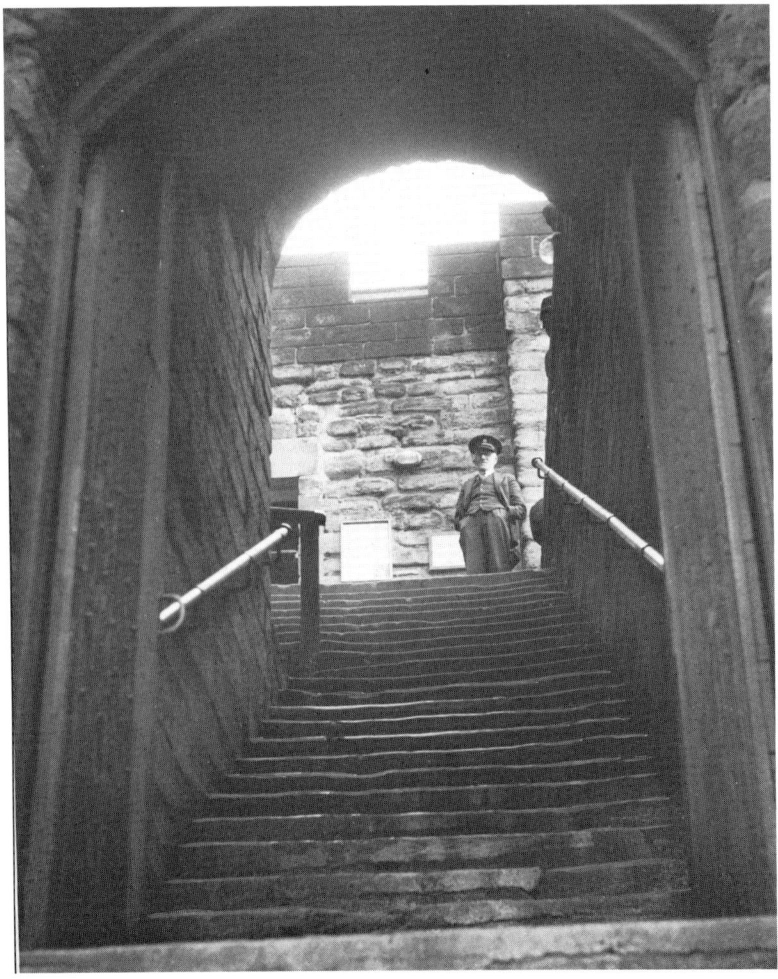

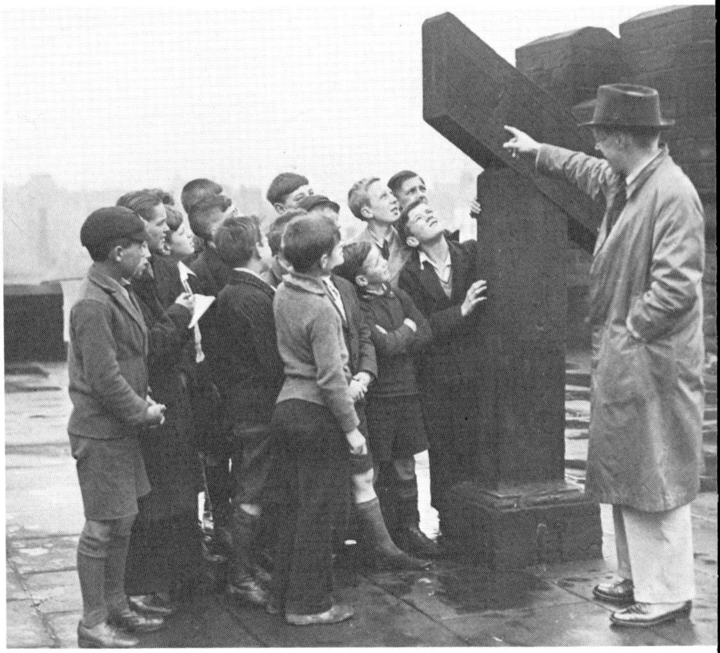

236. A seventeenth century sun-dial provides interest – or boredom – for a party of boys from South Benwell School in September 1937.

235. *Left:* Mr John Murdy, warden of the keep of Newcastle's Royal Castle, May 1962.

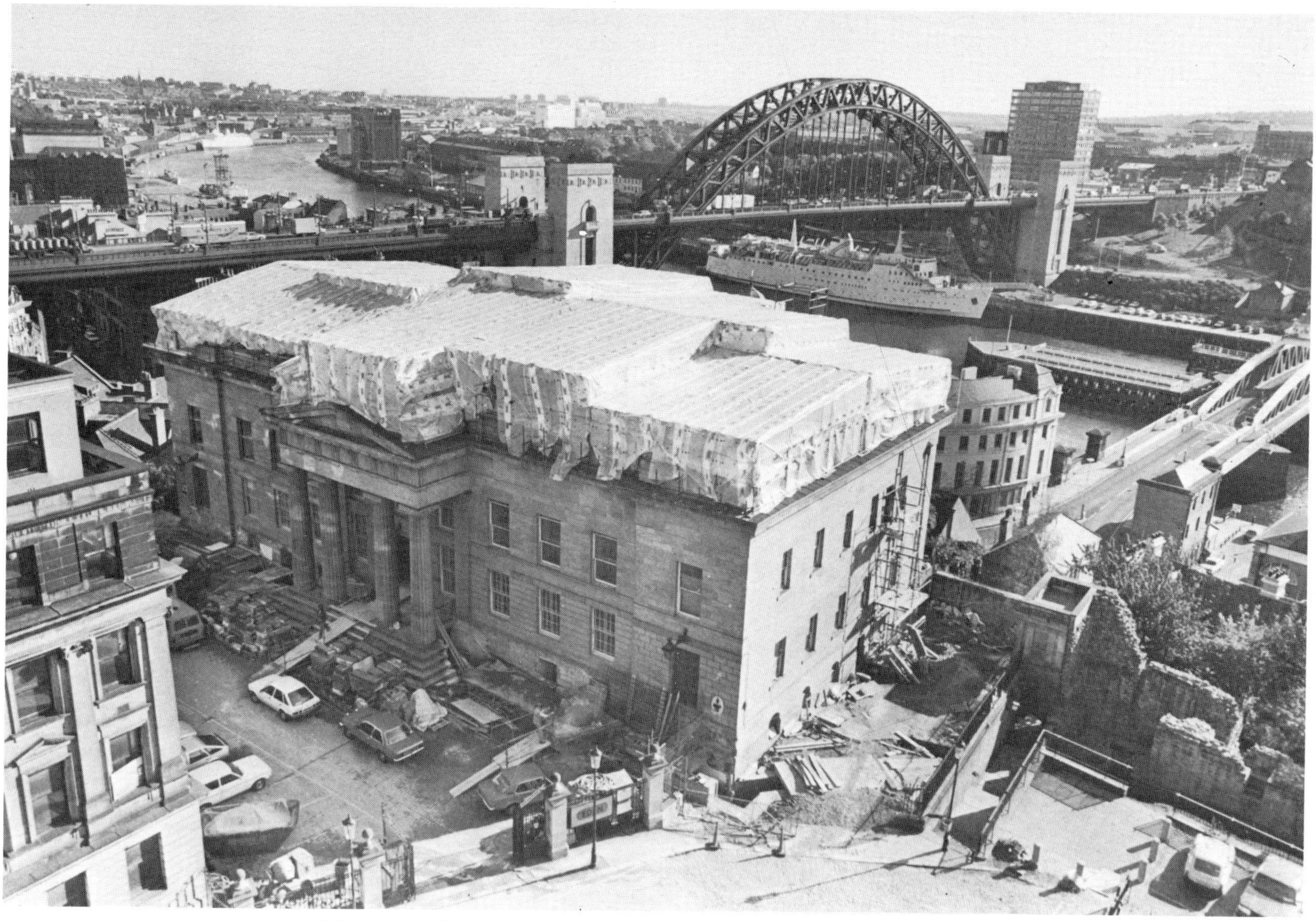

237. Restoration work proceeds at the old Crown Court in October 1986.

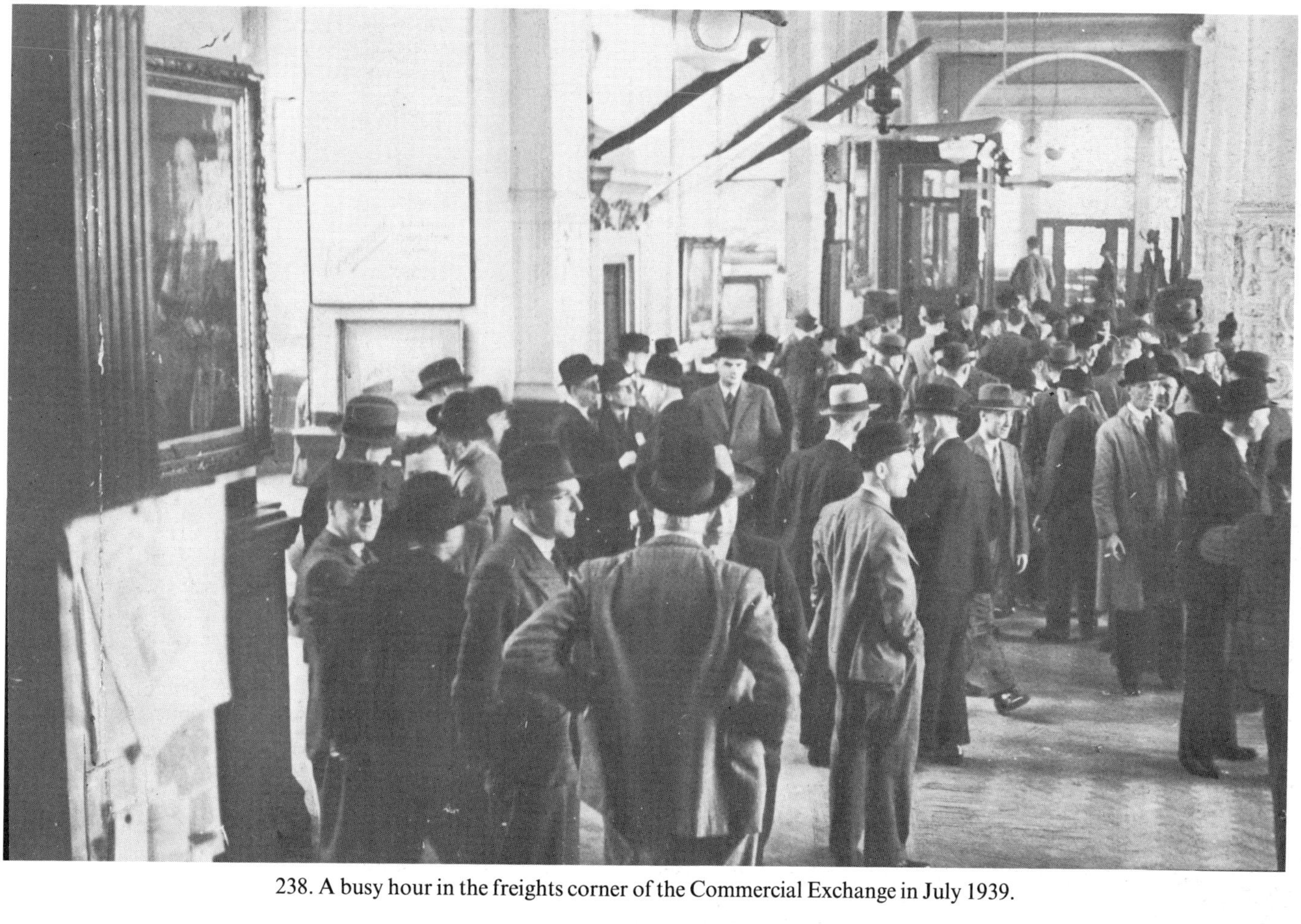

238. A busy hour in the freights corner of the Commercial Exchange in July 1939.

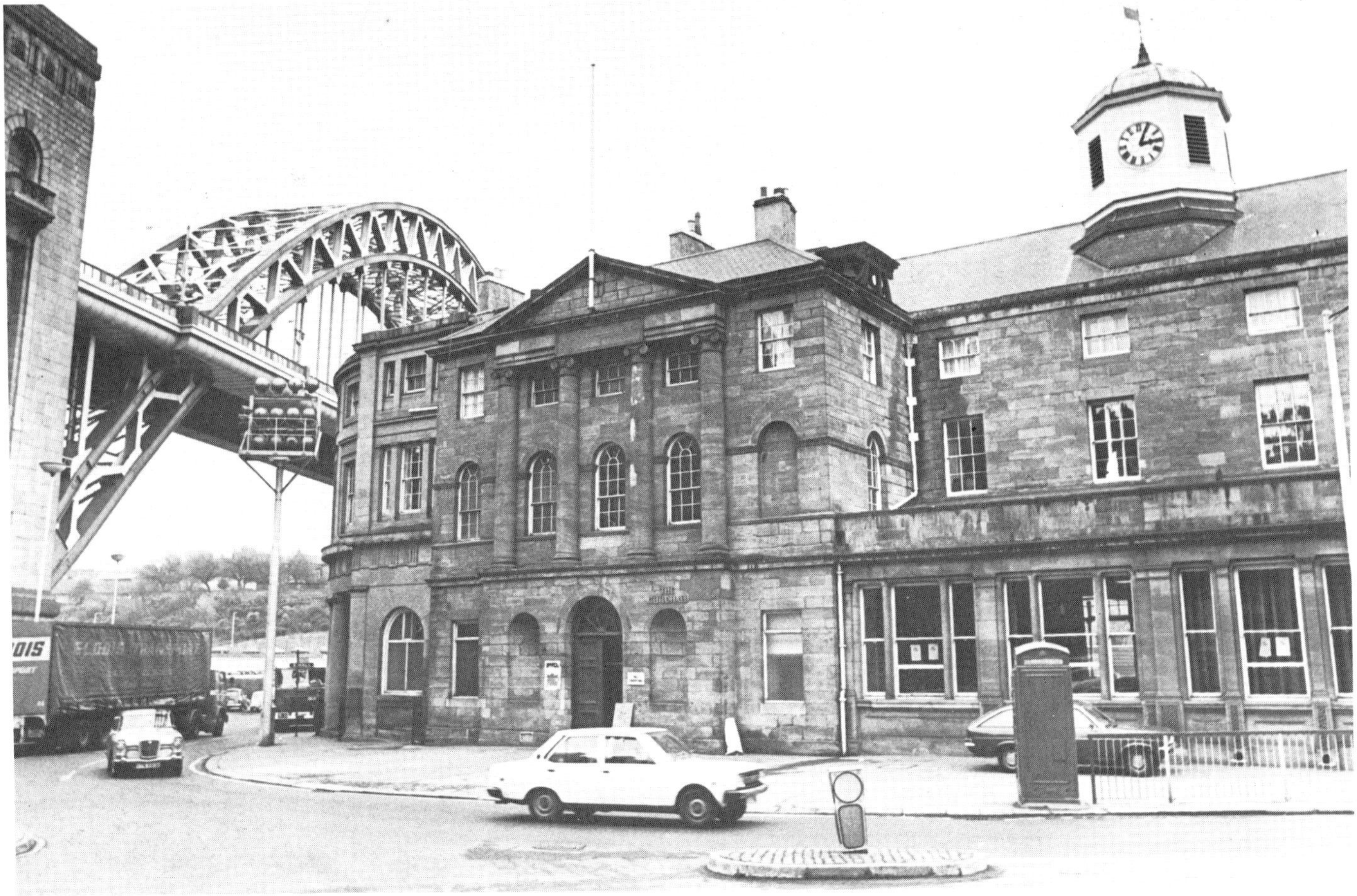

239. The Guildhall.

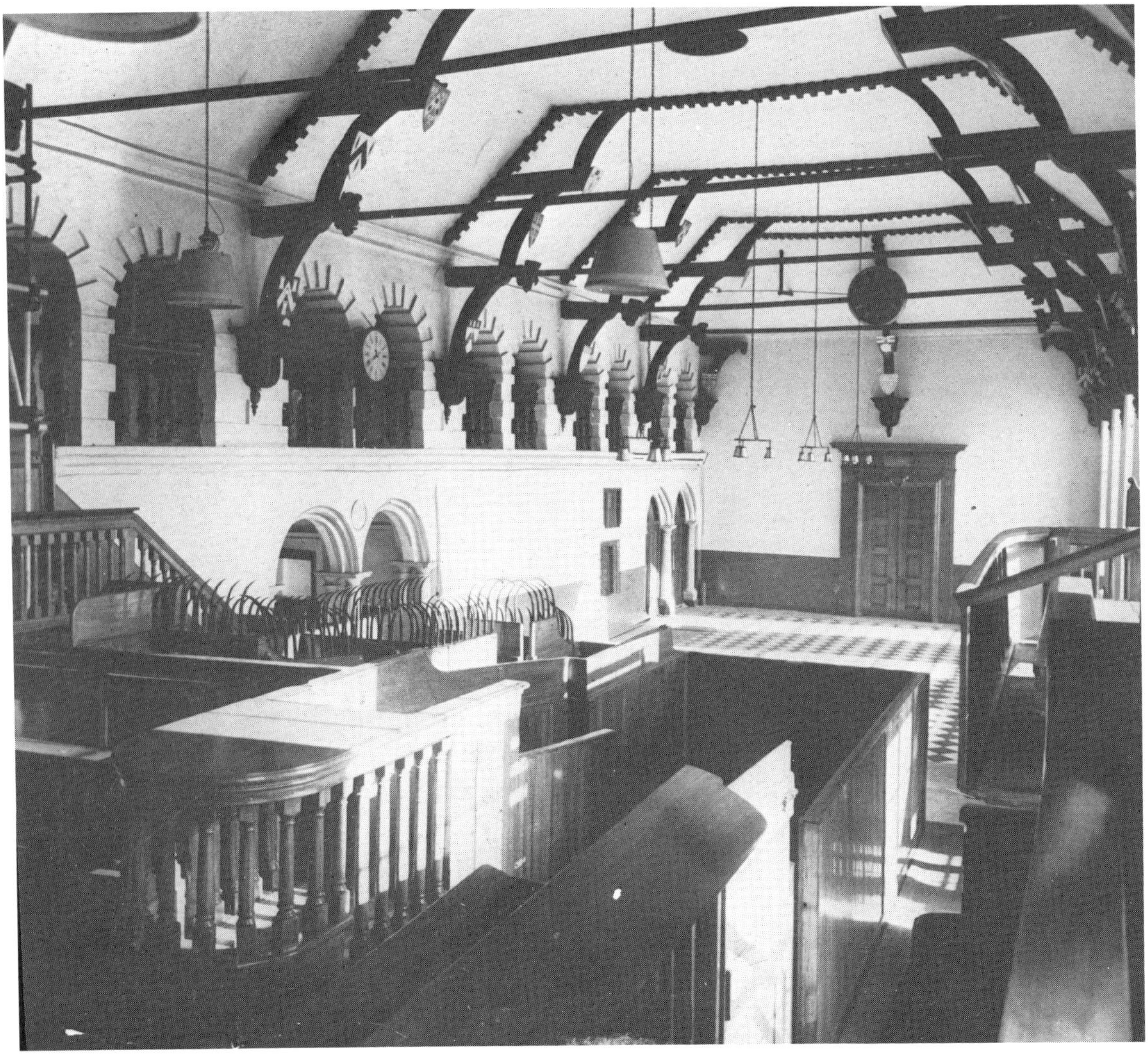

240. *Left:* A general view of the interior of the Guildhall, which was built between 1655 and 1658 at a cost of £10,000. In this view, the camera is looking to where the public would stand to watch a trial. The box with the bars is the dock where the prisoners stood, to the dock's left is counsel, to its right the witnesses, and behind was where the Judge sat.

241. *Opposite page:* Newcastle Prison c1925 when it was announced that it was to be closed and prisoners transferred to Durham Gaol.

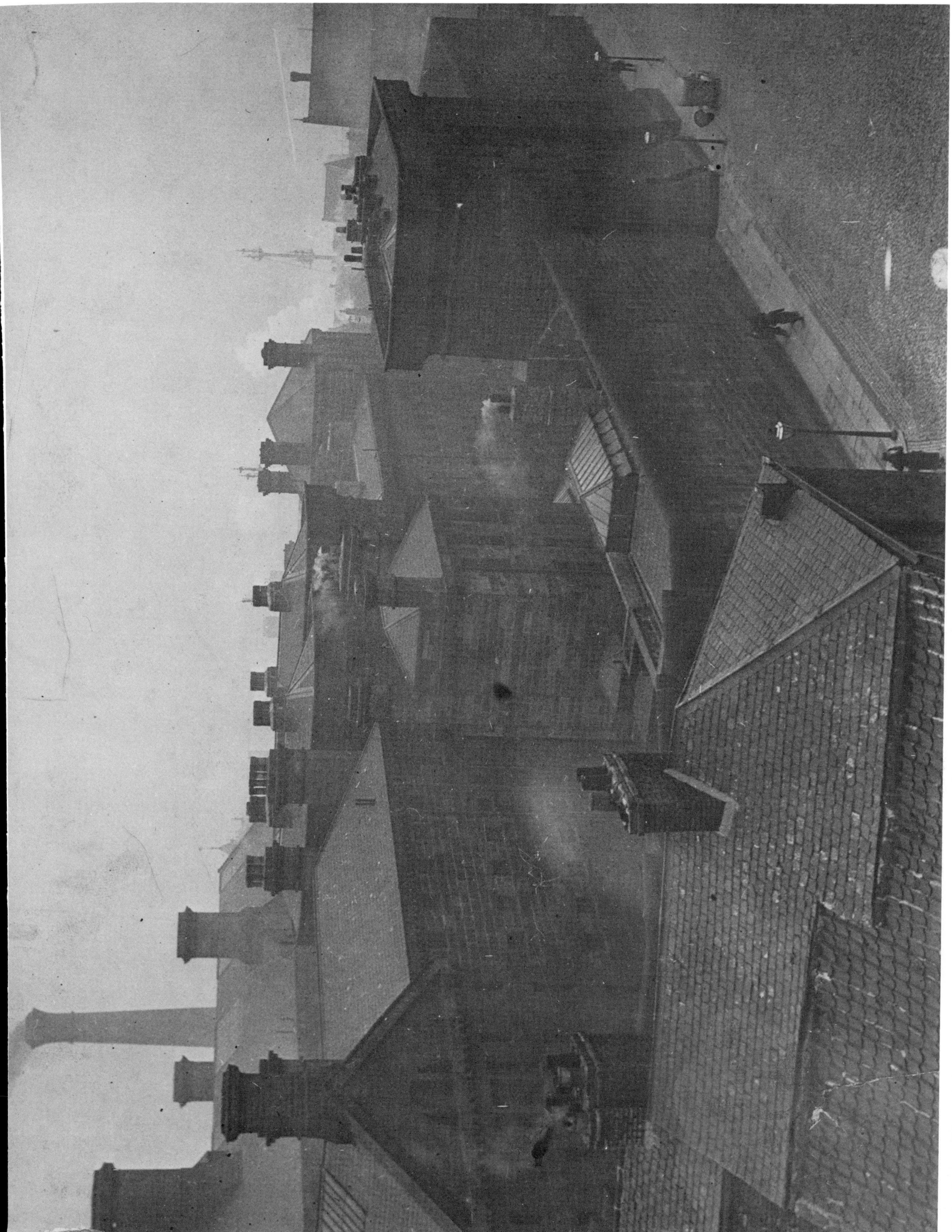

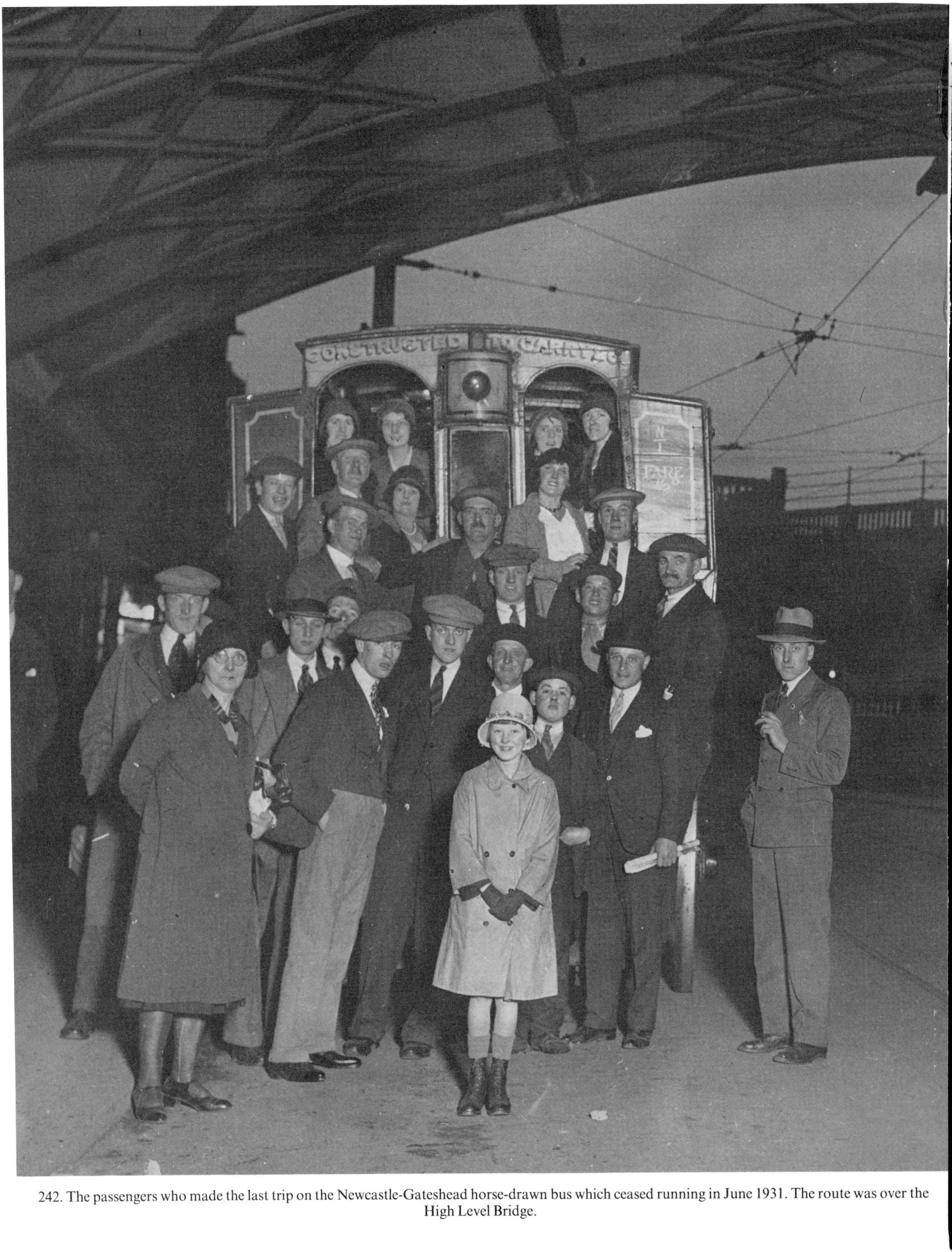

242. The passengers who made the last trip on the Newcastle-Gateshead horse-drawn bus which ceased running in June 1931. The route was over the High Level Bridge.